The History
&
Haunting
of
Salem:

The Witch Trials &
Beyond

Rebecca F. Pittman

Editors: Dan Scherer and Rusty Judd

Cover design and creation: Rebecca F. Pittman

Front cover photo of George Jacobs painting, courtesy of the
Peabody Essex Museum, Salem, MA.

ISBN: 978-0-9983692-2-8

DEDICATION

For those who refused to renounce their faith, even in the face of death.

Bridget Bishop, Sarah Good, Elizabeth How, Susannah Martin, Rebecca Nurse, Sarah Wildes, George Burroughs, Martha Carrier, John Willard, George Jacobs, Sr, John Proctor, Alice Parker, Mary Parker, Ann Pudeator, Wilmot Redd, Margaret Scott, Samuel Wardwell, Martha Corey, Mary Esty, and Giles Corey. Died in prison: Ann Foster, Lydia Dustin, Sarah Osborne, and Roger Toothaker.

"Maybe you who condemn me are in greater fear

than I who am condemned."

--Giordano Bruno

CONTENTS

ACKNOWLEDGMENTS

To write a book covering an event as historically important as the Salem Witch Trials is a daunting pursuit. I am eternally indebted to the amazing people who gave me their time and their expertise to make this book so much better than it would have been without them.

Thank You! to:

Marilynne K. Roach (author, historian, & artist); Richard B. Trask with the Danvers Archival Center; Rachel Crist with the Salem Witch Museum; KrisTina Wheeler & Claire Kallelis with the Hawthorne Hotel; Barbara Bridgewater (owner of the John Proctor house); Rebecca Beatrice Brooks (The History of Massachusetts blog); Tania Quartarone and Claire Blechman with the Peabody Essex Museum; Benjamin Ray with the University of Virginia; Julie Arrison with The House of the Seven Gables; and my editors Dan Scherer and Rusty Judd (who did so much to add their polish). And to those people who contributed their stories, photos, and time in answer to my questions, my sincere appreciation.

And to Sidney Perley, whose research and dedication to this subject has influenced so many authors, historians, and scholars.

The
History

Preface

In writing *The History and Haunting of Salem: The Witch Trials and Beyond*, I was faced with the reality that so many dedicated historians and gifted writers have gone before me, and will, no doubt, come after. The unprecedented events of 1692 in a remote and relatively unimportant town called Salem Village continue to capture our imagination and beg for answers. Why? Why here? Why did a populace dominated by men, in an era where women were relegated to childbearing and running a home, and children were deemed invisible unless spoken to, suddenly act with credulity to claims of witches and the Devil from girls as young as eight years of age? How were Christian women such as Rebecca Nurse and Martha Corey suddenly stripped of their church covenants and hanged?

What happened in Salem Village, and the neighboring towns of Andover, Beverly, Topsfield, Billerica, Waverly, Boston, and more? Was it a perfect storm of events that eroded friendships and put trust to naught? Many of the girls who led the witch trial attacks had witnessed brutal slayings of family and neighbors at the hands of Indian tribes. Wars with the natives, French, and Canadians were still raging as accused "witches" huddled in area prisons awaiting their fate. Traveling through the woods at night was akin to playing Russian Roulette. At the same time, Massachusetts was without a charter; something that played heavily in the lawlessness of the witch trials. Increase Mather was petitioning the King of England for the important papers that would allow the New England state to steer its way through troubled waters. By the time he returned home to Boston with the governing laws that may have stemmed the flow of madness in Salem Village, it was too late.

And what of the religious discord in the Village? The new Reverend Parris was literally begging for firewood and his wages to survive, yet he found himself squarely in the crosshairs of a feud that separated the very members of his congregation. As he spewed forth warnings of the Devil from the pulpit—partly in an effort to shame the members into honoring his calling and fulfilling their promise to him of a fair living—he was fueling the fear and distrust already so prevalent in that small community.

When you add the discord between neighbors over land, inheritance, and various squabbles, you have the makings of a cyclone that ravaged this small rural hamlet.

There are layers to the story of the Salem Witch Trials that cannot be ignored. Salem Village was a small town, virtually ignored by the prosperous seaport of Salem Town, only a short distance away. They were farmers, trying to eke out a living from hard ground, marshes, and craggy hillsides. Salem Town, on the other hand, was seeing immense prosperity with its burgeoning import and export business in the sea trades. When Salem Village came begging to the town magistrates of their sister city for help in the beginning months of the witch outbreak, they were told to "fend for yourselves."

Even the governing and military heads in Boston saw the witch hysteria as something they could work to their advantage. They had bungled many of their military attempts in the war with France and the Indians. What better than to blame their thwarted efforts on the Devil?

It is difficult for those of us in a world filled with technological devices, space travel, and quantum physics' revelations, to understand a religious sect who believed without question that the forces of evil lived among them, as surely as the sun rose and set. The Prince of Air and Darkness traveled with the 9,000 men, women, and children aboard the 17 ships that left England (and the Anglican Church) behind in the early 1600s. Later, as many as 20,000 dissenters would follow. The Puritans created a new religion, one of total purity and separation from the pagan beliefs they found in the Catholic Church of England under the Stuart's rule. They came to the shores of New England to build their "city on the hill," a beacon of God's laws that would shine across the frigid waters of the Atlantic and chasten the English courts.

Thousands of executions had been going on in Europe for decades. Witches were burned at the stake in numbers that would baffle the mind today. The Puritans of New England believed inexplicably that if hardship fell upon their neighbor, then God had found them wanting. Crops and livestock that perished, dissonance in the household, stillborn babies…these were signs that the involved parties had sinned and the Devil had visited them—or sent his witches—to obtain a pound of flesh. Children were told that they would go to hell or were "children of Satan" if they misbehaved. Hell was preached from the pulpit more often than words of hope and peace. It was an atmosphere of fear, born from myriad events, afflicting a small, insignificant colony.

Massachusetts Bay Colony was settled by unrelenting laws that would not tolerate any deviation from it. They considered themselves the Chosen People and those found straying beyond the harsh confines of the rules were subject to public humiliation. The pillories and stocks were wooden frames with holes for the heads and hands, where the disobedient were locked for hours and sometimes days in the village common on full display. Women were branded with signs or things attached to their clothing that labeled them with sins that varied from scolding one's husband to adultery. Giles Corey was pressed to death beneath a board laden down with large rocks when he refused to plead innocent or guilty of witchcraft before the 1692 witch trial committee. Hangings were a public affair, and children were in attendance. These public humiliations and executions were a warning to others who thought of going off the Puritan beaten path. Children were not cosseted in the harsh New England households and communities. Their souls were at stake, and if seeing their neighbor dangling from a tree limb instilled the fear of God in them, then it was a necessary lesson.

The colonies were ruled by men. Women were to bear the children, tend the gardens, make candles, quilts, and clothing, and obey. Above all, obey. Some were lucky enough to have grown female children to help them, or servants. The chores and meals were a tedious rhythm to each day. Men worked tirelessly in a wilderness that often seemed determined to maintain its invincible tree lines and rocky landscape. Marshes were sprinkled throughout the territory; a breeding ground for mosquitoes and disease.

The household leaders, however, were afforded the variety and companionship of their male neighbors that women were denied. The village males would go off and hunt and fish after the harvest was gathered. They attended meetings and discussed church and village politics. For the wives and daughters, the sparse walls of their rudimentary homes were their world. Trips to the market, a quilting bee, or to church, were looked upon as a holiday from the drudgery they inherited along with their mother's broach. Church meetinghouses became the place to catch up on gossip concerning neighbors, and juicy nuggets of information about nearby towns.

This religious grapevine had tendrils that reached unprecedented distances in the winter of 1692.

The Puritans of the Massachusetts Bay Colony became more unrelenting and intolerant than the Church of England from which they had escaped. They brought much of the religious dogma with them, along with their family heirlooms, chosen pieces of furniture and pewter. The smoke of thousands of witches roasting upon wooden pyres in European court yards clung to them as surely as the salt scenting the sea air. Then why, in this obscure village of farmers, has 19 hangings, one man pressed to death, and five deaths from imprisonment, continued to be the fascination and incredible touchstone for the term "Witches?" It is precisely for the impossible conditions that created this sad bookmark in American history that we cannot look away.

As with my other books in *The History and Haunting* series, I set up the atmosphere of the happenings based on archived documents, testimony, and history of the area. It is my way of pulling you into the story. It's a nod to Truman Capote's non-fiction novel *In Cold Blood.* The facts are real, the telling of them is my own particular style.

The final section of the book offers insights into haunted locations around Salem and events that still impact the town today, such as the continued fascination with the movie *Hocus Pocus.*

It is my sincere hope that this book offers another viewpoint and insight into one of America's tragedies. These were real people who in another time, during different circumstances, may have survived. Their story is one of acute courage and faith. They are due our empathy and our admiration, along with our curiosity.

Quotes and testimony from the witch trial era have been left untouched, spelling errors and all. I felt it gave authenticity to the text.

Rebecca F. Pittman
June 25, 2019

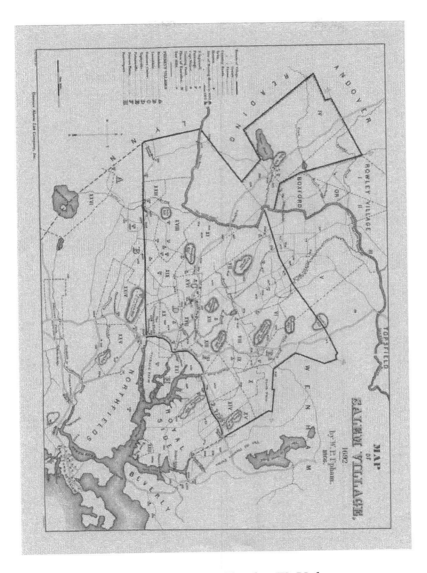

Salem Village 1692. Charles W. Upham.

PROLOGUE

The moon pressed hard through the sullen clouds in an effort to see its reflection in the steel-gray waters of Salem Harbor. Winter lay claim to the hamlets, fields, and houses that clung to the hard ground in a terra firma patchwork quilt. Their boundaries were documented only as rough lines drawn upon crude maps, their ambiguity creating a constant source of contention among the neighboring towns. It was early January 1692.

As smoke curled from the chimneys of homes—both rudimentary and monied alike—something moved in the smoke-laden night air. It brushed through the bare branches of towering oaks and traced unseen fingers along the rooftops of Salem Village. Whisperings, like gossip on the wind, blended with the brine-scented breeze coming from the harbor in Salem Town. Strange shadows escaped from brush and moved along rutted roadways, lingering near the parsonage and meetinghouse, and slipping up to peer into the windows of Ingersoll's Ordinary. The unseen entity moved among the various dwellings, assessing its inhabitants, and planning the machinations that would rip this New England village apart.

Wooden doors held secure by iron latches would falter, proving there was nothing impervious to the insidious force lurking just above the roofline. Nightmares among the inmates, already fueled by fears of Indian attacks, cruel winter conditions, a charter-less government, and fiery lectures from the pulpit warning of damnation and hell, would be made of more terrifying stuff in the weeks and months to come. Not one soul in Salem Village and the neighboring towns would be safe from the outcry of "Witch!"

As the moon slipped behind a bank of clouds, Sarah Good lay wrapped in a ratty blanket inside a barn, the only refuge offered to her after a day of begging. Her four-year-old daughter Dorcus pressed up against her in a fetal position, soft rumblings of hunger coming from her small belly. Something swept through the cracks of weathered boards and she shivered. It was to be a long winter. Clergymen, cosseted with their scriptures in small rooms laced with woodsmoke, glanced at flickering candles as some unseen force bent the flames. Children moved closer to each other in shared beds and clutched their coverings tightly. Livestock moved restlessly; the forlorn bellowing of a cow sounding in the darkness. Tituba, a Spanish Indian slave, listened to the night sounds outside the parsonage where she lived; niggling's of fear pulsed in her veins. Sudden gusts of wind caused tree limbs to groan and thin branches to rattle, a sound not unlike witches cackling. Cats rose up suddenly from a sound sleep, their hackles raised, and hissed toward doorways.

And so, the stage was set. An invisible map of Essex County was put into place above Salem Village where chess pieces were set in place. The two Kings of England and France (who were battling over Massachusetts), took their respective places on the antiquated parchment map; their Queens standing steadfast in the milieu. The warring families of the Putnam's and Porters would don their Knightly helmets and move in ways that, within mere months, would find their neighbors jailed and some strung up and dropped from sturdy tree limbs. The Castles of government in nearby Boston would fall beneath the depravity that would throw their gavels back into their faces. The Pawns would, of course, be the gaggle of young girls who would be the trumpeters of death.

The unseen hand lingered over the game board, deciding its first move. It came to rest upon the first piece that was to be played—a Bishop—better yet—a Reverend.

Chapter One

The Bishop

The Winter of Discontent

Reverend Samuel Parris sat in his study and pulled his candle closer in hopes the meager flame would add warmth to the frigid room. Outside, the January wind howled and snow coated the rippled glass window panes with frost. The thoughts that taunted him as he sat hunched over his next sermon were definitely not ones found in scripture. The fire he tended in the twin fireplaces of his parsonage was dependent on firewood that the Salem Village inhabitants had agreed to furnish as part of his contract for signing on as Reverend. Yet, here he suffered through yet another winter as the villagers refused to donate the fuel. He blew on his fingers, and set again to writing, the cold ink reluctant to flow across the parchment.

Reverend Samuel Parris

A muffled cough sounded from the parlor below, reminding him of his wife Elizabeth's declining health; the lack of heat, no doubt, contributing to her illness. He bristled, once again thinking of the discord within his own congregation that kept him rationing his diminishing woodpile. Nearly half of the village was against him. His sermons from the pulpit warning of the retribution that would befall those who did not honor Christ (and in direct alliance, himself) had done nothing but remind the people the Devil was among them. The sermon he delivered on November 22, 1691, had been a firm reminder: "The Lord said unto my Lord, 'Sit thou at my right hand, until I make mine enemies, they footstool.'" The "enemies" had only trudged home after the Sunday meeting to their own warm fires and grumbled against their neighbors.

"What am I doing here?" played like a refrain in his tired mind. He knew the fate that had befallen the three clergymen before him. Two were hounded out of town (John Bayley and George Burroughs), and only Deodat Lawson had met with some popularity, but chose to leave the cantankerous bickering and feuds of Salem Village by signing on as chaplain for a military expedition to Maine. The appointed governor, Sir Edmund Andros headed the expedition in 1687. Soon after his return to Salem Village, Lawson's wife and daughter died. As was the prevalent mantra in the small hamlet, some villagers felt his tragic loss was punishment by the Devil for deserting them. He moved to Boston in a fury where he finally became the Pastor of Scituate, Massachusetts. But Salem Village had not seen the last of him. He returned during the Witch Trials of 1692 to look into the outbreak. The result was a 10-page pamphlet titled *A Brief and True Narrative of Some Remarkable Passages Relating to Sundry Persons Afflicted by Witchcraft at Salem Village.*

Parris rubbed a hand across his clammy brow and thought of the enormity of tragedies that surrounded his small village. Small pox had broken out in nearby Salem Town, no doubt brought in by ship where the disease had broken out earlier. Indian raids still ravaged the coastline, burning and destroying towns only 57-miles away, such as York, Maine. Many of his parishioners were refugees from the milieu, and several young girls, whose faces looked up to him from their pews on the Sabbath, were orphaned and working as maids in village homes. Mercy Short was one such survivor who had witnessed unimageable atrocities at the hands of the Wabanaki

Indians when in 1690 they attacked Salmon Falls, New Hampshire (now Brunswick, Maine.)

Mercy was the daughter of Clement and Faith Short and sister to nine siblings. Her mother and father and three of the children were slain before her eyes. Fifteen-year-old Mercy was taken captive and marched through the harsh wilderness to Quebec where she would be sold as a captive. During the frightening pilgrimage, Mercy witnessed one teenage girl beheaded as a warning to the others should they try and escape. A small boy was murdered and chopped up before her, and one of her Salmon Falls neighbors, Robert Rogers, was stripped and tied to a stake and forced to endure horrors that haunted the young girl's dreams years later.

Cotton Mather, the minister from Boston who would play a large role in the Witch Trials, wrote of Rogers' slaying, the Wabanakis "danc'd about him, and at every Turn, they did with their knives cut collops of his Flesh, from his Naked Limbs, and throw them with his Blood into his Face."

Mercy Short was one of the lucky few who was ransomed in 1691, only a year before the witchcraft outbreak began in Salem Village. She became a servant in the household of a wealthy merchant's widow, Margaret Thatcher, in Boston. The following May, 1692, she happened across Sarah Good, the second victim of the witch trials, who was being held in the Boston Prison. Sarah asked Mercy for some tobacco. The young 17-year-old threw wood shavings in the face of the accused witch instead, shouting "Here's tobacco for you!" Later that night, Mercy finally lost touch with reality and broke out in violent fits, unable to sleep or eat. Cotton Mather was her acting minister at the time and took her into his home to try and exorcise the demon tormenting her. He also studied her and wrote about the incident.

Reverend Samuel Parris continued to stew. Massachusetts seemed doomed! The colony had been without a lawful charter from England for five years now. They were essentially steering a rudderless ship. Increase Mather, Cotton's father, was even now in England begging King James to reinstate their charter that had been taken away earlier after the Puritans refused to honor the church dictates of the British Isle from which they had escaped. When they threw the England-appointed governor Sir Edmund Andros in prison, their charter was revoked.

Without the charter, inhabitants of the New England settlement faced the realization that the land they had cleared, farmed, and built their homes upon, was now without valid claim. Tensions and land boundary disputes erupted. Salem Village quarrels taken to Boston's General Court were slow in being resolved. If they appealed to the magistrates in Salem Town, they were basically told they were on their own. Salem Village, known as The Farms, had been negotiating with the prosperous seaport of Salem Town for years to gain their autonomy and stop paying taxes for things that did not benefit them, such as road repairs and help with the town's poor. "Let us pay to fix our own roads and tend to our own poor," was basically the entreaty put forth repeatedly.

They also wanted their own church meetinghouse to alleviate the long walk to Salem Town to worship. Roads were barely passable, often no more than cattle trails, and weather conditions were harsh. They finally won the battle for the meetinghouse and the right to appoint their own pastor; other pleas for help fell on deaf ears.

The awarding of their own meetinghouse and clergyman became one more source of contention. The Puritans had a caste system in place. Church attendance was mandatory. However, not all church attendees were given the title of full member. Puritans had to prove through conversion that they were worthy of the distinction of the predestined elect, a body of people who were guaranteed an entrance into Heaven. Other villagers could attend church meetings, but they were not allowed to partake of the Sacrament service that followed the general meeting. The church also rejected the Half-Way covenant, which allowed infants of at least one church member to be baptized, whether they had joined the Salem Village church or not. This further inflamed the villagers to the point that nearly three-fourths of the adults were against him. In essence, the congregation was separated into the haves and the have-nots, and the have-nots resented it. When a committee of Parris supporters taxed the village in an effort to pay the minister's salary, and came calling for a cord of their wood, tempers flared and the lines were drawn. This division would play out in the most heinous of acts.

Salem Village was adrift. They were neither a part of Salem Town, nor legally protected under Boston's higher councils. Without a charter to give guidelines and backing to the constant eruptions between neighbors, families, and businesses, Salem

Village was a powder keg with a fuse waiting to be lit. The struck match would come in the form of a simple conjuring trick using an egg and a glass of water.

Chapter Two

The Pawns

Something Wicked This Way Comes

The new year of 1692 brought with it a thick snow, eradicating the roads' boundaries and wrapping Salem Village's households in a feeling of isolation. Cabin fever was a very real thing when the winters were upon the spread-out homes of this small enclave. Sequestered in rooms that afforded little entertainment, the inhabitants looked out upon a world of white. In Reverend Samuel Parris' home, the firewood was used sparingly, adding to the feeling of hopelessness that pervaded the clergyman's thoughts. His wife was often bedridden, and there were four children living beneath his roof. Not even Christmas had colored the home in boughs and presents. Christmas and Easter were considered pagan holidays and were not celebrated in Puritan homes. Winter brought only the relief that perhaps Indian attacks would be fewer in the deep drifts of snow.

Legends have abounded as to whether the witchcraft outbreak began in the kitchen of the parsonage where Tituba, the slave Parris brought with him from Barbados, may have been teaching conjuring and spells. Parris had failed to make a going concern of the plantation his father left to him, and now found himself in New England, first as a merchant, and finally as the minister for a small, bickering village. He had brought with him three slaves: Tituba and John Indian, and a young black male who died at the age of sixteen.

No specific documents but two survive that point specifically to Tituba teaching Parris' young nine-year-old daughter Betty and her eleven-year-old cousin Abigail fortune telling and spells. The only recorded account comes from Reverend Hale's passage in his *Modest Enquiry into the Nature of Witchcraft* (1702). He wrote, concerning the events of 1692, "I knew of one of the Afflicted persons, who (as I was credibly informed) did try with an egg and a glass to find her future Husbands Calling; till there came up a Coffin, that is, a Spectre in likeness of a Coffin. And she afterward followed with diabolical molestation to her death; and so dyed a single person." (The original spelling has been kept from the document.)

The other mention of this incident was also by Hale, and he documented it during his visit to Betty Parris at a later date. It will be shown later in the book.

Tituba and the children.

Many attribute Hale's description to Abigail Williams. He was one of the first on the scene to witness the frightening antics of she and Betty Parris and the Venus Glass conjuring may have slipped out. Abigail was orphaned, and living with her Uncle's family in the parsonage. Her role may have been slightly more elevated than that of servant, as she was, after all, Reverend Parris's niece, but her dull routine would have involved unrelenting boredom and household chores. Abigail did die single, at the age of 37. Others of the witch trial accusers also died without marrying, leaving Hale's accreditation to one of the "Afflicted" somewhat ambiguous. Betty Parris married and bore five children, dying at the respectable age of seventy-seven.

Young Elizabeth (Betty) Parris was by all accounts a nervous child. Her mother was often ill and her father preached fire and brimstone with aplomb. Tales of Indian attacks and burned villages were not fabrications but a living, breathing reality—one that many of the orphaned village girls told with relish. Her father's constant diatribe about the lack of firewood and essentials may have haunted her. Her daily scripture study reinforced that the Devil was real and hell was wide open for those who strayed, even in thought. Children were taught to speak only when bidden. The Puritan form of love was founded on "spare the rod and you spoil the child." For a nine-year-old, the world was a foreboding place.

Many of the young women who cried "Witch," and were later grouped as "the Afflicted," were in their teens and early twenties. Even Ann Putnam, Sr., one of the few married adult accusers, was only twenty-eight. These girls were becoming women, their hormones and repressed natures straining at the Puritan bit with which they'd been fitted. There was no outlet for pent-up frustrations and drama. While occasional harvest festivals and dances occurred in the village, along with some singing and a few lawn games, the Puritan belief was that frivolity was of the Devil's making. The mantra "Idle hands are the Devil's workshop" acted as a yardstick for righteous living. Teenagers in the twenty-first century are no different. The term "that's a teenager for you" validates the common interpretation that this is a time of life when acting out, rebelling, and "finding oneself" is a matter of course. For Salem Village in 1692, hemmed in by an isolating winter, it only took one young woman defying the rules to set off a maelstrom.

It is generally believed the strange behavior of Betty Parris and Abigail Williams began to manifest in mid-January. A week later, on Monday, January 25, York, Maine was attacked by roughly 150 Wabanki Indians. They captured most of the town's houses, burned others, and destroyed livestock and inhabitants. Nearly 50 villagers were murdered and another 100 taken captive. One of the butchered was Reverend Shubael Dummer, proving the clergy were not a protected people. Reverend George Burroughs from Wells, Maine (who would later be one of the accused in the witch trials' outbreak) looked upon the burned ruins of York and said, "God is still manifesting his displeasure against this Land, he who formerly hath set his hand to help us, doth even write bitter things against us."

This was the underlying belief in New England. The "Chosen

People" were beginning to believe they were now chosen not by God, but his nemesis, the Devil. What had they done to incur such wrath? Who among them was bringing on this continuous affliction?

It was in the very home that George Burroughs had once inhabited as the former Reverend of Salem Village that the first signs of something amiss began to manifest. If the two children living there had, indeed, been playing with magic, had the threat of the Devil tormenting those who defied the Puritan laws taken hold in their young minds? For Betty, whose father was, after all, the Reverend and religious leader in the village, the guilt of trifling with things she knew were forbidden may have unnerved a mind already beset with fears.

Legend has it that the two girls (and possibly other teenagers in the nearby households) had asked Tituba to show them how to see the roles of their future husbands. For these girls, the man they might one day marry held all their future hopes. Unmarried women were sometimes left destitute or reliant on others to provide them with a home. A rich husband was desirable, but in a village where the eligible young men may have been few, the uncertainty of their future as a spinster or matron was a daily reality. Many people dabbled in "white magic," feeling the need to have some control over their lives. It was strictly forbidden, yet it was common knowledge it was practiced behind closed doors. Cotton Mather had remonstrated against it in his sermons and writings.

One such device for peering into the future was called the Venus Glass. An egg white was dropped into a glass of water and gently stirred. As the albumen settled, it was thought to take the shape of the future husband's occupation. Thus, a scythe portended a farmer, an apron a butcher, etc. According to Reverend Hale's account, one such conjuring revealed the shape of a coffin. This may have been enough to unhinge young Betty Parris' already guilt-ridden mind. Did the coffin mean her own death for dallying with the Devil's magic? It is at this gathering, that legend puts the beginning of the witchcraft madness.

Shortly after January 15, 1692, Abigail Williams began to exhibit strange behavior that revealed itself as strange utterances and staring for long periods of time at the space before her. Betty soon followed suit, or she may have been the first but their symptoms worsened quickly. The children crawled beneath furniture and shrieked at unseen horrors.

Reverend John Hale from neighboring Beverly was the first to report on the strange behavior of the girls. Reverend Parris may have reached out to him as a fellow clergyman, in hopes of keeping the girl's maladies from the gossiping villagers. Hale later wrote that the girls "were sadly Afflicted of they knew not what Distempers." They "were bitten and pinched by invisible agents; their arms, necks, and backs turned this way and that way, and returned back again, so as it was impossible for them to do to themselves, and beyond the power of any Epilepick Fits, or natural Disease to effect. Sometimes they were taken dumb, their mouths stopped, their throats choked, their limbs wracked and tormented so as might move a heart of stone, to sympathize with them, with bowels of compassion for them." Reverend Hale also stated "I will not enlarge in the description of their cruiel Sufferings, because they were in all things afflicted as bad as John Goodwin's Children at Boston, in the year 1688." (Spelling errors are retained for the integrity of the text.)

Deodat Lawson witnessed the recent afflictions of the four children of John Goodwin in Boston, Massachusetts. They were believed to be bewitched in June of 1688. One of the young girls, Martha Goodwin, would have to be restrained to keep her from running into the fireplace where a fire was lit. Lawson wrote that the children exhibited strange behavior: "Yea, they would fly like geese; and be carried with an incredible swiftness through the air, having but just their toes now and then upon the ground, and their arms waved like the wings of a bird." An elderly Catholic woman, Mary Glover, was accused and arrested for bewitching the children. She was hanged the same year, only four years before the 1692 Salem hangings.

An earlier famous account of a young woman's affliction came from England and was presented before King James I in 1605. Anne Gunter showed pins sticking into her flesh, and stunned the onlookers when she vomited pins from her mouth and expelled them through her nose and even her urine. King James I, a man well studied in the art of witchcraft, accused her of fraud. She admitted to it finally and the case was noted in several publications.

On March 13, 1664, two elderly widows from Lowestoft, England, Rose Cullender and Amy Denny, were accused of witchcraft after 13 indictments were brought against them alleging, they had bewitched several people, including children. The two women were hanged on March 17, 1664, a mere four days after their trial. The case was publicized in a 60-page pamphlet titled *A Tryal of Witches, at the Assizes held at Bury St. Edmunds for the County of Suffolk; on the Tenth day of March 1664.* It was published in England in 1682, only ten years before the Salem Village witchcraft outbreak. It is significant as the parallels of the afflicteds' symptoms. The resulting aftermath is eerily similar to those of the Salem accusers.

The report states that Samuel Pacy of Lowestoft refused to sell Amy Denny some fish on several occasions. After denying her for the third time, Pacy's daughter Deborah "...was taken with most violent fits, feeling most extreme pain in her Stomach, and Shreeking out in a most dreadful manner like unto a Whelp, and like unto a sensible Creature." During the trial, Pacy testified that his daughter "...in her fits would cry out of Amy Duny [ms] as the cause of her Malady, and that she did affright her with Apparitions of her Person."

Rose Cullender was also accused of appearing to Deborah and her older sister Elizabeth in visions, threatening them. The two women were examined for "Devil's Marks" by a team of six matrons. These marks were supposed to prove that the accused was a witch and the marks were where she suckled her familiars (animals such as snakes, birds, and other small creatures that did her bidding). Marks were found on Rose Cullender and this evidence was presented to the court.

The trial began on March 10, 1664. By then, the afflictions had spread to three other girls who were neighbors of the Pacy's: Jane Bocking (14 years old); Susan Chandler (18 years old); and Ann Durrant (between 16 and 21 years of age). The girls fell into strange fits during the trial, shrieking out and then suddenly struck dumb. Elizabeth Pacy was only cured from her fits by the touch of Amy Denny's hand, a method used in the Salem Witch Trials as well. Supposedly, if an afflicted person is touched by the witch that hurts them, the curse goes back into the tormentor, curing the victim. The two women were found guilty of witchcraft after only a 30-minute deliberation. They were hanged on March 17, 1662.

In the Lowestoft case, one of the bewitched girls "ran round about the house holding her apron, crying hush hush." Abigail Williams was noted as "sometimes making as if she would fly, stretching up her arms as high as she could, and crying 'Whish, Whish, Whish!'". Deodat Lawson witnessed Abigail run toward the fireplace "and had attempted to go into the fire," just as Martha Goodwin had during "her affliction," only a few years earlier.

Both of these famous accounts of witchcraft trials were in publication and no doubt read and commented upon. Abigail and Betty read their scriptures daily, and it is not without reason to assume they read, or were told, of the perils of children who tempted the Devil with their misbehaving.

The similarities between the behavior of the girls associated with the Salem Village outbreak and those of earlier publicized trials, are too similar to ignore. The Salem girls also produced pins protruding from their bodies during the witch inquisitions, fell into fits, and at times, were struck dumb. Testimony of being pinched by unseen apparitions (or specters) was a common complaint. Pinching was also used as a reprimand by parents for minor offenses. Pins were found in every household and each maid was taught sewing and quilting. To secret pins in one's clothing was an easy thing to do. There is also the question of whether the girls may have helped each other in their duplicity as their fame escalated and their need to provide more visible evidence became necessary—such as producing a broken knife blade and bite marks upon their wrists.

According to Reverend Hale's account "Mr. Parris, seeing the distressed condition of his Family, desired the presence of some Worthy Gentlemen of Salem, and some Neighbor Ministers to consult together at his House; who when they came, and had enquired diligently into the Sufferings of the Afflicted, concluded they were preternatural, and feared the hand of Satan was in them."

The group of ministers advised Reverend Parris "that he should sit still and wait upon the Providence of God, to see what time might discover; and to be much in prayer for the discovery of what was yet secret. They also Examined Tituba, who confessed the making of a Cake…and said her Mistress in her own Country was a Witch, and had taught her some means to be used for the discovery of a Witch and for the prevention of being bewitched, etc. But said that she her self was not a Witch."

The above narrative was printed in a publication called *A Modest Inquiry*, by John Hale in 1702, ten years after the 1692 witchcraft outbreak. That he was on the scene and witnessed the events in person holds great weight.

Reverend Parris did as he was told and waited. It was perhaps his hope the whole thing would blow over and spare him the humiliation of admitting to the village already at war with him that the Devil had chosen his household, daughter and niece, to manifest his evil machinations. But the girls' afflictions worsened and the gossip was spreading. Parris finally turned to physicians for help.

On February 24th, it is believed William Griggs, a physician from nearby Ryal (a sub-section of Salem Village), examined the girls and diagnosed what everyone was thinking—the children were "under an Evil Hand." William Griggs was the only doctor in Salem Village at the time of the witchcraft outbreak. He was one of Parris' supporters in a village fractured by religious conflict. That Parris trusted Griggs and called upon him in the hopes of finding a physical malady rather than a diabolical one would have been natural. Griggs lived with his wife and their ward, Elizabeth Hubbard, a little over a mile away from the parsonage.

Finally, on February 25, 1692, Reverend Parris and his wife Elizabeth left the two girls alone with Tituba and John Indian to attend a Thursday lecture in a nearby town and talk with other clergymen about their problem. This innocuous trip was to become a turning point in what may have been two young girls' antics to gain attention. It may have begun innocently enough with Betty's nerves getting the best of her. But suddenly, her parents, who had been involved with their own burdens, were paying attention to her. She was put to bed and prayed over. Her chores may have been passed to Abigail. Seeing the benefit of acting out, Abigail may have followed suit. Here was a reprieve from the tedium of the daily routine. Adults were focusing on them! People were coming from other villages to witness the theatrics carried out within the austere parsonage walls.

Tituba took advantage of her master's and mistress's absence to take matters into her own hands and make a "Witch Cake." It is known that a neighbor, Mary Sibley, instructed Tituba as to the ingredients needed. Betty and Abigail may have watched as the slave mixed together rye meal and the girls' urine into a mound and then baked it in the fireplace. Once it was ready, it was fed to a dog and the small party watched the animal with trepidation. The belief was that part of the witch was in the afflicted girls. Taking some of their urine and putting it into a cake would then extract some of the curse from them. Once the cake was fed to the dog, the afflicted girls might find relief and the witch might reveal itself. There is no record of whether anything came of the antidote to *maleficia*. We do know Reverend Parris later found out about it and was furious.

Tituba had used the Devil's magic to combat the Devil, thereby inviting him into their home. Worse, it validated Betty's worse fears; that they had tempted Satan and his witches by conjuring with a Venus Glass. Suddenly, it was no longer a game or a bid for attention. The cake was real. The counter-magic baked into it must be real. Therefore, witches in Salem Village must be real!

It was also at this time, according to Tituba's testimony during her inquisition, that the Devil appeared to the Parris' slave.

Chapter Three

The Pawns Gather Forces

"Who Afflicts Thee?"

While many of the village farms were widely strewn, some homes were close enough to be easily assessed from one to another. Such was the case of Mary Walcott, a 16-year-old girl who lived just north of the Parris' parsonage. Elizabeth Booth, 18-years-old, and Susanna Sheldon, 19-years-old, lived far enough away from the parsonage that their indoctrination into the circle of girls may have come about after a Sabbath sermon at the meetinghouse.

While the Sheldon home was near Ipswich Road (the main artery running through Salem Village and leading south into Salem Town and north toward the meetinghouse, Topsfield, Andover, and Wenham), it would still require walking over a mile to get to Tituba's kitchen where some harmless conjuring may have attracted the teenagers; not an unheard of walking distance in those days, but formidable in the winter snow. Ironically, Susanna would pass the entrance of the Rebecca Nurse farm on her way to the parsonage or meetinghouse. Rebecca was an elderly church-covenanted woman who would bear the distinction of one of the oldest female "witches" to be hanged as a result of the girl's "crying out" against her.

Elizabeth Booth lived still farther south and was a neighbor of John and Elizabeth Proctor. She was no doubt friends with their maid servant, Mary Warren. Elizabeth was typical of the girls who found themselves in the witchcraft milieu as the first accusers. Her family life was not a happy one. Her mother had been widowed twice, leaving Elizabeth without a father in a barren wilderness where a male was essential. The family, consisting of herself, her mother, her sister Alice, and brother George, struggled to keep food on the table. She would be one of the most outspoken of the girls, especially in her verbal attack on John and Elizabeth Proctor, and a Marblehead fisherman's wife, Wilmot Reed. Later, in September, Elizabeth's 14-year-old sister Alice and 16-year-old sister-in-law Elizabeth Wilkins (who had married Elizabeth's brother George after finding herself four months pregnant with his child) joined the "afflicteds'" ranks. Alice and Elizabeth Booth's more audacious claim during the trials was that fifty specters had joined the Devil in their home on the outskirts of Salem for a communion of bread and wine.

We do not know if more and more girls heard of the Venus Glass conjuring trick and crept through the woods and muddy roads to the parsonage in hopes of divining their futures. We do know, the afflictions spread rapidly now, and other households were filled with the sounds of wailing as the girls were pinched and tormented by unknown forces.

Elizabeth Hubbard was ward to Dr. William Griggs; the physician called into the Parris home to examine the girls. His dour prognosis that they were "under an Evil Hand" would have been known to Elizabeth, an orphaned 17-year-old, who had been an indentured servant in Boston, until her "owner" Issac Griggs and his wife died in 1689. Dr. William Griggs was Isaac's father, and he paid the courts for Elizabeth's contract. As the only young person living in the elderly physician's home, most of the chores fell to her.

As would soon be seen in the upcoming line-up of witches, the young women acting as accusers "cried out" against adults who had been, in one way or another, the target of gossip and unsavory stories overheard within their own homes. Their elders regaled certain villagers for any number of crimes—from boundary disputes to jealous rivalries. Dr. Grigg's may have complained about Elizabeth Proctor's inadequate dealings as an ad-hoc physician, someone who may have been competing for some of his medical practice. Elizabeth Hubbard was overheard to say the stomach pains of a neighbor, James Holton, were the work of John and Elizabeth Proctor. She claimed the Proctor's specters attacked her. Elizabeth was responsible for filing forty witchcraft petitions and testifying thirty-two times. The fact she was 17-years-old qualified her as a legitimate witness, giving her accusations, and that of the other older girls, free rein to point and cry "Witch!" But in the early days of February, no names of witches had yet been declared.

Sarah Churchill and Mary Warren soon joined the ranks of the afflicted girls. The village's astonishment at the nature of the fits and the number of households falling beneath the "Evil Hand" were the only thing people could talk about. The girls were relieved of their chores as they writhed and babbled; piteous performances that touched all but a few hearts. There were older and wiser heads that looked at their antics with disgust. They are only "causing mischief" was one statement used against the girls. The majority of the people crowding into Reverend Parris' small parlor, however, looked on with fear and trepidation. Not a few villagers secretly gloated at the minister's misfortune.

Sarah Churchill was in her early-to-mid-twenties. Sarah, like many of the other girls, had witnessed the atrocities of Indian attacks. She had been sequestered inside a garrison house in Saco, Maine and watched as the natives burned her grandfather's home, along with many others of the settlers who had fled across the river to the protection of the garrison. Her grandfather later died of his wounds. Sarah was not an orphan, like many of the other "afflicted," but she was eventually reduced to acting as a maid servant to George Jacobs, Sr., a salty-tongued elder who would fall beneath the shadow of witchcraft. Mary Walcott, the Parris' closest neighbor (and one of the first to show signs of witchcraft after Abigail and Betty's original outbreak) was Sarah Churchill's relative. Nathaniel

Ingersoll, owner of the tavern that would act as forum for the first witch inquests, was also a relative. Ingersoll's Ordinary was a stone's throw from the parsonage and meetinghouse.

Sarah had originally been a reluctant recruit into the enclave of accusers. She, Mary Warren, and Mary Watkins admitted later to faking their seizures. When her faint attempt at seizures stalled, Mercy Lewis (out of fear the rest of them would be found out) pressured her into confessing her master, George Jacobs, Sr., had beaten her with his walking sticks and called her a "bitch witch." Sarah went on to accuse Jacobs' granddaughter, Margaret Jacobs, claiming the two had forced her to sign the Devil's Book. They ended up in prison. But Sarah's outcry backfired and she found herself accused and thrown into jail. She confessed again that she had lied, and in June, she was released.

Mary Warren, age 20, was another casualty of the Indian wars. She and her parents had escaped the bloodshed in Maine, but her mother and father later died. She was alone in the world, with the exception of a sister who was a deaf-mute.

Mary ended up in the home of John and Elizabeth Proctor. Their family was a large one with eleven children and another on the way. John ran a tavern from the farm, taking full advantage of the acreage's position where Ipswich Road branched into other roadways. Travelers from Salem Town, going north past Gallows Hill and heading to Lynn, Boxford, Topsfield, or Reading, could stop for some ale and "vittles." By all accounts, John Proctor was a harsh, no-nonsense type of man. His portrayal as the sympathetic figure in Arthur Miller's *The Crucible* may be a watered-down version of the farmer's true nature. Mary Warren would testify that John threatened to "burn her out" of her hysterics during the witch trials by forcing "hot tongs downe her throat." He shouted "If ye are afflicted, I wish ye were more Afflicted." When she cried out "Why?" he answered, "Because you goe to bring out Innocent persons."

John Proctor is one of the few adults who actually took action against the young women's fits. He told one neighbor. Samuel Sibley, that the best way to handle his "Jade" was to thrash it out of her, and to tie her to her spinning wheel to keep her busy. In the beginning, Mary Warren was not as verbal as the others in her testimonies, fearful of John Proctor's wrath. When John and Elizabeth were accused and subsequently jailed for witchcraft, Mary may have feared she would now have nowhere to go. In early April, shortly after their imprisonment, her fits disappeared. In gratitude, she posted a note on the meetinghouse board, thanking Providence for curing her. The other girls, fearing she might betray them as frauds, turned on her and accused her of witchcraft, saying the only reason she was cured was because she had joined the Devil. She was thrown into jail.

Elizabeth Hubbard accused Mary Warren on the day of her inquisition, that she claimed the afflicted girls were only play acting. Rather than look into the allegations that the girls were faking (even though innocent people may hang for it), the magistrates continued on with the trial. Mary protested her innocence as the afflicted girls fell to the floor in fits. As the questions became pressing, Mary too dropped to the floor in convulsions. She was taken from the room. Upon being returned to the unrelenting questions, and pressed to name witches, she again fell into fits and was removed, thus effectively avoiding pressing charges against the Proctors, or anyone else. Even when taken away to be questioned in private, she waffled on her answers.

In prison, she see-sawed back and forth between accusing others and recanting. "Yes," she had put a pin into a poppet (crude doll associated with witchcraft) that Elizabeth Proctor owned. But then, "No," she had never seen any poppets, but went on to name witches who had brought her the dolls. "Yes," she made a mark in the Devil's Book, but only with her fingertip. Her stories were so convoluted that the magistrates finally let her out of jail and focused on her testimony against accused witches. At this point, she joined forces with the other girls, and the Proctors became her main target.

During the 1690s, the legal age for a child to testify in court for a major offense was 14-years-old and older. Adults could testify to a younger child's behavior, but the child could not appear under oath. For that reason, Reverend Parris' daughter, Betty (age 9) and his niece Abigail (age 11) could not be credible witnesses. That would soon change. At this time, they were still being asked "What afflicts thee?" But as older girls from neighboring households began showing symptoms of bewitchment, namely Elizabeth Hubbard (age 17), the tide changed. Elizabeth Hubbard, and Ann Putnam Jr. (age 12) were the first newcomers to exhibit fits on February 25, 1962. Suddenly, the adults were not asking "What afflicts thee?" but "*Who* afflicts thee?"

This simple transfer of a single word began an event in history that will forever associate Salem Village (today's Danvers, Massachusetts) with the most famous witch trials in America. The answer to "*Who* afflicts thee?" would open the Devil's Book to names eagerly put forth by villagers with an axe to grind. The girls would indeed become pawns in a deadly game of revenge and greed.

Chapter Four

A Village of Hatred

The impetus for the witchcraft outbreak can only be understood by looking at the layers of festering strife that was the foundation of Salem Village as surely as the bedrock it was built upon. The innocent victims that were executed in 1692 were not "cried out" upon at random. The "afflicted" girls were as puppets, and it was the dissatisfied adults of Salem Village that were pulling their strings.

The large statue that commands the Commons area in today's Salem is that of Roger Conant, the town's founder in 1626. Conant knew, as those who came after him, that the location was a prime spot for fishing and as a trading post for the West Indies, Europe, and beyond. The area grew with the influx of Puritans making their way to the Promised Land. Soon, it became necessary to stretch the town's boundaries northward where the soil was fertile enough to supply the food needs of a growing populace. Land grants were given out to people who could farm the land. As the years went by, several men prospered in this interior farmland, about seven miles inland from Salem Town. Names such as Putnam, Porter, Ingersoll, and Hutchinson would appear as large land owners, and would become prominent participants in the Salem Witch Trials of 1692.

It is here the conflict began between "The Farmers" of Salem Village and the "Sea Merchants" of Salem Town. Salem Village produced the food and the tax revenues Salem Town depended upon, yet the rural community had no rights. They were forced to pay taxes that improved the roads and conditions of the Town, while living without any real autonomy of their own. Other neighboring areas of Salem Village also strained at the bit and became independent towns; Marblehead in 1648, Wenham in 1643, Manchester in 1645, and Beverly in 1668. Salem Village tried, in vain, to create its own infrastructure. Despite hundreds of petitions, court appearances, filings, and pleadings, Salem Village did not receive its autonomy until 1752.

In 1667, several of the Salem Village "farmers" appealed to the Essex County court to have the members of the village relieved of sending their men to take their turn at Salem Town's night watch. This is where two men or more were ordered to spend the night in the watch tower to alert the town of Indians or other dangers that appeared. The General Court granted their request, yet continued to order the Salem Village farmers to take their turn. Thirty-one farmers appeared again at court with the following grievance:

"Some of us live ten miles, some eight or nine; the nearest are at least five miles from Salem meeting-house…and then 'tis nearly a mile farther to the sentry-place…so that some of us must travel armed eleven miles to watch…which is more than a soldier's march that is under pay. And yet, not excused from paying our part to all charges, both ecclesiastical and civil, besides the maintenance of our families these hard times, when the hand of God is heavy upon the husbandman."

The Salem Farmers had no meetinghouse, minister, or church of their own and were forced to walk the above-mentioned miles to attend religious services each week. The time and mileage to fulfill the watch duty added to their grief. The Court finally capitulated and changed the ruling to "all farmers dwelling above four miles from the meetinghouse," were exempt from duty. Nathaniel Putnam, among others, refused to comply. He was fined £20 and instructed to offer a public apology. (Public humiliation was always at the foreground of the Puritan society.)

The Putnams' name appeared again on court documents when John and Thomas Putnam appeared before a Salem Town meeting with a petition signed by twenty-eight farmers. The manifesto informed the Town that the farmers were refusing to pay the new tax for construction of a new Town meetinghouse. Salem Village wanted their own meetinghouse and minister, once again bemoaning the great distance they had to travel to attend services, despite the fact they were considered part of Salem Town's religious congregation. George Corwin, a Salem merchant, acting Marshall, and meeting moderator, rebuffed the Putnams and declared they were out of order. It only strengthened the growing tension between town and village. It was clear the wealthy sea merchants of Salem Town were running the show.

Finally, after applying continued pressure to the General Court in Boston, the villagers were granted the right to build their own meetinghouse and hire a minister. They were not released from paying other civil taxes that still tied them to the town of Salem and its own interests. The General Court instructed that a five-man Committee be elected to assess which households were paying taxes in support of a new minister. The village elected its committee on November 11, 1672, and the meetinghouse plans began, along with a search for their very own minister.

Salem Village may have won the battle to have its own religious services and meetinghouse, but the war between the seaport town of Salem and the rural farmland of Salem Village was far from over. The Town continued to regulate everything from the price of the villagers' farm goods for sale, to their constables, road layouts, and land grants. Salem Village was split in its loyalties, with some of its inhabitants still firmly intrenched in Salem Town's identity, while many of the villagers strived valiantly to increase their autonomy and fight the constant restraints placed upon them.

1672 saw the Town wielding its power when it continued to tax the villagers for repairs and improvements to the Town meetinghouse. When Nathaniel Putnam refused, a Town constable seized two-and-a-half acres of Putnam's land, that was literally in his front yard. It wasn't until 1713, that the villagers were finally released from paying the taxes for the Town's meetinghouse. Salem Town held all the cards, and as strife continued, many believed it was the Devil doing the shuffling.

More and more the Salem villagers appealed to the Salem Town meetings to allow them to become a separate and fully independent town. They were refused and admonished for "the restless frame of spirit" that pervaded their small community. This "restless frame" of mind was only enhanced with boundary disputes between itself and the neighboring towns who had effectively become independent from Salem Town. Topsfield, Andover, and Wenham, who hemmed in Salem Village, bitterly fought over land rights. If the landowner's land was found to have tiptoed over the imaginary boundary line into another township, then that property was subject to be taxed by the offended municipality. As Salem Village was still considered only the ugly step-child of Salem Town, without authority or even its own constables, the feuding became, at times, violent, as the villagers felt the futility of their situation. Lawsuits, appeals, petitions, and face-to-face quarreling put neighbor against neighbor.

In 1679, Salem Village had acquired the reputation of a community where "brother is against brother and neighbors are against neighbors, all quarreling and smiting one another." The area was known for its "uncomfortable divisions and contentions." The wife of John Dodge of Salem Village declared that "if Wenham men came there for rates she would make the blood run about their ears." A Wenham neighbor laughed at her and said she didn't frighten him. At that, she "caught him by the hair of his head and with her other hand struck him on the face in a furious manner."

The importance of Salem Village's precarious and unprecedented structure cannot be stressed enough. They were without government, not only because Massachusetts was currently without its charter, but closer to home, Salem Town regulated their every move. They were taxed, land grants given and withheld, their very living determined by a Town that would, on one hand, set the rules, yet on the other hand, tell them they were on their own with their disputes. Surrounding townships considered them a non-issue; an ineffectual square acreage sometimes called the "parish" in Salem Town. It was a rudderless ship headed for dangerous waters.

Who Is in Charge?

The village of Salem was steeped in bitter disputes, that even the hard-won victory of having its own meetinghouse and minister became a hotbed of contention among the residents. The question arose "who had the power to call and dismiss a minister?" This should have been the right of church members. Yet when James Bayley was voted for as minister in 1673, he was elected by *all* the householders in Salem, not just those perched on pews each Sabbath. This irregular authority would play out over the years with continued rancor.

James Bayley, tired of the fighting and contention over his calling, left Salem Village in 1680. Nathaniel Putnam was elected by the "inhabitants" (church members and non-members) to find a new minister. Reverend George Burroughs was hired, and his fate was sealed.

George Burroughs was twenty-eight years old in 1680 when he accepted the role as religious helmsman in the quarreling village of Salem. He was a Harvard graduate, and went to Falmouth, Maine to preach in 1670. Falmouth (today's Portland) sat on Casco Bay and was attacked by Indians in 1676, during King Phillips War. Many lost their lives during the milieu. Reverend Burroughs took many of the survivors to Salisbury, Maine, where he lived until he received the offer from Salem Village to come there and act as their minister. Burroughs, who had no doubt heard of the contentious villagers, agreed, with one caveat:

"In case any difference should arise in time to come, that we engage on both sides to submit to counsel for a peaceable issue."

This plea for a "peaceable" resolution during tough times was not to be. By 1682, Burroughs was embroiled in legal disputes. The villagers were once again divided over their support of a minister. April of 1682, Jeremiah Watts wrote that the disputes were putting "brother against brother, and neighbors against neighbors." Less than one year later, Reverend Burroughs' salary was being withheld. Finally, Burroughs stopped showing up for his Sabbath meetings. Casco Bay had been rebuilding since the Indian desecration, and Burroughs was being asked to come back. But leaving Salem Village would prove to be no easy exit. Not if the Putnams had a say in it.

In September 1681, George Burroughs's wife died. Captain John Putnam loaned Burroughs' money to buy the customary funeral wine. He had also advanced credit to the Reverend on other occasions to buy merchandise from Boston. Burroughs promised to pay Putnam back from his salary as Reverend. However, the good Salem villagers reneged on paying Burroughs and he was unable to repay Putnam. Burroughs had returned to Casco Bay at this point and was ordered back to Salem to make an accounting for the debt. He returned on May 2, 1683, not quite two months after abandoning his post at the Salem Village church. A marshal (probably George Corwin) arrested Burroughs upon his return at the instigation of Captain John Putnam for default on his payment of debt.

According to the County Court Records, "Just as Burroughs began to give his accounts, the marshal came in and, after a while, went to John Putnam, Senior, and whispered to him. And said Putnam to him, "You know what you have to do; do your office." Then the marshal came to Mr. Burroughs and said, "Sir, I have a writing to read you." Then he read the attachment, and demanded goods. Mr. Burroughs answered that he had no goods to show, and that he was now reckoning with the inhabitants, for we know not yet who is in debt, but there was his body.

"As we were ready to go out of the meetinghouse, Mr. Burroughs said, "Well, what will you do with me?" Then the marshal went to John Putnam, Senior, and said to him, "What shall I do?" The said John Putnam replied "You know your business." And then the said Putnam went to his brother, Thomas Putnam, and pulled him by the coat, and they went out of the house together, and presently came in again. Then said John Putnam, "Marshal, take your prisoner, and have him up to the ordinary and secure him till the morning." The "ordinary" was the name for Ingersoll's Ordinary, a tavern only a stone's throw from the Salem Village meetinghouse where the first witches were brought for questioning in 1692.

Putnam's suit against Burroughs was eventually settled out of court. The disgraced Reverend left Salem Village under a cloud of angst and acrimonious feelings between himself and the inhabitants. He returned to Casco Bay where he lived for nine years. On May 4, 1692, he was brought back to Salem as a prisoner, not for unpaid debts, but as the accused ring leader of a coven of witches.

Deodat Lawson was the next chosen lamb to the slaughter. He was offered the position as village minister. In 1684, his belongings were brought from Boston to Salem harbor. His career as a preacher had floundered at Edgartown, on Martha's Vineyard. He had pursued other occupations in Boston in the ministry, but without success. It was this disrupted life that brought him to accept Salem Village's offer. But, as before, it was not long before the church was fractured.

Captain John Putnam and his nephew, Thomas Putnam, Jr., put forth the concept of a full-fledged covenanted church and the ordination of Lawson as the Salem Village minister. This was a formality not instigated with Bayley and Burroughs. A group of men opposed the idea and would play a prominent role in the witch trials to come. They were Joseph Hutchinson, Job Swinnerton, Joseph Porter, and Porter's brother-in-law, Daniel Andrews. The divided parties locked horns and the dissension escalated.

January of 1687, the four men mentioned above went to the villagers and encouraged them to form a committee to bring them their "grievances relating to public affairs of this place." Joseph Hutchinson owned the land the church meetinghouse was built upon and had bequeathed it to the Village in 1673 as use for the building. He now, in a petulant move, fenced in certain sections of the land and began farming it. The Village Committee, which included several Putnams, complained that "he hath so hedged in our meetinghouse already that we are all forced to go in at one gate."

Hutchinson shot back "They have no cause to complain of me for fencing in my own land; for I am sure I fenced in none of theirs. I wish they would not pull down my fences… As for blocking up the meeting-house, it was they did it, and not I, in the time of the Indian wars, and they made Salem pay for it. I wish they would bring me my rocks they took to do it with, for I want them to make a fence with."

For once, Salem Town got involved, no doubt to further its own ambitions in an attempt to keep Salem Village tied to its ecclesial apron strings. A three-man committee consisting of John Hathorne, Bartholomew Gedney, and William Brown, Jr. advised not to adopt Deodat Lawson's ordination as the matter had "not been so inoffensively managed as it might have been." They went on to admonish the villagers for their continued "uncharitable expressions and uncomely reflections tossed to and fro" which represented "the effects of settled prejudices and resolved animosity." Their final admonition would ring true as a tragic prophesy:

These continued behaviors will "have a tendency to make such a gap as we fear, if not timely prevented, will let out peace and order and let in confusion and every evil work."

Lawson left, unable to endure the constant upheaval over what should have been a joining of a community in the happy prospects of a church where brotherly love and peace would be proffered. As mentioned in an earlier chapter, he signed on as chaplain for a military expedition lead by Sir Edmund Andros, the England-appointed governor.

Sir Edmond Andros

The dark force that swept through Salem Village had found a home there—in the shuttered houses where vitriol dripped from tongues; in Ingersoll's Ordinary where men met and vilified each other over land disputes and petty quarrels; and where church members, cosseted in their righteousness, played spin the bottle with which neighbor was to live and which to die upon the gallows. It had been all too easy to stir this cauldron of discontent and hatred in this small fractured village.

Somewhere in the winter darkness, the unseen hand slid the new Bishop into place, brushed phantom fingers across the Castles and Pawns in uncertainty, and finally moved the Knights into their familiar L-shaped pattern. It would prove to be the most-deadly game with ramifications that still echoed through the decades.

Chapter Five

The **Knights**
The Putnams and the Porters

Salem Village was divided, geographically, politically, economically, and morally. The Puritans who had come here to build a shining beacon on the hill, had extinguished the flame with bitter jealousies and hatred. As 1692 would attest, it was a community ripe for the picking by an "Evil Hand."

The division of Salem Village is all-important to understanding the insidious days that were to come. What had begun as a promising partnership between farming and seaport towns, had gone awry when prominent families, in better placed geographical locations, began gathering the lion's share of the swell. Salem Town was dependent on Salem Village's food supply, not only for its own sustenance, but for the revenue their exported products created. Not only food stuffs but timber was supplied by the farmers. And herein, lies the rub.

The village farming acreage was shrinking. Third generation sons were taking their inherited lands and farming them themselves. This split up what was once large family holdings in one or two generations. Add to that the fact that Salem Village had nowhere to grow. It was hemmed in by towns to the north, east, and west that had gained their independence and drawn boundary lines. Salem

Town and the sea blocked their expansion to the south. Is it any wonder that land disputes were so common?

The farmers with land on the east side of the village had a distinct advantage over those who had chosen farming acreage on the west. The east-side was closer in proximity to Salem Town and its import/export trade. This area offered flat meadows and access to several rivers and Salem Harbor, giving it front row seats to the wharves and landings where goods were conveyed. They were closer to the waterways and roads leading from the Town and Boston, such as Ipswich Road. The eastern farmers were at least three miles closer to the bustling seaport town of Salem and its trading posts. The western farmers were, by contrast, trying to eke out a living in areas disrupted by swampy marshes and rocky outcroppings.

The eastern villager's proximity to Ipswich Road and its myriad travelers and tradesmen is very significant. Not only did the location offer the landowner the prime spot for sawmills and taverns, it gave this populace a feeling of connection with Salem Town and the news that came and went from that community and Boston. The western villagers, in turn, were more remote and cut off from the perks their eastern neighbors enjoyed. Three taverns lay on a branch of Ipswich Road and were within the boundaries of Salem Village. Joshua Rea, Jr. and Walter Phillips ran licensed "watering holes," while Bridget and Edward Bishop raked in the money from their popular unlicensed tavern. John Proctor's was farther removed in the southern part of Salem Village. Ingersoll's Ordinary was located along Andover Road, and typically served the western farmers and travelers heading north.

John Proctor had petitioned the Salem Committee to allow him to operate a tavern in his house on one of Ipswich Road's arteries. His home he said was "in the common roadway, which occassioneth several travelers to call in for some refreshments as they pass along. I do therefor earnestly request you that you would be pleased to grant me liberty to set up a house of entertainment to sell beer, cider

[and] liquors." Proctor was granted his license but the caveat was that he could sell only to outsiders and strangers.

While Puritans partook of wine and ale with their meals, they were concerned about the bawdy nature of the people taverns attracted. It is no surprise therefore, that three of the tavern owners became victims of the witchcraft outbreak. Bridget Bishop and John Proctor were hanged as witches in 1692.

As the Witch Trials play out, you will see a distinct dividing line between those who lived along Ipswich Road and those who did not. When Reverend Parris's position as pastor was put forth for the inhabitants' vote, only two living along the Ipswich Road were in favor of him. Twenty households voted against him. The eastern village farmers were more in tune with their prosperous benefactor—Salem Town. To them, the complaints coming forth from the western farmers were causing problems and worsening relationships with the seaport town. For the western inhabitants, they saw themselves cut off from the benefits flowing to their eastern neighbors, and so they were predominantly pro-Parris. Parris and the meetinghouse church represented some solace that they were breaking away from Salem Town and structuring their own government where they would pay taxes only for their improvements and needs. Of these pro-Parris farmers, most were not affluent. The names of Putnam, however, would fill the records of the Salem Village church, and therein lay all the difference.

Reverend Parris's supporters were made up of church members (those covenanted to accept the sacrament) who were of negligible wealth, although some, like the Nurse's and Putnams, had money. The majority (who were not covenanted members) were poorer still and made up the larger body of villagers who supported Parris and his church. It is important to note that the pro-Parris faction played the leading role in the witch trial prosecutions. These people were less-wealthy, cut-off from the income-producing rivers and wharfs, and owning less land.

It is also important to remember the underlying core of this populace. Westerner or Easterner, these people came together to create a community built on piousness and religious fervor. The anxiety felt throughout Salem Village in the days leading up the to the witchcraft hysteria was due to that same unrelenting mantra that said if there was trouble, it was due to personal failings. Morally, something was amiss. And while the simple farmers of the western acreage could look with self-righteous malice toward Salem Town with its capitalist interests and desire for fancy homes and ever-growing economic security, they still felt the pangs of guilt and fear that they were not without fissures in their holiness. And for the eastern faction, did their Puritan conscience whisper to them in the still hours of the night, asking "Which Master do you serve? God or money?"

The pro-Parris villagers perhaps saw their neighbors tied to Salem Town as they would those of Sodom and Gomorrah. Wasn't it their right, nay, their duty to weed out those that were standing in opposition to the Puritan way of life? Did not the Bible teach that to destroy the enemy that was morally tainted was better than to see the righteous falter? If nothing else, then for the sake of the community and their hard-won division from England's church and its archaic ways. Weren't they morally within their rights to take matters into their own hands to preserve the righteousness of their "city on the hill" and the futures of their children? And, as Salem Town had left them politically severed and without even a constable of their own, did it not fall to them to mete out justice? Didn't it fall to them to fashion a noose?

It's obvious that the divisive nature of the days of 1691/1692 had flooded the small hamlet of Salem Village with so many oppositions that it is hard to single out the most-destructive element that threw the town into the Devil's maw. The warring families of the Porters and Putnams, however, would be the pivotal catalyst that ended in the death of their neighbors and one-time friends. These Knights of the most-prominent families in Salem Village would move toward each other on a chessboard made of patches of farmland and clash in ways in which only the Prince of Darkness could revel.

The Porters and the Putnams

John Putnam sixty-five, and John Porter forty-eight in 1644, were the patriarchs of two families so similar that it was only logical the two men would move in similar circles inside the Salem Village community. They were chosen to walk the streets of the village each Sabbath and report on any inhabitants who were not attending church "such as either lie about the meetinghouse without attending to the word or ordinances, or that lie at home or in the fields." Both men had moved to Salem from the south of England and both men prospered. There were differences, as well, not the least was the almost twenty-year age difference between them. Porter's offspring were quite young while Putnam's were grown.

John Putnam accrued land grants to the tune of 800 acres by the time of his death in 1662. Porter, on the other hand, had amassed close to 2,000 acres when he died 14 years after Putnam in 1676. Both men had three living sons, each burying two. The Putnam second generation living in Salem consisted of Thomas (born in 1615), Nathaniel (born in 1619), and "Captain" John (born in 1627). The Porter brothers were Joseph (born in 1638), Benjamin (born in 1639), and Israel (born in 1644). All of the Putnam and Porter siblings were well off as tax records of 1681 proved. The Putnam brothers paid over twice what the other villagers paid in taxes, and the Porters were wealthier still. It is a conundrum then to see these two similar families, leaders of the community, heading up the two disparate parties that were pro- and anti-Parris. It would be the village's undoing.

During Reverend Parris' ministry, not one of the Porter family members or their in-laws joined the village church. In contrast, ten of the Putnam men and seven of their wives joined the church under Parris' ministry. The Putnam name appeared ad nauseum on all petitions and church documents, a reflection that they comprised one-fourth of the congregation. Church records indicated that "At a Church-meeting at Brother Thomas Putnam's house..., [it was] voted that our Brethren John Putnam, Senior, and Nathaniel Putnam and Deacon [Edward] Putnam and John Putnam Junior be appointed to meet...the dissenters...to treat in order to amicable issue." Only young Joseph Putnam joined the ranks of the anti-Parris campaign, but with good reason. He had married Israel Porter's daughter, Elizabeth, and their union would ignite a powder keg.

The Putnam family were represented by the Devil's black Knight. They pushed the witch trials forward with a fervor that was unrelenting. Robert Calef, a witch trial historian and author of *More Wonders of the Invisible World* (1700) wrote "that family of the Putnams, who were the chief prosecutors in this business." The Putnam family (a total of eight members) went on to accuse forty-six witches! Ann Putnam, Junior, daughter of Thomas Putnam, Junior, would be a driving force in the accusations, although she was only 12-years-old.

With the Putnams piling wood upon the witchcraft pyre, the Porters had reason to be fearful. They remained in the background with only a few exceptions. Israel's son John selected Sarah Bibber, the least respectable of the witch accusers, to cast doubt on her testimony. Sarah was from Wenham, a neighboring town, and possibly just far enough outside the village parameters to be fair game. Israel Porter stood up for Rebecca Nurse when she was accused and circulated a petition he drew up in her defense. Thirty-nine villagers signed it. Israel had been at Rebecca's bedside a few days before her arrest and found her feeble, yet pious in her suffering. The name Porter only appeared a few times during the 1692 witch hysteria, yet they were there, in the background, watching and waiting.

As noted earlier, those Salem inhabitants living in the eastern-most territory of the village had a great advantage over their neighbors who were farming to the west. One of the most-prosperous eastern land owners was Israel Porter. His father John Porter (who had once walked the rutted village roads with John Putnam, Senior in search of Sabbath Day slackers) was one of the leading merchants in Salem Town in the 1660's. He was granted land on the waterfront for a new wharf and warehouse. This put the Porter family directly within the Town boundaries. Their extensive land holdings were now on both sides of the dotted line that separated Salem Town from Salem Village. In 1670, Porter joined Joseph and John Hutchinson to build a saw mill on one of the rivers that fed the village proper. Once it was damned, the road leading to Thomas Putnam's farm became flooded. Thomas filed suit stating the dam had been flooding the single access road to his farm for months at a time. "To be this long-kept prisoner will be a way to ruin me and mine forever," he complained. Turning a deaf ear, Porter built a second saw mill on the Fish River at Ipswich Road's crossing, in partnership with a member of the Endicott family.

Sidney Perley, renowned Salem historian, wrote in his *History of Salem* the following accolades allotted to John Porter during his lifetime in Salem Village/Town:

"In 1647, John Porter was foreman of the Essex County Grand Jury. In 1646, he was elected as a Salem Town Selectman. In 1668, he was a deputy of the General Court, and became a deacon in the Salem Town church in 1661, where his pew was directly behind that of George Corwin and William Hathorne, wealthy merchants and powerful men in Salem Town government. Even though John Porter lived respectively within Salem Village, upon his death he left a bequest to the Salem Town church, and nothing to the village church where Reverend Bayley was then acting minister."

It is clear that the lines drawn in the hard ground of Salem Village kept the Putnam family on one side, and the Porter clan on the other.

The Third Generation of Putnams and Porters

It is with the third generation Putnams that the framework of the witch trials is built. The contentions between the second generation of Putnams and Porters may have cleared the way for what was to come, but it is primarily Thomas Putnam Jr.'s family that held the torch and pitchfork aloft and bid others to follow.

Thomas Putnam, Sr. married Ann Holyoke in 1643. They bore eight children, two of which were male. Thomas Putnam Jr. was born in 1653 and Edward Putnam in 1654. As the eldest, Thomas Junior expected to inherit a sizeable estate from his father, who was, at that time, the wealthiest man in the village. He realized the property, upon his father's death, would be divided up between he and his brother, and that his sisters' dowries would be taken care of. Still, his prospects looked bright. His future took on even more promise when he married Ann Carr in 1678.

Ann Carr was the daughter of George Carr, a wealthy man from nearby Salisbury. Carr owned 400 acres of farmland and a ship works in Salisbury. Upon his death, Carr's estate was more than £1,000, a sizeable amount in 1682. Thomas had married a woman whose future looked every bit as bright as his own, and their alliance opened the door for Putnam to become involved in his rich father-in-law's myriad businesses. Only four years after Thomas and Ann married, however, that magic bubble of prosperity and bliss burst.

Upon George Carr's death, his widow and two of his sons took control of the estate. About 60 percent of Carr's estate, which included the ship works and a ferry business, was given to the two sons, with the other six children receiving bequests that amounted to about 10% of the inheritance. In 1682, Thomas Putnam Jr., along with some of Carr's family, filed a protest that the widow and her sons (acting as executors) were cheating the daughters (and their husbands) out of their rightful inheritance. Their pleadings proved ineffectual, and Ann Carr Putnam walked away with a fraction of what she and her husband Thomas had expected.

Ok. Alright. All is not lost. Thomas still had his father's vast holdings to look forward to as the eldest son in Thomas Sr.'s lineage. Thomas expected to inherit almost 300 acres along with the family homestead. The eldest son typically received a double portion which would further fill his coffers. His future, though not as dazzling as he had first expected through his union with a Carr, was still glittering enough to satisfy him and his desire for wealth and status. But like the tides that filled Salem Harbor, only to be sucked away when the waters ebbed, the unseen force hovering over Salem Village would block the Black Knight using the harshest blow of all.

In a move no one saw coming, the elderly Thomas Putnam Sr. decided to take a second wife in 1666, one year after his first wife died. Perhaps the last three numbers in this date were indicative of the evil forces at work against Thomas Putnam Jr. For it was with this new wife, Mary Veren, that the prodigy son, Joseph, would be born in 1669.

Mary Veren was the widow of Nathaniel Veren, a Salem ship captain who, along with his two brothers, were affluent merchants in Salem Town. Mary owned her own house in Town that she had purchased from one of her brothers-in-law. Another Salem merchant, selectman, Timothy Lindall, became her son-in-law. His name would appear again in the witchcraft debacle. She bore Putnam Sr. a son, Joseph, the only offspring of their union.

It was with this birth, and the consequent actions of Mary and Thomas Sr., that a bitter hatred would be fueled that would see Thomas Putnam, Jr's name on so many witchcraft accusations. As stated earlier, he made at least thirty-five complaints against innocent souls, and testified against seventeen. His wife Ann Carr Putnam, their twelve-year-old daughter Ann Jr., and their servant Mercy Lewis were among the most vocal and vociferous of the accusers. Thomas also recorded 120 depositions against accused "witches." His detailed accounts of the depositions of witnesses was written in a way to promote the guilt of the accused during a trial.

His efforts were rewarded with a high success rate of guilty charges.

For whatever reason, when Thomas Putnam Sr. died in 1686, he left a will, with the approval of his wife Mary, leaving the largest part of his estate to Mary and their son Joseph (then 16-years-old). According to Paul Boyer and Stephen Nissenbaum's book *Salem Possessed* (1974), they referred to Eben Putnam's *History of the Putnam Family* (1891), giving the details of the will that gave the widow and Joseph "the best part of the estate, including ample family farmstead, the household furnishings, all the barns and outbuildings, and agricultural equipment, and many of the most fertile acres that had been granted to old John Putnam forty years before."

The will reaffirmed Putnam Sr.'s bequests of farms for his two sons Thomas and Edward from his first marriage, and dowries for his daughters. Yet, this fell short of the inheritance the Putnam siblings had expected. The fact that their father's will had made the unusual caveat that Joseph could take over his inheritance at age 18 instead of the usual 21-years of age, fanned the flames. This meant that within only two years, young Joseph would be one of the richest Putnams in Salem Village. The final burn came inside the will's fine print—Israel Porter, the Putnam nemesis, was named overseer of the estate, with the widow Putnam and young Joseph acting as executors.

Thomas Jr., his brother Edward, and their brothers-in-law Jonathan Walcott and William Trask took it to court. They asked that Thomas Putnam Jr. be named executor so that a fair accounting of the estate might be undertaken. They claimed they were "extremely wronged" and blamed the widow Putnam for the unfair distribution of property. Mary Veren Putnam hired a Salem Town attorney and the opponents' suit came to naught.

And so, without any effort on his behalf, Joseph Putnam, age 18, became the largest heir to the Putnam estate on September 14, 1687. The yardstick of his wealth is measured in the 1690 tax records. Joseph's taxes were 40% higher than his older half-brothers, and all of the third-generation Putnams. The betrayal was far from over.

In 1690, only two years before the witchcraft outbreak, Joseph Putnam, now 20-years of age, married Elizabeth Porter, the sixteen-year-old daughter of the Putnam enemy, Israel Porter. Joseph was now ensconced in the Porter clan, merging the wealth of Salem Village's two most-affluent families. He would now enjoy the benefits of his alliance with the prosperous Salem Town sea merchants while his half-brothers continued to toil in rock-infested farmland, cut off from growth and any hopes of furthering their position in life. Not that the Putnam men were not considered prosperous in their farming endeavors and leaders in the community, but their achievements paled when compared with that of their younger half-brother who was taking full advantage of his mother's political and economic connections in Salem Town.

Thomas Putnam Jr. home, circa 1691
Salem Village (now Danvers, MA)

Mary Veren Putnam died in April of 1695 and fired the final shot heard through the Putnam households. In her will she left everything to Joseph and cut off Thomas Jr., Edward and Deliverance (Putnam) Walcott, leaving them a mere 5 shillings each because they "brought upon me inconvenient and unnecessary charges and disbursements at several times." Joseph, meanwhile had now aligned himself with the Porter kinsmen who were anti-Parris and influential in what lie ahead: Joseph Porter and Daniel Andrews, along with aforementioned Timothy Lindell. Daniel Andrews would be accused of witchcraft in less than two years.

Did Israel Porter play puppet master in the whole affair? He was, after all, the one to draw up Thomas Putnam Sr.'s will. He was overseer for Mary Veren Putnam's estate at Putnam Sr.'s passing. Had he introduced Joseph to his daughter Elizabeth in a plot to unite a Putnam with a Porter? Was it he who influenced the changing of Joseph's age to inherit from 16 to 18 in fear something may happen if Mary (Joseph's mother) died before he came of age? He married off his daughter Elizabeth as soon as she turned 16. Had even the Devil underestimated the craftiness and cunning of the White Knight in this deadliest of chess games?

Chapter Six

"She's a Witch!"

Late February, 1692, found the roads of Salem Village weighted down with mud and sludge from a sudden thaw. Winter had taken a breath, promising Spring, and what many considered a season of fresh hope. But in the parsonage of Reverend Samuel Parris, hope seemed far away. The plague afflicting his daughter and niece was spreading to other girls in other households. Some evil force was at work in his parish. As the religious leader of that faction, it fell to him to explain it to his congregation and offer a promise of healing. His precarious position with the strong opponents he faced daily within the village boundaries was tripled with this new development. It appeared to all around him that the Devil had chosen *him* and *his home* to begin the recruitment of innocent lives. Only two possibilities existed now in the minds of the villagers—either the girls were themselves witches, or they had been bewitched. Perhaps due to their tender age and their relationship with the town reverend, the latter was the only possibility considered.

Several ministers from neighboring towns came to the parsonage to witness for themselves the sufferings of Betty Parris and Abigail Williams. We know Reverend John Hale from Beverly was one of them according to his accounts of the meeting. From Salem Town came the Reverend Nicholas Noyes, and Captain Stephen Sewall. There may have been others, but it is these names that appear on documents. After seeing the girls, the ministers called for a public fast. During the meeting, many of the girls sat as if in a trance.

45

Abigail Williams, however took advantage of the gathering and shouted out in shrieks that unnerved the congregation and the ministry.

The traveling clergy had to finally admit "the hand of Satan was in them." They placed the odious responsibility to ferret out the cause of the afflictions squarely into Parris's lap. Basically, he was told "It started in your home; you fix this. Find out who is doing this to the girls." To soften the blow, they told Parris he could put a good face on it to his congregation by noting the Devil had chosen him due to his post as leader of the church in Salem Village—in other words, good vs evil. Parris' sermons show his attempt to allay the suspicion that he was in want of moral virtues and therefore fodder for the Devil's dealings.

Tituba

The girls seemed to have worsened after Tituba's counter-magic with the "Witch Cake." It was Tituba Indian Betty and Abigail witnessed stirring the rye meal cake into a ball of white magic. It is perhaps for that reason, that when Reverend Parris pressed them with the question "*Who* Afflicts Thee?" that Tituba's name was finally uttered. Cornered, the two girls had two choices: admit they had been faking (after noted clergy had traveled miles to pray over them), or, name a name. There was no other way out of it.

It has long been considered true that little Betty Parris loved Tituba. The slave probably had the lion's share of caring for the child as Elizabeth Parris was often ill and in bed. Here may have been the cuddling and comforting the 9-year-old needed to allay her nervous fears. She may have fallen asleep to Tituba's stories of the Old World, and become drowsy from the sing-song rhythm of the slave's strange and exotic songs. It was later written down that Betty cried out "Oh, Tituba!" This may have been misconstrued as an accusation rather than a frightened plea for help or from anguish.

Tituba was a black Spanish Indian. With Indian attacks an ongoing terror, was it easier to name someone who resembled the enemy that had slaughtered so many of the village kin? From reports, we see Abigail as a stubborn and outspoken young girl. Had Tituba reprimanded her in the past for poor behavior at home? Was Abigail, only a ward of the family, jealous of Tituba's attention to Betty? There were two other small children in the household at the time, but history makes hardly any mention of them. Obviously, they were not among the "afflicted."

Sarah Good

Thursday, February 25, 1692, Ann Putnam Jr. became the next girl to "cry out" against a witch in the village. She chose a woman that would, in the villagers' mind, be no loss—Sarah Good.

Sarah Good was considered a scourge to a town steeped in piety and the outward appearance of cleanliness and moral rectitude. At 38-years of age, Sarah was forced to beg from her neighbors for food, and often shelter. She was dirty, foul-smelling, and smoked a pipe. She, along with her five-year-old daughter Dorothy (Dorcas), roamed the muddy streets and knocked on doors in search of another day's sustenance. Many gave her food, in an effort to get rid of her. Even then, if the offering was paltry, or none at all, she walked away "muttering."

Goody Good had reason to "mutter." Life had not been kind to her. With events that strangely mimic those of Thomas Putnam Jr., her inheritance was taken from her. Sarah's father had been an affluent innkeeper in Wenham, a village just north of Salem Village. She was one of seven children sired by John Soulart. At the age of eighteen, her father drowned. Some called it a suicide. Sarah's mother soon married another, and her new step-father lost no time in commandeering Soulart's estate, which consisted of seventy-seven acres and five hundred pounds sterling. Sarah Good, like Thomas Putnam Jr. before her, battled for her rights at the General Court in Boston in 1682, only ten years before she was to be hauled into another court and accused of witchcraft. The Boston court awarded her a small plot of land along with three acres of meadow land her father had left her.

Sarah married Daniel Poole, who, celebrated their good fortune, by ordering himself a fine suit of clothing and two dresses for Sarah. He suddenly died, leaving her with the debt for the clothing, amounting to seven pounds. To pay his funeral expenses, she sold a horse, two cows, and a good deal of her personal property. She married William Good a year later. William was a weaver and she may have felt her life would change for the better. But alas, her late husband's creditors relentlessly pressed for the debts Daniel Poole left owing. Sarah was forced to sell off part of the land she had fought for so diligently in court. In only a short time, she had sold it all, and her new husband and she were destitute. They began begging off their neighbors for food and other needs, despite the 17th-century warning from Town selectmen that those falling on hard times were not to beg for hand-outs.

Sarah became a bitter woman, shrew-like and vindictive. She was forced to approach the affluent for crumbs; people she had once equaled in rank and status when her wealthy father was alive. The hardships took their toll on her husband. He testified against her during her arrest on April 30th, stating he "was afraid that she either was a witch or would be one very quickly." When asked why he thought that, William Good replied that she treated him badly and that she was "an enemy to all good." Five days later, he told the magistrates that he had seen what looked like a witch's teat, or wart, just below Sarah's right shoulder that he had not noticed before. Was it there to suckle a witch's familiars?

The couple had made many enemies of the villagers as they went about begging for help. Mary and Samuel Abbey had felt pity for the homeless couple and given them shelter under their roof, only to ask them to leave due to Sarah's tirades. Sarah and Thomas Gadge turned her away, fearing that in her filthy condition she may be carrying smallpox. Henry Herrick's father had refused to allow her to sleep in his barn in fear her pipe would burn the place down. And so, became the life of Sarah Good. It would pale in comparison to what was coming next.

Sarah Good's arrest

On Saturday, February 27, young Elizabeth Hubbard was walking back from Thomas Putnam's to Doctor Griggs home where she lived. She had been visiting with her friend, Ann Putnam Jr. It was a long walk on that second to the last day of February. 1692 was a leap year, and thus an extra day was added to a calendar that would become infamous. Doubtless due to Ann Putnam Jr.'s tales of Sarah Good haunting her, Elizabeth, in an excited state spotted a black wolf stalking her. Her first thought was that Sarah Good, the witch afflicting Ann Jr., had sent one of her familiars to follow the girl home. Or worse, was the wolf actually Sarah Good in an animal's form?

The wind cut through her cape and stung her face as she quickened her pace. The rutted and muddy road seemed to mock her haste as it slowed down her hurried footsteps. The farms were spread out here and most were set far back from the road. Israel Porter's farm was one such home she passed, so far removed from Ipswich Road that one could barely see it. She crossed Porter River at Goff's Bridge and hurried the final yards to the Griggs' home across from Leach's Hill. Gusts of wind raised her cape and tugged at her dress; each assault confirming a witch was after here. Sarah Good may have even sent the tempest that was flooding the roads and farmland. She hurried through the door, slamming it and latching the hook. A howling sounded from outside the wooden door. Was it the wind or a wolf frustrated at losing its prey?

On this same day, Elizabeth Hubbard also began to be tormented by yet another spirit, that of Sarah Osborne.

Sarah Osborne was not the wandering beggar that Sarah Good portrayed. She had married Robert Prince in 1662, becoming the mistress of a one-hundred-and-fifty-acre ranch in Salem. Prince's sister was married to a Putnam, Captain John Putnam, who lived next door. Prince died in 1674, willing his land to Sarah, with one caveat. She was to divide the land between their sons, James and

Joseph, when they came of age to inherit. John Jr. and Thomas Putnam Jr. were made executors of his will.

Sarah was now a widow with two small sons and a farm to run. She hired a young Irishman, Alexander Osborne, buying him as an indentured servant for fifteen pounds sterling. Nothing wrong with that. The trouble began when Alexander, many years Sarah's junior, moved into the main house and a romance blossomed, much to the chagrin of the "pious" Puritans. Even when they married, the stain of misconduct was not erased. Adding to her unpopularity, Sarah moved to contest her late husband's will in an effort to control the property. It may be, she thought her new marriage might bring additional offspring. For whatever reason, the legal battle raged on. In fact, Sarah Osborne would be hanged as a witch before the suit was settled.

Sarah Prince Osborne's house in Salem Village (Danvers, MA)

The Sabbath fell on the following day, February 28, 1692. The weather was formidable with strong gales and torrents of rain. The four girls had "cried out" against three witches: Tituba, Sarah Good, and Sarah Osborne. Their hysterics and fits were so grievous that it was decided to take action. Thomas Putnam Jr. (Ann Jr.'s father), his brother Edward, Joseph Hutchinson, and Thomas Preston (who was a son-in-law to Rebecca Nurse) faced the storm and rode to Salem Town to put forth the official complaints against the three women. They charged that Tituba Indian, Sarah Good, and Sarah Osborne were under "suspicion of witchcraft" due to the "much mischief done to Elizabeth (Betty) Parris, Abigail Williams, Ann Putnam Jr. and Elizabeth Hubbard...sundry times within this two months, and lately also done, at Salem Village contrary to the peace of our Sovereign Lord and Lady William and Mary, King and Queen of England."

John Hathorne and Jonathan Corwin, magistrates of Salem Town, swore out the arrests. The constables from the territories where the women lived were to arrest them and take them to Nathaniel Ingersoll's Ordinary in Salem Village by ten o'clock the following morning to be questioned. Ingersoll's Ordinary, though functioning as a tavern, was frequently used as a meetinghouse for more than just drinks and meals. Other than a gathering place for local gossip, it was the only communal building in that area large enough to hold a sizeable group meeting for more official needs. The watch house was across the street and could hold prisoners temporarily if needed.

It is probably not lost on the reader how prominently Thomas Putnam Jr.'s influence is already seen in the arrests. It was his daughter who claimed Sarah Good was tormenting her. Elizabeth Hubbard followed suit after visiting Ann Jr. at the Putnam home. Thomas was the executor to the late Robert Prince's will that his widow, Sarah Osborne, was trying to refute. Only Tituba Indian was outside the Putnam's net. It may have been little Betty Parish crying out "Tituba...she...oh Tituba!" when asked about witches, that sealed Tituba's fate. Betty may have only been crying because she had witnessed the slave making a "Witch Cake" and it frightened her. But to those in attendance at the Parris home, it sounded like an accusation. And the witch hunt was on.

Chapter Seven

"Why Do You Hurt These Children?"

March 1, 1692 dawned on a village that must have been shaken to its core. This was no longer idle gossip after Sabbath meetings, or sniggering from those delighted with Reverend Parris's misfortunes. There were three among them who had been singled out as witches in a community that believed whole-heartedly that not only were the Devil and his minions real, it had been proven when thousands of witches were executed in England, a homeland they had vacated not that long ago. Some of these Puritans may have witnessed the human sacrifices themselves.

The two magistrates chosen by the General Court of Boston to handle the inquisition into possible witchcraft dealings were John Hathorne and Jonathan Corwin. Neither man was schooled in the predicts of law, nor was any other person at that time in Massachusetts. Graduates of Harvard at that time could claim a diploma in medicine or the ministry---those were the only two disciplines offered. For a witchcraft trial, the two men turned to their first source, the Holy Bible. Yet here, the instructions on how to detect a witch, let alone to question one, were absent. Only one sentence was offered, and it was a strong one, "Thou shall not suffer a witch to live." They turned next to other writings on the subject including the revered Cotton Mather's *Memorable Providences*.

It is important to note that the men overseeing the initial questioning and later, the trials themselves, were flying by the seat of their pants in the legal arena. In their minds, witches were not presumed innocent until proven guilty. If they had been "cried out" upon, especially by innocent babes, then there must be merit in the accusations. "There is no smoke without fire," may have been a unspoken mantra. The three accused were walking into a situation they could not hope to win.

John Hathorne

Jonathan Corwin

The magistrates prepared for the inquisition. They agreed on the terms by which an accused person could be found guilty as a witch:

- The finding of a Devil's "teat" or mark (an unusual growth or protuberance) on the accused's body, proving they suckled their familiars, such as small birds, reptiles, etc.
- An outbreak of misfortune or mischief following a disagreement with a neighbor. (A "neighbor" had a broader meaning than one who lived nearby.)
- "The Devil could not assume the shape of an *innocent* person in doing *mischief* to mankind" offered, perhaps, more than just a guideline for the court. It helped put the blame on the Prince of Air and Darkness if a guilty verdict was proffered, if only for mischief. (The italics are those of the author.)
- The Touch Test. As mentioned earlier, it was believed if a witch touched a person they had afflicted, the victim would be "cured" upon the touch of the witch attacking them. Over and over in the upcoming witch trials, the "Touch Test" was used, with much effect. The shrieking, tormented girls would quiet upon being touched by the accused.
- Spectral Evidence was also taken into consideration, a

practice that Cotton Mather later vociferously denounced. Basically, it said the witch did not have to afflict the victim in person, it could send its ghost or spirit to do its bidding. While it mimicked the second "proof" listed here, there were two forms of taking on a shape: The Devil assuming the "shape of someone," and that of a witch's shape (spirit or ghost) appearing to and even afflicting a person. Many accused witches were in jail when their shapes were said to be flying about Salem and attacking myriad victims.

Looking for a "Witch's Teat"

It is interesting to note that a test used in Europe and even within Connecticut, was not one put forth for Salem's trials. Increase Mather had decided "Swimming the Witch" was inhumane and not without misconceptions. The test went this way: A suspected witch had one finger tied to her opposite toe (thereby binding her), and lowered by rope into a body of water. Some tests show the victim tied to a chair and then lowered by a rope or pole into the water. If the accused sank, she was innocent. If she floated, she was a witch.

This was due to the belief that once she signed a pact with the Devil, she was refuting her Christian baptism, and therefore any water would refuse to accept her. The problem with this test, is that the innocent victim often drowned before she could be pulled back out. It was a "damned if you are and damned if you aren't" proposition.

Swimming the Witch bound finger to toe (above), & with a chair.

As Magistrates Hathorne and Corwin rode into Salem Village, they may well have been surprised at the fanfare that greeted them. The villagers had practically proclaimed a holiday from work and domestic duties to be in attendance for the preliminary questioning of the three suspected witches. People thronged the street and heralded their approach. Nathaniel Ingersoll was, no doubt, already figuring the influx of cash that would fill his coffers as the crowds filled his tavern. He had created an ad hoc court room by setting a long table with chairs at the far end of the largest room where the two magistrates and their scribe, Ezekiel Cheever would sit. Young Joseph Putnam, the prodigal brother, would also take notes.

The three prisoners, Tituba, Sarah Good, and Sarah Osborne were already at Ingersoll's awaiting the arrival of Hathorne and Corwin. They had spent the night at Ipswich Jail and been brought in by horseback early that morning. All but Tituba, who walked the short distance from the parsonage to the tavern. Sarah Good had put up a fight at the jail, and on the way to the tavern that morning had jumped from the horse she was riding tandem with Constable Samuel Braybrook. He had to chase her down more than once and probably figured he wasn't getting paid enough to deal with this scurrilous female. Sarah Osborne had been bedridden and flung into jail the night before. She was there now at Ingersoll's, feeble, yet defiant. She yelled out that she was more likely to be a victim of witchcraft than to be a witch!

It fell to Goodwife Hannah Ingersoll to check the three women for witch's teats, an odious detail added to her home acting as trial central for the moment. Every inch of an accused witch was to be searched and a pin stuck into any suspicious outgrowth found. If it bled, it was normal, if it didn't, it was suspicious. It was during this time that William Good, Sarah Good's husband, stopped by and told Hannah Ingersoll to look for a mark he noticed beneath his wife's right shoulder that he said he had not seen there before. So much for the marital bond.

The stage was set as a crisp March wind whipped frocks and capes into a frenzy and set doors and windows to chattering. A morbid excitement filled the streets. Here was something to break up the unrelenting boredom of the daily life of Salem Village—and perhaps a chance to rid the good people of some of those denizens they would just as soon live without.

Ingersoll's Ordinary in Salem Village (Danver's, MA)

As Hathorne and Corwin rode up to Ingersoll's Ordinary, they knew at once the tavern could not hold the throngs of people who had come not only from the village, but from the nearby towns of Beverly, Topsfield, Ipswich, and Salem Town. The General Court believed that the general populace was entitled to watch the proceedings, and it has always been the Puritan way to offer up the evil-doers to public ridicule and humiliation. Therefore, Ingersoll was told to grab the table and chairs and lug them down the street to the meetinghouse. His financial hopes may have been dashed, but they needn't be. The tabs for ale, food, boarding, and sundry services for the out-of-town men and horses, as the inquisition and subsequent trial continued for over a year, kept his cash box full. He was the closest game in town for the entire witchcraft show, being only several yards from the Salem Village meetinghouse. People flowed to his door during each break in the proceedings and the ale flowed.

The meetinghouse was hurriedly arranged into a court room. The long table and chairs were placed beneath the pulpit, and a "bar" created by reversing a tall chair or adding a platform. The four afflicted girls—Abigail Williams, Betty Parris, Elizabeth Hubbard, and Ann Putnam Jr.—were, for the first time ever, given the prime seats on the front row of pews. They were the star witnesses. Each reported having seizures that morning and appeared distraught and anxious. The rest of the large room was packed to the rafters with eager onlookers; the wind howling around the eaves outside like a warning banshee.

Sarah Good, Sarah Osborne, and Tituba were brought into the meetinghouse. All eyes were upon them. Were these really witches? Did little Betty Parris look upon her beloved Tituba with pity and guilt? The prayer was said and the room called to order. Sarah Good would go first. Tituba and Sarah Osborne were taken back to Ingersoll's, or the watch house (which was directly across the street from Ingersoll's) until it was their turn.

The following is the written account of **Sarah Good's** (G) interrogation by **John Hathorne** (H), the magistrate from Salem Town. Ezekiel Cheever is transcribing. The spelling has been preserved:

The examination of Sarah Good before the worshipfull Assts John Hathorne Jonathan Curren (Corwin).

(H.) Sarah Good what evil spirit have you familiarity with (S G) none (H) have you made no contract with the devil, (g) good answered no (H) why doe you hurt these children (g) I doe not hurt them. I scorn it. (H) who doe you imploy then to doe it (g) I imploy no body, (H) what creature do you imploy then, (g) no creature but I am falsely accused (H) why did you go away muttering from mr Parris his house (g) I did not mutter but I thanked him for what he gave my child (H) have you made no contract with the devil (g) no (H) desired the children all of them to look upon her, and see, if this were the person that had hurt them and so they all did looke upon her and said this was one of the persons that did torment them -- presently they were all tormented. (H) **Sarah good** doe you not see now what you have done why doe you not tell us the truth, why doe you thus torment these poor children (g) I doe not torment them, (H) who do you imploy then (g) I imploy nobody I scorn it (H) how came they thus tormented, (g) what doe I know you bring others here and now you charge me with it (H) why who was it. (g) I doe not know but it was some you brought into the meetinghouse with you (H) wee brought you into the meetinghouse (g) but you brought in two more (H) Who was it then that tormented the children (g) it was osburn (H) what is it that you say when you goe muttering away from persons houses (g) if I must tell I will tell (H) doe tell us then (g) if I must tell I will tell, it is the commandments I may say my commandments I hope (H) what commandment is it (g) if I must tell you I will tell, it is a psalm (H) what psalm (g) after a long time shee muttered over some part of a psalm (H) who doe you serve (g) I serve God (H) what God doe you serve (g) the god that made heaven and earth. though shee was not willing to mention the word God her answers were in a very wicked, spitfull manner reflecting and retorting aganst the authority with base and abusive words and many lies shee was taken in.it was here said that her housband had said that he was afraid that shee either was a witch or would be one very quickly the worsh **mr Harthon** asked him his reason why he said so of her whether he had ever seen any thing by her he answered no not in this nature but it was her bad carriage to him and indeed said he I may say with tears that shee is an enimy to all good.

(Essex County Court Archives, Salem -- Witchcraft
Vol. 1 no. 11)

Ezekiel Cheever's handwritten deposition of Sarah Good

It is obvious that the presumption of guilt was there from the beginning—a premise that tainted the witch trials from this time forward. The very early questions are to ask her about her allegiance to the Devil and "why do you torment these children?" She finally points out that two others were brought in with her, Tituba and Osborne. It must have been one of them. Interestingly, she chooses Osborne over Tituba to accuse. Perhaps Osborne has turned her away in the past or done her some wrong. Perhaps, it is because Osborne still has a nice house and has not been brought low as she, Sarah Good, has. The afflicted girls had tried out their roles that would pervade each questioning. They screamed out, writhed on the floor, and went into fits when Good looked at them. The astonishment of the congregation must have been formidable. And, unfortunately, the girls were now well aware that their theatrics were not only allowed, but condoned. The game was on.

Sarah Good was returned to Ingersoll's, and Sarah Osborne was brought in. The questioning began along the same lines:

Examination of Sarah Osborne. Recorded by John Hathorne. 1, 1692.

Sarah Osburn her examination (H) what evil spirit have you familiarity with (O) none. (H) have you made no contract with the devill (O) no I never saw the devill in my life (H) why doe you hurt these children (O) I doe not hurt them (H) who do you imploy then to hurt them (O) I imploy no body (H) what familiarity have you with Sarah Good (O) none I have not seen her these 2 years. (H) where did you see her then (O) one day agoing to Town (H) what communications had you with her, (O) I had none, only how doe you doe or so, I did not know her by name (H) what did you call her then Osburn made a stand at that at last said, shee called her Sarah (H) Sarah good saith that it was you that hurt the children (O) I doe not know that the devil goes about in my likeness to doe any hurt Mr Harthorn desired all the children to stand up and look upon her and see if they did know her which they all did and every one of them said that this was one of the woman that did afflict them and that they had constantly seen her in the very habit that shee was now in, thiere evidence do stand that shee said this morning that shee was more like to be bewitched than that she was a witch Mr Harthorn asked her what made her say so shee answered that shee was frighted one time in her sleep and either saw or dreamed that shee saw a thing like an indian all black which did pinch her in her neck and pulled her by the back part of her head to the dore of the house (H) did you never see anything else (O) no. it was said by some in the meetinghouse that shee had said that shee would never be teid to that spirit any more. (H) what lying spirit is this hath the devil ever deceived you and been false to you. O) I doe not know the devil I never did see him (H) what lying spirit was it then. (O) it was a voice that I thought I heard (H) what did it porpound to you. (O) that I should goe no more to meeting but I said I would and did goe the next Sabbath day (H) were you never tempted furder (O) no (H) why did you yeild thus far to the devil as never to goe to meeting since. (O) alas. I have been sike and not able to goe. her housband and others said that shee had not been at Meeting this yeare and two months.

(Essex County Court Archives, Salem – Witchcraft Vol. 1, no. 11)

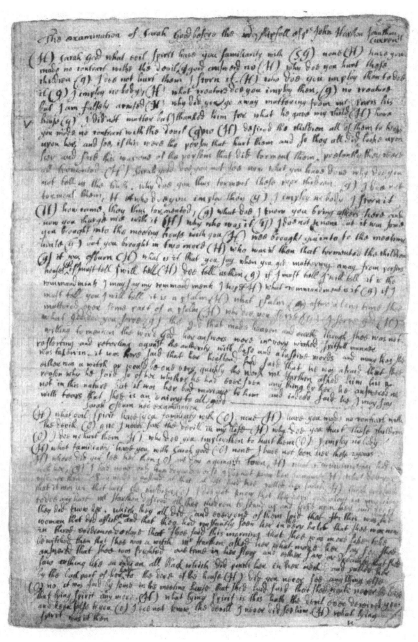

John Hathorne's handwriting/Sarah Osborn deposition

Osborne tries to prove that she had been visited and tested by the Devil as a victim, not as an accomplice. Stating she returned to church despite being ordered not to, she hoped, would gain her favor. Church attendance was all-important in this small Puritan community, as witnessed by John Putnam and John Porter's earlier roles as the Sabbath day name takers of those who were not in the pews.

One of Osborne's statements would come back to haunt her, and others. Her mention of seeing "a thing like an Indian all black" was too close to home for Tituba and her husband John Indian. With Indians still attacking and slaughtering villages along the east coastline, it was a double whammy to be both black and nicknamed "Indian." As we will see, Tituba finds a way to craftily handle the situation, while John Indian's defense is to join the "afflicted" before he too is accused of witchcraft.

The court recessed for the noon meal. Sarah Osborne was returned to a room at Ingersoll's while the magistrates, constables, and the Marshall ordered up ale and food from the happy Ingersoll. Sarah Osborne was ill, and may have been grateful her interrogation was not a lengthy one. Tituba would not fare as well.

Chapter Eight

The Devil's Book

Grey clouds hugged the bare branches that rattled in the wind like clacking bones as Salem Village hurried back to the meetinghouse for what was to be the highlight of the day—the questioning of Tituba Indian, the woman who many believed was the start of it all. Hadn't the girls told of the slave's conjuring in the parsonage kitchen? A sacrilege at any location, but that it happened beneath the eaves of the Village's religious leader made it even more damnable. Hadn't Tituba invited the Devil into the home by making a "Witch's Cake?" Hadn't the innocent young Parris daughter Betty cried out her name when asked "Who afflicts thee?"

The villagers, dressed in their Sunday finest, jostled for the pew seating. Many were forced to stand, pressed in like sardines, an air of excitement and nervousness pervading the cold room. Even old Giles Corey had come from his farm to watch the proceedings, despite his wife Martha's angry admonishment. She had even ripped his saddle from his horse in an effort to make him stay at home, citing the inquisitions as madness. The afflicted girls sat, once again, at the front of the room, looking quite agitated and pale. This accused witch was different. Tituba had lived with Abigail and Betty, nursed them, cared for them, and tried to help ferret out the cause of their pain. But more than that, Tituba came with the real threat of revealing their own sins to the congregation. They had conjured with the Venus Glass along with her.

Reverend Parris must have felt the weight of nervous dread as he watched the door for the arrival of Tituba. He had attacked her for her violation of his house rules against dabbling in magic, and had erupted over the knowledge of the "Witch's Cake creation. He accused her of inviting the Devil into his home and making the girls' torments more grievous. In a fearful rage he hounded her with accusations and questions, finally thrashing her when she would not give him the answers he wanted. She repeatedly cried out that she was not a witch, which only brought more beatings and wrath. For Reverend Parris, it became imminently important that the blame be removed from his doorstep, namely himself and his daughter Betty and niece, Abigail. Therefore, Tituba had to confess to being a witch. It was the only way he could begin to weave back together his tattered image and save his household from ruin.

It was this frightened Tituba that was finally escorted into the frigid meetinghouse by Constable John Herrick. At first, there was a gasp of anticipation and fear, but as she was brought before the magistrates, the four girls suddenly fell into fits and wailings that shocked the crowd. This was the most-frightening display yet. Abigail and Ann Putnam, Jr. shrieked and cried that they were being pinched and tortured. It was several minutes before order could be restored and the questioning begun.

One has to wonder if Tituba looked at Betty with shock and gut-wrenching sadness? What more betrayal could the young girl offer? To be found guilty of witchcraft was hanging. For the girls, they feared what Tituba might reveal about their secret conjuring, and perhaps their fakery. As a preventive measure, to make sure the magistrates saw how badly she was afflicting them, their screams and contortions were amplified far above the antics portrayed during Sarah Good's and Sarah Osborne's questioning. The atmosphere in a place set aside for worship became one of chaos and fear.

John Hathorne finally regained control of the crowd. The girls rose from the floor where they had been writhing, dusted off their white aprons, and returned apprehensively to their seats. The villagers tried to steady their racing hearts and turned their eyes to the cowering black woman who stood before the magistrates' table. Once again, John Hathorne conducted the questioning in his usual abrasive manner. Jonathan Corwin appeared happy to let him do so. Ezekiel Cheever sat ready to transcribe the on-goings. As Tituba's trial lasted three days, the notes were copious indeed.

[March 1, 1692]

The Examination of Titibe

(H) Titibe what (sp) evil spirit have you familiarity with (T) none (H) why doe you hurt these children, (T) I doe not hurt them (H) who is it then #(the de) (T) the devil for ought I (ken) know (H) did you never see the devil,, (T) the devil came to me and bid me serve him (H) who have you seen) (T) 4 women #(and) sometimes hurt the children, (H) who were they? (T) goode Osburn and Sarah good and I doe not know who the other were Sarah good and osburn would have me hurt the children but I would not shee furder saith there was a tale (tall) man of Boston t (w)hat shee did see (H) when did you see them) (T) Last night at Boston (H) what did they say to you they said hurt the children (H) and did you hurt them (no) (T) no there is 4 women and one man they hurt the (s) children and then lay all upon hure and they tell me if I will not hurt the children they will hurt me (H) but did you not hurt them (T) yes but I will hurt them no more (H) are you not sorry you did hurt them. (T) yes. (H) and why then doe you hurt them) (T) they say hurt children or wee will doe worse to you (H) what have you seen a man come to me and say serve me (H) what service (T) hurt the children and last night there was an appearnce that said (K) Kill the children and if I would no go on hurtang the children they would doe worse to me (H) what is this appearance you see (T) sometimes it is like a hog and some times like a great dog this appearance shee saith shee did see 4 times (H) what did it say to you (T) (it s)the black dog said serve me but I said I am afraid he said if I did not he would doe worse to me (H) what did you say to it (T) I will serve you no longer then he said he would hurt me and then he lookes like a man and threatens to hurt me. shee said that this man had a yellow bird that keept with him and he told me he had more pretty things that he would give me if I would serve him (H) what were these pretty things (T) he did not show me them (H) what else have you seen (T) two cats a red cat and a black cat (H) what did they say to you (T) they said serve me (H) when did you see them last (T) Last night and they said serve me but (shee) said I would not (H) what service (T) shee said hurt the children (H) did you not pinch Elizabeth Hubbard this morning (T) the man brought her to me and made hur) me pinch her (H) why did you goe to

Thomas putnams Last night and hurt his child (T) they pull and hall me and make goe (H) and what wold have you doe Kill her with a knif Left. fuller and others said at this time when the child saw these persons and was tormented by them that she did complain of a knif that they would have her cut her head off with a knife (H) how did you goe (T) we ride upon stickes and are there presently (H) doe you goe through the trees or over them (T) we see no thing but are there presently (H) why did you not tell your master (T) I was afraid they said they would cut off my head if I told (H) would not you have hurt others if you cold (T) they said they would hurt others but they could not (sh) (H) what attendants hath Sarah good (T) a yellow bird and shee would have given me one (H) what meate did she give it (T) it did suck her between her fingers (H) Did not you hurt mr Currins (Corwin's) child (T) goode good and goode Osburn told that they did hurt mr Currens child and would have had me hurt him two but I did not (H) what hath Sarah Osburn (T) yesterday shee had a thing with a head like a woman with 2 leeggs and wings Abigail williams that lives with her uncle mr Parris said that shee did see this same creature #(with goode osburn and it turned into the shape of goode osburn & yesterday being(?)) and it turned into the shape of goode osburn (H) what else have you seen with g osburn (T) an other thinge hairy it goes upright like a man it hath only 2 leeggs (H) did you not see Sarah good upon elisebeth Hubbar last Saterday

(T) I did see her set a wolfe upon her to afflict her the persons with this maid did say that shee did complain of a wolf (T) shee furder said that shee saw a cat with good at another time (H) what cloathes doth the man #(we) go in (T) he goes in black cloathes a tal man with white hair I thinke (H) how doth the woman goe (T) in a white whood and a black whood with a top knot (H) doe you see who it is that torments these children now (T) yes it is goode good she hurts them in her own shape (H) & who is it that hurts them now (T) I am blind now I cannot see.

Tituba's answers to Hathorne's questions are remarkable. While Osborne and Good stubbornly refused to admit they were witches or in allegiance with the Devil, sly Tituba listens for clues from the magistrate on how she should respond. Perhaps partly due to the beatings she has received at Reverend Parris' hand, and partly due to her own reasoning, she confesses, but with several caveats. One, she is sorry and will not hurt the children again. She only did so because she was afraid for her own life. Second, she is literally joining the girls as a witness against Osborne and Good by saying it is they who told her to hurt the children, and they go in shapes to afflict the girls, such as the wolf that followed Elizabeth Hubbard home only two days prior. She speaks of yellow birds, dogs, and hogs, all known creatures of the Devil and associated with evil in the Puritans' minds. The Bible even told of the Devil departing a possessed man and entering into the bodies of wild pigs.

Thirdly, Tituba avoids answering questions requiring detail that can be confirmed or discredited. When asked if she flew above the trees or through them on her "stick," she says basically, you don't get to see anything…you just suddenly arrive at your destination." At the end of her trial, the girls once more go into fits. Tituba is asked "Who is it that hurts them now?" She shuts it all down by saying "I am blind now. I cannot see."

For Tituba, a natural born storyteller, who cast her spells of magic over the drowsy heads of Abigail and Betty in the candlelit evenings at the parsonage, this was her finest hour. She would tell the young girls of exotic places, colorful birds, spices, and enchantments. But now, with the growing knowledge that the congregation of white people were hanging on her every word—and believing her!—it must have been a heady experience. Magistrates from Salem Village were almost panting for her information while a white male scribbled furiously to take down her every word. For the first time in her life, she had power. No longer Parris's slave, but the catalyst that could turn this village on its ear, and hopefully, pardon herself from the accusation with which she was branded.

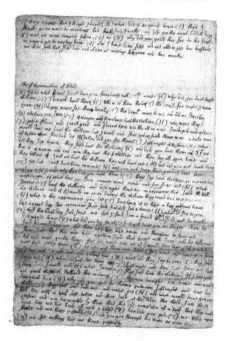

A page from Tituba's examination. Ezekiel Cheever is scribe.

Second Examination of Tituba, as recorded by magistrate Jonathan *Corwin
*Corwin uses a simple Q & A to indicate the questions & answers.

[March 2, 1692]

Q. What Covenant did you make w'th that man that Came to you? what did he tell you. A. he Tell me he god, & I must beleive him & Serve him Six yeares & he would give me many fine things. Q. how long agone was this? A. about Six Weeks & a little more, fryday night before Abigall was Ill. Q w't did he Say you must doe more? did he Say you must Write any thing? did he offer you any paper? A. yes, the Next time he Come to me & showed mee some fine things, Something like Creatures, a little bird Something like green & white. Q. did you promiss him then when he Spake to you then what did you answer him A. I then Sayd this I tould him I Could nott believe him God, I tould him I ask my maister & would have gone up but he stopt mee & would nott lett me Q. whatt did you promiss him? A. the first Tyme I beleive him God & then he was Glad. Q. what did he Say to you then? what did he Say you must doe? A. this he tell me they must meet together: Q. W'n did he Say you may meet together? A. he tell me Wednesday Next att my m'rs house, & then they all meet together & thatt night I saw them all stand in the Corner, all four of them, &

the man stand behind mee & Take hold of mee
to make mee stand still in the hall. Q. where was
your master then? A. in the other Room. Q. time
of Night? A. a little before prayr Time. Q. what
did this man Say to you when he Took hold of
you? A. he Say goe ibto the other Room & See
the Children & doe hurt to them. and pinch them
& then I went in, & would nott hurt them a good
while, I would nott hurt Betty, I loved Betty, but
they hall me & make me pinch Betty & the next
Abigall & then quickly went away altogether &
I pinched them. Q. did thay pinch A. Noe, but
they all lookt on & See mee pinch them. Q. did
you goe into that Room in your own person &
all the rest? A. yes, and my master did nott See
us, for they Would nott lett my Master See. Q.
did you goe w'th the Company? A. Noe I stayd
& the Man stayd w'th me. Q. whatt did he then
to you? A. he tell me my master goe to prayer &
he read in book & he ask me what I remember,
but don't you remember anything. Q. did he ask
you noe more but the first Time to Serve him or
the Second time? A. yes, he ask me againe, &
that I Serve him, Six yeares & he Com the Next
time & show me a book. A. and when would he
Come then? A. the next fryday & sHow me a
book in the day Time betimes in the morneing.
Q. and what Booke did he bring a great or little
booke? A. he did nott show itt me, nor would
nott; but had itt in his pockett. Q. did nott he
make you write yo'r Name? A. noe nott yett for
my #(mistris) mistris Called me into the other
roome. Q. whatt did he Say you must doe in that
book? A. he Sayd write & Sett my name to itt.

Q. did you Write? A. yes once I made a marke in the Booke & made itt w'th red like Bloud. Q. did he gett itt out of your body? A. he Said he must gett itt out the Next time he Come againe, he give me a pin Tyed in a stick to doe itt w'th, butt he noe Lett me bloud w'th itt as yett butt Intended another Time when he Come againe. Q. did you See any other marks in his book? A. yes a great many some marks red, Some yellow, he opened his booke a great many marks in itt. Q. did he tell you the Names of them? A. yes of Two noe more Good & Osburne & he Say thay make them marks in that book & he showed them mee. Q. how many marks doe you think there was? A. Nine. Q. did thay Write there Names? A. thay Made marks Goody Good Sayd she made hir mark, butt Goody Osburne Would nott Tell she was Cross to mee. Q. when did Good tell you, she Sett hir hand to the Book? A. the same day I Came hither to prison. Q. did you See the man thatt morneing? A. yes a litle in the morneing & he tell me the Magistrates Come up to Exam in me. Q. w't did he Say you must Say? A. he tell me, tell nothing, if I did he would Cutt my head off. Q. tell us True how many Woemen doe use to Come when you Rid abroad? A. foure of them these Two Osburne & Good & those Two strangers. Q. you say that there was Nine did he tell you whoe they were? A. noe he noe lett me See but he tell me I should See them the Next Tyme Q. What Sights did you see? A. I see a man, a dogge, a hogge, & Two Catts a black and Red & the strange monster was Osburnes that I mentioned before. this was was the hayry

Imp the man would give itt to mee, but I would nott have itt. Q. did he show you in the Book w'ch was **Osburne** & w'ch was Goods mark? A. yes I see there marks. Q. butt did he Tell the Names of the other? A. noe S'r Q & what did he Say to you when you made your Mark? A. he Sayd Serve mee & always Serve mee. the man w'th the Two women Came fro Boston. Q. how many times did you goe to Boston? A. I was goeing & then Came back againe I was never att Boston. Q. whoe Came back w'th you againe? A. the man Came back w'th mee & the woemen goe away, I was Nott willing to goe? Q. how farr did you goe, to what Towne? A. I never went to any Towne I see noe Trees, noe Towne. Q. did he tell you where the Nine Lived? A. yes, Some in Boston & Some herein this Towne, but he would nott tell mee whoe thay were

(Salem Selections, Massachusetts Box, Essex Co. Manuscripts & Archives, New York Public Library, New York, NY.)

Reverend Parris must have felt the hand of death squeezing the life from him as Tituba confessed before the villagers and magistrates that the tall man and others had chosen the parsonage for their meeting. Things weren't bad enough for him already. Note how Tituba first puts Parris in a different room, and then handily says he couldn't see what was going on anyway as the tall man would not let him see them. She is careful not to use the word "Devil" when speaking of the man with the book of witch's names signed in blood. When asked how often she flew to Boston, she quickly backtracks and basically says "I was going, but I came back.

I didn't go to Boston." She also says she saw no other towns. Was this because she feared being asked for details about places she had never seen. Better to just say, "I didn't go there." It is fair to say, this uneducated woman was craftier than any of the accused to come before the stand. And it is no wonder, she was one of the few early prisoners to escape hanging.

For Tituba, Sarah Good, and Sarah Osborne, life would never be the same. One would die shortly in jail, one would hang, and one would be sold to further her servitude. The dank jail at Salem Town became Tituba's and Sarah Osborne's home, beginning that afternoon. Sarah Good was taken back to Essex County jail at Ipswich. It's not certain if her captors were aware she was pregnant. Her layers of dirty skirts may have hidden her condition. Her daughter Dorothy (Dorcas) was handed over to her father William, who would now have to find food and shelter for the child.

The inhabitants of Salem Village flooded out of the meetinghouse and into the biting March cold. Excited voices wafted on the wind as they discussed the surreal court drama they had just witnessed. Were they safe now? The three witches were on their way to jail. Surely thick walls and guards would allow the Village residents to sleep soundly tonight. If they thought the three witches' imprisonment would put an end to the fevered attack on Salem village, they underestimated the force they were dealing with.

William Allen and John Hughes walked home along the muddy road from the meeting they had just attended in the meetinghouse that convened after the witchcraft hysteria earlier that day. It was a meeting for the men of Salem Village to discuss more earthly matters such as the ongoing war with Salem Town for their separateness and autonomy. The moon struggled to throw some light on the dark silhouettes below, as the wind continued to drive sodden clouds across its face. The two men thought back to the juxtaposition of the two meetings they had attended that day: one dealing with the evil forces of the Devil and witches, and the other concerning the maintenance of Salem Town's roadways. It was a strange reality, to say the least.

Suddenly, Allen and Hughes paused, as a repetitive sound they could not identify echoed from bare trees and jagged rocks. Up ahead, something sat on hulking black haunches and waited for them. As they mustered their courage and took tentative steps toward the beast, the shape suddenly broke into three women, who swiftly fled, vanishing into the night. In their fevered excitement from the day's hearings, they swore the women were none other than Sarah Good, Sarah Osborne, and Tituba Indian.

At Doctor Griggs home, neighbors had gathered to talk to Elizabeth Hubbard. They were dismayed to see that not only was the girl's suffering not at an end now that her attackers were in jail, she was worse than ever. She cried out that she was being pinched and jabbed by the shape of Sarah Good. Samuel Sibley (the husband of Mary Sibley who instructed Tituba on the making of the "Witch Cake") was one of the neighbors in attendance and was shocked as Elizabeth cried out, "There stands Sarah Good upon the table by you, with all her naked breast, and bare footed, and bare legged. OH, nasty slut! If I had something, I would kill her." Sibley grabbed his walking cane and struck at the place Elizabeth was pointing to, though he could see nothing. "You have hit her right across the back!" Elizabeth yelled. "You have almost killed her!"

As for the flesh-and-blood body of Sarah Good, she was on the run through the bitter March night without shoes or stockings. She had escaped her captures at Constable John Herrick's farm where she was spending the night on her way to the Ipswich jail. Leaving her shoes and stockings behind, she fled into the night. With nowhere to go, and her feet stinging and cut from the rocks and frozen ground, she gave up and returned to the shelter of her captures. John Herrick and his wife noticed Sarah's arm was bloody, no doubt from tearing through tree branches as she fled. Yet when word spread of Elizabeth Hubbard's attack by Sarah Good's specter that same night, and of Sibley hitting it with a cane, Good's wounds took on a more ominous tone. The bloodied arm took the place of where Hubbard *said* she was struck with Sibley's cane— her *back*. The fact that Elizabeth had said Good's specter was standing there "bare footed and bare legged" struck an even more chilling chord, as indeed, Good had left her shoes and stockings behind in her escape. Whether or not she was bare-breasted at some point that evening was not reported on.

Sarah Good was far from giving up her escape attempts. As one of her guards, Samuel Braybrook, rode with Sarah behind him pillion-style to the Ipswich jail the next day, she slid off the horse and tried to run. The beleaguered guard grabbed her and plunked her back upon the horse. She swore at him and berated him the entire three-hour journey as they covered over 10 miles, including passing the home of Sarah's childhood where she had seen happier times before her father's suicide. Here she was, strapped to a horse behind a man carrying her to jail to await a trial where, if found guilty, she would be strung from a tree and hanged. How cruel life had been to Sarah Good. Braybrook reported Sarah had tried to kill herself during the sojourn to the jail, but he did not say how.

In Salem jail, Sarah Osborne and Tituba were being questioned once again by Hathorne and Corwin. Tituba continued to play the victim card and expanded on how the evil entities had forced her to pinch and torment Betty Parris and Abigail Williams. She elaborated on the Devil's Book she had been told to sign, and how she was given a pin and a stick with which to draw her blood to sign her name on the brittle pages where nine other names were scrawled in scarlet. She told of the Devil's threats to hurt her if she spoke of the book and other things she had witnessed; even decapitation.

As if on cue, Tituba screamed out that she was being hurt by Osborne and Good's spirits. A woman was brought in and told to search the slave for any marks to verify what she was telling them. Sure enough, they found some. Reverend Hale wrote of the incident that the woman found "marks of the Devil's wounding of her." When Tituba was searched for witch's teats by Goody Ingersoll at the tavern the day before, the marks had not been there. Tituba was gaining the sympathy of the magistrates as they watched invisible demons tormenting her for her bravery in confessing. In comparison to Osborne's and Good's stubborn refusal to admit to any evil doing, it weighed particularly well in the tormented slave's favor.

What's interesting is whether or not Tituba had picked up some of the tricks used by the afflicted girls. Had she, herself, made the marks on her body in preparation for further questioning? If Osborne knew of being named again by the servant, how did it make for the two women sharing a room in the squalid jail? As for Sarah Osborne's accusation of seeing an "Indian—all black," Tituba had handled that during her turn before the magistrates. She testified of a "tall man in *dark clothes* with white hair...from Boston." As Tituba was the only one of the three witches to confess, her words carried more weight. With her cunning, she had turned Osborne's accusation of a black man into a man in all black...and put him in Boston for good measure. No one ever accused John Indian, and Osborne's words on the subject were forgotten.

Just in case, John Indian took up his role as one of the afflicted of Salem Village. Just after Tituba was jailed, he began to have fits so fearful that some said he looked "like a beaten creature." He chose Ingersoll's Ordinary for many of his "attacks" where there was always an ample crowd. As to what happened to Reverend Parris' household, with their only house slave in jail, and their other servant putting on a side show at the local tavern, is not commented upon. Elizabeth Parris was sickly, and Abigail and Betty were still twitching and shrieking into the night.

Meanwhile, the evil spirts were flying with aplomb about the rooftops of Salem Village. The Devil's fingers were moving the chess pieces frantically as the inhabitants of the small hamlet batted at nightmares and started at moving shadows. John Hughes, one of the two men who had seen "the beast in the roadway" the night before, was once again haunted by strange occurrences. A white dog followed him from a visit to Samuel Sibley's at eight o'clock when the Spring hours were already dark. That night a strange cat appeared on the end of his bed. It was glowing with an eerie light. He kicked at it, and the cat disappeared before his eyes.

His friend, William Allen, who had also seen the beast the night before, was faring no better. As shadows moved about his bedchamber, one became the likeness of Sarah Good. She glowed with a strange light that illuminated Allen's bed as she sat down upon his foot. He kicked at her, and she, like the cat of Hughes' nightmares, vanished.

The spectral attacks continued throughout the village, although the four girls seemed to quiet somewhat. They may have been putting a finger to the judicial wind to see which way it was blowing, or they may have realized that with Tituba actually confessing to their accusation of witchcraft, they'd just plunged down the rabbit hole. Ann Putnam Jr. however, was still active. She now added little five-year-old Dorcas Good to her spectral attackers, and that of an unknown woman. When Ann refused to sign the Devil's Book the specter of Dorcas was offering her, Ann claimed the little demon bit and choked her as viciously as any adult. The list of accused witches was just getting started.

Chapter Nine

Prison, Prayers, & Pranks

Salem Village peered from their windows at the frigid March nights with fear. Indians presented a very real and physical danger. Safeguards could be put in place for that: doors bolted, men in the watch towers, guns loaded. But this... How does one prepare a defense against an unseen enemy that can pass through a locked door and window as easily as air through a crack in the wall? What does one do when innocent shapes take on nefarious meanings? The moonlight shining down on the shingled and thatched rooftops of the village sent shadows from the tree trunks and boulders—skeletal fingers of smoke that reached out to pull innocent victims into the underworld. Evil was here, and perhaps, with God's grace, was safely confined in Salem Jail.

Sarah Good was finally transported from Ipswich jail three days later to join the other two accused witches in Salem Jail. Hathorne and Corwin continued to examine the three women, but only Tituba elaborated and embellished her tales of the "tall man," and of Osborne and Good's revenge upon her for confessing. Tituba, on a roll now, told the magistrates that the death of Deodat Lawson's wife and child all those years ago had been the result of witchcraft. How much more was there to know? How far back had Salem Village been in the clutches of the Devil without them knowing?

The web of familial and neighborly connections that had been spun for generations, was being pulled taut. Almost without exception, the accusers were related in some way to each other, or had some common bond. The Devil's pawns had had a taste of power and now they were out in full force.

Elizabeth Proctor

Sunday, March 6, 1692, Ann Putnam Jr. put a name to the "unknown woman" who accompanied Dorcas to her room and helped in the spectral attack. During the Sabbath services, she pointed out Elizabeth Bassett Proctor, wife of John Proctor, as one of the witches that had choked and bitten her three days earlier. Ann said she had seen Goody Proctor during the spectral attack, but did not recognize her until she saw her today sitting in one of the pews. Elizabeth Proctor may have been an easy target. It was no secret that the Proctors were not in sympathy with the girls' antics, to the point that John Proctor had punished his maid Mary Warren for her part in it. The Proctors lived just south of Salem Village's boundary and ran a tavern that had seen some scandal. Gossip reported that Proctor served liquor to "a drunken Indian." Mary Warren reported arguments between her master and mistress, and even Proctor's son, Benjamin, had confessed his father often kept "unseasonable time" and would drink to excess. The Proctors were not one of the tax-payers for Salem Village due to their location. All-in-all, the Puritan tongues wagged and there was a sense of impropriety concerning the family.

Elizabeth Proctor was John Proctor's third wife. She had inherited six of his children from his two prior marriages and had born five of her own. At the time of the witchcraft outbreak, she was pregnant with her sixth. Unlike the demur, withering female portrayed in Arthur Miller's *The Crucible*, she was a hard-headed, and at times, shrewish taskmaster. She ran the tavern while John tended the farm or was away. It was said that if a customer couldn't pay, they would have to hand over something she could pawn for the sum. These traits were not in alignment with the Puritan mantra of a wife being submissive to her husband and a beacon of purity and gospel values for her offspring. In short, the eyes of Salem Village were upon her.

Elizabeth Hubbard knew Mary Warren, in fact she had been to the Proctors the same day Sarah Good (in the shape of a wolf) had chased her home. As mentioned earlier, Elizabeth Hubbard lived with Dr. Griggs, and had made cutting remarks about Elizabeth Proctor's medicinal practices. Had Dr. Griggs put the bug in Hubbard's ear that Elizabeth Proctor was practicing some kind of ad hoc medicine that could be aligned with black magic? Elizabeth Proctor's grandmother had been accused of witchcraft in 1669. As we will see, she would not be the last of the accused to be tied to ancestral witchcraft proceedings.

No doubt, Mary Warren had confided in Hubbard about the Proctor's skepticism concerning the girls' afflictions. John had even made the cutting statement "She must have her fits forsooth" when Mary was ordered (against his protests) to testify in court. To him, the girls were faking it, and he had no time for such nonsense. Samuel Sibley got an earful of Proctor's tongue-lashings. He told the man that if the "afflicted" continued on with their fakery "we should all be devils and witches quickly." Joseph Pope overheard "Proctor say that if Mr. Parris would let him have his Indian, he the said Proctor would soon drive the devil out of him." He chose the wrong people in whom to vent his anger. These rantings, to men who were in the households as witnesses for some of the torment the girls were experiencing, would soon spread his vitriolic chastisements to those who could do him the most harm.

The following day, on March 7th, Governor Phipps and Increase Mather boarded the ship that would finally bring the longed-for charter home to Massachusetts. The sea voyage across the Atlantic would take 66 days, or longer. By the time they arrived, they would find many of their fellow Puritans festering in jails, and the cry of "Witch" echoing throughout the countryside. In fact, by the time they arrived in May, the accusations had reached a staggering amount.

The three women awaiting their fate in the cold and dank Salem Jail were suddenly rousted from their beds of hay and lead out into the March morning. If they were in hopes that they were being freed, they were sadly mistaken. They were loaded onto a cart and the day-long ride to Boston began. There, they would be housed in a new prison, a stone edifice in the heart of the market place of Boston. Believed to be one large communal room with possibly a few smaller rooms abridging it, it was well known for its odor of feces, vomit, rotting food, and tobacco. Unlike Salem's Jail, which had weathered wooden walls with a stone basement, Boston's prison walls were thick stone with a bare floor covered in filthy straw. Lice was a common affliction. Visitors to the jail compared it to hell.

From the moment the three women were unceremoniously thrown into the large common room, the jailer, John Arnold, began a tally for their "housing fees." They were to be charged two shillings, sixpence per week. They were also charged for shackles that were clamped to their ankles in the hopes of keeping their specters from flying about and afflicting the victims. Anything else they asked for was put on the bill. Many of the witchcraft accused were reduced to penury because of the jail debts they accrued. Those who could not pay the bill when the trials finally ended over a year later, would remain jailed. If family members could not bring them food, they were given a small portion of bread and water a day. Many of their possessions were confiscated and sold off in the name of paying off their debts. That many of their treasured heirlooms ended up in the hands of Sheriff George Corwin of Salem was a known fact.

Within this dark and forsaken world of noise, odor, and disease, Sarah Good gave birth. It is not certain at what date she delivered the child. There is no record of it, only to say that it died not long after. No baby could have survived through the freezing nights and the stench. With the foul food the prisoners were served, Sarah's milk was insufficient. And so, it is with this early death that the girls of Salem Village claimed the life of an innocent baby. There would be many more deaths to come.

On March 11th, Reverend Parris once again invited Reverend John Hale from Beverly and other pastors to his home to pray over his children. Public fasts had been held earlier and the inhabitants admonished to look within themselves for the answers of why this evil should befall the small village. As always, it was the shortcomings of the people, some slip of conscience or deed, that must have turned God away from them.

The ministers prayed over Abigail and Betty. For the most part, the two sat quietly, with the exception of some twitching and muttered words. It was well-known young Betty had been in a terrible state ever since Tituba was jailed. No doubt from guilt and fear, the little girl's fits and tortured soul were a piteous thing to behold. Elizabeth Parris appealed to her husband to let Betty be sent away to their relative Stephen Sewall's home in Salem Town until things settled down. The child's health was at stake. Betty was sent away and her name no longer appeared on court documents as one of the accusers in the witch trials. Abigail was left at the parsonage to carry on with her daily campaign of hatred.

In Boston, the question remained, what to do with the witches they had now imprisoned? Witchcraft was a hanging charge. Tituba had said there were at least nine other names scribbled in the "tall man's" book. That meant a witch conspiracy. They were without the charter and the legal structure to move forward. Sir William Phips was on his way to act as the newly-appointed Massachusetts governor over the deposed Andros. Until he arrived with the charter, the witches would just have to wait in jail. All the magistrates could do was continue to ferret out the rest of the coven afflicting Salem Village with malicious intent. They may have prayed that Tituba's nine names were now down to six. Elizabeth Proctor and little Dorcas had just been accused, but had yet to be brought forward. If they were found probably guilty and jailed, that would leave only four. Only four.

Sarah Good, Sarah Osborne, and Tituba remained shackled throughout the candle-less nights. Sarah Good had been allowed her pipe, and begged tobacco from any that came through the jail hallway. Perhaps no longer having to seek food and shelter, even in these hellacious conditions, was a welcome respite for Good. She may have believed it would all blow over when the magistrates came to their senses. It was now Spring—plowing and planting season. There was no more time for such silliness. But the "silliness" was finding a momentum that would shock the world for centuries.

Martha Corey

Without a legal compass with which to steer, the magistrates turned to previous writings that dealt with prior witchcraft trials and how to conduct them. One such publication was Richard Bernard's *Guide to Grand Jury Men.* Among other guidelines laid out within the pages, he admonishes that the suspected witches, the afflicted, and the witnesses should be questioned "apart, & not in the hearing one of another." The inquisitions put forth of the three originally accused witches in Salem Village in the Winter/Spring of 1692 had already blown that concept out of the water. It had been a public circus with the accused, witnesses, and afflicted on full display for all to see. This obvious sharing of knowledge contaminated any fair trial the accused could hope for. The girls were already comparing notes and being fed names by their elders with a grudge to bear.

Elizabeth Proctor and little Dorcas Good had been named by Ann Putnam Jr. as specters who had harmed her. Still, no warrants had been issued for them. The five people so far accused had fallen outside the walls of the church, as none of them attended on a regular basis and were not part of the covenanted members. It was with Ann Jr.'s next accusation that the pillars of the Puritan community would shudder and eventually find itself tied with nooses.

Martha Corey was a woman somewhere around 70-years-of-age when she found herself as the next villager to be accused of witchcraft. This was to be a shock to the Puritans who had, so far, seen only the derelict of the community accused. Martha was a covenanted woman of the church. Yet there were those who felt her past still followed her as a shadow at noonday. Martha was once married to Henry Rich, and the mother of his son. At some point, rumors began to spread that Martha had given birth to a mulatto son, Ben, in 1677, obviously not squired by Rich. She raised the boy away from prying eyes in a boarding house while Rich was left to raise their Caucasian son, Thomas. Henry Rich was reportedly a murderer, another nail in Martha's pious coffin. We don't know what became of him, but we do know she married Giles Corey in 1690, only two years before she joined the ranks of the accused. Corey was responsible for getting Martha into the Salem Village church with full honors. The marriage, however, must have been a tumultuous one, for Giles was heard to say "that what he knew about her if it ever got out would fix her business."

On March 12, 1692, Ann Putnam Jr. added a new name to her spectral attackers. She claimed Martha Corey was coming to her at night and tormenting her. As Corey was a member of the church, Ann's uncle, Edward Putnam, and neighbor Ezekiel Cheever, decided to ride over to the Corey farm and question Martha before word got out that she had been identified as a possible witch. They asked Ann before they departed to describe the clothing Martha Corey had worn when Ann was attacked by her specter. Ann, conveniently, told the men she could not see the Invisible World right now as the specter of Martha Corey had warned her that her "sight" would not return until that evening when Corey would be back to "pay her off" for betraying her.

It is obvious that Martha Corey is being given advantages the other accused witches were not afforded due to her name being among the church elite. The two men set off for the long ride to the Corey farm, which was just south of the Salem Village boundary. In fact, of those that would be accused in the witch trials, the Proctors were the Corey's closest neighbors. Traveling past several hills and village farms, they finally arrived at the Corey's home, finding Martha there alone.

Martha's derision of the visit did not bode well for her. She met the two men with a sneer and announced "I know what you are come for. You are come to talk with me about being a witch, but I am none. I cannot help people's talking of me."

Had Martha looked over the motley crew of the three witches accused and jailed so far and seen that they fell into the unsavory category for various reasons? Sarah Osborne had been accused, and she had a checkered past with multiple marriages and scandals. Was it reasonable to assume her name would come up due to her un-Puritan-like past? Martha would also become one of the girls' most-outspoken opponents, calling them out as faking their fits. Her question to the visiting men's accusation that Ann Putnam Jr. had said Martha's ghost had attacked her the night before was one perhaps anyone with a brain would ask:

"But does she tell what clothes I have on?" Putnam and Cheever may have paused in surprise at this question, as young Ann had just dodged this very question earlier. Martha repeated it, obviously trying to get her point across to these men that the accusations were nonsense with nothing specific with which to hang a witch. When they told her Ann could not describe her clothing, as Martha's specter had blinded her vision until later tonight, Corey grinned and shrugged, as if to say, "There you go! How convenient!"

Her defiance may have perturbed the two men, who were both deacons, because they warned her that by being accused herself, it reflected upon the entire church of covenanted villagers. She seemed not to care about the others, in fact showed no pity for the ones already jailed, calling them "idle slothful persons" who "minded nothing that was good." She reminded them that she was now a Christian woman who delighted in the word of God. It was obvious Martha Corey felt elevated over those other souls of Salem Village who were not "Gospel Women." It was also obvious that she looked upon the entire affair as humorous and a waste of her time.

But Martha went too far in her rejection of the girls' "crying out."

"I do not believe that there are witches," she announced haughtily.

To the two deacons of the church standing before her, this was blasphemy. God was real, and his nemesis the Devil was real. To deny one was to deny the other in the Puritan mind. To denounce witches, the Devil's handmaidens, was an insult to the church.

Ignoring the growing anger in the two men, Martha once again reminded them that she had nothing in common with the three accused witches. "I am a Gospel woman," she announced again. It would become her mantra in the coming days.

"Woman, outward profession of faith cannot save you!" they declared and left her house.

Putnam and Cheever made the long ride north back to Thomas Putnam's house near Hathorne's Hill, to check on Ann. She had been quiet all afternoon during their absence. No doubt the report was made to the Putnams of Martha's declarations of innocence. Ann Jr. may have worried that this church woman was slipping through her fingers. As soon as the two deacons departed for their homes, she once again fell into fits and screamed that Martha Corey had indeed returned that night for her pound of flesh.

Martha Corey was not out of the woods. For Mary Warren, the Proctor's twenty-year-old servant, claimed that the specter of Martha had appeared to her that night as well. According to Mary, she had reached out in a daze toward Corey's shimmering shape and pulled her to her lap where she was seated. But as the shape drew nearer, she saw it was John Proctor. "It is nobody," Proctor cried in exasperation, "but it is my own shape you see. I see there is no heed to any of your talkings, for you are all possessed with the Devil, for it is nothing but my shape."

The rumors of Martha Corey's "witchcraft" spread to the neighboring farm of Joseph Pope. The hysteria swept over Bathshua Pope, his wife, causing her to become temporarily blind. Though it was the Sabbath, the witches seemed to be zipping about Salem Village upon their sticks in a frenzy.

Chapter 10

A Cauldron of Fear

The inhabitants of Salem Village may have looked out upon the Spring thaw that March and seen not the promise of new birth, but a plague of death. What was happening to their "city on the hill?" Biblical references for the name Salem were ones of hope and promise: "And Melchizedek king of Salem brought forth bread and wine; and he was the priest of the most high God." (Genesis 14:18) "In Salem also is his tabernacle, and his dwelling place in Zion." Salem came from Hebrew Shalem, usually said to be another name for Jerusalem, and to mean "peace." The happenings in Salem that muddy month of March brought anything but peace to its community and those of the neighboring towns who watched on in horror.

The dilemma was this—the Puritans believed the Devil was very real and that witches were as deadly a threat as the Indians burning villages along the coastline. Others had been tormented in recent years in Boston and other places, and the accused offenders hanged. It was not a stretch to believe it was happening here, though "why?" probably bothered the righteous among them even more. What sins had been committed within their boundaries that would bring God's wrath upon them? For to deny the Devil was to deny God. They were two sides of a religious coin. In the early months of 1692, the face of that coin was showing something definitely un-God-like.

Perhaps the most-relevant quote concerned a prior reverend of Salem Village, George Burroughs, who would find himself accused not just of witchcraft, but as the ringleader of the coven. Thomas Putnam Jr. referred to him as "a wheel within a wheel." It meant one of the witches was a warlock, and not just any warlock, but a reverend!

The dichotomy was that there were two puppet masters involved in the witch trial accusations. The villagers who saw the girls' afflictions as real, believed the Devil was behind it. Those few who saw the accusers as faking their fits, saw something quite different. Someone besides the Prince of Air and Darkness was pulling the "afflicteds' strings. Did they have one puppet master manipulating the second? Did Satan, in his invisible chess game, maneuver the Bishop and Knight (among others), and those pieces, in turn, maneuvered the pawns? It may well have been a "wheel within a wheel" for many of the denizens of Essex County.

The weight of naming a member who fell under the church covenant was still bearing down upon the selectmen of Salem Village. Thomas Putnam Jr., perhaps aware that the blame would fall upon him and his household, wanted to make sure his daughter Ann had indeed been attacked by Martha Corey's shape. He sent for the woman to come and see Ann in person. Martha may have welcomed the invitation to put an end to the nonsense once and for all. An arrogant, abrasive woman, she clearly saw herself as above these shenanigans. If this young whelp of a girl could fool these foolish grown men with her antics, it was up to her, Martha, to unveil the "pretty little trick." It was a mistake she would live to regret. "Pride goeth before the fall" was never more relevant than Martha's haughty arrival at the Putnam home on March 14, 1692. The fact that Abigail Williams was now accusing Corey as attacking her, along with Elizabeth Proctor, was, as yet, unknown to the "Gospel Woman."

The moment Martha Corey stepped across the threshold of Thomas Putnam Jr.'s home, she may have realized her mistake. She had only heard reports of the girls' sufferings and terrifying fits and wailings. But now, upon coming face-to-face with Corey, Ann Jr.

shrieked and fell to the floor, contorting into unbelievable spasms of her head, hands, and feet. It appeared that some unseen force was choking her. Her parents, Thomas and Ann Putnam Sr., watched on in horror. Edward Putnam, Ann Jr.'s Uncle, and Mercy Lewis, the Putnam's 17-year-old maid, also watched the spectacle in astonishment. Ann, gasping and choking, managed to yell out that it was Goody Corey afflicting her. The moment she cried out Martha's name, Ann's tongue thrust from her mouth and her teeth clamped down upon it as if to bite it off. It was clear to those watching that the witch Corey was trying to silence the girl.

Ann regained control of her speech long enough to scream out, "There is a yellow bird a sucking between your fore finger and middle finger. I see it!"

Puritan children were raised on the Bible. They read their scriptures daily. That the Bible associates "birds of the air" as evil is found in many verses: Matthew 13:4—the birds eating the seeds are called "the wicked one." Mark calls them "Satan" and Luke references them as "the Devil." Therefore, "birds of the air" are a negative symbol. Revelation 18:12 came closest to aligning with what the children of Salem were going through: "And [an angel] cried mightily with a loud voice, saying Babylon the great is fallen, is fallen, and has become a habitation of demons, a prison for every foul soul, and a cage for every unclean and hated bird!" The color yellow was associated with envy and jealousy.

Upon Ann's accusation of seeing a yellow bird suckling between Corey's fingers, the woman instinctively rubbed at the spot. Ann declared the bird vanished. It was not lost on the spectators that Sarah Good had also been accused of suckling yellow birds. Ann next accused Martha of being responsible for Bathshua Pope's blindness on the previous Sabbath by clamping spectral hands over the woman's eyes. It was with the next outburst that the small company of witnesses came undone.

Ann looked into her parents' fireplace and claimed she saw a man roasting on a spit. "Goody Corey," Ann screamed, "you be a turning of it!" With that, Mercy Lewis, who had been watching with rapt attention, grabbed up a stick and swung at the hearth where Ann was pointing. Stories of Indians burning their victims with fire over a roasting pit was well known. Mercy Lewis, witnessing such heinous acts with her own eyes during the attacks in Maine, was perhaps the most susceptible to the vision Ann was seeing. It was also a reference to the attacks by a witch on the Goodwin children mentioned earlier. Cotton Mather in his *Memorable Providences* claimed that in 1688 the young John Goodwin, eleven-years-old at the time, said he was "being roasted on an invisible Spit, run into his Mouth, and outa his Foot, he lying, and rolling, and groaning."

Upon Mercy's strike, the roasting spit vanished, only to reappear again. Ann cried the man roasting had looked at her. Mercy swung again.

"Do not if you love yourself," Ann screamed to warn the maid. The hysteria gripped both girls as Ann screamed that Goody Corey had struck Mercy with an iron rod for interfering. Both the girls fell screaming to the floor, writhing in pain, and begging Corey to leave the house. But the show was not yet over. Mercy wailed that there were other witches in the room—shadowy forms she could not make out.

"I won't, I won't," she cried. "They would have me to write." The convulsions continued until the Putnam men asked Martha Corey to depart. What she felt as she stepped into the late afternoon light is anyone's guess. The first shivers of fear may have played across her nerves as she made her way home in the failing light.

The Putnam household was not yet done with the paranormal. Mercy Lewis, the Putnam's maid, grew worse. It took several men to hold her down as her fits became more severe. They finally managed to seat her into a chair and watch her. Around 11:00 that evening, to their horror, they claimed they watched as Mercy's chair, with the girl still seated in it, inched toward the fire blazing in the Putnam hearth. The men grabbed the chair and said it kept moving, dragging them along with it, until Edward Putnam blocked the chair's path and lifted it. She was only inches from going feet first into the flames.

It is with tales from witnesses, such as this retelling, that many wonder how such things could happen if not a result of unseen forces. That's a fair question. Mass hysteria seems unlikely, as the three men claim to have been holding onto the chair. Was it a case of poltergeist activity associated today with a teenager's raging emotions; their negative energy causing objects to move and even fly about a room? Emotion has incredible strength, as shown in the report of a terrified mother lifting a car from a trapped child. Had Mercy Lewis's long skirts hidden her feet moving the chair initially? With the men holding onto the chair had she continued to rock it back and forth as they struggled to get hold of it? We will never know.

Back at the Corey farm, earlier that week, animals at the home began to act strangely. An ox, that had, only moments before, walked from the woods, suddenly fell to the ground and began dragging "his hinder parts as if he had been hipshot," Giles Cory claimed. Then moments later, it was back up on its feet as if nothing had happened. Their cat was "strangely taken on the sudden" and looked near death. Martha advised Giles to knock it on the head. Giles was hesitant to kill it. Moments later, it too jumped up and was fully recovered. As Giles contemplated these strange events, he began to notice his wife Martha acting oddly late at night. He watched her kneeling before the fireplace, as if in prayer, but no words came from her mouth.

Martha Corey's spirit was still active, according to Elizabeth Hubbard who said Goody Corey's shape appeared to her on March 15th. But Martha Corey was not the only church-going woman being named by mid-March.

Ann Putnam Jr. declared a new specter had appeared to her. She saw the apparition of a pale woman seated in her grandmother's chair. The witnesses in the room around her asked breathlessly who she saw. She waffled, saying the shape was indiscernible at first, but said she thought she could recognize where the woman sat in the church meetinghouse on Sundays. Ann Putnam Sr., her mother, and their maid Mercy Lewis, persisted as Ann Jr.'s vague answer as to "Who is it?" brought forth no one's name. Exasperated, Mercy and Ann Sr. began suggesting names of who the woman might be. The young girl finally agreed to one of the names, perhaps the one put forth with the most vigor. This was an elderly church covenanted woman, held in high regard through the community. She was a member of the church in Salem Town, but regularly attended Reverend Parris's assembly, as the meetinghouse was very near to her farm. Her name as an accused witch would rock the village, and cause an outpouring of shock and protestation. Ann Putnam Jr., egged on by Mercy Lewis and Ann Putnam Sr., had just looked into the Invisible World and plucked out 71-year-old Rebecca Nurse. On March 15th, Abigail Williams also claimed to see Goody Nurse as one of the witches tormenting her.

Rebecca Nurse's sister, Mary Esty, lived just over the northern Salem Village boundary in Topsfield. It was the Nurse's native township. Many of the Putnam farms lay near this boundary and land disputes between the Topsfield farmers and Putnam clan were well-known. Hemmed in and prevented from expanding their land holdings, the Putnams continually disputed the two towns' boundary lines. It was such a reported grievance that led Rebecca Nurse's son-in-law, John Tarbell, to call upon the Thomas Putnam Jr. household after the accusation against his mother-in-law was made. He asked young Ann "Who was it that told her that it was goody nurs?" (Misspellings are extant.)

According to Tarbell's written account, Mercy Lewis, the Putnam maid, said "it was goody Putnam that said it was goody nurse: goody Putnam said it was mercy lewes that told her: thus they turned it upone one an other saying it was you & it was you that told her." The salient point is that Ann Jr.'s "special powers" of discernment as to whose specter she saw, was provided to her by a household with an agenda of its own. Some authors of the witch trials have put forth valuable theories that Ann Sr. was jealous of Rebecca Nurse. The woman owned a prosperous farm and had given birth eight times—all babies alive and thriving. Mrs. Putnam may have associated the elderly Nurse with her own step-mother who had deprived her of her inheritance, as had her husband Thomas been cheated out of his.

Meanwhile, reports from nearby Andover and Ipswich were coming in. Odd events, that before the witchcraft hysteria may have been looked at as a strange coincidence, were now viewed with more nefarious meanings. Neighbor was looking at neighbor with eyes of suspicion. One had to think again before bickering with another. If the butter soured, the well ran dry, or a person became suddenly ill after an argument over the cost of goods, the failings were now looked at as the workings of the devil. It was not a safe time in Essex County.

Ann Putnam Senior

The tormented girls had rattled the village with their tales of flying specters, wracked limbs, and bite marks. But now older women were joining the ranks of the accusers. Bathshua Pope had already claimed unexplained blindness, and it was Ann Putnam Jr. who had blamed it on Martha Corey. Other adult women began "crying out," including Sarah Bibber, a malicious woman who was not averse to spreading gossip and rumors of scandal. She and her husband worked as hired help and her voice would be raised against the accused on several occasions. A widow, thought to be Margaret Goodale, also joined the accusers. Her inclusion would prove a detriment to Giles Corey, who had been accused of murdering her stepson.

Among these matrons stepped Ann Putnam Sr, a beleaguered woman with demons of her own that spilled over to the witch trials.

Ann Carr Putnam Sr., as mentioned earlier, was married to Thomas Putnam, Jr. Both had been cheated out of their inheritances by family members. Ann had lost seven newborns during her prolific pregnancies. Her sister before her had also been "cursed" with a plethora of stillborn babies. Ann's older sister, Mary, had been married to Reverend Bayley, the same minister that had been hounded by inhabitants of Salem Village until he could no longer take the subterfuge. His young wife felt the malice of the community keenly, especially when she buried one infant after another while dealing with the stress of a bickering congregation. She finally died, beaten down and broken-hearted.

For Mary's younger sister Ann, it would be something that haunted her dreams. Often, she saw her sister Mary and her dead babies come to her in her dreams in their winding sheets they were buried in. They reached out to her in piteous supplication for help. As Ann was herself suffering from the loss of children, she may have felt that the same hatred in the village that had done her sister to death was also responsible for her own misfortune. To her unstable mind, her sister's spirit was begging her to ferret out the parties responsible for her losses.

Some authors have theorized that Ann Sr. sent her twelve-year-old namesake to the Parris parsonage to divine from Tituba's fortune-telling what the Putnam future might hold. With the plague of losses the elder Ann had dealt with over the years, perhaps the uncertainty the future held was too horrifying to face. When her daughter began manifesting what appeared to be a witch's revenge, did it unsettle her already fragile mind with guilt for what she had brought about? Shortly after Martha Corey's accusations became public, Ann Sr. began to see into the Invisible World as well. Saddled with more of the chores that young Ann and her maid Mercy Lewis had gotten out of in their afflicted states, five other children to care for, and a husband's growing anger at the people in the village he felt had wronged him, she was becoming increasingly unhinged. To add to her stress, she found she was again pregnant. All the old fears of stillborn babies came back to haunt her.

It is staggering to see the impact this one Putnam family had on the witchcraft trials. Thomas Putnam Jr. would become responsible for filing half of the twenty-one formal complaints. It is proposed that he and his wife whispered the names of these suspected witches to his daughter Ann, or she overheard the names tarnished over the years beneath her father's roof. Ann Jr., the most prolific of the accusers, would go on to name nineteen people, eleven of whom were hanged. Her name appeared on no less than four hundred witchcraft documents.

It was a house fueled by perceived wrongs, slights, and misfortunes. The lid put on a simmering pot of rage had just blown. The Putnams found relief in their sufferings by pulling down those whom they felt had cost them monetarily and spiritually. As Ann Sr. lay on her bed that March afternoon, hoping for a moment's rest, saying "she was wearied out,." she was instead visited by Martha Corey's evil specter. According to Ann Sr., Goody Corey "fell upon me…with dreadful tortors and hellish temtations." Ann claimed the witch brought her "a little red book in hir hand and a black pen urging me vehemently to writ I her book." Shortly thereafter, Rebecca Nurse's specter joined Corey's shape in their assault on Mrs. Putnam, repeatedly torturing her because "I would not yeald to their Hellish temtations." She told others only the divine saving grace of God had kept her from being destroyed.

The list of accusers was growing. Abigail Williams was now joined by Elizabeth Hubbard, Mercy Lewis, Ann Putnam Sr., and soon, Mary Walcott. Little Betty Parris had been whisked away to Salem Town in an effort to save the poor creature from further attacks. Sarah Bibber had posted an affidavit against Sarah Good, and Bethshua Pope had claimed temporary blindness due to witchcraft. Salem Village looked about the chaos, Bibles clutched to their bosoms, and wondered who would be next to stand before the magistrates to answer the cry of "Witch!"

Martha Corey's Warrant is Drawn Up

The March evenings in Salem Village were fraught with dread. As the sun sank into the wooded hills, the darkness brought with it the uncertainty of what lay ahead in the shadowed hours before dawn. Was that a form in a flapping cape riding atop a stick silhouetted against the moon, or a distant owl? Were the whispers overhead that of restless tree branches swaying in the breeze, or a coven of witches hissing names of victims into the night? Every shape caught in a candle's glow became sinister. Doors and windows were latched, but against what, and whom?

On March 19, 1692, Edward Putnam and Henry Kenney went to Salem Town to file a formal complaint against Martha Corey. Henry Kenney Jr. was married to Mercy Lewis's sister, Priscilla, and had either witnessed Mercy's attacks or was privy to the knowledge of them. The following account was filed:

> There being Complaint this day made before us, By Edward put- nam and Henery Keney Yeoman both of Salem Village, Against Martha Cory the wife of Giles Cory of Salem farmes for suspition of haveing Comitted sundry acts of Witchcraft and thereby donne much hurt and injury unto the Bodys of Ann Putnam the wife of Thomas Putnam of Salem Village Yeoman And Anna Puttnam the daugtter of s'd Thomas putnam and Marcy [Mercy] Lewis Single woman Liveing in s'd Putnams famyly; also abigail Williams one of mr parris his family and Elizabeth Hubert [Hubbard] **Doctor Grigs** his maid. You are therefore in theire Majest's names hereby required to apprehend and bring; before us. Martha Cory the wife of Giles Cory abovesaid on Munday next being the 21't day of this Instant month, at the house of Lt Nathaniell Ingersalls of

Salem Village aboute twelve of the Clock in the day in order to her Examination Relateing to the premises and hereof you are not to faile Dated Salem. March. the 19'th. 1691/2
p us
*Jonathan.Corwin
*John:Hathorne

Reverend Deodat Lawson traveled from Boston on that same day to see for himself what was happening in the village to which he had once administered. He had heard the report that Tituba Indian announced during her inquisition that his wife and child had died due to witchcraft. He booked a room at Ingersoll's Ordinary. The sun was sinking behind grey clouds and the atmosphere in the common room of the tavern took on an ominous feeling. It was not helped by the visit of young Mary Walcott (17-years-old), Reverend Parris's nearest neighbor, and cousin to Ann Putnam Jr.

Mary Walcott's father Jonathan had married Thomas Putnam's sister. Mary's own mother had died when she was eight, leaving six children, of which Mary was one of two girls. Her step-mother bore another seven children, again, two of them girls. The chores falling to the females of the house would have been arduous. Yet, Mary had it far better than many of the other girls her age in the village who had been orphaned by the Indian wars.

Mary had come to the tavern that evening with the appearance of only to say "Hello" to her former minister, Reverend Lawson. Nathaniel Ingersoll, the tavern's owner, was a distant relative of Mary's. After Mary had seen the Reverend, and was about to depart, she stopped inside the doorway and screamed. Something had bitten her, she wailed. Ingersoll grabbed a candle and held it near her wrist. He and Lawson looked at what appeared to be upper and lower teeth-marks. If Lawson thought this was unnerving, his visit to the parsonage that evening would give the visiting clergyman something to haunt his dreams. Voices on the wind taunted "Welcome back to Salem Village, Reverend Lawson."

Chapter Eleven

"They Are Distracted!"

That Saturday evening, March 19th, Reverend Lawson left Ingersoll's tavern and walked the short distance to Reverend Parris' house. What thoughts must have been raging through his mind after just witnessing Mary Walcott's bite marks? Was this really happening? He turned right onto the narrow road leading to the parsonage. The moon bobbed in and out of sight behind scurrying clouds, throwing shadows one moment only to withdraw them the next. He was relieved to see light shining through the rippled glass of the parsonage windows ahead. That relief would be short-lived.

There is no report to say whether Parris was happy to see the former minister of Salem Village, or fearful of what the Boston clergyman might witness within the walls of his home. The men had not long to wait.

Within a few minutes of Reverend Lawson's arrival, Parris's niece, Abigail began darting to and fro about the room, unable, apparently to sit still. She flapped her arms like a bird and whispered "Whish! Whish! Whish!" imitating the sound of wings flying. She was hurled about so violently at times that the men tried without success to restrain her. She suddenly stopped, and stared in horror at a corner of the room, pointing a trembling finger at empty air. She announced Goody Nurse's specter was hovering in the air. The others turned to look but saw nothing.

"Do you not see her?" Ann cried. "Why there she stands!" Nurse's shape obviously thrust out the ubiquitous book for Ann to sign as she yelled out, "I won't, I won't, I won't take it! I do not know what book it is. I am sure it is none of God's Book. It is the Devil's Book for aught I know." She suddenly ran for the fireplace and began picking up lit kindling, tossing the small sticks about the room. She ran at the flames as if to climb up the chimney. Parris told the shocked Reverend she had attempted to do so before. Just as the Lowestoft case mentioned earlier, the afflicted girl in that report ran about saying "Hush, Hush!" while flapping imaginary wings. She too had run toward the fire as if to be consumed by its flames. It is interesting how often the Salem Village girls' afflictions mirrored those of previous witchcraft reports.

That very evening, Giles Corey would report that he had been troubled during his evening prayers before retiring to bed. Complaining often that his wife Martha criticized his phrasing of prayers, he found now, as he knelt, that though he opened his mouth, he could not utter the prayer. "My wife did perceive it and came towards me and said she was coming to me," Giles reported. "After this, in a little space," he was able to pray.

A Witch Among the Righteous

The following day was the Sabbath. As the visiting Reverend, Deodat Lawson was invited to give the sermon. As the villagers took their seats, a gasp was heard from those who had heard the rumors of Martha Corey's specter attacking Ann Putnam Jr. and Sr. Bold as brass, Martha swept into the cold cavernous room and took her "rightful" seat among the other covenanted members. Reverend Lawson steadied himself and began the opening prayer, only to be interrupted by "several sore fits" from the girls reacting to Corey's presence. A psalm was sung with relative peace, but as the minister began his sermon, Abigail Williams blurted out "Now stand up and name your text!" Reverend Lawson, probably shaken by such an impertinent interruption, by a child no less, recovered and named the text upon which his sermon was predicated. "It is a long text," Abigail challenged impudently. No sooner had Lawson begun his talk, than Mrs. Pope, emboldened by young Abigail's outburst, yelled out, "Now there is enough of that!"

Horrified members of the congregation placed their hands on those disrupting the proceedings and admonished them to be quiet. It worked for a short period of time until Abigail supposedly saw the shape of Martha Corey depart the woman's body and float up to a beam in the meetinghouse ceiling. She cried out that Goody Corey was sitting "on a Beam suckling her Yellow Bird betwixt her fingers." Ann Putnam Jr.'s accusation of Corey's yellow bird had evidently been passed along to Abigail, perhaps within moments of entering the meetinghouse that morning.

All eyes turned upward to where the hysterical girl was pointing. Ann Putnam stated the bird had flown to Reverend Lawson's hat that was hanging on a peg behind him. The congregation's heads pivoted to that location. Those sitting near Ann hushed her. After some moments of confusion, the beleaguered minister continued and was able to finish his sermon. It was a short victory, for Abigail called him out again in the afternoon session, declaring "I know no Doctrine you had, If you did name one, I have forgot it."

For a child to act out in public this way in the Puritan community was unheard of. Obviously, the afflicteds' notoriety had emboldened them to act in more and more brash and abusive ways, even to the irreverent interruptions of a church service. The females "crying out" against their accusers were seeing unprecedented attention from the members of the community. Adult men, who were used to their wives and children being in a subservient position, were now praying over them and inviting neighbors to witness the fits and outbursts of their family. Children, who were relegated to a station not much above the servants who helped with the chores, were now being coddled and listened to! Their words were taken down by men who previously saw them as invisible. This was a new power, and one that would bring the small village to its knees.

Martha Corey left the meetinghouse in defiance, announcing again, that she was "a Gospel Woman," and even if the others could not see the mischief the girls were concocting, she could. Incensed at being ridiculed and accused of sitting astride a beam with a yellow bird in front of a congregation she felt superior to, this was the final straw. Enough was enough. As the following morning would show, it was only just beginning.

That night the specters were again flying through the eaves at the homes of Elizabeth Hubbard and Mary Walcott, who claimed to see Rebecca Nurse's shape, although they said she did not hurt them. Martha Corey, apparently no respecter of the Sabbath, sent her shape to torment Abigail Williams and Elizabeth Hubbard. It would be Corey's last outing as a specter before she was hauled Monday morning into the meetinghouse she had haughtily departed the previous Sabbath afternoon. At noon, Joseph Herrick, holding a warrant accusing her of witchcraft, escorted her into a packed assembly, numbering "many hundred," according to Deodat Lawson.

Martha Corey's Inquisition

Reverend Nicholas Noyes from Salem Town offered the opening prayer. Samuel Parris was offered the position as scribe, and the meeting's notes are seen in his neat hand. Ezekiel Cheever would be giving testimony during Corey's examination to report on the meeting he and Edward Putnam were party to at Martha's house nine days prior. He was therefore excused as the court's usual scribe for the proceedings.

Judge Hathorne once again commanded the room with his confident presence, and, once again, began with the presumption of guilt. (The spelling and verbiage are as it appeared on the document.)

Martha Corey during her examination. "We do not send for you to go to prayer!" Judge Hathorne.

[March 21, 1692]

21 March 1691/2

Mr Hathorne.

You are now in the hands of Authority tell me now why you hurt these persons

Martha Kory. (Corey)

I do not.

H) who doth?

K) Pray give me leave to goe to prayer

*This request was made sundry times

H) We do not send for you to go to prayer But tell me why you hurt these?

K) I am an innocent person: I never had to do with Witchcraft since I was born. I am a Gospel Woman

H) Do not you see these complain of you

K) The Lord open the eyes of the Magistrates & Ministers: the Lord show his power to discover the guilty.

H) Tell us who hurts these children.

K) I do not know.

H) If you be guilty of this fact do you think you can hide it.

K) The Lord knows --

H) Well tell us w't you know of this matter

K) Why I am a Gosple-woman, & do you think I can have to do with witchcraft too

H) How could you tell then that the Child was bid to observe what cloths you wore when some came to speak w'th you.

Cheevers.

Interrupted her & bid her not begin with a lye & so Edw'd Putman declared the matter

Mr Hath:

Who told you that

K) He said the child said

Cheev: (Cheever)

you speak falsly

Then Edw: Putman read again (from a deposition)

Mr H.

Why did you ask if the child told w't cloths you wore

K) My husband told me the others told

H) Who told you about the cloaths? Why did you ask that question.

K) Because I heard the children told w't cloaths the other wore

Goodm: Kory did you tell her (Goodman Corey)

*The old man denyed that he told her so.

H)Did you not say your husband told you so

K. (No Answer)

H.

Who hurtes these children now look upon them.

K.

I cannot help it

H.

Did you not say you would tell the truth why you askt that question: how come you to the knowledge --

K) I did but ask

H) You dare thus to lye in all this assembly You are now before Authority. I expect the truth, you promised it, Speak now & tell [what cloths] who told you what cloths

K.

No body

H.

How came you to know that the children would be examined what cloth you wore

K) Because I thought the child was wiser, than any body if she knew

H) Give an answer you said your husband told you

K) He told me the children said I afflicted them

H)How do you know w't they came for, answer me this truly,

will you say how you came to know what they came for

K) I had heard speech that the children said I [afflicted them] troubled them & I thought that they might come to examine

H) But how did you know it

K) I thought they did

H) Did not you say you would tell the truth, who told you w't they came for

K) No body

H) How did you know

K) I did think so

H) But you said you knew so

Child: H Q (Abigail Williams)

There is a man whispering in her ear,

H) What did he say to you.

K) We must not beleive all that these distracted children say

H) Cannot [he tell] you tell what that man whispered

K) I saw no body

H) But did not you hear

*No, here was Extream agony of all the afflicted

H) If you expect mercy of God, you must look for it in

K) Gods way by confession

H) Do you think to find mercy by aggravating your sins

K) A true thing

H) Look for it then in Gods way

K) So I do

H) Give glory to God & confess then

K) But I cannot confess

H) Do not you see how these afflicted do charge you

K) We must not beleive distracted persons

H) Who do you improve to hurt them

K) I improved none

H) Did not you say our eyes were blinded you would open them

K) Yes to accuse the innocent

Then Crossly gave in evidence

H) Why cannot the girl stand before you

K) I do not know.

H) What did you mean by that

K) I saw them fall down

H) It seems to be an insulting speech as if they could not stand before you.

K) They cannot stand before others.

H) But you said they cannot stand before you

Tell me what was that turning upon the Spit by you

K) You beleive the Children that are distracted I saw no spit

H) Here are more than two that accuse you for witchcraft. What do you say

K) I am innocent

Then mr Hathorn read farther of Croslys evidence

H) What did you mean by that the Devil could not stand before you

*She denied it

H) Sober witnesses confirm'd it.

K) What can I do many rise up against me

H) Why confess.

So I would if I were guilty

K) Here are sober persons what do you say to them

H) You are a Gosple woman, will you lye

*Abigail cryed out next Sab: is sacrament day, but she shall not come there

Kory

I do not care

H) You charge these children with distraction: it is a note of distraction when persons vary in a minute, but these fix upon you, this is not the manner of dis-traction --

K) When all are against me w't can I help it

H) Now tell me the truth will you, why did you say that the Magistrates & Ministers eyes are blinded you would open them

*She laught & denyed it.

H) Now tell us how we shall know
Who doth hurt these if you do not

K) Can an innocent person be guilty

H) Do you deny these words

K) Yes

H) Tell us who hurts these: We came to be a Terror to evil doers
You say you would open our eyes we are blind

K) If you say I am a Witch

H) You said you would show us

*She denyed it.

H) Why do you not now show us

K) I cannot tell: I do not know

H) What did you strike the maid at Mr Tho: Putmans with

K) I never struck her in my life

H) Here are two that see you strike her with an iron rod.

K) I had no hand in it

H) Who had. Do you beleive these children are bewitcht

K) They may for ought I know I have no hand in it.

H) You say you are no Witch, may be you mean you never Covenanted with the Devil. Did you never deal w'th any familiar

K) No never

H) What bird was that the children spoke of

*Then Witnesses, spoke

H)What bird was it.

K) I know no bird.

H) It may be: you have engaged you will not confess.
but God knows.
K) So he doth
H) Do you beleive you shall go unpunished
K) I have nothing to do w'th withcraft
H) Why was you not willing your husband should
come to the former Session here
K) But he came for all
H) Did not you take the Saddle off
K) I did not know what it was for
H) Did you not know w't it was for
K) I did not know that it would be to any benefit
*Some body said that she would not have them help to
find out witches.
H) Did you not say you would open our eyes why do
you not
K) I never thought of a Witch
K) Is it a laughing matter to see these afflicted persons
H) She denyed it
H) Severall prove it
K) Ye are all against me & I cannot help it
H) Do not you beleive there are Witches in the
Countrey
K) I do not know that there is any
H) Do not you know that Tituba Confessed it
K) I did not hear her speak
H) I find you will own nothing without severall
witnesses & yet you will deny for all
*It was noted w'n she bit her lip severall of the afflic-
ted were bitten. When she was urged upon it that she
bit her lip saith she what harm is there in it.
Mr. Noyes .
I beleive it is apparent she practiseth Witchcraft in the
congregation there is no need of images

H) What do you say to all these thing that are apparent

K) If you will all go hang me how can I help it.

H) Were you to serve the Devil ten years tell how many

*She laught

*The Children cryed there was a yellow bird with her When Mr Hathorn askt her about it she laught

When her hands were at liberty the afflicted persons were pincht

H) Why do not you tell how the Devil comes in your shape & hurts these; you said you would

K) How can I know how

H) Why did you say you would show us

*She laught again

H) What book is that you would have these children write in

K) What book: were should I have a book I showed them none, nor have none nor brought none.

*The afflicted cryed out there was a man whispering in her ears.

H) What book did you carry to Mary Walcott

K) I carryed none: if the Devil appears in my shape

*Then Needham Said that Parker some time agoe thought this woman was a Witch

H) Who is your God

K) The God that made me

H) Who is that God

K) The God that made me

H)What is his name

K) Jehova

H) Do you know any other name

K) God Almighty

H) Doth he tell you that you pray to that he is God Almighty

K) Who do I worship but the God that made [me]

H) How many Gods are there

K) One

H) How many persons

K) Theree

H) Cannot you say so there is one God in three blessed persons (The Father, the Son, and the Holy Ghost)

*(then she was troubled)

H) Do not you see these children & women are rational & sober as their neighbours when your hands are fastened Immediately they were seized with fitts & the standers by

*[Partially illegible on account of fold in paper.] said she was squeezing her fingers her hands being eased by them that held them on purpose for triall Quickly after the Marshall said she hath bit her lip & immediately the afflicted were in an uproar

H) [torn] why you hurt these, or who doth

*She denyeth any hand in it

H) Why did you say if you were a Witch you should have no pardon.

K) Because I am a Woman

Salem Village March the 21't 1691/2

The Rever't mr Sam'll parris being desired to take in wrighting the Examination of Martha Cory , hath returned it as afores'd Upon hear- ing the afores'd and seing what wee did then see, togather with the charges of the persons then present Wee Committed Martha Cory the wife of Giles Cory of Salem farmes, unto the Goale in Salem as p mittimus then Given out *John Hathorne *Jonathan. Corwin { Assis'ts

(Reverse) Martha Kory Exam (Essex Institute
Collection, no. 1, James Duncan Phillips Library,
Peabody Essex Museum)

Martha Corey had done herself few favors with her continual
scorn and inappropriate laughter throughout her examination. She
was caught out in her futile attempts to explain how she knew the
two men were going to ask her about her clothing she wore while
tormenting Ann Jr. She offered up lie after lie to save her skin. It
did more to bury her than to save her. The spectators, packed in
elbow-to-elbow, were watching as these seemingly helpless victims
were bitten, bound, and tortured, yet this brazen woman laughed at
their plight. And so, Martha Corey was taken away to the Goal (Jail)
in Salem Town. As the night seeped into that dungeon of stink and
squalor where she sat shackled, was she laughing now?

Samuel Parris's handwritten notes/Corey Examination.

Chapter Twelve

"What Sin Unrepented Of?"

Martha Corey's examination had not gone well for the magistrate, John Hathorne. In short, he had lost total control of the proceedings. At one point, during the shrieks and stomping feet, Martha had leaned wearily upon the bar in front of her. Bethshua Pope screamed out that Martha's leaning was causing her great stomach pains. She hurled her muff at the accused witch. Seeing it land without harm, Mrs. Pope removed her heavy shoe and threw it at Corey, hitting her squarely in the head. The chaos in the room had reached a fevered pitch.

It was at this point that the girls declared there was a black man whispering into Martha's ear. Another looked out the meetinghouse window and screamed that at least two dozen witches were arriving in the pasture outside for their black sabbath with the Devil. The afflicted said they heard the thrumming of a drum calling the witches to a blasphemous meeting just outside the sanctity of the village church meetinghouse.

"Don't you hear the drum beat?" a girl cried out. "Why don't you go, gospel witch?" she yelled at Corey, mocking her constant declaration that morning that she was "a Gospel Woman." "Why don't you go too?"

Hathorne was feeling the wheels come off the cart as the thunderous screams and vibrations of stomping feet filled the room. Where Sarah Good had been stubborn, Martha Corey had vehemently denied all charges and pressed that it was the girls who "were distracted." This was a church-covenanted woman, no slave or homeless beggar. Even when Joseph Herrick had gone to the Corey farm to fetch Martha, the constable found Giles Corey suddenly standing up for her. Herrick had seen a jar of salve on the table at the Corey house. Witches were known to concoct ointments and potions. What was in the jar, he had asked. Giles came to Martha's defense and told the constable it was something Major Bartholomew Gedney, a local doctor, had given her the recipe for.

As Martha was led away to jail, she screamed, "You can't prove me a witch!" The afflicted victims in the meetinghouse room felt they had done just that, their fits subsiding as Corey was yanked outside.

Tituba, Sarah Good, and Sarah Osborne had now been languishing in jail almost three weeks. Sarah Good's infant was dead. Martha Corey's imprisonment, a woman whose name ranked with the church elite, must have come as a shock, and perhaps, the knowledge that this "crying out" against villagers had just taken on a very threatening tone. The signed warrant for the next accused would underscore their fears that no one was immune to the gavel of witchcraft in Salem Village.

Rebecca Nurse

Rebecca Towne Nurse had led an exemplary life. She was a devout wife, mother of eight, and church goer. Rebecca could be seen each Sabbath seated in her usual spot at the church meetinghouse, with the exception of the prior week. She had been sick in bed for nearly nine days.

Rebecca was one of the many who immigrated to Massachusetts from England in 1621. Her family settled in Topsfield where she and her seven siblings were taught the hardships of working a farm. Their acreage was modest at the time, and sat just over the Salem Village border to the north. Property disputes over boundary lines ensued over the years, with the Putnams being the more frequent antagonists.

In 1640, Rebecca married Francis Nurse. He brought his new bride to Salem Village to a small farm. Francis was a hardworking woodworker, and had served as a constable and juryman. In 1678, he had the good fortune to acquire a sizeable farm of 300 acres from James Allen. It was a lease-to-buy option, where Nurse would pay off the lease based on what the property brought in. Their new prosperous endeavors were not applauded by all in the village, especially the Putnams. The farm set back from the road and was surrounded with open meadows and wooded acres. It was a setting anyone would covet.

Rebecca Nurse homestead in Danvers, Ma (Salem Village)

The farm was paying off handsomely by 1690, only two years before the witch outbreak began in Salem Village. Nurse had made each payment on time and his tax bracket has risen a sharp 39%. All eight of their children were grown and thriving; their four grown sons and four daughters and their spouses helped with the burgeoning farm. Only the daughter, Sarah, was not yet married. While most might congratulate the Nurses on their hard-won advancement, most people were not of the Puritan hierarchy. Gossip wagged its ugly tongue. How had this family of no real account in the pages of landed Gentry rise to so great a height? Had other forces been at work to fill their coffers and cradles? Many in the village thought the Nurses, though Godfearing, hardworking people, had gotten above themselves.

Orchard Farm butted up against the Nurse farmland, flanking Cow Horse River. Old Zerubbabel Endicott had thought the Allen acreage rightfully his for years. James Allen, the very man who was leasing the property to the Nurse family, had married an Endicott, who died shortly thereafter. Rather than the property reverting back into the Endicott portfolio, Allen retained the land, including a copse of prime woodland in the north-west corner of his farm. Fights broke out between Endicott and Francis Nurse and his sons when they repeatedly cut wood from the lot. Endicott filed a lawsuit, but it came to naught. It had been many years ago, but memories in Salem Village had long shadows.

Now, at 71-years-of-age, Rebecca's health was failing. She was hard of hearing and had been bedridden as the screams of "witchcraft" filled the meetinghouse not more than a mile or two away. She had heard the stories of poor Reverend Parris' daughter and niece. She turned to her Bible for comfort and prayer as she lay in her white shrift and bedcap on the second floor of her spacious farm house. Her family tended to her, and as always, she counted her blessings for such love and support.

Rumors of her own mother being a witch in Topsfield seemed far away. Joanna Towne had been rumored to deal in witchcraft when Rebecca was younger and the land disputes were at a peak. Nothing came of it. The stain of witchcraft was suspected to run in the family, as many accused in Salem Village would soon realize. Rebecca's two sisters, Mary Esty and Sarah Cloyce would too be called before the magistrates in the coming months. Had the current gossip of witches flying about the village brought home the pain those accusations had caused the Towne family so long ago?

For now, Rebecca found solace in her scriptures and frequent attention from those who loved her. It was therefore no surprise to have several visitors come into her room the morning of March 22nd to see how she was.

Elizabeth and Israel Porter, along with Porter's brother-in-law Daniel Andrews and Rebecca's brother-in-law Peter Cloyce, surrounded her bed and looked down with sympathy at the frail elderly woman before them. She seemed humbled and happy to see them.

Main floor room in the Nurse farm house.

The Porters and Daniel Andrews did not attend the Salem Village church. They were Salem Town members; those same members who had supported the anti-Parris movement. Rebecca was a member of the Salem Town church as well, but attended the much-closer meetinghouse in the Village. It may have been for that reason the party came to see her. Francis Nurse was no doubt known to them as a devout yeoman and for his work in the court system. But was it another reason that brought Porter and Andrews to Rebecca's bedside? For it was not just a visit of solicitation—they had come with some grievous news. News that was a direct result of Ann Putnam Jr.'s accusations against Rebecca. Porter, who had thus far kept his nose out of the growing Village chaos, may have seen this blatant attack of a pillar of the church and community as too much. The Putnams were the Porter's enemies for two generations now. Was it just Israel's concern for the woman that brought him there that day, or a perceived advantage that might drive a wedge between the Reverend Samuel Parris supporters?

Little did the small company of people standing within Rebecca's bed chamber know that the audacious claims of Ann Putnam Sr. were just revving up. The following day, Wednesday, March 23, Deodat Lawson witnessed her in the throes of an attack by the specter of Rebecca Nurse. They were in a battle over scriptural references with Ann screaming out, "Goodwife Nurse, be gone! Be gone! Be gone! Are you not ashamed? What hurt did I ever do you in my life? Your name is put out of God's book and it shall never be put into God's book again!" As Lawson scribbled down notes of the attack, Ann took the chance to portray herself "clothed with the white robes of Christ's righteousness" and therefore Nurse's specter could not hurt her, even though she at one point became as stiff as a board and her husband Thomas could not bend her as he tried to pull her to his lap.

Was Ann Putnam Sr. taking her revenge upon a matron who symbolized all she was not—surrounded by living children? Or, did it have to do with the Nurse's meteoric rise to wealth? Had Thomas Putnam coveted the farmland rented out to the Nurses?

One of Rebecca Nurse's sons-in-law was Thomas Preston. He was one of the men who had sworn out the original complaint against

Tituba Indian. Rebecca was, no doubt, well informed of the Parris household's afflictions. It was to that topic that she opened the conversation with her welcome company.

"I go to God for them," she said meekly, referring to Abigail Williams and Betty Parris. "But I am troubled, oh I am troubled at some of their crying out. Some of the persons they have spoken of, are, as I believe, as innocent as I am."

This statement may have caused the small group of visitors to pause, for it was for that reason they had traveled there along the Ipswich Road. Rebecca was ill with a stomach complaint, and may have looked particularly ashen and weak. How were they to tell her of the accusations against her spreading like wildfire through the village?

Finally, as softly as they could, they told the frail bedridden woman that Ann Putnam had "cried out" against her, and now many others were naming her as their tormentor. Putnam had even accused Rebecca of pressing her to sign the Devil's Book in the presence of Reverend Deodat Lawson.

One can only imagine the astonishment felt by this pious woman. Perhaps it was a trick of her hearing loss. Surely, they could not have just spoken such incredible words! But as she looked at their pained and stoic faces, the reality of it bore down upon her. After several moments, she said in a voice so hushed that it was almost inaudible.

"Well, if it be so, the will of the Lord be done," she whispered. But as the importance of the accusation hit home, fear gripped the frail woman. "As to this thing I am innocent as the child unborn," she pleaded, "but surely, what sin hath God found in me unrepented of that He could lay down such an affliction on me in my old age?"

The Porters came away determined to make a record of their conversation and observations during Rebecca Nurse's visit. Elizabeth Porter was Judge John Hawthorne's sister. Surely her testimony of the righteousness of this woman would carry some weight with her brother. Daniel Andrews and Peter Cloyce would witness the document. It took only one day for the warrant for Rebecca Nurse's arrest to be drawn up.

[March 23, 1692]

To the Marshall of Essex or his deputie

There Being Complaint this day made (before us by Edward putnam and Jonathan putnam Yeomen both of Salem Village, Against Rebeca Nurce the wife of franc's Nurce of Salem Village for vehement Suspition, of haveing Committed Sundry acts of Witchcraft and thereby haveing donne Much hurt and Injury to the Bodys of Ann putnam the wife of Thomas putnam of Salem Village Anna puttnam the dauter of Said Thomas putnam and Abigail Williams &c
You are therefore in theire Majesties names hereby required to apprehend and bring before us Rebeca Nurce the wife of franc's Nurce of Salem Village, to Morrow aboute Eight of the Clock in the forenoon at the house of Lt Nathaniell Ingersoll in Salem Village in order to her Examination Relateing to the aboves'd premises and hereof you are not to faile Salem March the 23'd 1691/2 per us *John. Hathorne] Assists*Jonathan Corwin] Assists
March 24'th 1691/2 I have apprehended the body of Rebeca Nurse and brought her to the house of Le't Nath. Ingersal where shee is in Costody per *George Herrick Marshall of Essex

The following morning, Rebecca Nurse was brought to Ingersoll's Tavern, only a short distance from her beloved home. She was taken into a room and stripped of her clothing. Mrs. Ingersoll and two midwives searched her body for witch's marks as the sickly woman shivered before them. One of the women announced she had found an unusual protrusion on the poor woman's genatalia. Humiliated and nauseous, Rebecca choked out that it was no more than a result of childbirth. It was noted on the record as evidence of a witch's teat. The woman helped her to redress and she was led down the street to the crowded meetinghouse. All of the afflicted were there, not just those names on the arrest warrant. Sarah Bibber had also joined the ranks of the tortured. Ann Putnam Sr. got the show started by convulsing before the meeting began.

Judge Hathorne looked at the forlorn woman who stood before him at the bar. Unlike Martha Corey's abusive taunts, this frail elderly woman seemed confused and frightened. She had just been accused, while standing naked and prodded before her neighbors, of bearing a witch's mark. After been bedridden for almost nine days, she leaned upon the bar for support and hoped her hearing would not fail her.

It was then, with a somewhat softer tone that Hathorne ordered the proceedings to begin. His sister Elizabeth Porter may have pleaded with him in Rebecca's favor. Reverend John Hale from Beverly gave the opening prayer, while Samuel Parris scribbled away. Jonathan Corwin sat at Hathorne's elbow, and once again, was happy to let the more-boisterous man handle the circus. Marshall George Herrick led the prisoner in, supporting her as she took each unsteady step. The girls immediately began to moan as she made her way to the front of the room.

Rebecca Nurse illustration with Marshal George Herrick beside her.

The examination of **Rebekah Nurse** at **Salem Village March 24, 1692**

Mr. Harthorn. What do you say (speaking to one afflicted) have you seen this Woman hurt you? Yes, she beat me this morning H) Abigial . Have you been hurt by this Woman? A) Yes *Ann Putman in a grievous fit cryed out that she hurt her. H) Goody Nurse , here are two An: Putman the child & Abigail Williams complains of your hurting them What do you say to it N). I can say before my Eternal father I am innocent, & God will clear my innocency H) Here is never a one in the Assembly but desires it, but if you be guilty Pray God discover you. Then **Hen: Kenny** rose up to speak H) Goodm: Kenny what do you say? * Then he entered his complaint & farther said that since this Nurse came into the house he was seizd twise with an amaz'd condition H) Here are not only these but, here is the wife of Mr Tho: Putman who accuseth you by credible information & that both of tempting her to iniquity, & of greatly hurting her. N). I am innocent & clear & have not been able to get out of doors these 8. or 9. dayes. H) Mr Putman: give in what you have to say *Then **Mr Edward Putman** gave in his relate H) Is this true Goody Nurse: I never afflicted no child never in my life. H)You see these accuse you, is it true N)No. H) Are you an innocent person relating to this Witchcraft. *Here Tho: Putmans wife cryed out, (**Ann Sr.**) Did you not bring the Black man with you, did you not bid me tempt God & dye How oft have you eat and drunk y'r own damaon H) What do you say to them? N) Oh Lord help me, & spread out her hands, & the afflicted were greviously vexed H) Do you not see what a solemn condition these are in? when your hands are loose the pesons are afflicted. *Then **Mary Walcot** (who often heretofore said she had seen her, but never could say or did say that she either bit or pincht her, or hurt her) & also **Eliz: Hubbard** under the like circumstances both openly accused her of hurting them H) Here are these 2 grown persons now accuse you, w't say you? Do not you see these afflicted persons, & hear them accuse you. N) The Lord knows I have not hurt them: I am an innocent person H) It is very awfull to all to see these agonies & you an old Professor thus charged with contracting with the Devil by the effects of it & yet to see you stand with dry eyes when there are so many whet – N) You do not know my heart. H) You would do well if you are guilty to confess & give Glory to God N)I am as clear as the child unborn H) What uncertainty there may be in apparitions I know not, yet this with me strikes hard upon you that you are at this very present charged with familiar spirits: this is your bodily person they speak to: they say now they see these familiar spirits com to your bodily [spirits com to your bodily] person, now what do you say to that N) I have none Sir: H) If you have confess & give glory to God I pray God clear you if you be innocent, & if you are guilty discover you And therefore give me an upright answer: have you any familiarity with these spirits? N)No, I have none but with God alone. N) How came you sick for there is an odd discourse of that in the mouths of many – H)I am sick at my stumach – H) Have you no wounds. N) I have none but old age H) You do Know whither you are guilty, & have familiarity with the Devil, & now when you are here present to see such a thing as these testify a black man whispering in your ear, & birds about you what do you say to it N) It is all false I am clear. H) Possibly you may apprehend you are no witch, but have you not been led aside by temptations that way. N) I have not. H) What a sad thing it is that a church member here & now an other of Salem, should be thus accused and charged *Mrs Pope fell into a grevious fit, & cryed out a sad thing sure enough: And then many more fell into lamentable fits. H) Tell us have not you had visible appearances more than what is common in nature? N) I have noe nor never had in my life H) Do you think these

129

suffer voluntary or involuntary N) I cannot tell H) That is strange every one can judge N) I must be silent H) They accuse you of hurting them, & if you think it is not unwillingly but by designe, you must look upon them as murderers. N) I cannot tell what to think of it. *Afterwards when this was som what insisted on she said I do not think so: she did not understand aright what was said H) Well then give an answer now, do you think these suffer against their wills or not. N) I do not think these suffer against their wills. H) Why did you never visit these afflicted persons. N) Because I was afraid I should have fits too. *Note Upon the motion of her body [had] fitts followed upon the complainants abundantly & very frequently. H) Is it not an unaccountable case that when you are examined these persons are afflicted? N) I have got no body to look to but God. *Again upon stirring her hands the afflicted persons were seized with violent fits of torture. H) Do you beleive these afflicted persons are bewitch. H) I do think they are. H) When this Witchcraft came upon the stage there was no suspicion of Tituba (Mr Paris's Indian woman) she profest much love to that child Betty Paris, but it was her apparition did the mischief, & why should not you also be guilty, for your apparition doth hurt also. N) Would you have me bely my self -- *she held her Neck on one side, & accordingly so were the afflicted taken. Then Authority requiring it Sam: Paris read what he had in characters taken from Mr Tho: Putmans wife in her fitts H) What do you think of this N)I cannot help it, the Devil may appear in my shap..

(Reverse) This a true account of the sume of her examination but by reason of geat noyses by the afflicted & many speakers, many things are pretermitted.

Nurse held her neck on one sid & Eliz: Hubbard (one of
the sufferers) had her neck set in that posture whereupon
another Patient Abigail Williams cryed out set
up Goody Nurses head the maid's neck will be broke &
when some set up Nurses head Aaron wey observed
that Betty Hubbards was immediately righted
Salem Village March. 24'th 1691/2 The Rever't Mr
Samuell parris being desired to take in wrighting the
Examination of Rebekah Nurse hath Returned itt as
aforesaid
Upon heareing the afores'd and seeing what wee then
did see together with the Charge of the persons then
present -- wee Committed Rebekah Nurse the wife
of fran's Nurce of Salem village unto theire Majest's
Goale in Salem as p[er] a Mittimus then given out, in
order to farther Examination *John Hathorne]
Assis'ts *Jonathan. Corwin] Assis'ts

The Porter's, Daniel Andrews, and Peter Cloyce presented
their petition in Rebecca's favor that same day, which
shows the speed with which they gathered 39 signatures
from those opposed to her arrest. Mr. Cloyce would come
to see his own wife, Sarah, Rebecca's sister, also accused
of witchcraft in the coming days.

(Statement of of Israel Porter , Elizabeth Porter , Daniel Andrew and Peter Cloyce for Rebecca Nurse)

[March 24, 1692]

We whos nams Are under writen being desiered to goe
to goodman nurs his hous to speeke with his wife and to

tell her that several of the Aflicted persons mentioned her: and Acordingly we went and we found her in A weak and Lowe condition in body as shee told us and had been sicke allmost A weak and we asked how it was otherwis with her and shee said shee blest god for it shee had more of his presents in this sickens then sometime shee have had but not soe much as shee desiered: but shee would with the Apostle pres forward to the mark: and many other places of scriptur to the Like purpos: and then of her owne Acord shee begane to speek of the Afflliction that was Amongst them and in perticuler of Mr Parris his family and How shee was greved for them though shee had not been to see them: by Reason of fits that shee formerly use to have for people said it was Awfull to:behold: but shee pittied them with: all her harte: and went to god for them: but shee said shee heard that there was persons spoke of that wear as Innocent as shee was shee belived and After much to this purpos: we told her we heard that shee was spoken of allsoe: well she said if it be soe the will of the Lord be done: she sate still awhille being as it wear Amazed: and then shee said well as to this thing I am Innocent as the child unborne but seurly shee said what sine hath god found out in me unrepented of that he should Lay such an Affliction upon me In my old Age: and Acording to our best observation we could not decern that shee knewe what we came for before we tould her

*Israel porter *Elizabeth porter To the substance of what is Above we if caled there too: are Ready to testifie on: oath *Daniell Andrew *Peter Cloys

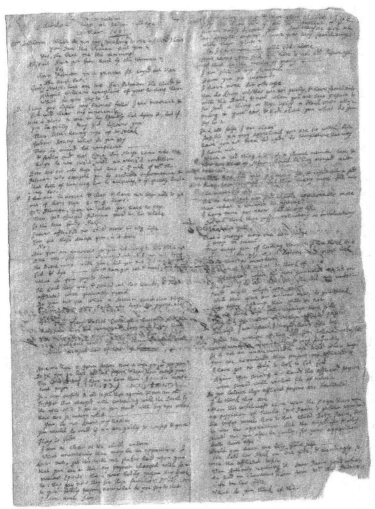

Samuel Parris's script of Rebecca Nurse's examination, March 24, 1692.

Something we see here in Hathorne's questioning of Rebecca is the offering of a loophole for her. For the first time, he basically says, "Well, perhaps you are not a witch. Maybe you were tempted to do something?" He reminds her more than once that it is a sad thing for a church woman to be so accused, and reminds her that another, Martha

Corey, is, even now, in jail. Mrs. Pope at this accusation screams out "A sad thing indeed!" The usual "black man and birds" are offered up from the same chorus of voices. Mary Walcott had cried out that Rebecca had bitten her, and raised her arm to show the fresh bite marks.

At one point, Deodat Lawson had to leave, possibly to prepare his next sermon. He was no doubt relieved to step from the crowded meetinghouse into the reasoning light of day. Little did he know, the afflicted had just accused Rebecca Nurse's shape of riding astride a horse behind the Devil around the meetinghouse. Lawson was a short distance away when the roar of shrieking girls was so loud, he paused and looked back at the building in horror. Mrs. Putnam had to be carried by her husband from the church after she became paralyzed. Once outside the doorway, she regained control of her body.

The noise had been so loud that at times Reverend Parris could not hear well enough to transcribe all the testimony. As for poor Rebecca Nurse, the one sentence that may have filtered through her deafened ears was the magistrate's reprimand, "They accuse you of hurting them and if you think it is not unwillingly but by design, you must look upon them as murderers." Hathorne had played a two-handed bid for a confession. Firstly, it was a manipulation to make the old woman feel ashamed for denouncing the children's' claims against her. Why, did she think these innocents were murderers? For their accusations, if found warranted, would result in the death of those they named. Would she, a woman who had enjoyed a long life already, deny them theirs by basically accusing them of being capable of murdering the accused people with their testimonies of torture?

And even more poignant, by using the word "murderer," he was reminding Rebecca that she faced a hanging charge if she did not confess and repent, as Tituba had done. It was with this admonition that the poor woman was hauled away to Salem Jail to join Martha Corey, another "Gospel Woman" of the Puritan faith.

A waning moon, that had been full only two days before, shone down on Salem Village. Rebecca Nurse had been introduced to her new quarters. Gone were the fresh linens and plump pillows her family had provided for her. Bread and water were now her fare until her family brought her fresh food from home. Her fellow inmates snored and wheezed their way through the long night. It had happened so fast. Pray God it would end as quickly. And through his grace, let no more be accused!

Chapter Thirteen

The Youngest Witch of All

Dorcas Good, Sarah Good's young daughter who had walked the streets with her mother begging food and lodging, was arrested along with Rebecca Nurse March 23, 1692, and brought to Ingersoll's Ordinary on the 24th. She sat in the tavern and could hear the screams coming from the meetinghouse during Rebecca Nurse's examination. The child was only four or five years of age. Did she comprehend what was happening? Her mother had been gone for three weeks, leaving her with a less than enthusiastic father. To the Ingersolls, who had been reluctant witnesses to the witch hysteria, what did they feel as they watched the dirty and hungry little girl huddled near the door, Deputy Samuel Braybrook standing guard over her?

[March 23,1692]

To The Marshall of Essex or his Dep't. You are in theire Majests names hereby required to bring before us **Dorcas Good** the Daugter of W'm Good of Salem Village tomorrow morneing upon suspition of acts of Witchcraft by her committed according to Complaints made against her by **Edw'd Putnam** & **Jonat putnam** of Salem Village.and hereof faile not Dated Salem.

March 23d 1691/2 Per us *John Hathorne]
Assists. *Jonathan. Corwin] Assists.
March 23d. 1691/2. I doe apoint mr Sam'll
Bradbrook to bee my lawffull Deputy, to serve this
summons and to make A true Returne per *George
Herrick Marshall of Essex.
(Reverse) March 24. 1691/2 I have taken the body
of Dorcas Good and brought her to the house of leut
Nath: Ingersol and is in Costody #[there] *Sammuall
brabrook Marshall's Deputy.

(Essex County Court Archives, Salem -- Witchcraft
Vol. 1, no. 61)

Examination of Dorothy Good,
as Told by Deodat Lawson)

[March 24,1692]

The Magistrates and Ministers also did inform me, that
they apprehended a child of Sarah G. and Examined it,
being between 4 and 5 years of Age And as to matter of
Fact, they did Unanimously affirm, that when this
Child, did but cast its eye upon the afflicted persons,
they were tormented, and they held her Head, and yet so
many as her eye could fix upon were afflicted. Which
they did several times make careful observation of: the
afflicted complained, they had often been Bitten by this
child, and produced the marks of a small set of teeth,
accordingly, this was also committed to Salem Prison;
the child looked hail, and well as other Children. I saw
it at Lievt. Ingersols After the commitment of Goodw.

N. [Goodwife Rebecca Nurse] Tho: Putmans wife was much better, and had no violent fits at all from that 24th of March to the 5th of April. Some others also said they had not seen her so frequently appear to them, to hurt them. Notes: Goodw. N. is Rebecca Nurse. The examined child is Dorothy Good.

(Deodat Lawson. A Brief and True Narrative of Some Remarkable Passages Relating to Sundry Persons Afflicted by Witchcraft, at Salem Village Which happened from the Nineteenth of March to the Fifth of April 1692 (Boston: Benjamin Harris, 1692), p. 9.)

The examination of poor Dorcas (Dorothy) had gone like the others. Declarations of pinching, choking, and biting. The small teeth marks were to prove they came from a smaller mouth than the older accusers could have produced. How easy was it to secret one's hands beneath an apron and press the smallest fingernail into the skin repeatedly in crescent shapes? Mercy Lewis, Ann Putnam Jr., and Mary Walcott gave written depositions to the magistrates listing their afflictions at the hand of the youngest witch of all.

Little Dorcas joined Martha Corey and Rebecca Nurse in Salem Town's wooden jail, while her mother, Sarah Good, still sat with Tituba in Boston's stone prison. She would be reunited with her mother on April 12th, but not until others shared the cart ride and ferry to Massachusetts' capital. Mention was made that Dorcas was questioned by magistrates John Hathorne and Jonathan Corwin, along with Deodat Lawson and Salem minister John Higginson, at the home of the prison keeper William Dounton. It may be the child was given special consideration due to her age and kept at the house until her proper trial was arranged, or, she was brought there out of earshot and influence of the other jail inmates.

The child unwittingly played along with the questions presented to her. She announced she had a little snake that suckled on her hand. She was asked to indicate where, and she pointed to a red mark the size of a flea bite on her forefinger, just below the joint. To make matters worse, when she was asked if "the black man" gave her the snake, the little girl cried, "Oh no! My mother did."

It was easy to convince the members of the Massachusetts Bay Colony that witchcraft ran in the family. That compass would point toward other family members of the accused in the days to come. For now, unsuspecting little Dorcas Good had just helped to put a noose around her mother's neck.

The next arrest warrant on the suspicion of witchcraft wouldn't come until April 8th. Despite the lull, apparently the Devil's chess game took no such vacation. Complaints of spectral attacks, including by those already imprisoned, swarmed about the 550 Salem Village inhabitants like angry bees. Witnesses dashed from one house to another to witness and document the plethora of curses befalling the band of victims. Even little Betty Parish, sequestered at her relative Stephen Sewall's home in Salem Town, was not freed from the bedlam.

Betty's tortures were extreme. Her description of her torments is interesting. If you listen closely, you will hear Tituba's descriptions at her examination—an examination for which Betty was present. Mrs. Sewall asked the afflicted girl what specter was tormenting her. Betty replied a man's dark shape came to her promising her gifts and a trip to a golden city, if she would sign his book and obey him. Tituba had spoken of a "black man" who offered her "pretty things" and trips to cities if she would sign his book. Perhaps, Betty's guilt-ridden mind was reliving her friend's testimony, or, Betty, quite possibly, believed Tituba's visions and feared the man was after her as well.

Reverend John Hale visited Betty at the Sewall home. He had been one of the first to witness her ailments at the parsonage in February. Mrs. Sewall had tried to alleviate Betty's nightmares by telling her the man was the Devil and "a liar from the beginning." She told Betty to bid him go back to where he came from and leave her alone. Reverend Hale recorded that this admonition of Mrs. Sewall's had helped ease Betty's torments. He spoke at length with the girl, and she confessed to him about the conjuring she had participated in at the parsonage. She admitted to using eggs in a glass of water. "After her confession of it, and manifestation of repentance for it, and our prayers to God for her, she was speedily released from those bounds of Satan," Hale wrote in his notes.

What concerned Reverend Hale was the ignorance of what these little forays into magic could do. It is similar to the wanton use of Ouija boards today, seeing it only as a parlor game. Repeatedly, the use of these boards has been warned against as a portal for inviting evil spirits into the home. Hale feared that by using sorceries such as fortune telling, the girls were, in effect, acting as witches. He backed off from proclaiming them so by adding the caveat, they were not witches yet "because such persons act ignorantly, not considering they hereby go to the Devil." He did warn that the afflicted parties "are in their fits tempted to be witches."

Many witch trial scholars over the years have wondered why the accusers weren't, in fact, first looked upon as witches themselves. It was a fine line between afflicted to afflicter. The magistrates, constables, village adults, and visiting dignitaries were willing to hear these young women, along with a few matrons, and listen with credulity to their claims. One has to wonder, were the trials serving more than just as a means to rid the village and surrounding towns of witches? Were they a threshing floor for unwanted inhabitants and revenge for petty grievances?

Deodat Lawson Tries to Stem the Tide

Once Rebecca Nurse and Dorcas Good had been taken away to jail, the meetinghouse returned to a more sanctimonious function, based on the nature of some of the members filling the pews. It was Thursday, and Salem Village's turn to host a weekly Lecture. The room was packed, as many people from surrounding towns who had just witnessed the examinations of Goody Nurse and Dorcas Good remained. Ingersoll's cash box overflowed as trial attendees walked the several yards from the meetinghouse to his front door. Now, the throngs reclaimed their seats, or pressed into standing positions against the walls. This would be a sermon they needed to hear. Were they doomed? Was the witch hunt at an end? For those who had listened to the accused women's testimonies, one thing was clear—the "tall black man" mentioned by the afflicted and "witches" alike, had not been brought to the bar. It had only been women and a small female child dragged before the magistrates. In their gut they knew; this was not over.

It may have been a rattled Deodat Lawson who took the steps up to the pulpit. He was the invited minister for this sermon. After what he had witnessed only hours before in this very room, how did he now speak to these people who were so eagerly looking to him for guidance and explanations. He decided to hit it head on.

He named his text, Zechariah 3:2, and began "And the Lord said unto Satan, "The Lord rebuke thee, O Satan. Even the Lord that hath chosen Jerusalem rebuke thee. Is this not a brand plucked from the fire?" The "brand plucked from the burning," was a reminder that repentance and good deeds could save a soul. Jerusalem also referenced the word Salem, and alluded to the city being the first among the cities forged from the Wilderness. His next warning was meant to hit a little closer to home for the "afflicted" sitting with rapt attention in the meeting, for once, quiet. They had captured two more apprentices of the Devil earlier, and were appeased for a time.

Lawson looked out into the congregation and said the Devil had the power to do many things, from physical ailments to mental contortions. He can "raise mists of darkness and ignorance in the understanding," he said pointedly, along with "false representations to the eyes." If the girls twitched uncomfortably in their seats at the words "false representations," his next statement, unfortunately, offered confirmation of their alleged afflictions.

Giving credibility to the spectral evidence that far outweighed any forensic proof of witchcraft, he said, the afflicted might fall victim by allowing Satan to "use their bodies and minds, shapes, and representations to affright and afflict others at his pleasure." While his point was that Satan could misrepresent individuals by appearing in their likeness and doing harm, the fevered minds of those that had just witnessed the examinations and outpouring of pain from the victims, heard only that specters could visit and hurt. He pressed his point by referencing Martha Corey and Rebecca Nurse, church-covenanted women, as Satan's ploy to divide the church. Lawson warned these women had not yet been given a legal trial, and had not been proven guilty. To assume they were "would be a matter of deep humiliation to such as are innocent."

Then, using the Puritan whip so long employed by the ministers, he admonished the people before him to look to themselves first to see if they were without blemish, or had, even unknowingly, brought the Devil's afflictions upon the community. As others had noted of the Village, "their inveterate anger and ill-will makes way for the Devil. Give no place to the Devil by rash censuring of others without sufficient grounds, or false accusing any willingly."

Here was the reprimand that should have given the girls, Ann Putnam Sr., Bathshua Pope, John Indian, and the Putnam men, pause. Deodat Lawson had just pointed out that by accusing falsely you were opening yourself to the Devil. This was against God's laws. Without preamble he took on the means used by the girls that many believed started the whole thing. He warned that the use of egg and water, Bible and Key, shears and sieve, the burning of hair, or the use of urine (as in Sibley's witch cake), were trifling with white magic and inviting Satan into their homes and hearts.

Impassioned by his need to get his message across to the congregation he yelled, "Arm! Arm! Arm!" against Satan's army. "Let us admit no parley, give no quarter. Prayer is the most proper and potent antidote against the old serpent's venomous operations...Pray! Pray! Pray!" Each person was to look to themselves and "put on the whole armor of God." He finished on a hopeful note, reminding the villagers that God had already defeated Satan. "All Satan's strugglings now are of a conquered enemy."

These words may have held little comfort for the four women held in jails with the threat of a noose waiting for them. And as for Lawson's basic warning, that in effect was a nod to Jesus's words, "Those among you who are without sin, cast the first stone." The afflicted not only refused to lay down their stones, they suffered more slights from the Invisible World that very evening.

John Proctor rode his horse north from his farm toward the village proper. He passed Felton's Hill, Sarah Phillips home, and crossed the wooden bridge spanning Endicott River. He was in a black mood. He was on his way to fetch back his absent maid, Mary Warren, who had appeared as a witness the day before and stayed over at the village. He stopped into Walter Phillips tavern, where he vented his disapproval of the whole witchcraft affair to Samuel Sibley, and possibly others overhearing his heated remarks. He told Sibley he would rather have given up forty pence than let his "jade" attend the exams in the first place. He said of the afflicted girls, "They should all be at the whipping post," and as for the rest, he yelled, "Hang them! Hang them all!"

Whether Proctor was speaking of the accusers that he was sure were faking their miseries, or the witches already accused, is not clear. But his words "Hang them all!" would come back to him, and to his wife, Elizabeth Proctor. For on March 26th, only two days after Deodat Lawson's poignant sermon, the specter of Elizabeth Proctor and Martha Corey, once again, attacked Mercy Lewis. More damning yet to the Proctors, John's words had been spewed into the ears of Samuel Sibley, who was none other than Mary Walcott's Uncle. He was also the husband of Mary Sibley who had helped in the making of the "Witch Cake." If John Proctor didn't fear the power of the young women fueling the witch hunt, he soon would.

Chapter Fourteen

Elizabeth Proctor, Come Forth!

Although incarcerated, the specters of Rebecca Nurse and Dorcas Good continued to prey upon the afflicted girls. Ann Putnam, Jr., never calm for long, accused Rebecca Nurse of whipping her with a chain. Her Uncle, Edward Putnam, claimed to have seen marks resembling chain links upon the child's skin. Others present said they saw the marks as well, along with bite marks. As the afflicters were already in shackles within jail walls, did Ann Jr. and others continue to accuse them for good measure, or was it to remain in the lime light until new witches were named?

Meanwhile, Thomas and Ann Putnam Sr. took advantage of their maid's newest torments. Mercy Lewis was suffering fits and exclaimed "There she is!" at empty air. When Samuel Barton and John Houghton arrived at the Putnam home to help the young woman, Thomas and Ann Sr. told the men Mercy had accused Elizabeth Proctor during her seizures. Mercy seemed hesitant to agree with the Putnam's naming of Proctor, saying if she did say her name, it was while she was delusional. This is one of the more obvious attempts documented to show how the manipulation of the witch trials was by "suggesting" names to the girls.

Abigail Williams was also "crying out" against Elizabeth Proctor. A new name had been added to the cauldron of lies.

As Ipswich and Andover began to suffer their own accusations of witchcraft among their townsfolk, Governor Phips was on his way back from England aboard the *Nonsuch*, carrying with him the precious charter that had been long-awaited. If ever there was a need for some legal foundation for the Massachusetts Bay Colony, it was now. Four accused witches were in jail (five counting little Dorcas Good), and reports of others were swirling about the wooden-framed houses of Salem Village.

Rebecca Nurse's kinsmen were still active in their efforts to get the elderly woman freed from jail. It may have been one of the reasons Ann Jr., and Abigail Williams continued to accuse her shape of coming to them with ever-increasing vengeance.

Rebecca's sister, Sarah Cloyce, attended the Sabbath at the village meetinghouse March 27th. Reverend Samuel Parris had reclaimed his pulpit after the visiting Deodat Lawson had returned to Boston. Where Lawson's sermon had been one of hope and guidance in overcoming the current ills of the village, Parris took another tact. Lawson had admonished the congregation to look to themselves for the reason things had gotten out of control, and to resist the urge to blame others that had not been proven guilty before a proper tribunal. Parris planted the Devil firmly back in the middle of the church, and agreed with Lawson that some of the church elite could indeed be among his followers.

"Have I not chosen you twelve," Parris intoned, "and one of you is a Devil?" His text referred to Jesus's words concerning Judas Iscariot's betrayal of Him. But to the sensitive hearing of some in the congregation that morning, it was too much to bear. Sarah Cloyce, Rebecca Nurse's sister, suddenly stood up and made her way to the rear of the building. As others looked on with surprise, she flung open the church door and stepped out, flinging it shut behind her with a bang! The afflicted girls pounced on her dramatic exit and embellished it. They later testified that not only had she departed the church before partaking of the Lord's Supper afterwards, a communal event only those members under the covenant could do, but that they saw her curtsy to the Devil at the gate outside and sign his book.

Parris swung at the consciousness of the attendees again, making sure his point that those awaiting trial for witchcraft were probably rightly accused. "Pray we also that not one true saint may suffer as a devil either in name or body. The Devil will represent the best saints as devils if he could, but," Parris said, driving the stake home, "it is not easy to imagine that his power is of such extent."

As many in the village had spoken out against the girls, Proctor and Martha Corey among them, Parris may have worried that if the majority of the "saints" felt his own daughter and niece had made up the accusations, and that the results of their words were already damning lives, it would be his head that would roll. It was one of two courses to take: either denounce the girls as frauds, or admit strongly the Devil was to blame and was inflicting even church-covenanted members.

Those elite stayed after the lesser villagers returned to their homes that Sabbath day, each taking the bread and wine offered to them in remembrance of Jesus's body and blood. It was at this time that Parris asked the men present to vote by a show of hands how many would accept Mary Sibley's apology for her part in creating the "Witch Cake" and possibly escalating the diabolic forces at work. The men all raised their hands in her support. The picking and choosing of who was a witch and who was not in the eyes of Salem Village is interesting. Here is a woman who instructed Tituba on the ingredients of a "Witch Cake," acknowledging her understanding and use of magic, and yet, she is not accused of witchcraft. The girls participated in the egg and water fortunetelling and are displaying strange maladies that could be interpreted as witchcraft possession, yet none are arrested. Mary Sibley was Mary Walcott's Aunt. Had that relationship kept her from the gallows?

As the hysteria of March ushered the calendar forward, Abigail Williams saw to it that the last day of that month would not be forgotten. She claimed no less than forty other witches had come to her Uncle's pasture behind the parsonage for their own communal supper. Raw meat replaced the while bread, and a blood-red drink replaced the wine, as the specters of Sarah Good and Sarah Cloyce served those in attendance.

"Oh Goodwife Cloyce!" Abigail screamed, "I did not think to see you here! Is this a time to receive the sacrament? You ran away on the Lord's Day, and scorned to receive it in the meetinghouse, and is this a time to receive it? I wonder at you!"

The audaciousness of this 11-year-old girl is astounding. One can only imagine the shock and rage of Reverend Parris. His sermon, only four days prior, had been a cloaked ploy to distance himself from the fact that the Devil had chosen his house to begin his campaign of evil. Even devout church members could be under Satan's attack, he had preached. But his niece Abigail had just put him right back into the thick of things by declaring the Devil was hosting his communal feast within the parsonage boundaries!

How could one look at Abigail's vision of this heinous sacrament and not feel she was trying to hurt her Uncle in some way? Was it because Betty had been the golden child and not an orphan like herself? Betty had been sent away for protection, while she, herself, was left to deal with witches attacking her at every turn. For whatever reason, Abigail was out to hurt as many people as possible. She threw in Rebecca Nurse's spectral torture at the same time Sarah Good and Sarah Cloyce were pouring the Devil's wine. As for Reverend Parris, his moving sermon had done nothing to turn the hearts of the villagers toward him—his salary once again went unpaid.

April Brings New Victims and Torments

Rebecca Nurse's spectral shape was far more active than the elderly matron had been for decades. It flew in and out of homes with shocking regularity. Abigail was going after another of the village denizens. She claimed Elizabeth Proctor had become a vicious specter, pinching the girl "grievously" and tearing at her bowels in a fierce rage. Stephen Bittford, a Salem Village farmer, awoke to find Rebecca Nurse, along with Elizabeth and John Proctor's spirits, inside his room. He claimed to have suffered "a very great pain in my neck and could not stir my head nor speak a word."

Mary Warren seemed to be the only one of the group of accusers that was punished for her outcries against her neighbors. John Proctor would brook none of her foolishness. After bearing her home from the meetinghouse examination of Rebecca Nurse and Dorcas Good, he carried out his threats and piled on the work. He may have beat her, for Mary had a sudden change of heart. He accused her of crying out "against innocent persons." She ceased her fits and tacked a note to the meetinghouse board outside asking the church members to share with their prayers of gratitude that she had been delivered from Satan and was no longer suffering attacks.

Her relief was short-lived. Reverend Parris read her note to the congregation on Sunday, April 3rd. The villagers questioned Mary after church, asking what had brought forth the change? She answered, "The afflicted persons did but dissemble." She may have hoped the listening crowd would see the statement as the girls had been led astray by false visions from Satan, and that they were confused. The very definition of dissemble is "to hide under false appearance," or to "simulate." But it can also mean "to conceal facts under pretense." The mumblings from the crowd at her statement must have been ones of astonishment. What did this mean? There were people in jail.

The horror of the other afflicted people at being found out would have been chilling. What if Mary went further and admitted they were faking their symptoms? There was only one thing to do. The others put forth their own remedy for Mary's sudden healing—she must have signed the Devil's Book. Now that she had joined his ranks, the witches had no need to torment her any longer.

If Mary's declaration that she had been healed caused concern among the accusers, it did not show in Abigail's continued outbursts. Perhaps to include Mary Warren's employers as a possible coven of witches running the Proctor's tavern, Abigail experienced not only torture by Elizabeth Proctor's hand, but of John's as well. "Are you come too?" she cried of John. "You can pinch as well as your wife."

Enough was enough. Mary Walcott's torments had prompted her father Captain John Walcott. along with Nathaniel Ingersoll, who was his nephew and Mary Walcott's relative, to ride to Salem Town and swear out complaints against Sarah Cloyce (Rebecca Nurse's sister), and Elizabeth Proctor (who was pregnant at the time). The document accused the two women of torturing not only Mary Walcott, but Abigail Williams, Ann Putnam Jr., John Indian, and Mercy Lewis, who was Sarah Cloyce's niece. The arrest warrants were drawn up by Hathorne and Corwin on April 3rd, 1692. They may have felt control of the situation slipping away as more names of suspected witches crossed their desks. They decided to consult with a higher authority in Boston before serving the warrants.

It was obvious the town members with an agenda had brushed off Mary Warren's "dissembling" account, and were going ahead with the witch hunt. In fact, reports of Sarah Cloyce's specter, along with those of Rebecca Nurse, and Martha and Giles Corey, and even Dr. Grigg's wife Rachel, were flooding in. Benjamin Gould had awakened to see his neighbors, the Coreys, standing by his bed staring at him. A sharp pain in his foot and sides followed.

By April 8th, Hathorne and Corwin took action. Boston had offered to send constituents of the Governor's Council of Assistants to be present at the next examination. Salem Town was selected for this meeting. The drawn-up warrants for Sarah Cloyce and Elizabeth Proctor were issued.

Rebecca Nurse's family rallied around Sarah Cloyce as they had Rebecca, even before the warrants had gone out. On March 28th, Daniel Elliott, Cloyce's stepson-in-law, and William Rayment from Beverly, had been visiting Ingersoll's Ordinary and found some of the afflicted girls there. They questioned the girls about the visions and afflictions they had endured. Mrs. Ingersoll was present and no doubt interested to hear their answers, as she was one who doubted their fits. William Rayment mentioned that Elizabeth Proctor's name had come up as one now afflicting the girls. Mrs. Ingersoll announced she could not believe it. Right on cue, one of the girls yelled, "There is Goody Proctor!" The visitors looked at the empty space she pointed to.

"Old witch!" cried another. "I'll have her hang."

The audacious announcement resulted in tempers flashing among those who were listening to the two girls. Mrs. Ingersoll scolded them. Rayment out-in-out told the girls he thought they were lying. "They seemed to make a jest of it," he reported later. This was new for the girls. They had always found a receptive crowd at Ingersoll's; people who hung on their every word and sympathized with their torments. But now, these adults were angry and accusing them of fakery. Nervously, one of the girls tried to shrug it off. "She did it for sport. They must have some sport," the report said later, repeating the girl's words.

Even then, along with Mary Warren's confession that they "dissembled," the trials went on. In fact, the list of accused witches would reach astonishing numbers.

(Complaint of Jonathan Walcott & Nathaniell Ingersonv. Elizabeth Proctor & Sarah Cloyce)

[April 4, 1692.]

This. 4'th Aprill. 1692. Capt Jonathan Walcott and Leut Nathaniell Ingerson personally Appeared before us & Exhibited there Compl't in behalfe of theyr Majestyes for them selves & Severall of theyr Neighbours against Sarah Cloyes wife of peter Cloyes of Salem

Village & [Eliz.] proctur the wife of Jno proctur of Salem for High Suspition of Severall Acts of Wichcraft donne or comitted by them upon the Bodyes of Abigall Williames & John. Indian of the family of mr Sam'll parris, & Mary Walcott daughter of one of the complaynants & Ann. Putnam and Mercy Lewis of the family of Thomas putnam Whereby great hurt & damage hath bin donne to the Bodyes of s'd persons & Therefore Craved Justice

(Reverse) Walcutt & Ingersol comp'ts

(Essex County Court Archives, Salem -- Witchcraft Vol. 1, no. 96)

(Warrant for the Apprehension of Elizabeth Proctor & Sarah Cloyce, and Officer's Return)

[April 4, 1692

There Being Complaint this day made (Before us) by Capt Jonat Walcott , and Lt Nathaniell Ingersull both of Salem Village, in Behalfe of theire Majesties for themselfes and also for severall of their Neighbours Against Sarah Cloyce the wife of peter Cloyce of

Salem Village; and Elizabeth Procter the wife of John Procter of Salem farmes for high Suspition of Sundry acts of Witchcraft donne or Committed by them upon the bodys of Abigail Williams , and John Indian both of Mr Sam parris his family of Salem Village and Mary Walcott daugter of one of the abovesaid Complainants, And Ann Putnam and Marcy Lewis of the famyly of Thomas Putnam of Salem Village whereby great hurt and dammage hath beene donne to the Bodys of s'd persons above named therefore Craved Justice.

You are therefore in theire Majest's names hereby required to apprehend and bring before us Sarah Cloyce the wife of peter Cloyce of Salem Village and Elizabeth procter the wife of John Procter of Salem farmes; on Munday Morneing Next being the Eleventh day of this Instant Aprill aboute Eleven of the Clock, at the publike Meetinghouse in the Towne, in order to theire Examination Relateing to the premises aboves'd and here of you are. not to faile Dated Salem Aprill 8'th 1692

To George Herick Marshall *John Hathorne of the County of essex*Jonathan. Corwin] Assists

Ingersoll's tavern and the meetinghouse continued to be the preferred scene for spectral attacks. Both places were, after all, a gathering place where there was sure to be a crowd. Only two days after the arrest warrants had gone out for Elizabeth Proctor and Sarah Cloyce, John Indian screamed out during the Sabbath meeting that Cloyce's specter had just bitten him and drawn blood. It was not a bad ploy for distancing himself from all the talk of a diabolic man with dark skin.

Ingersoll's, as always, filled after the services. Mercy Lewis suddenly fell to the floor at the tavern in a fit. Standing nearby was Ephraim Sheldon, who had also escaped Maine's Indian attacks along with Mercy. He claimed she cried out that it was Goody Cloyce attacking her. But when Mercy calmed down, she denied she had named Cloyce. Others weren't ready to let a good seizure go, and pressed the girl for a name of the specter attacking her. "Was it Goody Nurse? Goody Corey? Goody Cloyce?" Mercy persisted in saying she had seen "nobody," just as she had denied saying Elizabeth Proctor had attacked her at the Putnams, although Thomas and Ann Sr. claimed she did. Abigail decided to take over and interpret. She said she had seen all three specters attacking Mercy, and threw in Sarah Good as a bonus.

Elizabeth Proctor and Sarah Cloyce were transferred to Salem Town's meetinghouse on April 11, 1692, to stand before the magistrates and the afflicted. The Villagers left their chores, donned coats, cloaks and hats, and headed toward the seaport. The seven-mile trip to the harbor town, that had once caused an outcry for its distance for Sunday services and watch tower duty, was now traversed with eagerness. There was to be another trial, this time with Boston dignitaries in residence.

Chapter Fifteen

"Oh! You Are a Grievous Liar!"

Reverend Samuel Parris took his seat in the Salem Town meetinghouse and readied himself to take down the proceedings of the inquisitions into Sarah Cloyce's and Elizabeth Proctor's accusations of witchcraft. He stacked his parchment sheets and pulled the quill and ink bottle over to within reach. It was eleven o'clock and the air crackled with anticipation. The good Reverend may have felt relieved to have the upcoming hysteria away from his own meetinghouse in Salem Village. It was a physical distancing, if not a mental one.

Deputy Governor Thomas Danforth was in attendance, along with four assistants of the Governor's Counsel from Boston: James Russell, Isaac Addington, Samuel Sewall, and Samuel Appleton. They took their seats but saved the two dominant places for John Hathorne and Jonathan Corwin, who would, once again, act as judges. Reverend Nicholas Noyes opened the proceedings with a prayer. At its conclusion, the afflicted persons readied themselves. Elizabeth Hubbard chose to sit trance-like and stare at nothing in particular. She had been the first to name Elizabeth Proctor. Was she now regretting it as the weight of a legal proceeding, the accused's possible incarceration, and execution hung in the balance? A trance would excuse her from putting any damning words on paper.

It appears the two accused women were together in the room, rather than separated and brought in one-at-a-time, as had been previously done. The following account by Samuel Parris seems to show their testimonies and those of the witnesses were grouped.

Examination of Sarah Cloyce & Elizabeth Proctor

(Examination of Sarah Cloyse and Elizabeth Proctor)

[April 11, 1692]

At a court held at Salem 11th April 1692, by the honoured Thomas Danforth, Deputy Governor. Q. John [Indian]; who hurt you? A. Goody Procter first, and then Goody Cloyse . Q. What did she do to you? A. she brought the book to me. Q. John [Indian]! tell the truth, who hurts you? have you been hurt? A. The first, was a gentlewoman I saw. Q. Who next? A. Goody Cloyse . Q. But who hurt you next? A. Goody Procter . Q. What did she do to you? A. She choaked me, and brought the book. Q. How oft did she come to torment you? A. A good many times, she and Goody Cloyse . Q. Do they come to you in the night as well as the day? A. They come most in the day. Q. Who? A. Goody Cloyse and Goody Procter . Q. Where did she take hold of you? A. Upon my throat, to stop my breath. Q. Do you know Goody Cloyse and Goody Procter ? A. Yes, here is Goody Cloyse . (Cloyse) when did I hurt thee? A. A great many times. (Cloyse) Oh! you are a grievous liar. Q. What did this Goody Cloyse do to you? A. She pinched and bit me till the blood came. Q. How long since this woman came and hurt you? A. Yesterday at meeting. Q. At any time before? A. Yes a great many times. Q. Mary Walcot! who hurts you? A. Goody Cloyse. Q. What did she do to you? A. She hurt me. Q. Did she bring the book? A. Yes. Q. What was you to do with it? A. To touch it, and be well. -- Then she fell into a fit. Q. Doth she come alone? A. Sometimes alone, and sometimes in company with Goody Nurse and Goody Corey , and a great many I do not know. -- Then she fell into a fit again. -- Q. Abigail Williams! did you see a company at Mr. Parris's house eat and drink? A. Yes

Sir, that was their sacrament. Q. How many were there? A. About forty, and Goody Cloyse and Goody Good were their deacons. Q. What was it? A. They said it was our blood, and they had it twice that day. Q. Mary Walcot! have you seen a white man? Yes, Sir, a great many times. Q. What sort of man was he? A. A fine grave man, and when he came, he made all the witches to tremble. -- Abigail Williams confirmed the same, and that they had such a sight at Deacon Ingersoll's . Q. Who was at Deacon Ingersoll's then? A. Goody Cloyse , Goody Nurse , Goody Corey , and Goody Good . -- Then Sarah Cloyse asked for water, and sat down as one seized with a dying fainting fit; and several of the afflicted fell into fits, and some of them cried out, Oh! her spirit is gone to prison to her sister Nurse . -- Q. Elizabeth Procter ! you understand whereof you are charged, viz. to be guilty of sundry acts of witchcraft; what say you to it? Speak the truth, and so you that are afflicted, you must speak the truth, as you will answer it before God another day. Mary Walcot! doth this woman hurt you? A. I never saw her so as to be hurt by her. Q. Mary Lewis! does she hurt you? -- Her mouth was stopped. -- Q. Ann Putman , does she hurt you? -- She could not speak. -- Q. Abigail Williams! does she hurt you? -- Her hand was thrust in her own mouth. -- Q. John! does she hurt you? A. This is the woman that came in her shift and choaked me. Q. did she ever bring the book? A. Yes, Sir. Q. What to do? A. to write. Q. What, this woman? A. Yes, Sir. Q. Are you sure of it? A. Yes, Sir. -- Again, Abigail Williams and Ann Putman were spoke to by the court, but neither of them could make any answer, by reason of dumbness or other fits. Q. What do you say Goody Procter to these things? A. I take God in heaven to be my witness, that I know nothing of it, no more than the child unborn. Q. Ann Putman! doth this woman hurt you. A. Yes Sir, a great many times. -- Then the accused looked upon them and they fell into fits. Q. She does not bring the book to you, does she? A. Yes, Sir, often, and saith she hath made her maid set her hand to it. Q. Abigail Williams! does this woman hurt you? A. Yes, Sir, often. Q. Does she bring the book to you? A. Yes. Q. What would she have you do with it? A. To write in it and I shall be well. -- Did not you, said Abigal, tell me, that your maid had written? (Procter) Dear Child, it is not so. There is another judgement, dear child. -- Then Abigail and Ann had fits. -- By and by they cried out, look you there is Goody Procter upon the beam. -- By and by, both of them cried out of Goodman Procter himself, and said he was a wizard. -- Immediately, many, if not all of the bewitched, had grievous fits. -- Q. Ann Putman! who hurt you? A. Goodman Procter and his wife too. -- Afterwards some of the afflicted cried, there is Procter going to take up Mrs. Pope's feet. -- And her feet were immediately taken up. -- Q. What do you say Goodman Proctor to these things? A. I know not, I am innocent. -- Abigail Williams cried out, there is Goodman Procter going to Mrs. Pope , and immediately, said Pope fell into a fit. -- You see the devil will deceive you; the children could see what you was going to do before the woman was hurt. I would advise you to repentance, for the devil is bringing you out. -- Abigail Williams cried out again, there is Goodman Procter going to hurt Goody Bibber; and immediately Goody Bibber fell into a fit. There was the like of Mary Walcot , and divers others. -- Benjamin Gould gave in his testimony, that he had seen Goodman Corey and his wife, Procter and his wife, Goody

Cloyse , Goody Nurse , and Goody Griggs in his chamber last thursday night. -- Elizabeth Hubbard was in a trance during the whole examination. -- During the examination of Elizabeth Procter , Abigail Williams and Ann Putman , both made offer to strike at said Procter ; but when Abigail's hand came near, it opened, whereas it was made up into a fist before, and came done exceeding lightly, as it drew near to said Procter , and at length with open and extended fingers, touched Procter's hood very lightly. Immediately Abigail cried out, her fingers, her fingers, burned, and Ann Putman took on most greviously, of her head, and sunk down.

Salem, April 11th, 1692. Mr. Samuel Parris was desired by the honourable Thomas Danforth , deputy-governor, and the council, to take in writing the aforesaid examinations, and accordingly took and delivered them in; and upon hearing the same, and seeing what was then seen, together with the charge of the afflicted persons, were by the advice of the council all committed by us, John Hawthorne, John Corwin, Assistants.

(Thomas Hutchinson , History of Massachusetts-Bay, vol. 2, pp. 21-23 .)

(Council Record Pertaining to Sarah Cloyce, Martha Cory, Dorothy Good, Rebecca Nurse,

Elizabeth Proctor & John Proctor)

[April 11, 1692]

Salem At a Councill held at Salem. and pr'sent Aprill 11 -- 1692 Thomas Danforth Esq'r Dept. Gov'er
James   Russell -- Maj'r   Sam   Appleton John Hathorne Capt Samuell Sewall Isaac Adington Jonath' Corwin.
And John   procter of   Salem   farmes   being   then personally present was by Abigail Williams and Anna putnam Charged with severall acts of Witchcraft by him Committed on the person of Mrs pope the wife of mr Joseph pope and Others, who ware at s'd tyme accordingly afflicted apparent to all, likewise marcy Lewis and [] cott charged s'd John procter at s'd tyme upon w'ch s'd Jno procter & his wife and Sarah Cloyce ware all Committed to prison per advise of the Councill Also further Information being given against s'd Jno procter by mr Samueell parris. Aprill 12'th as appeares. Aprill 12'th 1692 John procter and Elizabeth procter his wife -- and Sarah Cloyce , also: Rebecka Nurse . Martha Cory and Dorothy Good ware sent to Boston Goale per Marshall Geo: Herrick -- upon high Suspition as aboves'd –

John Proctor received unwanted attention at his wife's examination that he had not expected. After Ann Putnam Jr. named "Goodman Proctor and his wife too" as the ones hurting her, the umbrella of suspicion began hovering above John's head. Others testified against him and he was lumped in with his wife and Goody Cloyce and taken to the Salem Jail around the corner from the meetinghouse. Those who had made the trip from the Village may have been disappointed that the inquisition was shorter than usual.

At one point during the questioning of Cloyce and Goody Proctor, the Lord's Prayer test was administered. The women were asked to repeat the prayer in front of the congregation. It was believed a witch could not recite the sacred prayer perfectly. One of the two accused, it is not said which one, fumbled saying "deliver us from all evil," instead of "deliver us from evil." Another mistake was made by saying "hollowed is his name," instead of "hallowed is his name." The word "hollow" appeared as an afront to the sacred deity. It is also rumored that John Proctor muttered during the proceedings against John Indian when the man was testifying against his wife. "I'll beat the Devil out of him," he reportedly said, "if I get him in my custody." Statements such as these did Proctor few favors. He was in enemy territory.

The following morning, April 12th, John Proctor was to be questioned in Salem Town while Samuel Parris took notes. A dog was reclining beneath the table where Parris sat. Marshal George Herrick left to bring Proctor over from the jail for his interrogation. Parris took the opportunity to put his notes from the previous day in order. His hopes were dashed when a number of the afflicted fell into fits. As Mary Walcott, Abigail Williams, and John Indian entered the meeting room, they screamed, "There is Goodman Proctor! There is Goodman Proctor in the magistrate's lap," Abigail screamed, and fell to the floor in convulsions. Mary Walcott took up a ball of yarn and quietly began knitting. Only after one of the men asked her if she too saw the specter of Proctor (who had yet to be brought into the room from jail) did she softly answer that she too saw him sitting in the magistrate's lap.

John Indian suddenly shouted for the dog resting beneath the table to run away for Goodman Proctor was on its back. He stared off into space and claimed he saw the specter of Sarah Cloyce. "Oh, you old witch," he yelled, and fell into such terrific fits that three men failed to restrain him. The others joined in with great shrieks and convulsions. Mary Walcott, still calmly knitting, quietly said it was John Proctor behind it all, along with his wife, and Goody Cloyce. The hysteria caused by John Indian and Abigail Williams was so great, that they were led from the room so that Parris could try to ready himself for the next proceeding. "I met with nothing but interruption," he wrote of the entire episode.

Mary Walcott, who was still seated calmly knitting away, had been silent. Just as Parris wrapped up his notes, she gave a little yelp and said, "There, Goody Cloyce has pinched me now." The pinch seemed to awaken her to her duties, for she suddenly yelled, "Oh, yonder is Goodman Proctor and his wife, and Goody Nurse and Goody Corey and Goody Cloyce and Good's child. Oh! Goodman Proctor is going to choke me!" She grabbed at her throat at invisible hands and made frightening gagging sounds. Her words had been a roll call for the accused witches, a reminder of those who should hang. There is nothing else in the records to show the proceeding against John Proctor, other than he was held over in Salem Jail, and taken away to Boston Prison.

With both Proctors in jail, their household was flung into instant disarray. The youngest child there was but three years old. John's son from a previous marriage, Benjamin Proctor, thirty-three-years-old, became their guardian. Their maid, Mary Warren, was useless during her fits and time away testifying against witches. The young man later said that he "helped bring up all my father's children by all his wives, one after another."

The Proctors' time in Salem Jail was a short one. The following morning, they were loaded onto a cart along with little Dorcas Good, Rebecca Nurse, and Martha Corey for their trip to the Boston Prison. Giles Corey was allowed to ride next to his wife, which shows his love for a woman he had helped indict. Without a wife at home, he had faced the harsh reality of running a farm without her help. His guilt at an unbridled tongue was, no doubt, weighing on him as well. He rode with her to the ferry and stopped. Martha Corey would never again walk through the doorway into her home. She would never tongue-lash him again or criticize his method of praying. It wouldn't matter for long, as Giles himself was soon on the radar of those hunting for witches.

The ride back to Salem Village from the hearings in Town was not uneventful. John Indian, riding behind a man on horseback, suddenly declared his hands were bound with invisible rope. He sunk his teeth into the shirt of the man riding in front of him in an effort to hold on. Edward Bishop, riding beside them, had had enough. He had witnessed John having "fits" at Salem Inn earlier that day and had beaten him in an effort to end the fakery. He and Proctor were of a like mind that the Indian was only joining in with the others for the notoriety. As John held onto the rider's shirt with his teeth, Bishop reached out and whacked his "bound" hands with a stick. John yelped and said he wouldn't do it again. Bishop announced in disgust that he didn't doubt it, and said he could end this nonsense now if he could likewise beat it out of all the afflicted persons. It was a declaration that would soon see his name on the list of witches.

Mary Walcott, Doctor Grigg's niece, likewise was followed home from the hearing by witches. For the first time, she witnessed the specter of Elizabeth Proctor. Mary was riding behind her brother Jonathan, and said Proctor's shape followed them all the way from Gedney's tavern in Salem Town until her brother stopped at Phillips' Ordinary for a drink, a distance of some miles. The sun was sinking as the party rode home, shadows slipping from the trees to run their truncated shapes across the rutted ground. Was that Elizabeth Proctor cackling from the boughs overhead? That hulking shape at the side of the road—a boulder or a witch huddled in wait? Perhaps it was Goody Proctor who had bound John Indian's wrists at the exact time hers were shackled in jail.

Sheriff George Corwin

With both Proctors in jail, a feat that had not presented itself before,

Sheriff George Corwin took action. While confiscating a convicted person's affects, after a proper trial and conviction, were considered legal in Massachusetts, confiscating their property only after an inquisition, was not. The Proctors were still due their proper trial, and were awaiting a charter to arrive from England to give them one.

Without preamble, George Corwin, the twenty-five-year-old nephew of Judge Jonathan Corwin, and son-in-law to Justice Bartholomew Gedney rode over to the Proctor farm and, in a word, began looting it. His name would be forever linked with his greed and heartlessness during the 1692/1693 witch trial tragedy.

John & Elizabeth Proctor homestead. This house was built upon the site of the original home, using some extant structures. It once fell within the southern border of Salem Village. It is now called Peabody, MA.

As Mary Warren, the Proctor children, and Benjamin Proctor watched helplessly, Corwin "came to their house and seized all the goods, provisions and cattle that he could come at, and sold some of the cattle at half price and killed others and put them up for the West Indies; threw out the beer out of the barrel and carted away the barrel, emptied a pot of broath [ms] and took away the pot and left nothing for the support of the children." It was the actions that Dicken's novels and nightmares were made of. For Mary Warren, who had played a part in the accusations and gossip concerning her employers, it was a reality too horrible to absorb.

Mary Warren

Mary Warren, the Proctor's maid, had not been in attendance the morning of April 11th as her mistress and master were ordered to jail. She had remained at home, no longer one of the afflicted after her revelation that she had been saved. Her note, posted to the Salem Village meetinghouse community board, and later read aloud in church by Reverend Parris, had led to much discussion and confusion among the villagers. For the afflicted girls, it had been the ultimate betrayal. If people believed, as Mary had said, that the girls "dissembled," they were in deep trouble. It was, instead, Mary whose troubles were just beginning.

Chapter Sixteen

Bishop, Hobbs, Corey & Warren

The following day, April 13, 1692, a Wednesday, saw no respite from the specters of jailed witches. Obviously, the ferry ride across the water from Salem to Boston's Jail, had not broken the witch's hold on Salem Village. Water was purportedly the purest element on earth, and therefore, witches could not survive it, as witnessed in the Swimming of the Witch test.

Even in modern day, people struggling with possession and demonic attacks have moved away across rivers and oceans in an attempt to leave the afflicter behind. One such story made it to the big screen. *The Entity* is based on a true story of Doris Bither, a single mother of four, living in Culver City, California, who was repeatedly attacked and raped by a demon. When every stratagem failed to rid herself of the entity, she finally moved, hoping that crossing water would end her terror. It didn't. The demon followed her.

In Salem Village that tortuous Spring, Ann Putnam Jr., Mary Walcott, Mercy Lewis, and Elizabeth Hubbard all reported being pinched, choked, and beaten by Rebecca Nurse, Martha Corey, and Elizabeth Proctor. Giles Corey's name was slandered as well as he reportedly beat Mercy Lewis so badly, she feared her back would break. Constable John Putnam had once remarked that he was not surprised to see Rebecca Nurse and her sister Sarah Cloyce arrested as everyone knew their mother Joanna Towne had always been suspected of being a witch. Soon after, he suffered with fits, and on

April 13th, his 2-month-old daughter began convulsing. He and his wife Hannah feared it was the revenge of the Towne sisters (Nurse and Cloyce) for John Putnam's muttering against them. The baby died two days later.

The afflicted girls were in need of flesh blood. They had carried out their goal, the witches were in jail. They added three more names mid-April; that of Bridget Bishop, Mary Warren, and Abigail Hobbs, a strange young woman from Topsfield, who had begun tormenting Ann Putnam Jr.

Abigail Hobbs was a 14-year-old refugee from the Casco Bay slaughter that Mercy Lewis had also witnessed. The two girls may have been distantly related by their Aunts' mothers-in-law. There was no doubt they knew one another in the small Falmouth community. There is also no doubt of where Abigail Hobbs' name was first muttered—the home of Thomas Putnam Jr. where Mercy Lewis resided as maid. It was Ann Putnam Jr. who first accused Hobbs of attacking her. The girl's wild reputation did little to help her situation.

Deliverance Hobbs, Abigail's step-mother, had lost control of her ward. Abigail was wild and rebellious. She roamed the woods at night, when most feared to do so. She talked back to her step-mother and reportedly flipped baptismal water into her face. For years she had been declaring she had signed the Devil's Book, nicknaming him "Old Nick." Her joy was to shock and show disdain for the modalities of a Puritan-structured community. Her step-mother had said, "she little thought to be mother of such a daughter."

Hobbs' specter reportedly choked and pinched Mercy Lewis, Mary Walcott, Ann Putnam, and Elizabeth Hubbard for not signing the book from the Devil. Meanwhile, Giles Corey and Mary Warren's specters were still active. On cue, Ezekiel Cheever and John Putnam, Jr. wrote out official complaints against Giles Corey, Bridget Bishop, Mary Warren, and Abigail Hobbs for their attacks on the afore-mentioned girls. Marshal George Herrick, who must have wondered at that time if he would eventually arrest the entire village of Salem, arrested the four newly named witches and took them to Ingersoll's that very day. It was April, 18, 1962.

There being Complaint this day made (Before us) by Ezekiell Chevers and John putnam Jun'r both of Salem Village Yeomen: in Behalfe of theire Majesties, for themselfes and also for theire Neigh- bours Against Giles Cory, and Mary Waren both of Salem farmes And Abigaile Hobbs the daughter of Wm Hobs of the Towne of Tops- feild and Bridgett Bushop the wife of Edw'd Bishop of Salem Sawyer for high Suspition of Sundry acts of Witchcraft donne or Committed by them, upon the Bodys of: Ann putnam . Marcy Lewis , and Abig'l Williams and Mary Walcot and Eliz. Hubert -- of Salem village -- whereby great hurt and damage hath benne donne to the Bodys of Said persons above named.therefore craved Justice

You are therefore in their Majest's names hereby required to apprehend and bring before us Giles Cory & Mary Waren of Salem farmes, and Abigail Hobs the daugter of Wm Hobs of the Towne of Topsfeild and Bridget Bushop the wife of Edward Bushop of Salem To Morrow about Eight of the Clock in the forenoone, at the house of Lt Nathaniell Ingersalls in Salem Village in order to theire Ex- amination Relateing to the premises aboves'd and here of you are not to faile Dated Salem April 18'th 1692 To George Herrick Marshall of the County of Essex -- *JohnHathorne
*Jonathan.Corwin Assis'ts

Giles Corey

The Salem Village Meetinghouse was once again open for all matters pertaining to witchcraft. Area farmers may have found it more and more disadvantageous to attend so many meetings as it was now Spring and there was much to do. The grass was growing taller and their scythes sat idle. Blossoming trees foretold the fruit that would come later. Fields had to be cleared, crops planted, and repairs undertaken incurred from the harsh winter's elements. It was becoming fearfully obvious that the witchcraft hysteria was not dying down with the imprisonment of a few people. Tituba had mentioned nine names in the Devil's book. Surely, they were close to finding them all.

Samuel Parris and Ezekiel Cheever both sat with quills poised as Magistrates Hathorne and Corwin sat the bench. Giles Corey, perhaps not as confident now that his wife was in jail, stepped forward. The afflicted were in place, and they took up the wail and accusations as always. Only Elizabeth Hubbard sat "dumb."

(The Examination of Giles Cory)

[April 19, 1692]

The examination of Giles Corey, at a Court at Salem Village, held by John Hathorn and Jona. Curwin, Esqrs. April 19, 1692.

Giles Cory, you are brought before authority upon high suspicion of sundry acts of witchcraft; now tell us the truth in this matter.

C) I hope through the goodness of God I shall, for that matter I never had no hand in, in my life. H)Which of you have seen this man hurt you? *Mary Wolcott, Mercy

Lewis, Ann Putnam, jr. and Abigail Williams affirmed he had hurt them

H) Hath he hurt you too? speaking to Elizabeth Hubbard. *She going to answer was prevented by a fit. H) Benjamin Gold, hath he hurt you? G) I have seen him several times, and been hurt after it, but cannot affirm that it was he. H) Hath he brought the book to any of you? *Mary Wolcott and Abigail Williams and others affirmed he had brought the book to them.

H) Giles Cory, they accuse you, or your appearance, of hurting them, and bringing the book to them. What do you say? Why do you hurt them? Tell us the truth. C) I never did hurt them. H) It is your appearance hurts them, they charge you; tell us what you have done. C) I have done nothing to damage them.

H) Have you ever entered into contract with the devil? C) I never did. H) What temptations have you had? C) I never had temptations in my life. H) What, have you done it without temptations?

B) What was the reason (said goodwife Bibber) that you were frighted in the cow-house? and then the questionist was suddenly seized with a violent fit.

*Samuel Braybrook, goodman Bibber, and his daughter, testified that he had told them this morning that he was frighted in the cow-house. Cory denied it. H) This was not your appearance but your person, and you told them so this morning: why do you deny it? What did you see in the cow-house? C) I never saw nothing but my cattle. *Divers[e] witnessed that he told them he was frighted. H) Well, what do you say to these witnesses? What was it frighted you? C) I do not know that ever I spoke the word in my life. H) Tell the truth, what was it frighted you? C)I do not know any thing that frighted me.

*All the afflicted were seized now with fits, and troubled with pinches. Then the court ordered his hands to be tied. H) What, is it not enough to act witchcraft at other times, but must you do it now in the face of authority? C) I am a poor creature, and cannot help it. *Upon the motion of his head again, they had their heads and necks afflicted.

H) Why do you tell such wicked lies against witnesses, that heard you speak after this manner, this very morning? C) I never saw any thing but a black hog. H) You said that you were stopt once in prayer; what stopt you? C) I cannot tell; my wife came towards me and found fault with me for saying living to God and dying to sin.

H) What was it frighted you in the barn? C) I know nothing frighted me there. H) Why here are three witnesses that heard you say so to-day.C) I do not remember it.

*Thomas Gold testified that he heard him say, that he knew enough against his wife, that would do her business .H) What was it that you knew against your wife? C) Why that of living to God, and dying to sin. *The Marshal and

Bibber's daughter confirmed the same, that he said he could say that that would do his wife's business.

C) I have said what I can say to that. H) What was that about your ox? I thought he was hipt.

H) What ointment was that your wife had when she was seized? You said it was ointment she made by major Gidney's direction. *He denied it, and said she had it of goody Bibber, or from her direction. Goody Bibber said it is not like that ointment. You said you knew, upon your own knowledge, that she had it of major Gidney. He denied it.

H) Did not you say, when you went to the ferry with your wife, you would not go over to Boston now, for you should come yourself the next week? C) I would not go over, because I had not money. *The Marshal testified he said as before. One of his hands was let go, and several were afflicted. He held his head on one side, and then the heads of several of the afflicted were held on one side. He drew in his cheeks, and the cheeks of some of the afflicted were suckt in.

*John Bibber and his wife gave testimony concerning some temptations he had to make away with himself. H) How doth this agree with what you said, that you had no temptations? C) I meant temptation to witchcraft. H) If you can give away to self murther [murder], that will make way to temptation to witchcraft.

*Note. There was witness by several, that he said he would make away with himself, and charge his death up- on his son. Goody Bibber testified that the said Cory called said Bibber's husband, damn'd, devilish rogue. Other vile expressions testified in open court by several others. Salem Village, April 19, 1692.

Mr. Samuel Parris being desired to take in writing the examination of Giles Cory, delivered it in; and upon hearing the same, and seeing what we did see at the time of his examination, together with the charge of the afflicted persons against him, we committed him to their majesties' gaol. John Hathorn

Robert Calef, *More Wonders of the Invisible World.* London (1700), reprinted in (Salem: John D. & T.C. Cushing, Jr. Cushing & Appleton, 1823): 310-312.

Corey was led away, and the young Abigail Hobbs brought in. It was oddly quiet in the meetinghouse when the teenager approached the bar. The usual outcries from the afflicted were absent. Strange…as this was a young woman who admitted and bragged about her association with "Old Nick."

Trial of Giles Corey.

Giles Corey

Abigail Hobbs

(Examination of Abigail Hobbs ,)

[April 19, 1692]

The Examination of Abigail Hobbs, at Salem Village,
19 April, 1692, by John Hawthorn and Jonath. Corwin,
Esqs., and Assistants.

Abig. Hobbs . you are brought before Authority to answere to sundry acts of witchcraft, committed by you against and upon the bodies of many, of which severall persons now accuse you. What say you? Are you guilty, or not? Speak the truth.

AH) I will speak the truth. I have seen sights and been scared. I have been very wicked. I hope I shall be better, if God will help me. H) What sights did you see? AH) I have seen dogs and many creatures. H) What dogs do you mean, ordinary dogs? AH) I mean the Devil. H) How often, many times? H) But once. H) Tell the truth. AH) I do tell no lye. H) What appearance was he in then? AH) Like a man. H) Where was it? AH) It was at the Eastward at Casko-bay. H) Where, in the house, or in the woods? AH) In the woods. H) In the night or in the day? AH) In the day. H) How long agoe? AH) About 3 or 4 years agoe. H) What did he say to you? AH) He said he would give me fine things, if I did what he would have me. H) What would he have you do? AH) Why, he would have me be a witch. H) Would he have you make a covenant w'th him? AH) Yes. H) And did you make a covenant with him? AH) Yes, I did, but I hope God will forgive me. H) The Lord give you Repentance. You say you saw dogs, and many sorts of creatures. AH) I saw them at that time. H) But have you not seen them at other times too? AH) Yes. H) Wher? AH) At our house. H) What were they like? AH) Like a cat. H) What would the cat have you do? AH) She had a book and would have me put my hand to it. H) And did you? AH) No, I did not. H) Well, tell the truth, did you at any other time? AH)Yes, I did, that time at the Eastward. H) What other creatures did you see? AH) I saw things like men. H) What did they say to you? AH) Why they said I had better put my hand to the Book. H) You did put your hand to the book you say? AH) Yes, one time. H) What, would they have you put your hand to their book too? AH) Yes. H) And what would they have you do then, would they have you worship them? AH) They would have me make a bargain for so long, and do what they would have me do. H) For how long? AH)Not for above 2 or 3 years. H) How long did they agree with you for? AH) But for (2) two years. H) And what would they then do for you? AH) They would give me fine clothes. H) And did they? AH) No. H) When you set your hand the last time to book, how long was that for? AH) It was for (4) years. H) How long is that agoe? AH) It is almost 4 years. The book was brought to me to get my hand to it for 4 years, but I never put my hand but that once at Eastward. H) Are you not bid to hurt folks? AH) Yes. H) Who are you bid to hurt? AH) Mercy Lewes and Ann Putman. H) What did you do to them when you hurt them? AH) I pinch't them. H) How did you pinch them, do you goe in your own person to them? AH) No. AH) Doth the Devil go for you? H) Yes. H) And what doth he take, your spirit with him? AH) No. I am as well as at other times: but the Devil has my consent, and goes and hurts them. H) Who hurt your mother last Lord's day, was it not you? AH) No. H) Who was it? AH) I heard her say it was Goody Wilds at Topsfield. H) Have you been in company with Goody Wilds at any time? AH) No, I never saw her. H) Well, who are your companions? AH) Why I have seen Sarah Good once. H) How many did you see? AH) I saw but two. H) Did you know Sarah Good was a witch, when you saw her? AH) Yes. H) How did you know it? AH) The Devil told me. H) Who was the other you saw? AH) I do not remember her name. H) Did you go and do hurt with Sarah Good ? AH) No, she would have me set my hand to her book also. H) What mark did you make in the Devil's book when you set your hand to it? AH) I made a mark. H) What mark? Have you not been at other great meetings? AH) No. H) Did you not hear of great hurt done here in the village? AH) Yes. H) And were you never with them? AH) No, I was never with them. H) But you know your shape appeared and hurt the people here. AH) Yes. H) How did you know? AH) The Devil told me, if I gave consent, he would do it in my shape. H) How long agoe? AH) About a fortnight agoe. H) What shape did the Devil appear in then? AH) Like a black man with an hat. H) Do not some creatures suck your body? AH) No. AH)Where do they come, to what parts, when they come to your body? AH) They do not come to my body, they come only in sight. H) Do they speak to you? AH) Yes. H) How do they speak to you? AH) As other folks. H) What do they speak to you, as other folks? AH) Yes, almost. *Then other questions were propounded to her, but she was taken D E A F: and Mary Walcott, Mercy Lewis, Betty Hubbard, Abigail Williams and Ann Putman jun'r , said they saw Sarah Good and Sarah Osborn run their fingers into the examinant's ears; by & by, she this examinant was blind, with her eyes quite open.

*A little after, she spake & said, Sarah Good saith I shall not speak; And so the Court ordered her, being seized with dumbness, to be taken away.

*Note. The afflicted, i.e., the bewitched persons, were none of them tormented during the whole examination of this accused and confessing person, Abigail Hobbs .

Note. -- After this examination, Mercy Lewes, Abigail Williams , & Ann Putman , three of the sufferers, said openly in Court, they were sorry for the condition this poor Abig. Hobbs was in, which compassion they expressed over and over again.

As with Tituba, who had been the first to confess her alliance with the Devil and beg forgiveness, Abigail Hobbs' confession mollified the afflicted girls. Here, they could afford to show mercy and benevolence toward this "poor creature." It was only those whose testimony refuted their claims that brought on their wrath and condemnation. And it was with one their own, that they now turned their attention. Mary Warren was next before the bar.

Chapter Seventeen

More and More Witches

If the crowd that had traveled to Salem Town to hear the inquests for the Proctors and Sarah Cloyce felt the journey was somewhat anti-climactic, they were getting their money's worth on April 19. Old Giles Corey had been accused and held over for trial, and Abigail Hobbs had actually confessed to witchcraft. Now, Mary Warren (who had been among the afflicted girls' circle prior to recanting her participation) and Bridget Bishop of Salem Town would stand before the magistrates. Four in one day! The crowd of onlookers could barely be contained within the wooden structure of the meetinghouse walls.

Mary Warren's Inquest

If Abigail Hobbs entrance had been surprisingly peaceful, Mary Warren's frightened advancement to the bar that afternoon was just the opposite. The group of afflicted girls realized what was at stake with this girl's testimony. Mary was twenty-years-old. Her testimony would carry more weight than 14-year-old Abigail Hobbs. If the magistrates found reason to believe the afflicted girls had been merely play acting for "sport," they would surely face dire consequences. This would need to be the show of a lifetime, and the girls began their torments without preamble.

(Examination of Mary Warren)

[April 19, 1692]

The examintion of Mary Warren At a Court in Salem VillageJohn Hauthorne] Esq'rs Jonath: Corwin] Esq'rs

As soon as she was coming towards the Bar the afflicted fell into fits. H) Mary Warren, You stand here charged with sundry acts of Witchcraft, what do you say for your self, are you guilty, or not?
W) I am inocent.
H) Hath she hurt you (speaking to the sufferers) *Some were Dumb. Betty Hubbard testifyed ag'st her, & then said Hubbard fell into a violent fit.
H) You were a little while ago an Afflicted person, now you are an Afflicter: How comes this to pass?
W) I looke up to God & take it to be a great Mercy of God.
H) What do you take it to be a great mercy to afflict others?
*Betty Hubbard testifyed that a little after this Mary was well, she the said Mary, said that the afflicted persons did but dissemble.
Now they were all but John Indian grievously afflicted, & M'rs Pope also, who was not afflicted before hitherto this day: & after a few moments John Indian fell into a violent fit also.
H) Well here was one just now that was a Tormentor in her apparition, & she owns that she had made a league with the Devil. *Now Mary Warren fell into a fit, & some of the afflicted cryed out that she was going to confess, but Goody Korey , & Procter , & his wife came in, in their apparition, & struck her down, & said she should tell nothing.

*Mary Warren continued a good space in a fit that she did neither see, nor hear, nor speak. Afterwards she started up, & said I will speak & cryed out, Oh! I am sorry for it, I am sorry for it, & wringed her hands, & fell a little while into a fit again: & then came to speak, but immediately her Teeth were set, & then she fell into a voilet fit, & cryed out, Oh Lord help me, Oh good Lord save me!

And then afterwards cryed again, I will tell, I will tell, & then fell into a dead fit againe.

And afterwards cryed, I will tell, they did, they did, they did, & then fell into a violent fit again.

After a little recovery she cryed I will tell, I will tell, they brought me me to it; & then fell into a fit again: which fits continuing, she was ordered to be had out, & the next to be brought in, viz: Bridget Byshop

Some time afterwards she [Mary Warren] was called in again, but immediately taken with fits, for a while.

H)Have you signed the Devils book?

W) No.

H) Have you not toucht it? W) No.

*Then she fell into fits againe, & was sent forth for air. After a considerable space of time she was brought in again, but could [not] give account of things, by reason of fits, & so sent forth.

Mary Warren called in, afterwards in private, before Magistrates & Ministers.

She said, I shall not speak a word: but I will, I will speak satan -- she saith she will kill me. Oh! `she saith, she owes me a spite, & will claw me off --

Avoid Satan, for the name of God avoid. And then fell into fits again: & cryed will ye; H) I will prevent ye in the Name of God, Tell us, how far have you yeilded?

*A fit interrupts her again.

H) What did they say you should do, & you should be well?

*Then her lips were bit so that she could not speak. so she was sent away

*Note That not one of the sufferers was afflicted during her examination after once she began to confess, tho they were tormented before.
Salem Village Aprill 19'th 1692.
Mr Samuell parris being desired to take in wrighting the Examination of Mary Warren hath delivered it as aforesaid And upon heareing the same and seeing what wee did then see, togather with the Charge of the afflicted persons then present. Wee Committed said Mary Warren
*John   Hathorne]   Assis'ts *Jonathan.   Corwin] Assis'ts

In between Mary Warren's breakdowns, Bridget Bishop was led into the meetinghouse to face accusations of witchcraft, something of which she had been accused in 1679. Of all the accused victims that stood before the magistrates, Bridget Bishop represented by far the most un-Christian-like opponent. Her story read like a tawdry novel, filled with whippings, domestic violence, her specter's lascivious nocturnal attacks on her male neighbors, and even jailtime.

Bridget was a thrice-married fifty-year-old woman by the time of her inquisition in 1692. She had married Samuel Wasselbee in England while in her twenties. After arriving in New England, she married Thomas Oliver from Boston. They later moved to Salem and turned the harbor town into an arena for their constant battles. Bridget's bruises were often apparent to the townsfolk. The couple had one child, a daughter, Christian. The fights, name-calling, and public displays of abuse became so bad that the couple were fined and publicly whipped. Unrepentant, the abuse continued and they found themselves before the court and jailed. Thomas's daughter Mary, from a former marriage, paid Thomas's fine, but left Bridget to the mercy of the court. None was given. She was forced to stand in the town Common wearing a sign upon her forehead that broadcast to all her failings. It was a public humiliation she would not forget.

Bridget's ill-temper and moral shortcomings brought her many enemies. She was accused of stealing more than once. Her specter had been seen by those who fell out of favor with her, or reported her. In 1682, a local woman, Goody Whatford, accused her of stealing a spoon. When Bridget verbally attacked her, Whatford said Bridget's specter had tried to drown her in Salem harbor. Bridget's husband Thomas died in 1687. The circumstances of his death were suspicious and tongues wagged. Undaunted, she married Edward Bishop in 1687. Shortly after, she was accused again of stealing, this time from Thomas Stacey's mill where a brass bearing went missing. Bridget was found with the bearing and claimed she found it in her garden. Unfortunately, her daughter Christian, unaware of the garden alibi, lied and said the bearing had belonged to her departed father.

Bridget was hauled away to jail where she spent three months. During that time, Thomas Stacey's son reported that an angry Bridget Bishop had sent her specter to throw him about their yard. Once released from jail, Bridget and her husband Edward moved from Salem Town to Salem Village. Bridget, now with an unrelenting eye to making money, kept her home in Salem Town and turned it into a tavern. She had a sizeable apple orchard on the property and found she could make a pretty penny selling apple cider…no doubt the fermented kind. Unlike John Proctor and other tavern owners, Bridget did not bother with obtaining a license. The tavern soon brought complaints from Salem's neighbors who reported "drinking and playing at shuffleboard" and that they feared the area youth were "in danger to be corrupted."

It was through her tavern ownership and dealings with the drunken clientele that some of the lewder reports of spectral visitations came from. Bridget's specter was accused of visiting men in their bed chambers at night and "taking advantage." Richard Coman, his wife laying by his side, reported Bridget came to him in the night and sprawled across his chest. William Stacey announced she had visited him as well and, along with Samuel Gray, claimed they awoke to find her ghost inserting something into their mouths. Worse yet, John Louder said Bishop came to him in the moonlight and sat astride his chest while trying to strangle him. She was accused of causing the death of children and livestock, along with reports of theft and even hiding poppets in the wall of her home. Poppets were crude dolls said to be used by witches to curse their victims. With Bridget's reputation, and her prior arrest for witchcraft in 1679, no one doubted the claims made against her. Nothing came of the earlier witchcraft accusation. This one would have a different ending.

Sample of a poppet doll in 1692.

(Examination of Bridget Bishop, as Recorded by Ezekiel Cheever.)

[April 19, 1692]
The examination of Bridget Bishop before the WorshipfullJohn Harthon and Jonathan Curren esq'rs

Bridget Bishop being now comeing in to be examined relating to her accusation of suspicon of sundry acts of witchcrafts the afflicted persons are now dreadfully afflicted by her as they doe say
H) Bishop what doe you say you here stand charged with sundry acts of witchcraft by you done or commited upon the bodyes of mercy Lews and An Putnum and others
B) I am innocent I know nothing of it I have done no witchcraft
H)Looke upon this woman and see if this be the woman that you have seen hurting you. * mercy Lewes and An Putnum and others doe doe now charge her to her face with hurting of them
H) M'r Harthon) what doe you say now you see they charge you to your face
B) I never did hurt them in my life I did never see these persons before I am as innocent as the child unborn
H) is not your coate cut
*answers no but her garment being Looked upon they find it cut or toren two wayes Jonathan walcoa[te saith that the sword that he strucke at goode Bishop with was not naked but was within

the] scabberd so that the rent may very probablie be the very same that mary walcoate did tell that shee had in her coate by Jonathans stricking at her apperance

*The afflicted persons charge her, with having hurt them many wayes and by tempting them to sine to the devils Booke at which charge shee seemed to be very angrie and shaking her head at them saying it was false they are all greatly tormented (as I conceive) by the shaking of her head

H) goode Bishop what contract have you made with the devill

B) I have made no contract with the devill I never saw him in my life. *An Putnam sayeth that shee calls the devill her God

H) what say you to all this that you are charged with can you not find in your hart to tell the truth

B)I doe tell the truth I never hurt these persons in my life I never saw them before.

(Mercy Lewis) oh goode Bishop did you not come to our house the Last night and did you not tell me that your master made you tell more then you were willing to tell

H) tell us the truth in this matter how comes these persons to be thus tormented and to charge you with doing

B) I am not come here to say I am a witch to take away my life

H) who is it that doth it if you doe not they say it is your likenes that comes and torments them and tempts them to write in the booke what Booke is that you tempt them with.

B)I know nothing of it I am innocent.

H) doe you not see how they are tormented you are acting witchcraft before us what doe you say to this why have you not an heart to confese the truth

B) I am innocent I know nothing of it I am no witch I know not what a witch is.

H) have you not given consent that some evill spirit should doe this in your likenes.

B) no I am innocent of being a witch I know no man woman or child here

* how came you into my bedchamber one morning then and asked me whither I had any curtains to sell

*shee is by some of the afflicted persons charged with murder

H) what doe you say to these murders you are charged with

(B) I am innocent I know nothing #[about] of it

*now shee lifts up her eyes and they are greatly tormented [again]

H) what doe you say to these things here horrible acts of witch craft

B) I know nothing of it I doe not know whither be any witches or no

H) no have you not heard that some have confessed.

B) no I did not. * two men told her to her face that they had told her here. shee is taken in a plain lie. now shee is going away they are dreadfully afflicted. 5 afflicted persons doe charge this woman to be the very woman that hurts them

[This] is a true account of what I have taken down at her examination according to best [un]derstanding and observation I have also in her examination taken notice that all her actions be great influence upon the afflicted persons and that have ben tortered by her *Ezekiel Cheever.

188

Ezekiel Cheever's organized notes, compared to Parris' jumbled run-on sentences, make it easier to discern the proceeding of that inquest. Cheever's father was a school master, and his eloquence is no doubt a result of much instruction. The questioning as to Bridget's coat being torn was the result of Mary Walcott insisting her brother Jonathan had struck at Bishop's specter with his sword, tearing her clothes. Reverend Parris noted "upon some search in the Court, a rent that seems to be answere what was alledged was found."

Bridget Bishop

Bridget was led away from the room, the wails of the afflicted ringing in her ears. "It was she that hurt me!" they cried. Samuel Gould later asked her, didn't it bother her to see how the afflicted were suffering. Her indifferent answer of "No," flew in the face of all the Puritan members who felt for the tortures of the brave girls who were trying to rid their village of evil. Bridget Bishop's and Abigail Hobbs' inquests also marked the beginning of catastrophic events. They were the first who fell outside the village proper. Bishop's tavern and original home was in Salem Town, and Hobbs was from Topsfield. The net was being thrown wider. Had it escaped the magistrate's notice, or had they felt the niggling fear of what was to come?

The four—Hobbs, Corey, Bishop and Warren—were taken to the Salem Jail. The former witches had been carted off to Boston, where little Dorcas was finally reunited with her mother Sarah Good. The Proctors had been separated, as men and women had different jail rooms. Large and without privacy, these communal areas were nothing better than cattle pens.

Mary Warren is Questioned in Jail

For the next two days, the magistrates took the opportunity to question Mary Warren while she was housed in the Salem Jail. This was their chance to ferret out from a former afflicted person just what was going on. Bridget Bishop, jailed along with Warren, may have questioned her extensively as well. This was her chance to try and catch the girls out in their lies. Mary, undoubtedly, would have preferred to be back in the protection of the Proctor home, back before all this started, even if it meant dealing with John Proctor's wrath.

(Examination of Mary Warren in Prison)

[April 20, 1692]

Mary Warrens Examination in Salem Prison

She Testifys that Her master Proctor was always very averse to the putting up Bills for publick prayer. Q: Did you not know it was the Devils book when you Signed? A: No, But I thought it was no good book. Q: after you had a Mark in the Book what did you think then? A:

190

Then I thought it was the Devil's book. Q. How did you come to know your Master, and Mistris were Witches? A. The Sabbath Even after I had put up my note for thanks in publick, my Mistris appeared to mee, and puld mee out of the Bed, and told mee that Shee was a witch and had put her hand to the Book, she told me this in her Bodily person, and that This Examinant might have known she was a Witch, if she had but minded what Books she read in. Q. what did she say to you before you tormented the Children? A. The night after she told mee she was a Witch, she in person told mee this Examinant, that my self and her son John would quickly be brought out for witches. This Examinant saith that Giles Cory in apparition told her, the night before that the Magistrates were goeing up to the farms to bring down more witches to torment her. Moreover being in a dreadful fit in the prison she Charged it on Giles Cory, who was then in Close prison, affirming that he came into the Room where she was, and afflicting her, Charged her not to Come into the Other Room while he was Examining. But being sent for and he Commanded to look upon her, He no sooner turned his face to her but shee fel into a dreadful fit again. and upon her Recovery Charged him to his face with being the procurer of it. Moreover the said Cory in prison formerly threatned her that he would fitt her for itt, because he told her she had Caused her Master to ask more for a peice of Meadow than he was willing to give she Likewise in her fitt in the Other Room before she had seen Giles Cory in person, Charging him with afflicting off her, described him in all his garments, both of hat Coat and Colour of them with a Cord about his wast, and a white Cap on his head, and in Chains, as several then in Company Can affirm.

(Essex County Court Archives, Salem -- Witchcraft Vol. 1, no. 115)

(Examination of Mary Warren)

[April 21, 1692]

Mary Warins examination April 21: 1692
Being Asked by the Hon'd Majestrates: whether the bible that then was showed her: was the book: that was brought: to her to touch: & that she saw the flurrish in answered no: she see she was decieved
being asked whether (Mercy) Lewis that she had signed to a book: told Mercy Lewis that she had signed to a book: answerd no
She was Asked: whether her: Mistris had brought a book to her to sign Answerd. heir Mistris brought none. but her Master brought one being Asked whether she signed to it: answerd: not unles putting her finger to it was signing
being Asked whether she did not se a spot where she had put her finger Answerd there was a spot: she was Asked what couller: the spot was: Answered: black
she was Asked whether. her Mast'r did not thretten her to run the hot tongs downe her throat if she did not sign Answered that her M'r threttned her to burn her out of her fitt
being Asked whether she had made a mark in the book Answered she made no mark but with her top of her finger. she was asked what she dipt her finger in when it made the mark: Answered: in nothing: but her mouth

she was Asked whether her finger was wett when she touched the book w't it Answered she knew not that it was wett: or whether it was wett w't sweat or with sider: that she had bin drinking of she knew not: but her finger did make a mark and the mark was black she was asked whether any but her M'r and Mr's was with her: when she was threttoned with the hott tongss: answerd none but them

she s'd her Mast'r put her hand to the book and her finger made a black spott which made her tremble: then she s'd she was undon body and soul and cryed out greivously. she was told that it was he[r] own Vollantary act: she would have denyed it: but she was told the devil could have done nothing: if she had not yeilded and that she for eas to her body: not for any good of her soul: had done it with this she much grieved: and cryed out: she s'd her Mast'r & Mistris thretned to drown her: & to mak her run through the hedges

she was Asked whether she had not seen her Mast'r & Mistris since she came to prison answerd she thought she saw her Mast'r & dare say: it was he: she was Asked wh[h]at he sayd to her: answerd nothing

after a fitt she cryed out I will tell: I will tell: thou wicked creature it is you stopt my mouth: but I will confess the little that I have to confess being asked: who she would: tell off whether goodwife Procter or no: answered o Betty procter it is she: it is she I lived with last

she then cryed out it shall be known: thou wrech: hast thou undone me body and soul. she s'd also she wishes she had made me mak: a through league she was again Asked what her finger was blacked with when she toucht the book.

Answered she knew not that her finger was black: till she se it black: the book and after she had put her finger to the book: she eat: bread and butter and her finger blacked the bred and butter also

being asked: what: her mistris now said to her: when she complaind of her mistris she s'd her mistris bid her not tell that her mistris was a wich

Coming out of another fit s'd she would tell she would tell: she s'd her Mast'r now bid her not tell: that he: had some times gone: to make away with himselfe for her Master had told her that he had bin about some times to make away with him self becaus of his wives quarrilling with him

being Asked how she knew: goodwife procter was a wich she coming out of a fit s'd she would: tell she would tell: and she s'd her mistris Procter s'd she might know she was a wich if she herkend to what she used to read she sayd her Mistris had many books, and her Mistris carried one book with her to Reddin when she went to se her sister

being Asked whether she knew her Mistris to be a wich before she touched the book: and how she knew it: she s'd her Mistris: told her she had set her hand to the devils book: that same night: that: I was thrown out of bed: s'd she: which was the same night after she had a note: of thanks giving: put up at the meeting hous

she s'd her mistris came to her: her body: not her shape as far as far as she knew she afirmd: her mistris was a wich being Asked whether: she had seen any of the wiches: since she came to prison: s'd she had seen [goodman Cory & Sara Good: they brought the book to her to sign

but she would not own that she knew her master to be a wich or wizzard being asked whether she did not know her finger would make a mark if she touched the book with it: she answerd no: but her master and mistris asked her to read:and she s'd the first word she read was moses: the next word she could not tell what it was but her m'r and mistris bid her: if she could not pronownce the word: she should touch the book

being asked why she would not tell the wholle truth: she s'd she had formerly not told all the truth. becaus she was thretned to be torn in peices: if she did_but now she would and had told the truth being Asked whether she did not suspect it was the devils book that she touched answerd she did not suspect it before: she se: her finger blacked it

she was Asked why: she yeilded to do as she did: answered that her Master s'd if she would not: when she was in her fit she should run: into the fire or: water if she would and destroy her selfe

being Asked whether she had not bin instrumentall to afflict the afflicted parsons Answerd no but when she: heard: they were aflicted in her shape: she began to fear: it was the Devill [that hurt in her shape]

being Asked whether she had images to stick pins or thorns into to hurt peple with: answerd no:

she was asked whether the devil never asked her consent: to: hurt in her shape answerd no: she had heard her master and mistris tell of immages and of sticking of thorns in them: to hurt people with

she was asked: whether she knew of any Immages in the hous: sayd no

being asked if she knew of any oyntment they had in the hous: she s'd her M'rs oynted her once:for some ayll she had: but it was with oyntment that came from Mrs Bassits of Linn the coullour of it was greenish she was asked how it smelt: sayd very ugly to her she s'd when: she toucht the book she went to put her finger to another line but still her finger went to the same place: where her finger had blackt

Mr Noys told her she had then touched the book twice: and asked her whether she did not suspect it to be the devils book before she toucht it the second time: she s'd she feare it was no good book: being asked what she ment by no good book: she s'd a book to deceiv.

Abigail Hobbs was also questioned while incarcerated in the Salem jail. Much to Reverend Parris' chagrin, she said she too was in attendance at the Devil's sacrament on the parsonage acreage. She names a Judah White from Boston as a witch.

(Examinations of Abigail Hobbs)

[April 20, 1692]

Abigail Hobb's Examination 20. Apr. 1692 in Salem Prison

This Examinant declares that Judah White , a Jersey maid that lived with Joseph Ing'rson at Cascoe, but now lives at Boston, with whome this Examinant was very well formerly acquainted, came to her yesterday in apparition, together with Sarah Good , as this Examinant was going to Examination, and advised her to fly, and not goe to be Examined, shee told them that She would goe; They Charged her if she did go to Examination not to Confess anything. She Said she would Confes all that She knew; They told her also Goody Osburn was a witch This Judah White came to her in fine Cloaths in a Sad coloured Silk Mantel, with a Top knot and an hood She Confesseth further that the

Devil in the Shape of a Man came to her and would have her to afflict Ann Putnam, Mercy Lewis, and Abigail Williams , and brought their images with him in wood like them, and gave thorns, and bid her prick them into those images, which She did accordingly into Each of them one.and then the Devil told her they were afflicted which accordingly they were and Cryed out they were hurt by Abigail Hobbs . She Confesseth, She was at the great Meeting in Mr Parris's Pasture when they administered the Sacram'tt, and did Eat of the Red Bread and drink of the Red wine att the same Time.

Meanwhile, in Topsfield, Deliverance Hobbs, mother of Abigail (now jailed) reported spectral attacks of her own. Perhaps from fear that she too would be named a witch as the step-mother of the recently accused Abigail, or in a pro counter-attack against one of the accusers, Deliverance claimed the specters of Mercy Lewis, and Goody Sarah Wildes came to her beneath the light of a full moon and nearly tore her to pieces! So now, we have the tables turned and one of the afflicted is accused. While Mary Warren's name had been accused earlier, it was done by the circle of afflicted girls to save themselves. This was the first to be uttered from someone outside the "pack."

In a spectral version of witchcraft ping pong, Abigail Williams returned the favor, and said the specter of Deliverance Hobbs came to her with the ubiquitous book to sign. "I have signed the book and have ease," Hobbs' specter said. "Now do you sign, and so shall you have ease." But it was not to Goody Hobbs that Ann replied. Reportedly she scorned a new specter, crying "Oh, dreadful, dreadful! Here is a minister come. What? Are ministers witches, too? Whence come you? And what is your name? For I will complain of you though you be a minister, if you be a wizard."

Abigail declared she had been tortured for refusing to sign the book he also placed before her. She finally spewed out the name so many had been waiting to hear ever since Tituba's declaration that a "black man" had shown her a book with nine other names. Triumphantly, Ann Putnam Jr. declared the new specter was none other than that of George Burroughs, the swarthy-complexioned former minister who had abandoned them for Casco Bay, after being sued by the Putnams for punitive damages. Mercy Lewis, the Putnam's maid, had spent time with Burroughs in Casco during the Indian attacks before coming to Salem Village. And now, here was young Ann Putnam naming him, and not just naming him, but building his coffin with her accusations.

According to Ann, Burroughs' specter bragged that he had killed his first two wives. He claimed to have also killed Deodat Lawson's wife and child to punish the man for deserting the village ministry in favor of excursions with Andros, thus fulfilling Tituba's earlier announcement that witchcraft had killed Lawson's wife and child. Burroughs then said the unthinkable. Ann claimed he boasted that it was he, not the Devil, who lured Abigail Hobbs to his fold. He was far more than just a witch. He was a conjurer.

That same night, around midnight, Mercy Lewis claimed the specter of old George Jacobs Sr. appeared as "an old, very gray headed man." Jacobs was a farmer from the Northfields section of Salem. She said Jacobs threatened to beat her if she did not sign his book. He also bragged of killing his first wife years before.

On April 21, 1962, warrants were drawn up for no fewer than nine people accused of witchcraft. Thanks to the reports of Abigail Williams, Ann Putnam Jr., Mary Walcott, and Mercy Lewis, the magistrates issued orders to bring in William and Deliverance Hobbs, Nehemiah Abbott Jr., Mary Esty (sister of Rebecca Nurse and Sarah Cloyce), and Sarah Wildes, all from Topsfield. Warrants were also drawn up against Edward and Sarah Bishop and Mary Black (Nathaniel Putnam's slave) of Salem Village. Salem Town's accused was Mary English, wife of a wealthy merchant, Phillip

English. George Burroughs name was not yet on the list, something Thomas Putnam Jr. would soon rectify.

Marshal George Herrick hitched up his horse and his trousers, and rode off to conduct what was becoming his routine business. By 10 o'clock the following morning, eight of the nine accused had been rounded up and delivered to Ingersoll's Ordinary. The wealthy Mary English was missing.

Chapter Eighteen

The Inquests Continue

By April 23, 1692, when the latest group of witches were arrested, the original two were still languishing in Boston Prison. Tituba, Sarah Osborne, and Sarah Good had been held prisoner since March 1st, first in Salem's Jail, and now in Boston. For almost two months they had awaited their fate with growing fear as the days went by. Rumors of more witches being charged were surfacing daily. Sarah Good may have muttered at having little Dorcas once more to care for. The poor child was given few comforts. Whatever sibling had been born to her mother while in jail had died. It was a hideous reality for one so young.

The other accused witches awaited their fate in Salem's Jail. Shackles were bolted to the walls and floor, and were used to hold prisoners—especially those whose shapes had been accused of sailing about the households of innocent villagers.

Abigail Hobbs and Mary Warren were repeatedly questioned while in jail. Mary told many stories concerning the Proctors, insisting they had presented her with the Devil's Book to sign. Reverend Nicholas Noyes showed her a Bible with many names scribbled in the front page. Family genealogy was often noted in family bibles. He asked if this might have been the book she saw, or one like it? She said it was not a Bible she saw. Mary said the Proctors had come to her with the strange book while she was buttering bread. They held out the open book and told her to read a verse from it. She remembered seeing the name "Moses." When she touched the book to bring it closer and see the rest of the text, a black mark appeared beneath her finger. It wasn't red like blood, she told Reverend Noyes. It was black. She was sure because when she picked up her buttered bread, the black mark on her finger left a black smear on her toast. She went on to say the Proctors threatened her with drowning, burning her, and forcing hot tongs down her throat. She accused Elizabeth Proctor of owning a "good many books" and carrying a small one in her pocket when she called on her sister in Reading. Mary swore she did not sign the Devil's Book. The Proctors had deceived her and only her fingertip had touched it, leaving a black mark. She vowed she had never given the Devil permission to use her specter and hurt others, and that she had never stuck pins in a poppet. For now, she would remain in Salem Jail.

The interior of Salem Jail's dungeon in 1935 before the building was torn down.

If Abigail Williams was feeling any remorse for the plight of her friend Mary Warren, it was not obvious. Without a sniffle or regret, she plunged ahead on her mission to lynch the villagers that she felt deserving of death.

At the same time Mary Warren was being questioned in jail, Abigail was once again parked outside Ingersoll's Ordinary where she continually found a willing group of people to perform before. This day was no different. The chosen spectator was Benjamin Hutchinson, who had arrived at his foster father's tavern sometime between 11 o'clock and noon. Abigail marched up to him and announced that their former minister, George Burroughs, had bragged to her about several murders. As Hutchinson listened in shock, the eleven-year-old told of Burroughs admitting to killing his first two wives *and* the wife of Reverend Lawson. To underscore Burroughs involvement with the Devil, she related how he bragged of his superhuman strength. Others had mentioned how strong the man was, especially as he was shorter than the average male at that time. He was swarthy in complexion, almost dark-skinned. Tituba had spoken of "a black man." The difference is, she had said the man she saw was "tall" and "from Boston."

Before Benjamin could recover from the girl's startling declarations, Abigail suddenly shouted "the little black minister" was watching them right now, from the road "just where the cart wheel went along." Her panic aroused the man who grabbed up "a three-grained iron fork" and threw it at the location to which Abigail pointed. The girl fell into a "little fit" and screamed "You have torn his coat, for I heard it tear!" "Whereabouts?" Hutchinson asked her? "On one side," she replied.

Benjamin, shaken and perhaps in need of a drink, entered the tavern with Abigail directly behind him. She was nowhere near done. "There he stands!" yelled Abigail, indicating a spot where the specter of Burroughs supposedly stood. Hutchinson drew his rapier but before he swung at it, the specter disappeared.

"There is a gray cat!" Abigail screamed. Hutchinson, feeling as though he had entered a haunted house, stabbed at the place the girl was pointing. "You killed her," she said breathlessly, and dropped into a convulsion. "Sarah Good carried her away," she said of the dead cat, once she had regained control of herself.

Abigail was only four years old when Reverend George Burroughs left Salem Village for Casco Bay in 1683. Mercy Lewis, the Putnam maid, however, had known him well. Burroughs's name had been slandered within the Putnam household during the time Burroughs was being sued by the Putnams for money he owed them. Mercy would have heard all of it. Was it she, or perhaps Ann Putnam Jr. who had shared these stories with Abigail?

It was Thursday, and the Lecture was dutifully conducted in the Salem Village meetinghouse. At its conclusion, a crowd ambled back to Ingersoll's around four in the afternoon. Once inside, Abigail Williams and Mary Walcott took center stage. They announced the specters of William and Deliverance Hobbs were attacking them. They yelled that Goody Hobbs had bitten Mary's foot as she passed their table. Benjamin Hutchinson, rapier at the ready, struck at the space they indicated.

The two girls cried out "You have struck her on the right side" near her eye. Warming to the sensation they were creating among the adults in the room, the girls ramped it up. As they pointed out more and more witches flying about the room, Hutchinson and Ely Putnam swung their swords randomly at each spot the girls revealed. "You have killed a great black woman of Stonington," one cried, "and an Indian that comes with her, for the floor is all covered with blood." Stonington was a town in Connecticut and it is unknown who the traveling specters were.

Abigail looked out from the tavern at Thorndike Hill and said she saw three dead witches laying on the hillside where a large gathering of witches was camped.

On Friday, April 22, 1692, reports of witches filling the sky had villagers' heads spinning. The court was due to convene for the inquest of the newly-arrested afflicters, yet rather than these proceedings stemming the tide of witchcraft, it appeared to have opened the flood gates.

Once again, Reverend Parris's pasture was filled with a coven of witches. The girls reported that the witches had tried to drag them along. Villagers had struck at the shapes in an effort to save the girls as the afflicted victims pointing here and there, crying out at the plethora of cape-flapping specters. A crowd had gathered, preparing to go into the meetinghouse for the inquisition. Parris's pasture ran behind the meetinghouse and farther back where many were standing about and talking. To suddenly hear that they may literally be standing amidst a witch's assembly must have been terrifying.

Abigail, bold as always, came hurtling through the parsonage door and loudly proclaimed that the pasture was filled with entire families of witches from Andover. Martha Carrier was sharing a pole ride with Ann Foster and Mary Lacy. With delicious excitement she told her story. The pole the witches were riding upon had broken and Foster grabbed Carrier around the neck to break her fall. Nonetheless, she hurt her leg. Then they had a picnic beneath a tree at the far end of the pasture by a stream where a cart path ran. As other witches arrived, the three nibbled on bread and cheese. It was a large gathering with the specters of imprisoned witches joining others that had yet to be apprehended. William Barker's specter from Andover claimed there were 105 swordsmen standing guard outside the meetinghouse. Then, George Burroughs' specter arrived with that of two other ministers, John Busse from Wells, Maine (who brought the meetings' wine from Boston), and an unnamed gray-headed man.

Abigail went on in a frenzied state of excitement. Burroughs, she said, had blown a trumpet to call two companies of witches, who arrived accompanied by a drum beat. Burroughs called the meeting of witches to order and told them to begin in Salem Village in their efforts to replace all of God's churches with the Devil's. Salem Village was the perfect place to start, he said, as the people here were already so divided. Then he told them to go throughout New England and build up the Devil's Kingdom. At noon, the witch's sacrament was served, Abigail continued, with Rebecca Nurse, Sarah Good, Sarah Osborne, and Sarah Wildes (the newly-accused witch) acting as deacons. They served the others the bloody sacrament. Later, a luncheon was offered that was of more meager fare: brown bread and cider. Burroughs sat at the head of the table with a man with a white high-crowned hat who many guessed was the Devil himself. The man read off a list of seventy-two names who were the new recruits of the Devil's Kingdom. This brought the list of witches to three hundred. Their King was to be George Burroughs, and their Queen, Martha Carrier.

The magistrates, meanwhile, had entered the meetinghouse in preparation for the inquest. Shocked and muttering, the crowd of villagers who had just listened to Abigail Williams' wild story of the Devil's covenant being hosted literally beneath their feet, flooded into the meetinghouse. Parris listed in his notes that morning that there were "much people, and many in the windows," the blocked light causing a gloom to fall over the interior.

Deliverance Hobbs, mother of Abigail Hobbs, who had already confessed to witchcraft, was the first to be examined. Knowing her daughter had admitted to being in league with the Devil, no doubt, made her despair of a fair inquest.

(Examination of Deliverance Hobbs)
[April 22, 1692]
(1) The Examination of Deliverance Hobbs . 22. Apr. 1692 At a Court held at Salem village by John Hauthorn] Esq'rsJonath: Corwin] Esq'rs

H) Mercy Lewes do you know her that stands at the Bar (for the Magistrates had privately ordered who should be brought in, & not suffered her name to be mentioned) Do you know her? speaking to another; but both were struck dumb. Ann Putman jun'r. said it was Goody Hobbs , & she hath hurt her much John Indian said he had seen her, & she choake him. Mary Walcot said, yesterday was the first time that she saw her i.e. as a

Tormenter H) Why do you hurt these persons? D) It is
unknown to me. H) How come you to commit acts of
Witchcraft? D) I know nothing of it. H) It is you, or your
appearance, how comes this about? Tell us the truth. D)
I cannot tell. H) Tell us what you know in this case. Who
hurts them if you do not? D) There are a great many
persons hurts us all. H) But it is your appearance. D) I
do not know it. H) Have not you consented to it, that
they should be hurt? D) No in the sight of God, & man,
as I shall answere another day. H) It is said you were
afflicted, how came that about? D) I have seen sundry
sights. H) What sights D) Last Lords day in this
meetinghouse & out of the door, I saw a great many
birds cats & dogs, & heard a voice say come away. H)
What have you seen since? D) The shapes of severall
persons. H) What did they say? D) Nothing. H) What
neither the birds, nor persons? D) No. H) What persons
did you see? D) Goody Wilds and the shape of Mercy
Lewes.. H) What is that? Did either of them hurt you?
D) None but Goody Wilds , who tore me almost to
peices. H) Where was you then? D) In bed. H) Was not
the book brought to you to signe? D) No. H) Were not
you threatened by any body, if you did not signe the
book? D) No, by no body. H) What were you tempted
to under your affliction? D) I was not tempted at all. H)
Is it not a solemn thing, that last Lords day you were
tormented, & now you are become a tormentor, so that
you have changed sides, how comes this to pass? *Abig:
Williams [cry out there] & Ann Putman jun'r cry out
there is Goody Hobbs upon the Beam, she is not at the
Bar, they cannot see her there: tho there she stood. H)
What do you say to this, that tho you are at the bar in
person, yet they see your appearance upon the beam, &
whereas a few dayes past you were tormented, now you

are become a Tormentor? Tell us how this change comes. Tell true. D) I have done nothing. H) What have you resolved you will not confess? Hath any body threatened you if you do confess? You can tell how this change comes. *She lookt upon John Indian , & then another, & then they fell into fits. H) Tell us the reason of this change: Tell us the truth what have you done? D) I cannot speak. H) What do you say? What have you done? D) I cannot tell. H) Have you signed to any book? It is very lately then. When was it? D) The night before the last. H) Well the Lord open your heart to confesse the truth. Who brought the book to you? D)It was Goody Wilds . H) What did you make your mark with in the book? D) Pen and ink. H) Who brought the Pen and Ink? D) They that brought the book, Goody Wilds. Did they threaten you if you did not signe? D) Yes, to tear me in peices. H) Was there any else in company? D) No, Sir. H) What did you afflict others by? Did they bring images? D)Yes. Who brought the images? Goody Wild & Goody Osburn . H) What did you put into those images. D) Pins, Sir.

H) Well tell us who have you seen of this company?

D) None but those two.

(Reverse side)

H) Have you not seen many? D) No. I heard last night a kind of Thundring. H)How many images did you use? D)But two.

H) Nay here is more afflicted by you, You said more. Well tell us the truth. recollect yourself. I am amazed. can you remember how many were brought? D) Not well, but severall were brought. H) Did not they bring the image of John Nichols his child? D) Yes. H) Did not you hurt that child? D) Yes. H) Where be those images, at your house? D) No they carryed them away again. H)

When? D) They carried some then & some since. H) Was it Goody Wild in body, or appearance? D) In appearance. H) Was there any man with them? D) Yes a tall black man, with an high-croun'd hat. H) Do you know no more of them? No Sir.

*Note All the sufferers free from affliction during her examination after once she began to confesse, tho at sundry times they were much afflicted till then.

*Note Whereas yesterday at Deacon Ingersols Mary Walcot & Abigail Williams cryed there stands Goody Hobbs , showing also where Benja. Hutchinson struck at her with a Rapier, & the afflicted that is the said Mary & Abigail said, oh you have struck her on the ride side: Whereupon the Magistrates asking her after the publick examination whither she had received any hurt yesterday, she said yes in her right side like a Prick & that it was very sore, & done when she was in a Trance, telling us also in what house and room it was done. Whereupon the Magistrates required some women to search it, who found it so as she had confessed. Also a little after the said prick in her side, she had som what in her left eye like dust, w'ch agrees with what the afflicted farther said that Benja. Hutchinson after wards toucht her eye w'th the same Rapier, & said pointing to the place there was a mark which the Marshall being by said so there was.

Salem Village Aprile the 22th 1692 Mr Sam'l parris being desired to take in wrighting the Examinaticon of Deliverance hobs hath delivered itt as aforesaid

And upon heareing the same and seeing what wee did see togather with the Charg of the afflicted persons against them, Wee Committed her.*John Hathorne

The Examination of (1) Deliverance Hobbs 22.Apr. 1692

Perhaps, one of the most confusing elements of the witchcraft phenomenon is that markings were found in places where the afflicted said they would be found upon the clothing and bodies of the "witches." Tears in clothing during that era would be common. Perhaps Abigail and others had already seen the tears or marks on a person before they went into their theatrics and matched their accusations accordingly. It would be a simple thing to do. Others may have fallen under a lucky guess, or the willingness of the villagers and magistrates to see what they were told to see.

What is particularly interesting with the inquest of Deliverance Hobbs, is that we see for the first time the magistrates testing the veracity of the afflicted girls. The accused names were heretofore always announced before the afflicter was brought into the room. This time, Hathorne deferred, and instead asked the girls who the woman was that was led in. Hobbs was from Topsfield, outside the village boundaries. Parris wrote "the Magistrates had previously ordered who should be brought in, & not suffered her name to be announced."

Hathorne asked Mercy Lewis and another girl, "Do you know her?" The two were "struck dumb." Ann Putnam Jr. offered the correct name. "It is Goody Hobbs and she hath hurt me much." Mercy Lewis had known the Hobbs family while living in Falmouth, Maine. She may have been distantly related to them. Unwilling to name a relation herself, had she given Hobbs' identity to Ann Jr. earlier? Hobbs' Topsfield property was adjacent to the Putnams' just over the Salem Village line. While no disputes between the two men are on record, had Ann Jr. been aware of the families?

(Examination of William Hobbs)

(The transcript is an alternate line Q & A. There were many tears in the manuscript.)

[April 22, 1692]
The Examination of William Hobbs At the Same Court

[H]ath this man hurt you?
[S]everal answered yes.
[Goo]dy Bibber said no.
[W]hat say you, are you guilty or not?
[I] can speak in the presence of God safely, as
[I] must look to give account another day, that I am as clear as a new born babe.
Clear: of what?
Of Witchcraft
Have you never hurt these?
No.
Have you not consented that they should be hurt?
Abigail Williams said, he was going to Mercy Lewes, & quickly after said Lewes was seized with a fit.
Then said Abigail cryed, he is coming to Mary Walcot , & said Mary presently fell into a fit also.
[How] can you be clear when the Children
[saw] somthing come from you & afflict
[th]ese persons?
Then they fell into fits & halloo'd [and]
[suffe]red greatly.
[torn] [ur] wife before you God wa [torn]
[torn] open her mouth, & she ha [torn]
[torn] session: And you seen to [torn]
[torn] before us.
[I a]m clear of any Witch.
[Wh]at do you call it, and over-look[ing of]
[the]m? you look upon them & they are [hurt]
[I h]urt none of them
[T]hen they all fell into great fits again
When were you at any publick Religious meeting

Not a pretty while
Why so?
Because I was not well: I had a distemper that none knows.
Can you act Witchcraft here, & by casting your eyes turn folks into fits?
You may judge your pleasure, my soul is clear.
Do you not see you hurt these by your look
No. I do not know it.
You did not answere to that question, dont you over-look them?
No I don't over-look them.
What do you call that way of looking upon persons, & striking them downe?
You may judge your pleasure.
Well but what do you call it?
It was none of I.
Who was it then?
I cannot tell who they are.
Why they say, they see you going to hurt persons & immediatly hurt persons.
Abig: Williams said he is going to hurt Mercy Lewes [torn] & imediately s'd Mercy fell into a fit, & divers others
Can you now deny it?
I can deny it to my dying day.
What is the reason you go away when [there] is any reading of the Scripture in your [family]
He denyed it.
Nathanael Ingersol & Tho: Haynes tes[tifyed] that this Hobb's daughter had told them [so] As soon as your daughter Abigail , & aft [torn] to day your wife confessed they left torturing & so would you, if you would confess: can you still deny that you are guilty?
I am not guilty.
If you put away Gods ordinances, no wonder that the Devil prevails with you. to keep his counsell. Have you never had any apparition.
No Sir.
Did you never pray to the Devill that your daughter might confess no more?

No Sir.
Who do you[r] wo[r] ship?
I hope I worship God only.
Where?
In my heart.
But God requires outward worship [torn]
not worship him in publick, ne [torn]
[torn] I worship him in my heart [torn]
[torn] worship him in your family [torn]
[torn] amily, speak the truth,
[torn] not given the Devil advant [torn]
[torn] gainst you thereby? [torn]
He was silent a considerable spa[ce] then said yes.
Have you not known a good while [how] that your daughter
was a witc[h]
No Sir.
Do you think she is a witch now
I do not know.
Well if you desire mercy from God, own the truth.
I do not know anything of that nature.
What do you think these people aile?
More than ordinary?
But what more than ordinary
-- silent
Why do you not answer what do they aile?
I do not know what they aile I am sorry
It is none of I.
What do you think they aile?
There is more than ordinary
What is that?
I cannot tell.
Do you think they are bewitcht.
I cannot tell
Not tell when your wife & daughter o [torn]
Did not you give consent that these should be [hurt]
Never in my dayes.
What do you think curd your wife she was
[torn] these the other day [torn]
[torn] nal God in Heaven knows. [torn]

[torn] know that. We do not ask that [but]
[whet] her you do not know what curd
[torn] t tell. I know nothing
[torn] man said he told me that if his wife
[torn] not write in the book he would kill her,
[torn] was the same time that she did signe
[torn] ppears by the time of her appearing as a
[torm] enter to Mr. Parris family & others
Did not you say so?
I never said so.
Salem Village Aprill 22th 1692
Mr. Sam'l parris being desired to take
[in] wrighting the Examination of
[Sar]ah Wilds and W'm Hobs delivered it as afores'd
[and up] on heareing the same and seeing
[what] wee did see at the tyme of her
[examin] ation togather with the Char[ge of]
[the af] flicted persons against he[r we]
[co] mmitted her to their M[aj'ts Goale]
*John Hathor[ne]
(Reverse)   Examination   of Sarah   Wilds & William
Hobbs 22. Apr. 1692

Sarah Wildes of Topsfield was examined next. Sarah was a 65-year-old woman with a checkered past. She had been accused of witchcraft in 1676. One of the accusers stated she had cursed his cartful of hay for borrowing her scythe without permission. The cart's wheel had broken on the road and the hay unloaded while it was fixed. Even after the repairs, the oxen refused to budge. A strange-looking dog appeared and spooked them. They bolted into a river, dumping the cart-load of hay and ruining it.

Sarah had also been accused of fornication and publicly whipped. Her marriage was contentious and long-standing hostilities resulted. One Mary Gould Reddington (stepmother of John Herrick) had confessed to Reverend Hale of Beverly that Sarah Wildes' specter had tormented her. And now, Deliverance Hobbs had accused her of witchcraft and that Sarah "tore me almost to pieces."

It was, perhaps, unfortunate that Sarah Wildes son, Ephraim, had been the constable enlisted to arrest Deliverance Hobbs. Hobbs accusation against Sarah may have been payback for Ephraim being the one to take her away under the accusation of witchcraft.

(Examination of Sarah Wildes)

[April 22, 1692]

The examination of Sarah Wilds At a Court held at Salem Village [April 22] 1692 by the worshipful:_ John Hathorn & Jonathan Corwin.

The Sufferers were siezed with sundry[?] the accused came into the Court H) Hath this woman hurt you? A) Oh she is upon the beam. Goody Bibber that never saw her before said she saw her now upon the beam, & then said Bibber fell into a fit H) What say you to this are you guilty or not? W) I am not guilty Sir. H) Is this the woman? speaking to the afflict[ed] *Thay all, or most, said yes, & then fell into fits. H) What do you say, are you guil[ty] W) I am not guilty Sir. H) Is this the woman? speaking to the afflicted *They all, or most, said yes,& then fell into fits W) I thank God I am free. H) Here is a clear evidence that [you have] been not only a Tormenter [but that] You have caused one to sig[ne the] book, the night before last [What do]you

214

say to this?W) I never saw the book in my life and I never saw these persons before *Some of the afflicted fell into fits H) [Do] you deny this thing that is apparent *All fell into fits, & con[firmed] that the accused hurt th[em] H) Did you never consent that [these] be hurt? D) Never in my life. *She was charged by some [with] hurting John Herricks mo[ther] The accused denied it. Capt'n How gave in a relation [and] confirmation of the charge before made. She was ordered to be taken away, & they all cryed out she was upon the Beam, & fell into fits.

While the others awaited their turn at the bar, rumors circulated that the missing Mary English had been at last apprehended in Salem Town. According to the report, Phillip and his wife Mary English were in bed when someone pounded on the door at eleven o'clock at night. Some believe Sheriff George Corwin was one of the men present who was let into the house by a startled maid servant. Phillip English, hearing the banging and the sound of his maid climbing the stairs, got up and began dressing. Before he had accomplished the act, the officers barged into the couple's bedchamber, drew back the bed curtains, and ordered Mary English to accompany them. She flat out refused, stating she did rise at such an hour. The men, not wanting to drag a wealthy woman from her bed, agreed to come back in the morning, and posted a guard at the house door.

Phillip and Mary English home in Salem Town, 1692.

Mary took her time the following morning as the guards fumed. She dressed, breakfasted with her family, and held a meeting with the household staff, before finally accompanying the men to Ingersoll's Tavern in Salem Village where she would spend the next three nights awaiting her inquest.

Chapter Nineteen

Mary Estes and Others

As the madness continued, several things became apparent. The accused were no longer living only within the Salem Village boundaries. Neighboring towns were fair game. It is also obvious that the girls were feeling their power. Where they had once contented themselves with accusing others of the kind of witchcraft that curdled milk or lamed cattle, their accusations now were far more serious. They claimed the specters of certain afflicters were admitting— *and* bragging—about murder! Were the girls ramping up the odds against those they were accusing? Spectral evidence of a witch abusing them might skate by. Why not add murder just to make sure the charges had some weight to them?

The witchcraft mania, that began as one small child became overcome with guilt and hysteria, spread so rapidly that it was hard to keep track of who was twitching when. It snowballed beyond the young women's ability to contain it. They had built the fire with the first fragile kindling, consisting of accusing the village throwaways of some pinching and torment. But each story and embellishment poured accelerant onto the flames until it became a raging bonfire, devouring all in its path. The girls could not have known at the beginning that they would be believed, let alone revered and instrumental in adults going to jail. The

Puritan society placed children firmly at the bottom of the totem pole. Normally, the only official documents their names might appear on were a mention of birth, marriage, and death. Now, their names were inked on more court depositions and recordings than they could have imagined a few short months ago. Certainly, in the back of their minds, they may have wondered when these people would awaken to the fact that they had been faking all of their afflictions. And when they did, what repercussions awaited children doing so much evil?

And of their antics...their "sport?" What if saying specters were doing most of the mischief didn't stick? Three "witches" had actually confessed, something that probably shocked the girls. It was akin to an author seeing his imaginary characters coming to life and mocking him. The girls had taken great strides to make their visons believable—even furnishing visons of torn cloth that actually appeared in the accused coats where swords had attacked spectral beings. Didn't that collaborate what they were saying was true? But...just in case...a charge of murder would carry the most weight of all. It would tie a very fine noose.

Nehemiah Abbot Jr., a weaver from Topsfield in his twenties was led into the room. Ann Putnam Jr. had identified him as one who afflicted her.

(Examination of Nehemiah Abbott, Jr.)

[April 22, 1692]

The examination of Nehemiah Abbot , at a court at Salem village, by John Hawthorne and Jonathan Corwin Esqrs. 22nd April 1692.

H) What say you, are you guilty of witchcraft, of which you are suspected, or not? A) No Sir, I say before God, before whom I stand, that I know nothing of witchcraft. H) Who is this man? *Ann Putman named him. Mary Walcot said she had seen his shape. H) What do you say to this? A) I never did hurt them. H)Who hurt you Ann Putman ? P) That man. A) I never hurt her. *Ann Putman said, he is upon the beam. H) Just such a discovery of the person carried out, and she confessed; and if you would find mercy of God, you must confess. A) If I should confess this, I must confess what is false. H) Tell how far you have gone, who hurts you? A) I do not know, I am absolutely free. H) As you say, God knows. If you will confess the truth, we desire nothing else that you may not hide you guilt, if you are guilty, and therefore confess if so. A) I speak before God that I am clear from this accusation. H) What, in all respects? A) Yes in all respects. H) Doth this man hurt you? *Their mouths were stopped. H) You hear several accuse you, though one cannot open her mouth. A) I am altogether free. H) Charge him not unless it be he. * This is the man say some, and some say he is very like him. H) How did you know his name? P) He did not tell me himself, but other witches told me. Ann Putman said, it is the same man, and then she was taken with a fit. H) Mary Walcot , is this the man? W) He is like him, I cannot say it is he. (*Mercy Lewis said it is not the man. They all agreed, the man had a bunch on his eyes. Ann Putman , in a fit, said, be you the man? ay, do you say you be the man? did you put a mist before my eyes? Then he was sent forth till several others were examined. When he was brought in again, by reason of much people, and many in the windows so that the accusers could not have a clear view of him, he was ordered to be abroad, and the accusers to go forth to him and view him in the light, which they did, and in the presence of the magistrates and many others discoursed quietly with him, one and all acquitting him, but yet said he was like that man, but he had not the wen they saw in his apparition, *Note, he was a hilly faced man and stood shaded by reason of his own hair, so that for a time he seemed to some by-standers and observers, to be considerably like the person the afflicted did describe.

Mr. Samuel Parris , being desired to take in writing the examination of Nehemiah Abbot , hath delivered it as aforesaid, and upon hearing the same did see cause to dismiss him.

JohnHawthorne

Jona. Corwin { Assistants.

Samuel Parris made note that the man did not have the wen next to his eye that the girls had mentioned. With so many people jammed onto the window sills, they used the dimness of the room as their excuse for mis-identifying him. For the first time in the witchcraft hysteria, an accused was let go. This altruistic act may have mollified the villagers that had seen no leniency for any brought before the bar. Perhaps the proceedings were fair after all. Perhaps justice was being carried out. The trial of Nehemiah Abbot caused the scales to tip slightly in the girls' favor.

The last witch of the day was the sister of Rebecca Nurse and Sarah Cloyce. Mary Esty filled out the triumvirate of daughters belonging to accused witch Joanna Townes. At 58-years-of-age, she was younger than her sister Rebecca, already in shackles in the Boston Prison. She was from Topsfield, along with the other accused questioned that day. Where Nehemiah Abbot had been shown mercy, Mary Estes' story is one of the more heartless to be recorded inside that shadowed court room. It is not surprising that the complaints against her originated with John Putnam. As mentioned before, the Putnams had long coveted the Esty farmland just over their border in Topsfield; in fact, Lieutenant John Putnam lived only about two miles from the Esty homestead, just below Solomon's Hill.

Just as Judge Hathorne had wavered in his suspicion of the elderly Rebecca Nurse when he saw her stand before him, barely able to support herself, he too felt the niggling of doubt at seeing Mary Esty. The woman held herself with such calm grace, that her spirit was felt among the spectators. She was not the spitfire her sister Sarah Cloyce had been. No one could picture this woman slamming a church door in the face of a minister or defying the magistrates. Nor, was she the frightened, tremulous personage of her older sister, Rebecca. Hathorne looked at the woman, and at the strange quiet of the afflicted girls as she was led to the bar and asked, "Are you certain this is the woman?" After all, they had just made a mistake with Abbot.

On cue, the spell was broken and the afflicted on the front row exploded with signs of demonic possession.

(Examination of Mary Esty)

[April 22, 1692]

The Examination of Mary Eastie . At a Court held at Salem village 22. Apr. 1692

By the Wop. [=worshipful] John Hathorne & Jonathan Corwin.

At the bringing in of the the accused severall fell into fits. H) Doth this woman hurt you? *Many mouths were stopt, & several other fits seized them Abig: Williams said it was Goody Eastie , & she had hurt her, the like said Mary Walcot , & Ann Putman , John indian said her saw her with Goody Hobbs . H) What do you say, are you guilty? E) I can say before Christ Jesus, I am free. H) You see these accuse you. E) There is a God H) Hath she brought the book to you? *Their mouths were stopt. H) What have you done to these children? E) I know nothing. H) How can you say you know nothing, when you see these tormented, & accuse you that you know nothing? E) Would you have me accuse my self? H)Yes if you be guilty. How far have you complyed w'th Satan whereby he takes this advantage ag't you? E) Sir, I never complyed but prayed against him all my dayes, I have no complyance with Satan, in this. What would you have me do? H) Confess if you be guilty. E) I will say it, if it was my last time, I am clear of this sin. H) Of what sin? E) Of witchcraft. H) Are you certain this is the woman? *Never a one could speak for fits. By and by Ann Putman said that was the woman, it was like her, & she told me her name; H) It is marvailous to me that you should sometimes think they are bewitcht, & sometimes not, when severall confess that they have been guilty of bewitching them. E) Well Sir would you have me confess that that I never knew? *Her hands were clincht together, & then the hands of Mercy Lewis was clincht H) Look now you hands are open, her hands are open. Is this the woman? *They made signes but could not speak, but Ann Putman afterwards Betty Hubbard cryed out "Oh. Goody Esty, Goody Esty you are the woman, you are the woman" H) Put up her head, for while her head is bowed the necks of these are broken. What do you say to this? E) Why God will know. H) Nay God knows now. E) I know he dos. H) What did you think of the actions of others before your sisters came out, did you think it was Witchcraft? E) I cannot tell. H) Why do you not think it is Witchcraft? E) It is an evil spirit, but wither it be witchcraft I do not know *Severall said she brought them the Book & then they fell into fits. Salem Village March 24'th. 1691/2 Mr Sam'l parris being desired to take in wrighting the Examination of Mary Eastie hath delivered itt as aforesaid

Upon heareing the aforesaid, and seeing what wee then did see, together with the Charge: of the persons then present Wee Committed s'd. Mary Easte to theire Majest's Goale

*JohnHathorne

*Jonathan. Corwin { Assists

Edward and Sarah Bishop's examination notes are not extant. Edward was the unfortunate man who had beaten John Indian on April 11th and admonished him at other times during his fits at Ingersoll's Ordinary. Many had learned it was not wise to antagonize one within the afflicteds' circle. The Bishops lived a stone's throw from Dr. Griggs' home in the Ryal sector of Salem Village. They ran an unlicensed tavern from their home, and had been in court many times. Christian Trask had accused Goody Bishop of being a witch only two years earlier. Elizabeth Hubbard, Dr. Griggs' niece, was one of the more forceful accusers, as she was the Bishop's neighbors. Accusations of public fighting abounded, and stories that the couple even sent their sons to "abuse" the neighbor's pigs.

Christian Trask went on to suffer fits and a "distracted" state after dealing with the Bishops, so much so, that Reverend Hale was called for. This is his report filed in May, 1962:

(The Rev. John Hale v. Sarah Bishop)

[May 20, 1692]

John Hale of Beverly aged about 56 yeares [torn] & saith that about 5 or 6 years ago e Christian the wife of John Trask (living in Salem bounds bordering on the abovesaid Beverly) beeing in full comunion in o'r Church came to me to [de] sier that Goodwife Bishop her Neighb'r wife of Edw: Bishop Jun'r might not be permitted to receive the Lords Supper in our church till she had given her the said Trask satisfaction for some offences that were against her.viz be- cause the said Bishop did entertaine people in her house at unseason- able houres in the night to keep drinking and playing at shovel-board whereby discord did arise in other families & young people were in danger to bee corrupted & that the s'd Trask knew these things & had once gon into the house & fynding some at shovel-board had taken the peices thay played with & thrown them into the fyre & had reprooved the said Bishop for promoting such disorders, But re- ceived no satisfaction from her about it. I gave s'd Christian Trask direction how to proceed farther in this matter if it were clearly prooved And indeed by the information I have had otherwise I doe fear that if a stop had not been putt to those disorders s'd Edw. Bishop's house would have been a house of great prophainness & iniquity.

But as to Christian Trask the next news I heard of her was that she was distracted & asking her husband Trask when she was so taken [he told] mee shee was taken distracted that night after shee [came from] my

225

house when shee complained against Goody Bishop.
She continueing some time Distracted wee sought the
Lord by fasting & prayer & the Lord was pleased to
restore the s'd [Trask] to the use of her reason agen. I
was s'th her often in [her] distraction (& took it then to
bee only distraction, yet fearing sometimes somw't
worse) but since I have seen the fitts of those bewitched
at Salem Village I call to mind some of hers to be much
like some of theirs. The said Trask when recovered as I
understood it did manifest strong suspicion that shee
had been bewitched by the s'd Bishop's wife & showed
so much aversness from having any conversation that I
was then troubled at it hopeing better of s'd Goody
Bishop at that time for wee have since [torn] At length
s'd Christian Trask [was] agen in a distracted fit on a
Sabboth day in the forenoon at the pub- l[i]ck meeting
to o'r public desturbance & so continued sometimes
better sometimes worse unto her death, manifesting that
shee under temptation to kill her selfe or somebody else.
I enquired of Marg'rt Ring who kept at or nigh the
house, what shee had observed of s'd Trask before this
last distraction shee told [mee.] Goody Trask was much
given to reading & search the pro- phecys of scrip[ture].
The day before shee made that disturbance in the
meeting [house she[e] came home & said shee had been
w'th Goody Bishop & that they two were now friend or
to that effect. I was oft praying w'th & councelling
of Goody Trask before her death and not many days
before her end being there shee seemed more rationall
& earnestly desired Edw: Bishop might be sent for that
shee might make friends with him, I asked her if shee
had wronged Edw. Bishop shee said not that shee knew
of unless it were in taking his shovel-board pieces when
people were at play w'th them & throwing them into the

fyre & if she did evill in it she was very sorry for it & desiered he would be friends with her or forgive her. this was the very day before she dyed, or a few days before. Her distraction (or bewitching) continued about a month and in those intervalls wherein shee was better shee earnestly desired prayers & the Sabboth before she dyed I received a note for prayers on her behalf w'ch her husband said was written by her selfe & I judge was her owne hand writing beeing well acquainted with her hand.

As to the wounds she dyed of I observed 3 deadly ones; apeice of her wind pipe cutt out. & another wound above that threww the windpipe & Gullet & the veine they call jugular. So that I then judge & still doe apprehend it impossible for her w'th so short a pair of cissars to mangle her selfe so without some extraordinary work of the devill or witchcraft signed. 20. may 1692 by *John Hale.

Edward Sarah Bishop house, Danvers, MA.

Reverend Hale wrote that he believed witchcraft was involved in

Goody Trask's death. This was very damning evidence as the only people named in the document were Edward and Sarah Bishop. After their questioning on April 22, 1892, they were ordered to jail to await their trial for witchcraft.

Mary Black

Mary Black was next. She was an African American slave who was believed to work for Nathaniel Putnam's son Benjamin. Mary was only the second black person to stand before the bar. Her predecessor, Tituba Indian, had a much lengthier examination than this accused.

(Examination of Mary Black and Clearance by Proclamation)

[April 22, 1692]
The examination of Mary Black (a Negroe) at a Court held at Salem Village 22. Apr. 1692 By the Magistrates of Salem

H) Mary, you are accused of sundry acts of witchcraft:
Tell me be you a Witch?
B)-- Silent.
H)How long have you been a witch?
B) I cannot tell.
H)But have you been a witch?
B) I cannot tell you.
H) Why do you hurt these folks
B) I hurt no body
H) Who doth?
B) I do not know.
[Benj'a Putnam] Her Master saith a man sat down upon the farm with her about a twelve month agoe.
H)What did the man say to you?
B) He said nothing.

H) Doth this Negroe hurt you?
*Severall of them said yes.
H) Why do you hurt them?
B) I did not hurt them.
H) Do you prick sticks?
B) No I pin my Neck cloth
H) Well take out a pin, & pin it again.
*She did so, & severall of the afflicted cryed out they were prick't. Mary Walcott was prick't in the arm till the blood came, Abigail Williams was prick't in the stomach & Mercy Lewis was prick't in the foot.

mr Samuell parris being desired to take in wrighting the Examination of Mary Black a Negro Woman delivered itt as aforesaid And upon heareing the same and seeing what wee did then see togather with the Charge of the afflicted persons then present Wee Committed s'd Mary black .   Per   us *John   Hathorne *Jonathan. Corwin { Assis'ts

Mary English's examination does not exist. We know she was the wife of Phillip English, a wealthy merchant in Salem Town. She helped him with business matters and may have run a shop out of their home, which was a common occurrence in those days. There were rumors that some of the less-fortunate Salem Town folk found her to be rather self-important—not a hanging crime, but in the witch trial climate, one could use all the friends one could make.

At the end of a long train of inquisitions, the magistrates and ministers sauntered up to Ingersoll's to dine and to make sure their horses were attended to. (Oats and hay were duly noted on Ingersoll's tab for the visiting dignitaries.) At the end of the day, Marshal Herrick took the strange menagerie to Salem's Gaol (jail). Among the prisoners were two tavern owners, a devout Christian woman, the mother of a confessed witch, a black slave, and a wealthy merchant. How the inmates at Salem Jail that night must have looked about themselves at their strange bedfellows. Did the poor among them secretly gloat at seeing the likes of a fine lady such as Mary English huddled in the filthy straw? The juxtaposition of souls accused of mounting poles and flying through the night air, dining with the Devil, and tormenting innocent children was a surreal reality to accept. But reality it was for these accused witches, and it came with iron shackles, slops, and a threadbare blanket.

Meanwhile, the Devil's minions were dining on their own fare at Parris's pasture outside the meetinghouse. No other mention was made of the diabolic sacrament that day, with one exception. Deliverance Hobbs reminded the magistrates of it when they came to the jail to question her later that day.

Chapter Twenty

Susanna Sheldon Enters the Frey

Deliverance Hobbs had barely chosen her spot in the large stone-walled dungeon, flanked by weathered boards, when she was visited by Hathorne and Corwin the following day. Her answers to their questions were shocking.

(Examination of Deliverance Hobbs in Prison)

[April 23, 1692]

The first Examination of Deliverance Hobbs in prison. She continued in the free acknowledging herself to be a Covenant Witch, and further Confesseth she was warned to a meeting yesterday morning, and that there was present Proctor and his Wife , Goody Nurse , Giles Cory , and his Wife , Goody Bishop alias Oliver , and Mr Burroughs was the Preacher, and prest them to bewitch all in the Village, telling them they should do it gradually and not all att once, assureing them they should prevail; He administred the sacrament unto them att the same time with Red Bread, and Red Wine Like Blood,   she   affirms   she   saw Osburn , Sarah

Good , Goody Wilds ; Goody nurse, and Goody Wilds distributed the bread and Wine, and a Man in a long crowned white Hat, next the Minister, and they sat seemingly att a Table, and They filled out the wine in Tankards, The Notice of this meeting was given her by Goody wilds . She herself affirms did not nor would not Eat nor drink, but All the Rest did who were there present, therefore they Threatened to Torment her. The meeting was in the Pasture by Mr Parris's House. and she saw when ran out to speak with them: But by that Time Abigail was come a little distance from the House This Examinant was strucke blind, so that she saw not with whome Abigail spake She further saith, that Goody Wilds to prevail with her to sign, told her that If she would put her hand to the book she w'ld give her some Cloaths, and would not afflict her any more -- Hir Daughter Abigail Hobbs being brought in att the same time while her Mother was present was immediately taken with a dreadful fitt, and Answered it was Goodman Cory , and she saw him, and the Gentlewoman of Boston striving to break her Daughters Neck.

We see here by Deliverance's own admission that she was present when Abigail William's came out from the parsonage door the day before and told the astonished crowd of villagers about to enter the meetinghouse, that there was a Devil's sacrament going on right behind them. Hobbs repeats Abigail's description of the man in a white high-crowned hat, and of the women witches who were serving the blood red meat and wine. Hobbs does depart from Abigail's story in a few instances. Deliverance is suddenly "struke blind" when it came time to identify who Abigail was conversing with during the Devil's sacrament.

Abigail said it was Sarah Cloyce, the Devil's deacon. Hobbs could not bring herself to name Cloyce, possibly because Thomas Cloyce, Sarah's brother-in-law, had been a neighbor in Falmouth, Maine, during the Indian wars there. She also mentions a solitary "gentlewoman" from Boston. Tituba's testimony mentioned "two women" from Boston, and a "tall black man."

As for Reverend George Burroughs, he now had three different witnesses accusing him of sitting at the head of the Devil's sacrament: Abigail Williams, Mercy Lewis, and Deliverance Hobbs. That he had a dark complexion and was not in favor with Salem Village denizens, did not help him.

Reverend Parris's pasture was becoming the hot spot for the Devil's call to witches. Abigail Williams had already mentioned it on March 31st, claiming similar deacons serving bloody meat and wine as those Deliverance Hobbs claimed to see. Williams had added a man with a white high-crowned hat to this more-recent meeting, and Hobbs dutifully picked up the ball.

For villagers passing the open meadow on their way to-and-from the meetinghouse and Ingersoll's Ordinary, it may have sent shudders along their spine as they eyed the quiet area. The rutted cart path that ran from Parris' home along the back of Ingersoll's and to the meetinghouse, was not the primary road. It traversed a small creek, and ended only a few feet from the meetinghouse on what is today's Forest Road. Ingersoll's Ordinary sat at the corner of today's Hobart and Centre Streets. The meetinghouse was a short walk down the main street from Ingersoll's, and a short cut along the cart path from the parsonage.

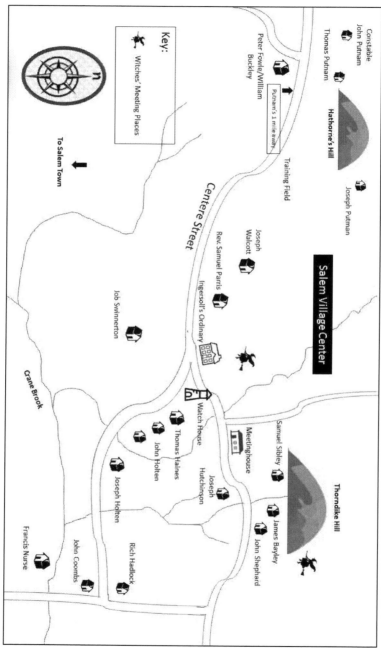

Salem Village Center as seen in 1692.
Map courtesy of Rebecca F. Pittman.

On April 24, 1892, a new young woman joined the group of accusers. Her name was Susanna Sheldon, an 18-year-old who was yet another survivor of the Indian wars of Maine. Her uncle had perished in the attack on Dunston. As the villages were being ravaged and people slaughtered, a local military commander, Captain Joshua Scottow, flinched at the anguished pleas from the settlers for help. He held off sending in troops, fearing he would be leaving other farmers vulnerable to attack. It would be the ruin of his reputation. One of his closest friends was none other than Reverend George Burroughs.

Susanna's family continued to suffer from the Indian wars. Her twenty-four-year-old brother Godfrey died in battle. Her father died from an infected wound in his leg only a year later. She was left with a brother Ephraim, four sisters, and her widowed mother in Salem Village.

The morning of April 24th, Susanna was attending church in Salem Town. She claimed she saw the specter of Phillip English climb over a pew and torment her. She said the specter of a Boston woman was with him. Phillip's specter followed her home and tried to get her to sign his Devil's Book outside the residence of William Shaw. The Devil was standing next to English, she continued, and he had dark hair and was wearing a tall-crowned hat. Susannah may have worked for William Shaw in his home by Proctor's Brook. Her family home was just south of Rebecca Nurse's farmland.

For the next two days, April 25th and 26th, Susanna was tormented again by Phillip English's specter during the day. That evening, she was attacked by the Devil and two women. Demanding to know the women's names, one answered her saying "old man Buckley's wife" from Salem Village. The other specter was Buckley's daughter. Susannah said the Devil had given the two Buckley women familiars to suckle—hideous hairless kittens with human ears. She claimed she had refused to sign the Devil's Book and he had smacked her in the head as the trio departed.

On the 26th, Susanna was found screaming and thrashing about in William Shaw's woodlot behind his house. Shaw's son found the girl in hysterics, claiming Goody Buckley had snatched her up into the air when she refused to sign her book and dropped her into the sticks. She also said Goodwife Whits of Boston had forced her way into the Shaw's home and pushed the Devil's Book toward the girl to sign.

Was this finally a name for the strange phantom woman of Boston? Who was Goodwife Whits?

The following day, April 27th, the specters of Mary English, Giles Corey, and Bridget Bishop accompanied the Devil in a visit to Susanna Sheldon. As she looked on in horror, they suckled their demon familiars—a yellow bird, a pair of turtles, and a snake. Though they bit her and threatened her, she refused to sign their book.

One day later, on April 28th, a Thursday, the specters of Giles Corey and Mary English forbade Susanna anything to eat. When the poor girl finally put a spoonful of food into her mouth, Corey struck her and said she would only eat when he gave her permission. Her hands were forced closed for a quarter of an hour. As she sat there unable to defend herself, the specter of Phillip English repeatedly tortured her to sign the book.

Ann Putnam Jr. was back on the scene claiming the specter of John Willard horrified her by showing her the murdered bodies of his first wife and Ann's own sister, Sarah in their winding sheets. Sarah was reportedly whipped to death at six weeks of age. He threatened to do the same to Ann. This is the first time we hear mention of one of Ann Carr Putnam's babies dying as a result of being whipped.

April 30th brought no respite to Susanna from the torments of the Invisible World. Goody Bishop, Mary English, Martha and Giles Corey, and the Devil showed up to torment the teenager. The specters kneeled in prayer to their leader, while Martha Corey suckled a hairless black pig. It was at this time that an odd confession was made by the specter of Bridget Bishop. According to Susanna, Bridget claimed she had been responsible for the death of John Trask's wife. It was Sarah Bishop who was accused of killing Christian Trask, according to Reverend Hale's account. Had Susanna mistaken the two names, or gotten a bad tip from one of the other girls?

Meanwhile in Boston, jailer John Arnold was under pressure to update his facilities to accommodate all the new witch prisoners being brought over from Salem Jail as they awaited their trials. He began repairs (and charged accordingly) to beef up the structure. The prison keeper's house could be rented out by a prisoner with deep pockets, which again, is not unusual. Lizzie Borden was kept in the jail matron's apartment, rather than a cell, during her inquisition for murder in 1892.

Elsewhere in Boston, Cotton Mather drew his shawl about his feverish shoulders and prayed for God's guidance against these "horrible enchantments and possessions broke forth upon Salem Village." The minister had been in the grasp of flu-like symptoms for months, saddled with his absent father's work load as well as his own. He worried over the use of "spectral evidence" to condemn a person, as the Devil could appear in an innocent's shape. He also wished to do for the afflicted victims what he had done for the Goodwin girl in 1689, when he took her into his home and tried to help free her of her demons. He had extended this same offer to six of the Salem Village's sufferers, but it fell on deaf ears. All he could do now was pray that his father Increase Mather and the new charter were almost upon Massachusetts' shores.

Before the *Nonsuch* could arrive back in the Massachusetts Bay Colony, the warrants for the arrest of a new batch of witches went out. On the final day of April, the complaint against Reverend George Burroughs was finally drawn up. Jonathan Walcott and Thomas Putnam Jr. saw to it. The list of complaints went on: Lydia Dustin of Reading; Susanna Martin of Amesbury; Dorcas Hoar and Sarah Morrell of Beverly; and Phillip English of Salem Town (Mary's harried husband). The accusers were Abigail Williams, Ann Putnam Jr., Mary Walcott, Mercy Lewis, Elizabeth Hubbard and the newly ordained Susannah Sheldon.

Hathorne and Corwin were kept busy that Saturday writing out warrants for the arrests. As Burroughs was in Maine, his capture would take a few days. The others were ordered to appear at Ingersoll's Ordinary in two days. The Sabbath would be observed after all, so the inquisitions would begin at 10:00 Monday morning.

But before the knock could come on his door, Phillip English, being tipped off from someone, fled to Boston to his friend George Holland's house.

April of 1692 would go out with the clanking of chains upon the ankles of the accused as their specters freed themselves and flew off to cavort about the countryside. One of the three originally accused witches, Sarah Good, flew into the home of Sarah Bibber, threw back her bed curtains, and ripped the sheets from Bibber's four-year-old child. John and Sarah Bibber clung to their toddler as the child was taken with sudden convulsions so strong, they could hardly hold her.

Over in Salisbury, Joseph Ring saw the shape of the newly arrested Susanna Martin staring down at him while in bed. He felt pinching sensations. John had long been a favorite of witches, it seems. For two years they would visit him and carry him off to their meetings. Once done with him, they would strike him mute so he could not tell of the things he witnessed. The last episode had been the previous August and he had not been able to speak since. Now, for some odd reason, Susannah Sheldon's specter's pinch had broken the spell and he could speak again.

And so, April, with its burgeoning blossoms and promise of fertile ground, ended with many of the villagers' neighbors absent from their ploughs and gardens. How many more would be cried out upon? Who was safe in this shining "city on the hill?"

Chapter Twenty-One

May Maleficium

The magistrates realized there would be no speedy ending to the witch hysteria. The number of complaints pushed across their tables was sobering. It was obvious this was not what they thought they were dealing with three months ago when two little girls cried out that they were being pinched and tormented. It should have been an easy thing to ferret out the culprit, and be done with it. With the arrests of Sarah Good, Sarah Osborne, and Tituba Indian, they may have congratulated each other on the speedy remedy to the malady suddenly afflicting Salem Village. But it was with Tituba's ominous warning that she saw *nine* names in the Devil's Book that the first harbinger of doom sounded. This would not end quickly. In fact, much more than nine witches were already jailed; and as May would prove, the witchcraft outbreak was just getting warmed up.

Maleficium is the power to work evil magic. The Puritans of the late 1600s believed without hesitation that evil walked among them. There was a God and there was his nemesis, the Devil. You spent your days in the service of God and did your best to live a Christian life, filled with hard work and long hours of scripture study. If you were good, the Devil and his helpers would pass you by. If you suddenly experienced a series of misfortunes, you would look to yourself and your household to see if some redemption was in order. And if it was apparent your house was in order, then the sudden loss of a cow, a stillborn child, a burned barn, or any number of tragic losses would turn one to look at one's neighbor, especially if that neighbor had reason to dislike you. It was that simple, and that deadly.

The specters of witches were not contained inside Salem Village, or even Salem Town. Reports of torturing were coming in from Stamford, Connecticut; Andover, Beverly, Ipswich, Reading, and Boston, Massachusetts, and were appearing on a daily basis. Residents barred their doors, said fervent prayers, and hoped the trials would begin soon. Inquisitions were fine, but until a legal trial could take place, there would be no resolution of the continued torment. The charter allowing such legal proceedings was crossing the seas, and would find its way to Boston on May 14, 1692. Only two more weeks. Increase Mather and Governor Phips would fix this. The villagers held out hope that this would soon be over. Yet arrest warrants flew about the countryside as feverishly as the specters of angry witches.

Monday morning, May 2nd dawned with the rumblings of thunder, a precursor of what was ahead for those filling the meetinghouse in Salem Village. By 10:00 am, the magistrates and scribes were ready for the first prisoner to plead her case. Several of the accused were not there. Phillip English was still hiding out at his friend's house in

Boston, Susanna Martin of Amesbury had not arrived yet (but was expected any minute), and George Burroughs would have to be brought from Maine. Gossip was already filling the packed room that Elizabeth Hubbard had been tormented the day before on the Sabbath by the specter of old George Jacobs Sr.'s daughter-in-law, Rebecca Jacobs. Another name added to the cauldron of suspected witches.

Dorcas Hoar of Beverly was called in, and the anticipation of another display of histrionics shot through the room.

(Examination of Dorcas Hoar)

[May 2, 1692]

The Examination of Dorcas Hoar . 2. May. 1692 .

Severall of the afflicted fell into fits as soon as she was brought in El iz: Hubbar d: said this woman hath afflicted me ever since last Sab: was seven night, & hurt me ever since, & she choakt her own husband. Mary Walcot said she told me the same Abi g: Willi ams saith this is the woman that she saw first before Tituba Indian or any else. An n Put man said this is the woman that hurts her & the first time she was hurt by her was the Sab: was seven night. Susa n: Shel don accused her of hurting her last moonday night. Abi g: Willi ams & An n Putm an said she told them that she had choakt a woman lately at Boston Eliz: Hubbard cryed why do you pinch me the mark was visible to the standers by. The Marshall said she pincht her fingers at that time.
(H) Dorcas Hoar why do you hurt these? D) I never hurt any child in my life. H) It is you, or your appearance D) How can I help it? H) What is it from you that hurts

these? D) I never saw worse than my self H) You need not see worse. They charge you with killing your huband D) I never did, nor never saw you before H) You sent for Goody Gale to cut your head off What do you say to that? D) I never sent for her upon that account. H) What do you say about killing your husband. *Susan: Sheldon also charged her that she came in with two cats, & brought me the book, & fell into a fit & told me your name was Goody Bukly [Buckley]. D) No, I never did, I never saw thee before. H) What black cats were those you had? D) I had none. *Mary Walcot , Susan: Sheldon, & Abigail Williams said they saw a black man whispering in her ears. D) Oh! you are liars, & God will stop the mouth of liars H) You are not to speak after this manner in the Court D) I will speak the Truth as long as I live. *Mary Walcot & Susan: Sheldon & Eliz: Hubbard said again there was a man whispering in her ear, & said she should never confess. Good y Bibb er free from fits hitherto said there was a black man with her & fell into a fit. H) What do you say to those cats that suckt your breast, what are they? D) I had no cats. H) You do not call them cats, what are they that suck you? D)I never suckt none, but my child. H) What do you say, you never saw Goody Bukly ? D) I never knew her. H) Goodm: Bukly testifyed that she had been at the house often. D) I know you but not the woman H) You said you did not know the Name. *Many by-standers testifyed she disowned that she knew the name D) I did not know the name so as to goe to the woman *Susan: Sheldon & Abig: Williams cryed there was a blew bird bird gone into her back. The Marshall struck, & several of the by-standers testifyed that they saw a fly like a Millar. H) What did you see goddy Bibber. who was looking up. *Goody Bibber was taken dumb. H) What can you have no heart to confess. D) I have nothing to do with witchcraft H) They say the Devil is whispering in your ear. D) I cannot help it if they do se it. H) cannot you confess what you think of these things? D) Why should I confess that I do not know. *Susan: Sheldon cryed O Goody Hoar do not kill me, & fell into a fit, & when she came to her self she said, she saw a black man whispering in her ear, & she brought me the book. D) I have no book, but the Lords book. H) What Lords book. D) The Lords book *Oh said some of the afflicted there is one whispering in her ears. There is some body will rub your ears shortly, said the examinant Immediately they were afflicted, and among others Mercy Lewes. H) Why do you threaten they should be Rubb'd? D) I did not speak a word of Rubbing. *Many testifyed she did. D) My meaning was God would bring things to light. H) Your meaning for God to bring the thing to light would be to deliver these poor afflicted ones, that would not Rubb them.

(On reverse side)

H) This is unusual impudence to threaten before Authority. who hurts them now. D) I know not. H) They were rubbed after you had threatened them. *Mary Walcot , Abigail   Williams & Eliz: Hubbard were carried towards her, but they could not come near her H) What is the reason these cannot come near you D) I can not help it, I do them no wrong, they may come if they will H) Why you see, they cannot come near you D)I do them no wrong

*Note. The afflicted were much distressed during her examination.

This is true account of the Examination of Dorcas Hoar without wrong to any party according to my original characters from themselves at the moments thereof Witness my hand *Sam Paris

Dorcas Hoar is not only accused of murdering her husband, something equally striking appears in this recorded testimony. Abigail Williams, for the first time since her original affliction in February, claims it was Dorcas Hoar she first saw—before Tituba, as her afflicter! She never mentioned this until now? Reverend John Hale had tried to downplay the rumors circulating about Dorcas Hoar in the early months of 1692, when "the Evil Hand" had been found within the walls of Parris's parsonage. Dorcas had been accused before of fortune telling in her home in Beverly, Reverend Hale's home town. Any rumors of "white magic" from months and years past now resurfaced with new import. Had Abigail mentioned Dorcas to Hale at that time? He was the first minister Parris called to his home when Abigail's and Betty's symptoms worsened in February.

Susannah North Martin waited at Ingersoll's Ordinary where she had been brought to await her turn at the meetinghouse. The sixty-seven-year-old widow was not new to witchcraft allegations. Her neighbors in Amesbury and Salisbury had been accusing her of malefic practices for over three decades. One such report came from William Brown who claimed his wife, Elizabeth, had been attacked by Goody Martin's specter who repeatedly stuck her with spectral "nayls & pinns." He swore out a formal complaint, which only exacerbated the problem. His wife fell into "a strange kind of distemper & frensy uncapible of any rasional action." Two doctors verified Brown's assessment of his wife's condition. Other depositions against Susannah Martin were filed by her neighbors accusing her of witchcraft. She had managed to dodge the noose for three decades. Had her luck run out?

Although court documents don't mention the body searches of each witch brought into Ingersoll's Ordinary, it may be assumed that each of the accused were put through the humiliating examination. Several midwives, along with Mrs. Ingersoll appear on documents as performing the unpleasant duty as they searched for witch's marks. Constable Orlando Bagley had brought Martin the twenty miles from Amesbury and dutifully left her to the magistrates.

(Examination of Susannah Martin)

[May 2, 1692]

The Examination of Susannah Martin. 2. May. 1692

As soon as she came into the meeting-house many fell into fits H) Hath this Woman hurt you? *Abig: Williams said it is Goody Martin, she hath hurt me often Others by fits were hindered from speaking. Eliz: Hubbard said she had not hurt her. John Indian said he never saw her Mercy Lewes pointed at her & fell into a fit. Ann Putman threw her Glove in a fit at her H) What do you laught at it? M) Well I may at such folly. H) Is this folly, to see these so hurt? M) I never hurt man, woman or child. *Mercy Lewes cryed out, she hath hurt me a great many times & plucks me down. Then Martin laught againe Mary Walcot said this woman hath hurt her a great many times Susannah Sheldon also accused her of hurting her H) What do you say to this? M) I have no hand in Witchcraft. H) What did you do? Did you consent these should be hurt? M) No never in my life.

H) What ails these people? M) I do not know. H) But what do you think ails them? M) I do not desire to spend my judgment upon it H) Do you think they are Bewitcht? M) No I do not think they are. H) Well tell us your thoughts about them? M) My thoughts are mine own when they are in, but when they are out they are an others H) You said their Master -- Who do you think is their Master? M) If they be dealing in the black art, you may know as well as I. H) What have you done towards the hurt of these? M) I have done nothing H) Why it is you, or your appearance M) I cannot help it That may be your Master that hurt them I desire to lead my life according to the word of God H) Is this according to the word of God? M) If I were such a person I would tell you the Truth H) How comes your appearance just now to hurt these? M) How do I know? H) Are you not willing to tell the Truth? M) I cannot tell: He that appeared in sams shape can appear in any ones shape. H) Do you beleive these afflicted persons do not say true? M) they may lye for ought I know. H) May not you lye? M) I dare not tell a lye if it would save my life H) Then you will not speak the truth will you? M) I have spoken nothing else. I would do them any good. H) I do not think that you have such affections for these whom just now you insinuated had the Devil for their Master *The marshall said she pincht her hands & Eliz: Hubbard was immediately afflicted. Severall of the afflicted cryed out they saw her upon the Beam. H) Pray God discover you if you be guilty. M) Amen, Amen. M) A false tongue will never make a guilty person. *You have been a long time coming to day said Mercy Lewes, you can come fast enough in the night M)No sweet heart -- *And then said Mercy, & all the afflicted beside almost were afflicted John Indian fell into a fit, & cryed it was that woman, she bites, she bites. And then said Martin was biting her lips.   H) Have not you compassion on these afflicted – M) No I have none *They cryed out there was the black man along with her, & Goody Bibber confirmed it Abig: Williams went towards her, but could not come near her. norGoody Bibber tho she had not accused her before: also Mary Walcot could not come near her. John Indian said he would kill her, if he came near her, but he fell down before he could touch her H) What is the reason these cannot come near you? M) I cannot tell it may be the Devil bears me more malice than an other. H) Do you not see God evidently discovering you? M) No, not a bit for that. H) All the congregation besides think so. M) Let them think what they will. H) What is the reason these cannot come to you? M) I do not know but they can if they will or else if you please I will come to them. H) What was that the black man whisperd to you? M) There was none whispered to me.

Samuel Parris is scribe.

Susannah Martin for the first time during the inquisitions turned the tables on the girls. When asked "Do you think they are Bewitcht?" she answered bluntly, "No, I do not think they are."   She then alluded to a fact the magistrates and all the adults of the Village had refused to consider, even when two of the afflicted girls had admitted they were faking their fits and calling out names "for sport."

"If they be dealing in the black art, you may know as well as I," she said. Goody Martin was saying the girls were consorting with the Devil by their ability to see into the Invisible World and view other witches. Perhaps that was why they repelled the Devil's Book—their signatures may have already been there. The girls were not distancing themselves from Satan…they were the instigators alarming the Villagers and inviting the Devil to make a home in Salem Village. It was a dangerous move, and one that fell moot.

Hathorne admonished Martin and told her God would discover her (find her to be a liar). "All the congregation besides think so." With those words, Susannah Martin's fate was sealed.

Sarah Morrell of Beverly was also a Falmouth, Maine refugee. Her father was captured in the Fort Loyal attack and taken to Canada as a hostage. Sarah, her mother, and sister ended up in Beverly. A family that may have been related to them—Robert Morrell family—lived for a time with Thomas Putnam's family in Salem Village. Sarah, or her sister Mary, had been brought into court on charges of fornication the summer of 1691, a reputation that did not bode well for those accused of witchcraft by the Puritan members.

Sarah Morrell's inquest testimony is lost to us, as is another accused the same day, **Lydia Dustin** of Reading, Ma. Lydia was an eighty-year-old widow, older than Rebecca Nurse by a decade. Along with Susannah Morrell, she too had long been accused of witchcraft. Although a member of the Reading Church, she had garnered a dubious fame throughout the town. In 1682, one of her neighbors (in a drunken stupor) threw rocks at her daughter's house while shouting "old-crooked back witch, your mother, you, and all your company of witches!" While ten years passing may have found the assault forgotten, a new accusation from a Reading villager, Mrs.

Mary Marshall, found Lydia Dustin held over in Salem Jail on the accusation of witchcraft.

(Warrant for the apprehension of **Lydia Dustin**, and Officer's Return)

[May 2, 1692]

To the Constable of reading You are in theyr Majestyes Names Required to Apprehend and bring before us Lydah Dasting of Reading Widdow in the County of Middlesex on Munday Next being the Second day of the Month of May Next Ensueing the date hereof, about Eleven of the Clock in the forenoone, att the house of Lev't Nath'll Ingersolls in Salem Village, in Order to hir Examination, relateing to high suspition of severall acts of Witchcraft done or Comitted by hir upon the Bodys of Marÿ Walcott , Ann. putnam , Mercÿ Lewis & Abigall. Williamesall of Salem Village: whereby great hurt [&] da[mbar]age hath bin done to the Bodys of Said persons according to Complaint of Capt Jonathan. Walcott & serg't Thomas putnam in behalfe of theyr Majestys for themselves & severall of theyr Neighbours, and hereof you are nott to fayle att your perrill. date Salem Aprill. 30'th 1692 Per us *John Hathorne
*Jonathan. Corwin { Assis'ts (Reverse)
Pursewence to a warant from yrs honrs baring date the 30 of aprill last for the aprihending and bringing of the person of Lidea Dasting in obediance ther to I have brought the said Lidea Dasting of Redding to the hous of Lu't   Ingersons in   Salem   viledg

dated in #[May: the:2d] Salem viledg the 2'd day of May 1692 Atest. *John Parker of Redding

The court wrapped up for the day, as they were still awaiting the arrival of George Burroughs of Maine. The four prisoners who had been examined—Sarah Morrell, Lydia Dustin, Dorcas Hoar, and Susannah Martin—were kept overnight, possibly at the watch house across from Ingersoll's. They were transported by cart the following morning to Boston Prison, rather than Salem's. The quickness of being arrested, questioned before the magistrates, and sent directly to prison, must have been terrifying. There was no room for pleadings or arguments once the gavel fell.

On the evening of the examinations of the four accused, Elizabeth Hubbard claimed that a little, black-bearded man in dark clothing appeared to her and declared he was George Burroughs. He opened a book and thrust it toward her to sign. She refused to sign it, shuddering at the blood-red names she saw scrawled there. He pinched her and left. It would be his *physical* form that appeared next.

Chapter Twenty-Two

The Witches' Ringleader

The reach of the afflicted girls had many baffled. How could they "cry out" against people they had never met, from towns they had never visited? It was enough to make a believer of anyone. Surely, these afflicted persons must have the gift of second sight—an ability to see things withheld from "normal" people. Yet, even with this belief, the majority of the "inhabitants" did not link the girls themselves to witchcraft. If it wasn't the Devil giving them powers to see into the Invisible World, then it was God using them as instruments to weed out the evil among them. For that reason, the girls were revered and praised. In today's terms, they were Super Stars.

George Burroughs

Reverend George Burroughs had more strikes against him than the other accused witches. He had abandoned Salem Village as their minister years earlier, due to the bickering of the church members and their reluctance to pay him his wages as their reverend. He had incurred the disfavor of the powerful Putnam family, and he was the husband of the late Sarah Ruck Hathorne—the sister-in-law of Judge John Hathorne, presiding judge over the witch trials. Mercy Lewis, one of the afflicted girls' most-vocal accusers, knew him well. Mercy had once lived in his home in Falmouth,

Maine after her own family was slain during an Indian attack.

George Burroughs, around 42-years of age in 1692, was a Harvard educated man who had studied at the prestigious college for a degree in ministry. Two of his classmates were well-known names to the Salem Village debacle: James Bayley, Salem Village's minister before Burroughs; and Samuel Sewall, who would later condemn the "little black minister" for witchcraft.

Burroughs was married three times, in rapid succession. His first wife, Hannah Fisher of Dedham, followed him to Falmouth (now Portland, Maine) after the inhabitants there offered him two hundred acres to be their minister. It was a remote location, sitting hard against the frontier wilderness. He preached there for two years until the village was attacked in 1676 during King Phillips War. Burroughs was hailed a hero for helping to evacuate the women and children to Cushing's Island after so many husbands and fathers were slaughtered. They lived on berries and fish until rescue could come for them.

Burroughs took his wife Hannah, who was pregnant at the time, and their other two children to Salem Village, as had many other war refugees. He had been offered a trial period as acting minister for the village. John Putnam offered them a home while the new parsonage was being built. The accommodations were cramped, and privacy scarce. John Putnam would later relate that Hannah had been "very good and dutiful" but Burroughs was "very sharp" with her. Putnam claimed Burroughs made Hannah sign and seal a statement saying she would never divulge his "secrets." Putnam complained that Burroughs would often involve his family in the minister's marital arguments.

Salem Village offered only heartache for George Burroughs. His wife lost the baby, and died during childbirth. This was the second child to die for the minister. Now faced with the cost of a funeral, he turned to his host, John Putnam to borrow the money, promising to repay it out of his minister's salary. Putnam loaned him the money, but Burroughs (as stated earlier in the book) was unable to pay it. A law suit from Putnam resulted after Burroughs returned to Maine.

In the meantime, Burroughs remained in Salem Village and within a year married the lovely widow of Captain William Hathorne of Salem Town, older brother of Judge John Hathorne. Sarah Ruck Hathorne bore him four more children. When Salem Village lived up to its reputation of slandering and indebting their ministers, Burroughs resigned his post as the Village's voice of spiritual reason, packed up his wife and children, and returned to Falmouth, despite the fact there were threats of Indian attacks. He was brought back to Salem to face Putnam in court. He narrowly missed jail time due to some friend's petitions in his favor. Free from the threat of imprisonment, George Burroughs would never be free from the bad taste he had left in the mouths of the villagers he deserted.

In 1689, Falmouth was once again attacked. Burroughs survived, but his wife did not. Her death was rumored to be from childbirth, not an Indian massacre. He shipped her remains to Salem Town for burial and moved to Wells Maine in 1690. Without delay, Burroughs remarried, this time to a woman named Mary, who gave him a daughter. A vicious attack on York, Maine fueled rumors that Wells might be next. He stuck it out. Burroughs taught school boys, preached on the Sabbath and Lecture Days, helped with military and civic duties, administered to the sick and grieving, and helped build the town. His strength was often reported upon as he felled trees, raised barns, and helped bring in supplies from the harbor.

George Burroughs "super human" strength would come back to haunt the small minister. Despite his stature, many people related stories of his prowess. Captain Simon Willard and Captain William Wormall shared their testimonies during the 1692 witch trials that they had heard stories of Burroughs single-handedly hauling in a heavy barrel of cider or molasses from an unstable canoe. He was accused of lifting a heavy seven-foot barreled musket with only his index finger.

More stories surfaced, about "the pretty little man" who was never single for long. Almost exotic in his looks, with his dark hair and complexion, the short and swarthy minister seemed to hold a fascination for all who met him. Some might say, to his wives' detriment.

Mary Webber, one of Burroughs' Falmouth neighbors during his time there with his second wife Sarah Ruck Hathorne, gave testimony that Sarah was afraid of her husband. According to Webber, Sarah told her that she had seen Burroughs chase something that resembled a white calf down their front stairs. Her husband seemed to have an uncanny ability to always know what she was thinking and saying, even in his absence. One of their maidservants, Hannah Harris, said Burroughs always seemed to know the two women's conversations, even when he wasn't around.

Sarah's brother, Thomas Ruck, recited the time he, Sarah, and George had been picnicking. George had gone off into the bushes to look for strawberries. As soon as he was out of sight, Sarah took the opportunity to tell her brother of her forebodings about her husband. When George returned, he mentioned the conversation and was determined to tell his side of the story. Surprised that Burroughs knew what they had discussed out of his ear shot, Thomas asked him how he knew what was said. Haughtily, Burroughs answered "My god makes known your thoughts unto me."

Burroughs' maidservant, Hannah, did little to help the minister after his arrest. She told all who would listen that she believed the minister hastened her mistress's death by not allowing her to rest after childbirth, but insisted that she stand at the door while he accosted her. She continued to say that her master had only baptized one of his nine children, and neglected the customary home prayers. She had admonished Sarah to send a letter to her father in Salem Town, telling of the wrongs of her husband, but Sarah was afraid to. Hannah sent the letter instead.

On May 2, 1892, George Burroughs was at dinner in his home with his wife Mary, and the children. A knock came at the door, and before any of them knew what was happening, Marshal Jonathan Partridge and some guards stormed into the home and arrested Burroughs. Partridge had complained about the length of the trip to escort Burroughs from Wells, Maine to Salem Town. He was ignored and the journey was begun. Gossip rumored that a terrible tempest had ensued to thwart Burroughs' extradition. Thunder roared and lightening flashed, as tree limbs thrashed and broke apart.

The party endured, and Burroughs was brought to Thomas Beadle's tavern in Salem Town. He was kept in a private room upstairs, away from the other prisoners. Some men dropped by to question Burroughs, including Captain Daniel King, a military leader who knew Burroughs from the frontier wars in Maine. King believed in the minister, saying "I believe he is a child of God, a choice child of God," and he believed God would prove Burroughs' innocence. Others, including, Eleazar Keyser, the brother of a Salem girl who had long been "distracted," said he believed Burroughs was the "ringleader" of all the witches.

Keyser overcame his fear and did visit Burroughs as he sat in Beadle's locked room. Burroughs, disgusted at his plight, and not wanting to be viewed as a local curiosity, refused to talk to the man, staring at him silently instead. Keyser's fears got the best of him and left. He said later that night at his home, he saw a dozen quivering globs of light, like jellyfish, shooting about in the dark. They disappeared and a strange glow appeared in the dark chimney of the room. Peering up into it, he claimed to see a ball of light shimmering. The maid backed up his story, saying she saw it too. But Keyser's wife said she saw nothing.

Eleazar Keyser's Deposition Against Burroughs

I did afterwards forbeare The same Evening after these words being alone in one Roome of my house and noe candle or light being in the s'd Roome the same afternoone I haveing Occation to be at the s'd Beadles house and [being] in the Chamber where mr George Burroughs Keept I observed that s'd Burroughs did steadfastly fix [his] eys upon mee, the same Evening being in my own house, in a Roome without any Light I did see very strange things appeare in the Chimney. I suppose a dozen of them. w'ch seemed to mee to be something like Jelly that used to be in the water and quaver with a strainge Motion, and then quickly diappeared soone after which I did see a light up in the chimney aboute the bigness of my hand some thing above the bar w'ch quivered & shaked. and seemed to have a Motion upward upon Which I called the Mayd, and she looking up into the Chimney saw the same, and my wife looking up could not see any thing, soe I did and doe very Certainly Concider it was some diabolicall apperition

Due to the gravity of a case instigated against a minister, other magistrates were brought to Salem Village to assist Hathorne and Corwin. Seated beside the two men at the meetinghouse table were William Stoughton and Samuel Sewall. Several depositions against the minister had been procured, along with a letter from Thomas Putnam to the magistrates telling of his fears on behalf of his beleaguered daughter Ann Putnam Jr., that there were disturbing events happening—"a wheel within wheel," hinting that a minister of God was within the grasp of the Devil.

Samuel Sewall   William Stoughton

The crowds were out in force to witness this former minister's examination, a man who had thumbed his nose at their torments and moved away. What did Judge Hathorne think of this man before him? Here was a man that both Susanna Sheldon and Ann Putnam had sworn to seeing the specters of his dead wives standing before them, accusing Burroughs of murdering them. If Judge Hathorne believed the two girls (despite the contradictions in their testimonies—Sheldon said the dead wives said Burroughs had choked and smothered them, while Abigail claimed they said he had stabbed and strangled them—then he believed Burroughs was guilty of killing his former sister-in-law.

For the man with renowned strength, who had taken on Indians, frontier hardships, and acted as the savior of a beleaguered town, it would take only a handful of young women to bring him to his knees.

THE LEGEND OF SALEM:
"THE REV. GEORGE BURROUGHS WAS ACCUSED OF WITCHCRAFT ON THE EVIDENCE OF FEATS OF STRENGTH, TRIED, HUNG, AND BURIED BENEATH THE GALLOWS."

Illustration of George Burroughs on Trial for witchcraft.

(Examination of George Burroughs)

[May 9, 1692]

The Examination of Geo: Burrough 9.May.1692
Before   Wm. Stoughton
Honoured John Hallum (Hathorne?)
Sam: Sewall Esqrs
Jonath: Corwin

Being ask'd w[hether] he partook of the Lords supper, he being (as he said) in full communion at Roxbury. He answered it was so long since he could not tell: yet he owned he was at meeting one Sab: at Boston part of the day, & the other at Charlstown part of a Sab: when that sacrament happened to be at both, yet did not partake of either. He denied that his house at Casko was haunted. Yet he owned there were Toads. He denied that he made his wife swear, that she should not write to her Father Ruck without his approbation of her letter to her Father: He owned that none of his children, but the Eldest was Baptised.
*The abovesd was in private none of the Bewitched being present
At his entry into the Room, many (if not all of the Bewitched) were grievously tortured.
Sus: sheldon testifyed that Burroughs two wives appeared in their winding sheets, & said that man killed them [words rubbed out] He was bid to look upon sus: sheldon. He looked back & knockt down all (or more) of the afflicted, wo stood behind him.

Sus: [one line too faint] The sholdiers 2. Mercy Lewis deposition going to be read & he lookt upon her & she fell into a dreadfull & tedious fit

Mary Walcott {testimony going to be read

1. Elis: Hubbard {& they all fell into fits Susan Sheldon
2. Susan Sheldon {affirmed each of them that Ann Putnam, junior {he brought the Book & [?] {have them write. Being askd w[hat] he thought of these things. He answered that it was an amazing & humbling Providence, but he understood nothing of it He said (some of you may observe, that) when They begin [to] name my name they cannot name it.

Ann Putnam, junior {testified that his 2 wives Susan: Sheldon {& 2 Children did accuse him

*The Bewitched were so tortured that Authority Ordered them to be taken away Some of them

Sarah Bibber testified that he had hurt her tho She had not seen him personally before as she knew

Abig: Hobbs Deliberance Hobbs {testimony read Elizer Keiser

Capt. Willard {testimoy about his great Jno. Brown {strength & the Gun. Jno. Wheldon

Capt. Putnam testified about the Gun.

Capt Wormwood testifyed about the Gun & the Mallossoes

He denied that about the Mallossoes About the Gun he said he took it before the lock & rested it upon his breast

John Brown test testifyed about a b[arre]ll [of] Cyder He denied that his family was affrighted by a white calf in his house.

Capt Putman testifyed that he made his wife enter into a covenant

11.May.1692

Abig: Hobbs in prison affirmed that Geo: Burroughs in his Shape appeared to her, & urged [her to set] hand to the Book, which she did; & after --wards in his own person he acknowledged to her, that he had made her set her hand to the Book.

George Burroughs was held over for trial, as were other defendants brought in that day under arrest for witchcraft. Their records did not survive. Ann Sears; Lydia Dustin's daughter, Sarah; and Bethia Carter were held over for trial. Constable Bock reported that all were in jail. However, twenty-one-year-old Bethia Carter Jr. was still free. She may have been questioned and released. That same day, Sarah Churchill, who had once been one of the afflicted, had accused her master George Jacob's Sr. of hurting her. He had called her a "Bitch Witch," and according to Mary Warren had tried to kill Sarah by leaning on her with his two canes as she convulsed. Sarah, after being interrogated, changed her story and confessed to witchcraft in the hopes of seeing leniency like Mary Warren before her. It didn't work. The magistrates were now leery of anyone changing their stories, especially with the nervous afflicted victims claiming she was free of pain only because she had joined the Devil.

That night at Ingersoll's, George Jacob's specter attacked Mercy Lewis, John Willard's shape came after Susanna Sheldon, and Elizabeth Coleson (Lydia Dustin's granddaughter) offered the afflicted a black coin if they would touch "the book." The specters flew, the prisoners languished away from the May sunlight in their jail rooms, as the afflicted of Salem Village turned their eyes to the Invisible World to see whom they would pluck from it next.

Chapter Twenty-Three

Family Against Family

On May 10, 1692, the latest prisoners were taken to Boston Prison via Nathaniel Ingersoll's rented cart. Once again, the ferry crossed from familiar farmland into a bustling harbor city with fine brick homes and ladies in fancy apparel. The bound hands of the accused would have caused all to stop and stare as the cart made its way to the austere stone prison. "Witches!" some may have whispered in fear, as the wooden wheels creaked past them. The news of Salem Village and the outbreak of evil flooding into its meetinghouse was well-known.

Also in Boston, was Lady Phips, eagerly awaiting the return of her husband, Sir William Phips, England's newly-appointed Governor of Massachusetts. She had held vigil while he was away these many months, campaigning for a new charter along with Increase Mather. Lady Phips, before marrying William, was the widow of Captain Roger Spencer and the daughter of John Hull. She counted Samuel Sewall (one of the witch trial magistrates) as a relative. She was used to finery and boasted a beautiful brick home in one of Boston's elite neighborhoods. Along with all of the Massachusetts Bay Colony, she watched the waters off Boston harbor for any sight of the *Nonsuch* rounding the rocks.

Back in Salem Town, the magistrates continued on with the arrests of yet more accused witches. Constable John Putnam was ordered to arrest John Willard (whose specter had just appeared again to Susanna Sheldon and threatened her if she testified against him). Putnam dutifully arrived at Willard's home in Boxford to take him in, but the man had fled. Based on Sarah Churchill's testimony of spectral abuse, an arrest warrant was also sworn out for George Jacobs Sr. and his granddaughter Margaret. They were brought to Thomas Beadle's tavern in Salem Town to allow the magistrates some respite from traveling to the Village. John Willard's arrest warrant also stated he was to be brought to Beadle's, a block east of the Salem Common. And so, George Jacobs Sr., leaning on his two walking sticks, went through an all-too familiar inquest.

George Jacobs Sr.

Trial of George Jacobs Sr. Photo courtesy of the Peabody Essex Museum.

(Examination of **George Jacobs, Sr.**)

[May 10, 1692]

The Examination of Geo: Jacobs Sen'r 10 May. 1692

H) Here are them that accuse you of acts of witchcraft J) Well, let us hear who are they, and what are they. Abigail Williams – Jacobs laught. J) Because I am falsely accused. Your worships all of you do you think this is true? H) Nay, what do you think? J) I never did it. H) who did it? J) Dont ask me. H) Why should we not ask you? H) Sarah Churchwell accuseth you, there she is. J) I am as innocent as the Child born to night, I have lived. 33. years here in Salem. What then? If you can prove that I am guilty, I will lye under it, Sarah Churchwell said last night I was afflicted at Deacon Ingersolls , and Mary Walcot said it was a man with 2 staves, it was my master. Pray do not accuse me, I am as clear as your worships; you must do right judgments. H) What book did he bring youSarah? S) The same that the other woman brought. J) The Devill can go in any shape. H) Did he not [be] appear on the other side of the river and hurt you, did not you see him. S) Yes he did. H) Look there, she accuseth you to your face, she chargeth you that you hurt her twise. Is it not true? J) What would you have me say? I never wronged no man in word nor deed. H) Here are 3 evidences. J) You tax me for a wizard, you may as well tax me for a buzard I have done no harm. H) Is it no harm to afflict these? J) I never did it. H) But how comes it to be in your appearance? J) The Devil can taken any likeness. H) Not without their consent. J) Please your worship it is untrue, I never showed the book, I am as silly about these things as the child born last night.

H) That is your Saying, you argue you have lived so long, but what then Cain might live long before he killed Abel, and you might live long before the Devill had so prevailed on you. J) Christ hath suffered 3 times for me. H) What three times. J) He suffered the Crosse & gall C) You had as good confesse (said Sarah Churchwell) if you are guilty. J) Have you heard that I have any witchcraft? C) I know you lived a wicked life. J) Let her make it out. C) Doth he ever pray in his family? Not unless by himself. Why do you not pray in your family? J) I cannot read. C) Well but you may pray for all that. Can you say the Lords prayer? Let us hear you? *He mist in severall parts of it, and could not repeat it right after Many Trialls. Sarah Churchwell) when you wrote in the book you was showed your masters name you said. Yes Sir. J) If she say so, if you do not know it, what will you say? H) But she saw you, or your likeness tempt her to write. J) one in my likeness, the Devil may present my likeness. H) Were you not frighted Sarah Churchwell, when the representation of your master came to you? C) Yes. J) Well: burn me, or hang me, I will stand in the truth of Christ, I know nothing of it. H) Do you know nothing of getting your son George and his daughter Margaret to signe? J) No nothing at all.

George Jacobs Sr. was held over at Beadle's Tavern for a second day of examination.

The 2nd Examination of said George Jacobs

[May 11, 1692]

The bewitched fell into most grevious fits and screhings when he came in. H) Is this the man that hurts you? *Abig

Williams cryed out this is the man and fell into a violent fit. Ann Putman said this is the man, and he hurts her, and brings the book to her, and would have her write in the book, and she should be as well as his Grand daughter. H) Mercy Lewis is this the man? L) This is the man (after much interruption by fits) he almost kills me.* Eliz: Hubbard said the man never hurt her till to day he came upon the Table. H) Mary Walcot is this the man? *After much interruption by fits she said this is the man, he used to come with two staves and beat her with one of them. H) What do you say, are you not a witch? J) No I know it not, if I were to dye presently. *Mercy Lewes went to come near him but fell into great fits. Mercy Lewes testimony read. H) What do you say to this? J) Why it is false, I know not of it, any more than the child that was born to night. *Ann Putman said yes, you told me so, that you had been so this: 40 years. Ann Putman and Abigail Williams had each of them a pin stuck in their hands, and they said it was this old Jacobs . Abigail WilliamsTestimony read. H) Are not you the man that made disturbance

(Reverse) at a Lecture in Salem? J) No great disturbance. Do you think I use witchcraft? H) Yes indeed J) No I use none of them.

During a lull in the proceedings, Sarah Churchill left the meetinghouse in an agitated state. Sarah Ingersoll (daughter of Nathaniel Ingersoll) had been in attendance at the trial. She lived around the corner from Beadle's Tavern. With her was George Jacob's daughter. They confronted Sarah, who they could see was close to hysterics. Sarah broke down and said she had been lying about it all, and others with her. There had not been a Devil's Book. When Goody Ingersoll told her that she had believed her when she confessed of witchcraft and signing the book, Sarah wailed "No, no, no! I never did." The magistrates had threatened to imprison her along with Burroughs if she did not confess, she wailed. She had told the original story for such a long time, and had been afraid to admit now it had all been a lie. She cried that they wanted to believe the worst. If she told Reverend Noyes only once that she put her hand to the Devil's Book, he would believe her, but if she told him the truth a hundred times, he would not.

As Susanna Sheldon made her way to court for day two of Jacobs's questioning, she claimed the specters of John Willard and an old man followed her, skimming over the river on something that resembled a dish. The physical form of John Willard had yet to be found. His specter, however was very active, tormenting Elizabeth Hubbard as well.

Sarah Osbourne Dies in Prison

As George Jacobs examinations were being held, jailer John Arnold entered the Boston Prison room and noted that Sarah Osborne had died. She had been imprisoned for nine weeks and two days. Sarah had been dragged from her bed where she had been ill for some weeks for her initial inquisition back in February. The unhealthy conditions and poor food had finally taken their toll on her frail body. It was reported on the jail bill that she still owed £1-3-0 for her room and board at the prison. As the other prisoners looked on in horror and defeat, the woman's limp body was carried away. The first arrow the girls had fired off three months earlier had found their mark. A "witch" was dead.

Margaret Jacobs, George Jacob Sr. granddaughter, was led in next. Oddly, her father, George Jacobs Jr. had not been arrested. George Sr. had been taken to the next room at Beadle's, his walking sticks still supporting his small frame.

For Margaret Jacobs, the frightening theatrics of the afflicted girls as she entered the meetinghouse were overwhelming. They were thrashing about and pointing at her. Her family had warned her that this might happen and urged her not to confess to witchcraft. The girls cried out that because she had recovered from her spectral torments, she must have signed the Devil's Book and was now free of his assaults. On and on it went, a swirling haze of threats and screaming accusations. The magistrates hammered at her that she must be causing the poor girls' fits. She would state later that all she recalled of the chaos was the threat of imprisonment and hanging if she did not confess. Broken down and in tears she confessed with a lie, but she did so to save her life.

Tituba had been the first to confess, believing that by so doing, she would not hang. This was erroneous. The promise of salvation to the confessors was not of this physical realm, but of the spiritual one. It was their *soul* that may be saved by renouncing the Devil and admitting to an alliance with him. So many took it to mean they would be spared execution.

Margaret Jacobs confession bundled in accusations against her grandfather George Jacobs Sr., George Burroughs, John Willard and a new name—Salem inhabitant Alice Parker. One of those in attendance at Margaret's examination was Joseph Flint. He secretly slipped to the next room to tell George Sr. that his granddaughter had just confessed to witchcraft. "If Margaret were innocent, and yet confessed, she would be an accessory to her own death," Jacobs muttered brokenly. It would not be long before more of the Jacobs' family would be arrested and brought in.

John Willard, still on the run, was actively sending his specter to assault other afflicted girls. On the day of Margaret Jacobs confession, his shape throttled Mercy Lewis. George Jacobs Sr.'s spirit knocked sixteen-year-old John DeRich into the river with one of his walking sticks. DeRich said he would have drowned had not a passing neighbor rescued him.

In Salem Jail, Margaret Jacobs, facing the cold reality of her imprisonment, was doubled over with fear that the Devil would come and take her for telling "such horrid lies." Abigail Hobbs was not helping her anxious state as she declared aloud that the Devil was indeed inside the jail room and was trying to force her to sign his book.

Magistrates Hathorne and Corwin visited the Salem Jail to question again the two confessors: Mary Warren (the Proctor's maid), and Abigail Hobbs. They found Hobbs more reluctant to talk, answering most questions with "I don't know." Her only admission at that time was she had been a witch for six years and had signed two covenants with the Devil: one for a four-year-term, and one for two years. They turned their attention to Mary Warren in hopes of better information. They got more than they bargained for, including the names of new witches tossed in as a bonus.

(Examination of Mary Warren)

[May 12, 1692]

Mary Warrens Examination May. 12'th 1692

Q. Whether you did nott know that itt was the Devill's book when you Sighned? A I did nott know itt then but I know itt now, to be Sure itt was the Devills book; in the first place to be sure I did sett my hand to the Devills book; I have considered of itt, Since you were here last, & itt was the Devills book, that my Master Procter brought to me, & he Tould me if I would Sett my hand to that book I should be well; & I did Sett my hand to itt, butt that w'ch I did itt was done w'th my finger, he brought the Book & he Tould me if I would Take the book & Touch itt that I should be well & I thought then that itt was the Devill's book. Q. Was there nott your consent to hurt the Children, when they were hurt? A. Noe Sir, but when I was Afflicted my master Procter was in the Roome & said if ye are Afflicted I don't think that's ye & you and all: I said master, w't make you Say soe he Answered because you goe to bring out Innocent persones. I Tould him that that could nott bee & Whether the Devill Took advantage att that I know not to Afflict them and one Night Talking about them I said I did nott care though ye were Tormented if ye charged mee. Q. Did you ever See any poppetts? An. yes once I saw one made of cloth in mistris Procters hand. Q. whoe was itt like or w'ch of the Children was itt for? An. I cannot Tell, whether for Ann. Putnam or Abigail Williams, for one of them itt was I am Sure, itt was in my mistris's hand. Q. what did you stick into that poppitt? An. I did stick in a pin about the Neck of itt as itt was in Procters hand. Q. how many more did you See afterwards? An. I doe nott remember that ever I saw any more. yes I remember one and that Goody Parker brought a poppitt unto me of Mercy. Lewiss & she gave me a needle & I stook itt some where about the wasts & she appeared once more to me in the prison, & She Said to me what are you gott here? & she tould me that she was Comeing here hirselfe. I had another person that appeared to mee, itt was Goody. Pudeator & Said she was Sorry to Se me there, itt was in apparition & she brought me a poppitt, itt was like to Mary. Walcott & itt was a peice of Stick that she brought me to Stick into itt & Somewhare about hir armes I stuck itt in. Q. where did she bring itt to you? An. up att Procters. Goody Parker Tould me she had bin a Witch these. 12. years & more; & Pudeator tould me that she had done damage, & Tould me that she had hurt James Coyes Child Takeing itt out of the mothers hand. A. Whoe brought the last To you? -- An. my mistris & when she brought itt, she brought itt, in hir owne person & hir husband w'th his owne hands brought me the book to Sighne, & he brought mee an Image w'ch looked yellow & I beleive itt was for Abigall Williams being like hir & I putt a thing like a thorne into itt, this was done by his bodily person after I had Sighned the night after I had Sighned the book: While she was thus Confessiong Parker appeared & bitt her Extreamly on hir armes as she affirmed unto us. Q. Whoe have you Sene more? An. Nurss & Cloys and Good's Child after I had Sighned. Q. What Sayd they to you? An. They Sayd that I should never Tell of them Nor anything about them & I have seen Goody Good hirself. Q. was that True of Giles Cory that you Saw him & that he Afflicted you the other day? An. yes I have Sene him often & he hurts me very much & Goody Olliver hath appeared to me & Afflicted me & brought the Book to Tempt mee, & I have Seen Goody. Cory. the first night I was Taken, I saw as I thought the Apparition of Goody Cory & Catched att itt as I thought & Caught my master in my lap tho I did nott See my master in that place att that Time, upon W'ch my master Said itt is noe body but I itt is my shaddow that you see, butt my master was nott befor mee as I Could descerne, but Catching att the Apparition that Looked like Goody Cory I Caught hold of my master & pulled him downe into my Lap; upon W'ch he Said I see ther is noe heed to any of your Talkings, for you are all possest With the Devill for itt is nothing butt my shape. I have Sene Goody Cory att my masters house in person, and she Tould mee that I should be Condemned for a Witch as well as she hirself, itt was att my masters house, & she Said that the Children Would cry out & bring out all. Q. was this before you had Signned? An. yes, before I had any fitts. Q. Now tell the truth about the Moutebank what Writeing was that? An. I don't know I asked hir what itt was about

(On Reverse) but she would nott tell mee Saying She had promised nott to Lett any body See itt. Q. well, but Whoe did you See more? An. I don't Know any more. Q. how long hath your Mast'r & Mistris bin Witches? An. I don't know, they never Tould me. Q. what likeness or appearance have you had to bew'ch you? An. they never gave me any thing. While I was reading this over upon the Comeing in of mr. Higginson & mr Hale as soon as I read the Name Parker, She Imediately fell into dreadfull fitts as she affirmed after his fit was over by the appearance of Goody Parker: & mr Hathorne presently but nameing Goody Pudeator & Tormented hir very much. and Goody Parker in the time of hir Examination in one ofWarrens fitts Tould this Examinant that she had bewitched the Examinants Sister & was the Cause of hir dumbness as alsoe that she had lately killed a man aboard a vessell & Tould me that his name was Michaell Chapleman aboard the vessell in the harbour after they Ware Come to Anchor & that he dyed with a paine in his Side & that she had done itt by strikeing Something into his Side & that she had strook this Examinants Sister dumb that she should never speak more. and Goody Pudeater att the same Tyme appeared & Tould this Examinant that She had throwne Jno Turner off of a chery Tree & almost Killed him & Goody Parker s'd that she had Cast away Capt Prices Ketch, Thomas Westgate master, & Venus Colefox in itt & presently Tould hir that Jno Lapthorne was lost in itt and that they Were foundred in the Sea and she Saith that Goody Pudeator Tould hir that she went up to mr Corwins house to bewitch his mare that he should nott goe up to the farmes to Examine the Witches, alsoe mr Burroughs appearing att the Same Tyme and Afflicting hir Tould hir that he went to Tye mr Hathornes horses leggs when he went last to Boston & That he Tryed to bewitch him tho he Could nott his horse: Goody Pudeator tld hir that she Killed hir husband by giving him Something whereby he fell Sick and dyed, itt was she Tould hir about .7. or 8. years Since. and Goody Parker Tould hir that she was Instrumentall to drowne Orn's Son in the harbor. also she s'd she did bewitch Jno Searle's boy to death as his master was Carrying him out to Sea soe that he was forced to bring him back againe: alsoe Burroughs Tould hir that he Killed his Wife off of Cape=Ann. Parker tould hir allsoe that Margarett Jacobs was a wittness against hir and did charge hir yesterday upon hir (that is Jacobs's) examinatio'n.

In one interview, Mary Warren's list of witches ran like a Who's Who in the Invisible World. Adding the names of Alice Parker and Ann Pudeator proved Mary was far from being done with her role as one of the accusers. She claimed that when she was living with the Proctors, poppets in the likeness of Abigail Williams and Ann Putnam were held out to her by her mistress Elizabeth Proctor where she was told to stab them in the neck with a pin. Even John Proctor concocted some yellow image in the likeness of Abigail Williams as they conjured up their evil. Without a doubt, Mary Warren had just signed the Proctors' death sentences.

Chapter Twenty-Four

The Charter Comes Home

The Devil's machinations were not always ones that could be labeled and tagged. So many of the strange afflictions befalling villagers defied explanation. How could they be anything but a result of the "Evil Hand" visiting them? That hand had pushed the pieces about its chessboard like one would direct players upon a stage. All had played their parts with more alacrity than "Old Nick" could have wished for.

None of the suspicious maladies befalling the victims visited by witchcraft could compare with the mysterious afflictions of the Wilkins family. And it would be the missing John Willard who would pray the price.

John Willard

John Willard was a young man in his twenties who was, once again, linked to the formidable Putnam family. He had worked as a hired hand on Thomas Putnam Jr.'s farm. When Thomas was away for extended periods of time, John was asked to keep an eye on Ann Putnam Sr. and the children. Ann had just given birth and was praying the child would reach adulthood, after losing so many others. It was not to be. The infant did not see its first birthday.

For some reason, the Putnams, including young Ann Jr., blamed John for her death.

John went on to marry the granddaughter of Bray Wilkins, a Salem Village farmer with a Hill and Pond named after him. Will's Hill and Wilkins Pond sat at the northwest corner of Salem Village, not far from the Boxford border, where John Willard lived. In 1692, Willard was hired to be the constable in Boxford and tasked with bringing in accused witches of that area. Perhaps it was his youth, or his morals, but he could not continue shackling and jailing his neighbors. He gave up his post. This did not set well with many who saw this as a suspicious act for someone who should be eager to rid the community of witches.

It was at this time that Ann Putnam Jr. began accusing him of witchcraft. The accusation troubled him so much that John Willard rode to his grandfather-in-law Bray Wilkins home and asked the older man to pray with him. Bray, oddly, refused, claiming a previous engagement.

On May 4, 1692, as the witchcraft arrests reached a fever pitch, John Willard arrived at a Boston dinner party Bray Wilkins was attending. John had asked his wife's Uncle, Henry Wilkins Sr. to accompany him, which he did. Sometime during the dinner, Bray Wilkins felt suddenly ill and went into a different room where he was overcome. He claimed he could not eat or urinate, and he felt "like a man on a Rack." Due to "a look" John had given him during the party, Bray believed "Willard had done me wrong." Willard left the party alone. Immediately upon his departure, Henry Wilkin's son Daniel blurted out "Willard ought to be hanged!" Henry was shocked at his son's outburst.

Bray Wilkins consulted a woman healer while in Boston, complaining of inexplicable pain and the inability to urinate. The woman asked "whether those evil persons" being accused of witchcraft in Salem Village had perhaps "done him damage." Bray had plenty of time to mull over the healer's dire statement as he made the long, thirty-mile trip from Boston to his home at Will's Hill.

Upon his arrival home, Bray was distressed to see that his grandson, seventeen-year-old Daniel (the very one who had blurted out that Willard "ought to be hanged!") was gravely ill. No one could decipher what was causing the young man's afflictions. His symptoms grew worse. By May 16, 1692, his family and neighbors were gathered in his room, beside themselves as they watched Daniel struggling for breath. Mercy Lewis and Mary Walcott were in the room and announced that they saw John Willard's specter choke the young man while the shape of Goody Buckley pressed down upon his chest. They claimed the specters said the boy would be dead within three hours-time, as they continued their assault on the suffering youth.

Henry and Benjamin Wilkins were also in the room. Henry watched as his son grappled with death, as the afflicted girls cried out that witches had set upon him. The men saw nothing but the dying young man. Neighbor Thomas Flint also said he saw no specters. It was too late to save him. Daniel Wilkins died that night.

A posse of men were rounded up to find John Willard who had gone into hiding. Six of the ten henchmen were Putnams. They found him tilling one of his meadows in Lancaster, and brought him in. They shackled him in the watch house across from Ingersoll's Ordinary, mainly due to the outcry of Ann Putnam Jr. and other of the girls who went into hysterics when Willard rode into town behind one of the men.

Constable John Putnam ordered twelve men to examine the body of newly-deceased Daniel Wilkins. What they found was staggering. The boy's back was covered with punctures as though he had been "pricked with an instrument about the bigness of a small awl." His throat was bruised as though he had been strangled. They turned him over and blood spurted from his mouth and nose. The men ruled out poison as there was no vomit, usually indicating poisoning of some kind. They ruled Daniel Wilkins had died "an unnatural death by some cruel hands of witchcraft or diabolical act." Things did not look good for John Willard.

(Warrant No. 2 for the apprehension of John Willard, and Officer's Return)

[May 15, 1692]

To the Marshall of the County of Essex or to the Constables in Salem or any other Marshal or Marshalls Constable or Constables within this theire Majest's Colony or Terretory of the Massachusetts in New England --

You are in theire Majest's names hereby required to Apprehend John Willard of Salem Village husbandman, if he may be found in your precints who stands charged with sundry acts of Witchcraft by him donne or Committed on the Bodys of Bray Wilkins. and Daniell Wilkins the son of Henery Wilkins both of Salem Village and others -- according to Complaint made before us by Thomas fuller Jun'r and Benj'n Wilkins sen'r both of Salem Village afores'd Yeomen; who being found You are to Convey from Town to

Towne from Constable to Constable, untill he be Brought before us or such as may be in Authority There, in Salem and hereof You are not to faile Dated Salem May the 15'th 1692
per us *John Hathorne] Assist's
*Jonathan. Corwin]

To be prosecuted according to the direction of Constable John Putnam of Salem Village who goes with the Same.]

(Reverse) I have apprehended John Wilard of Salam Veleg according to the tener of this Warrant and brought him before your Worsheps Date 18 may 1692 by me *John Putnam Constoble of Salam

On May 18, 1692, John Willard was led into the Salem Village meetinghouse for his belated inquisition. The fact that he had fled from the magistrates and caused two warrants to be made out for his arrest did not help with his cry of innocence. His was not the only examination to be held that day, but it was the longest and most-anticipated.

(Examination of John Willard)

[May 18, 1602]

The Examination of John Willard .18. May 1692
The afflicted in most miserable fits upon his this Examinants drawing near
After several of them were recovered, he lookt upon them, & they again fell into fits, whilst the warrant & returne was reading.

H) Here is a returne of the Warrant that you were fled from Authority that is an acknowledgment of guilt, but yet notwithstanding we require you to confess the truth in this matter.

W) I shall, as I hope, I shall be assisted by the Lord of Heaven, & for my going away I was affrighted, & I thought by my withdrawing it might be better, I fear not but the Lord in his due time will make me as white as snow.

H) What do you say? Why do you hurt these? It is you, or your appearance.

W) I know nothing of appearance.

H) Is this the man?

*Several of the afflicted said yes.

H) They charge you, it is you or your appearance.

W) I know nothing of appearance, & the God of Heaven will clear me.

H) They charge you, not only with this, but with dreadfull murders, & I doubt not if you be guilty, God will not want evidence.

*Eliz: Hubbard testifyed that he afflicted her, & then he lookt upon her & she fell into a fit.

Mercy Lewes testimony read.

H) If you desire mercy from God, then you must confesse & give Glory to God.

W) S'r as to sins I am guilty of, if the minister asks me I am ready to confesse

H) If you have revolted from God you are a dreadful sinner.

*Mary Warren cryed out, oh he bites me

Ann Putnam cryed out much of him

H) Open your mouth, don't bite your lips.

W) I will stand with my mouth open, or I will keep it shut: I will stand any how, if you will tell me how.

*Ann Putnams evidence read

H) Do you hear this evidence read?

W) Yes I do hear it.

*Susan: Sheldons testimony read

H) What do you say to this murdering & Bewitching your relations?

W) One would think (said he) that no creature except they belong to hell from their Cradle would be guilty of such things.

H) You say, you will bewitch your Grandfather because he prays that the Kingdom of Sathan may be thrown down

*The examinant began a large oration

H) We do not send for you to Preach.

*Ben: Wilkins testifyed for all his natural affections he abused his wife much & broke sticks about her in beating of her

H) You had need to boast of your good affections

W) There are a great many lyes told, I could desire my wife might be called

*Peter Prescot testifyed that he with his own mouth told him of beating his wife.

H) It seems very much one of your confidence & ability to speak, should be no more courageous than to run away: by your running away you tell all that you are afraid

*The examinant called upon Aaron Wey & urged him to speak if he knew anything against him

Aaron Wey if I must speak I will, I can say you have been very cruel to poor creatures.

H) Let some persons goe to him

*Ann Putnam said she would go.

He said let not that person but another come.

John Indian cryed out Oh! he cuts me.

Susan: Sheldon said there is the black man whispering in his ear, & he should not confess

H) What do you say to this?

W) S'r, I heard nothing, nor see nothing.

*Susan: Sheldon tryed to come near him but fell down immediately, & he took hold of her hand with a great deal of do, but she continued in her fit crying out, O John Willard , John Willard & #[the ex]

H) What was the reason you could not come near him?

S) The black man stood between us.

W) They cannot come near any that are accused.

H) Why do you say they could not come near any that were accused: You know Nehemiah Abbet [Abbot] they could talk with him.

*Mary Warren in a great fit carried to him & he clasping his hand upon her arm was well presently.

Why said he [Willard] was it not before so with Susannah Sheldon?

Because said she [Sheldon] the standers by you did not Clasp your hand before.

The like said the Constable and others.

They all or most testifyed that the dead those that he had murdered were now about him.

H) Do you think these are Bewitcht?

W) Yes, I verily believe it.

H) Well others they have accused it is found true on & why should it be false in you?

*Sus. Sheldon & Mary Warren testify that now h[torn] appearance come from his body & afflicts them.

H) What do you think of this? How comes this to pass?

W) It is not from me. I know nothing of it

H) You have taxt your self wonderfully, it may be you do not think of it.

W) How so?

W) You cryed up your tender affections and here round about they testify your cruelty to man & beast, & by your flight you have given great advantage to the Law, things will bear hard upon you, if you can therefore find in your heart to repent it is possible you may obtain mercy & therefore bethink your self

W) S'r I cannot confess that I do not know

Well but if these things are true Heaven & Earth will rise H) up against you.

W) I am as innocent as the child that is now to be born.

H) Can you pray the Lords prayer?

W) Yes.

H) Well let us hear you.

1. *He stumbled at the threshold (that is the beginning) & said Maker of Heaven & Earth.
2. He began again & mist It is a strange thing, I can say it at another time. I think I am bewitcht as well as they & laught
3. Again he began & said trespass against & mist us.
4. He began again, & cryed being puzled Well this is a strange thing
   W) I cannot say it
   *He begun again & could not say it
   W) Well it is these wicked ones that do so overcome me
   *Josh: Rea Sen'r gave in testimony that last night he said he hoped he should confess tho he had a hard heart, but, but he hoped he should confess.

H) Well say w't you will confess.

W) I am as innocent as the child unborn.

H) Do not you see God will not suffer you to pray to him, are not you sensible of it?

W) Why it is a strange thing.

H) No it is no strange that God will not suffer a wizard to pray to him. There is also the jury of inquest for murder that will bear hard against you. Therefore confess. Have you never wisht harm to your Neighbours?

W) Never since I had a being.

H) Well confess & give glory to God. Take counsell.

W) I desire to hearken to all good counsell. If it was the last time I was to speak I am innocent.

*This is a true account of the Examination of John Willard without wrong to any party according to my original from Characters at the moments thereof
Witness my hand *Sam: Parris

John Willard was held over for trial on the grounds of witchcraft for torturing Mercy Lewis, Ann Putnam Sr. and Jr., Susanna Sheldon, Abigail Williams, Mary Walcott, and

Elizabeth Hubbard. The death of Daniel Wilkins had not been formally laid at his feet. Meanwhile, Bray Wilkins had suddenly found relief from a blocked bladder. The instant John Willard was shackled, Bray received so much relief of his two-week malady, that it was hard to stop using the privy.

Over at Ingersoll's Ordinary, the place was bursting with accused witches awaiting their turn at questioning. Marshal George Herrick gratefully relinquished his charge of Rebecca Jacobs, Sarah Buckley, Mary Witheridge, Elizabeth Hart, and Thomas Farrar Sr.

Elizabeth Hart was led into the meetinghouse. An elderly woman from Lynn, Massachusetts, she confronted Ann Putnam Jr.'s accusations against her. Ann admitted that she had not recognized Hart at first.

Ann Putnam Jr.'s complaint against Elizabeth Hart:

[May 16, 1692]

The Deposistion of Ann putnam who testifieth and saith that I have often seen the apperishtion of gooddy heart among the witches butt I did not know who she was: nor she did me no hurt tell the 13th of may 1692: that she came to my father house parsonally and tould me who she was and asked me if she had ever hurt me: but ever sence that day she has hurt me most greviously severall times and urgeth me greviously to writ in hir book.

Elizabeth was held over and Sarah Buckley was ushered into the court room. Samuel Parris's written report was short and perfunctory, as though he was tiring of reporting the same redundant complaints of pinching, pulling hair, choking, and the like.

(Examination of Sarah Buckley)

[May 18, 1692]

Abig: Williams said this is the Woman that hath bit me with her scragged teeth a great many times

Mary Walcot , Ann Putman , & Susan: Sheldon unable to speak

Mercy Lewis said she see her upon her feet last night. Mary Walcottstestimony read

Eliz: Hubbard said I see her last sab: day hurt Mary Walcot in the meetinghouse but I do not know that she hurt me

Ann Putmans testimony read

Mary Warren said that she saw this Woman & a great company & that this Woman would have her the said Warren go to their Sacrament up to Mr Parris

#[Eliz: Hubbard] Suzan: Sheldon said this Woman hath tore her to peices & tempted her with the book

Ann Putman carried to this Examinant in a fit was made well upon the Examinants grasping her Arm

Suzan Sheldon the like.

Mary Warren the like.

When the examinant was pressed to confess she said she did not hurt them: she was Innocent --

Suzan: Sheldon said there is the Black man whispering in her ear

This is a true copy of the substance of the Original Examination of the aboves'd Sarah Buckley . Witness my hand upon my Oath taken this day in Court. 15 Sept'r 1692 *Sam Parris

The above record was used during Buckley's formal trial hearing in September. A formal court had not yet been formed as Massachusetts eagerly awaited the charter. It is clear the examinations of witches at the middle of May were cursory, hoping the law under the new charter would soon take over the onerous chores performed so far in Salem Village. It must be remembered that no one overseeing these examinations had a law degree. Harvard was not yet that legal giant it would become. It spewed out clergymen and doctors in the 17th century.

The men who sat at the bar were flying by the seat of their pants, relying on previous manuscripts from England and elsewhere that outlined the criteria for finding a witch guilty, which was whittled down to the "touch test", reciting the Lord's Prayer verbatim, the finding of witch marks upon their bodies, and that more than one witness to the act.. Increase Mather had done away with the "swimming the witch" test as he found it inconclusive and barbaric. Above all, a confession was the most-desired evidence, especially as spectral evidence was becoming increasingly problematic.

Thomas Farrar Sr. was another Lynn resident with a history of drunkenness. At seventy-five-years of age, he numbered among the older accused witches. Interestingly, Farrer's indictment was based largely on only Ann Putnam Jr.'s testimony against him, although it had been rumored, he had once struck a pregnant woman while she was riding, throwing her from her horse.

(Deposition of Ann Putnam, Jr., Thomas Putnam and Robert Morrill v. Thomas Farrer)

[May 16, 1692]

the deposistion of Ann putnam who testifieth and saith that on the: 8.th of may 1692 : there appeard to me the Apperishtion of an old gray-head man with a great nose which tortored me and almost Choaked me and urged me to writ in his book: and I asked him what was his name and from whence he came for I would complaine of him: and he told me he came from linne and people used to call him old father pharoah and he said he was my grandfather: for my father used to call him father: but I tould I would not call him: grandfather: for he was a wizzard and I would complaine of him: and ever sence he hath afflected me by times beating me and pinching me and all most Choaking me and urging me continewally to writ in his book we whose names are under writen haveing been conversant with Ann putnam have hard hir declare what is above writen what she said she saw & heard from the apperishtion of old pharoah and also have seen hir tortors: and perceived hir hellish temtations by hir loud out cries I will not writ old pharoah I will not writ in your book *Thomas putnam *Roburt Morrell

Mary Witheridge had the misfortune of being the daughter of Sarah and William Buckley. When her husband Sylvester Witheridge died, she moved in with the Buckleys along with her two small children. Elizabeth Hubbard was the most-vocal at Mary's short inquisition, stating "I have a considerable time ben affletid by Mary Witheridge: but on the 18'th may 1692 being the day of hir Examination mary witheridge did most greviously torment me dureing the time of hir Examination for if she did but look upon me she would strick me down or almost choake also on the day of hir Examination I saw mary witheridge or hir Apperance most greviously afflet and torment mary walcott sarah bibber and ann putnam and I beleve in my heart that mary witheridge is a wicth and that she has often affleted and tormented me and the afforesaid parsons by acts of wicthcraft."

Rebecca Jacobs

Rebecca was the wife of George Jacobs Jr., another of the Jacobs family to be summoned before the magistrates in Salem Village on May 18, 1692. Rebecca had been charged along with her husband, George Jacobs Jr. Her brother Daniel Andrews, also of Salem Town, along with her husband George, had fled "out of the country" and gone into hiding. When Constable Jonathan Putnam knocked on the Jacobs' door, it was Rebecca who answered it, standing there in a confused state, along with her four children (ages 2 ½ years to 15 years old). Rebecca had been unbalanced for some time. Her mother stated that Rebecca was "a woman crazed, distracted, and broken in her mind." Probably based on her apparent "distractedness," along with the fact that George Sr. and Margaret Jacobs (who had confessed to witchcraft) were imprisoned, and that they had a warrant for George Jr., the men took Rebecca with them. Her children ran down the road after them, crying. Daniel Andrews was their Uncle on their mother's side, but as he too had fled along with their father, they were taken in by neighbors.

Elizabeth Hubbard was Rebecca Jacob's chief accuser, claiming Jacobs had pinched her and choked her on many occasions, including today during the inquisition. The other afflicted girls seemed not to recognize Rebecca as she stood before the bar, until Hubbard cried out "Don't you know Jacobs, the old witch?" Hubbard hit the floor in a convulsion. Frightened by the outburst, Rebecca took the road others had before her and confessed to hurting the girls and covenanting with the Devil. Oddly, she also confessed to accidentally drowning her two-year-old Mary in a well seven years earlier. She was committed to jail to await trial.

Roger Toothaker

Roger Toothaker was a farmer from Billerica with an interesting reputation of detecting *maleficium* and punishing the wicked with countermagic. It was rumored his daughter had killed a suspected witch once with the use of his white magic. Toothaker had been living inside the Salem Town boundaries for about eight years, leaving his wife and children in Billerica to the mercy and charity of strangers. This was against Puritan law, where charity was thought to be akin to slothfulness. Hathorne issued a warrant for Toothaker to be brought from Salem Town to the Village meetinghouse, which was carried out that very day. A deposition presented to Hathorne and Corwin a few days later testified to the white magic carried out by Toothaker's daughter.

(Deposition of Thomas Gage and Elias Pickworth v. Roger Toothaker)

[May 23, 1692]

The Deposition of Thomas Gage Aged aboute [six &] thirty six years (of Age)

This Deponant saith & doth testifie that sometime this Last spring of the year, that Docter Toothaker was in his house in Beverly (upon some occasion) & we Descoursed aboute John Mastons Childe of salem that was then sick & haveing unwonted fitts: & Likewise another Childe of Phillip Whites of Beverly who was then strangly sick I perswaded sd Toothaker to goe & see sd Children and sd toothaker answered he had seen them both allready and that his opinion was they were under an Evill hand And farther sd Toothaker sd that his Daughter had kild a witch & I asked him how she Did it, & sd Toothaker answered readily that his Daughter had Learned something from him I asked by what means she Did it, & he sd that there was a [a] Certaine person bewitched & sd person Complained of beeing afflicted by another person that was suspected by the afflicted person: & farther sd Toothaker sd that his sd Daughter gott some of the afflicted persons urine & put it into an Earthen pott & stopt sd pott very Close & putt sd pott to a hott oven & stopt up sd oven & the next morning sd [witch] was Dead other things I have forgotten & farther

saith not ias Pickworth Aged aboute thirty foure years
testifieth to all that is above written
(Reverse) Sworne by Thomas Gage Salem Village
May. 23'd before us *John Hathorne]
Assists *Jonathan. Corwin] Assists

The *Nonsuch* Arrives!

On May 14, 1692, the fleet from England headed by the
frigate *Nonsuch* sailed into Boston harbor. Governor Sir
William Phips and Increase Mather were triumphantly
escorted to the Town House on High Street where a
candlelit ceremony was to take place, instating Phipps as
the Governor of Massachusetts. As it was a Saturday, the
festivities were cut short as the sun began to set, heralding
the Sabbath. The formalities would have to wait. The two
men were ceremoniously led to their waiting families in
Boston's North End without the usual fanfare of volley
rounds and bugle blasts, again, due to the ensuing Sabbath.

The charter was finally home in Boston. The legal means
to condemn a witch to death now loomed above the heads
of those waiting in prison, some of them for months.
Before the first trial could take place, However, more
witches were arrested and brought to Salem Village.

Typical cart from the colonial era. Nathaniel Ingersoll often rented his out for the transport of accused witches from Salem Jail to the Boston prison.

Chapter Twenty-Five

Homecomings and Heartbreaks

Sometime in mid-May, during all the arrests and hearings, the specter of **Abigail Soames** began torturing Mary Warren as the girl sat in prison. Abigail was a Salem Town resident who had once lived in Gloucester. The thirty-seven-year-old woman's shape was so unrelenting in its attack on Mary Warren, that Hathorne and Corwin issued a warrant for her arrest immediately. Constable Peter Osgood hastened to the home of Samuel and Elizabeth Gaskill in Salem, where Abigail was living and working at the time.

Wasting no time, Hathorne and Corwin ordered Mary Warren brought from Salem Jail to Thomas Beadle's tavern. She cried that the specter of Abigail Soames was following her and biting her as she entered Beadle's gate. Abigail Soames was brought into the room, and Mary dropped to the floor, screaming that the woman's spirit was biting her and jabbing her. Based on Mary's attack, the court ordered that the clothing of Soames be searched for any source of image magic (poppets). They found a "great crotching [crocheting] needle" in her apron.

(Examination of Abigail Soames)

[May 13, 1692]

Abigail Soame's Examination 13 May, 1692 at Salem

Upon the glance of her Eye she struck Mary Warren into a dreadful fit att her first appearance, and s'd Warren continually Crying out that it was this very Woman tho she knew her not before, only affirmed that she herself in apparition had told her that her name was Soams, and also did affirm that this was the very woman that had afflicted her all this day, and that. she met her as she was comeing in att the gate, and bit her Exceedingly. att her first Examining there was found in her Apron, a great Botching Needle, about the middle of it near her Belly, which was plucked out by one of the standers by. by ord'r of the Magistrates, which the s'd Soams affirmed she knew not how it came there. Mary Warren affirmed that she never saw the s'd woman before only in apparition, and then she told her that her Name was Abigail Soams and that she was sister to John Soams of Preston Cooper, and that she Lived att Gaskins, and that she had lain Bedrid a year. Being asked whether she was sister to John Soams she answered peremptorily she would not tell, for all was false that Warren said. furthermore Warren affirmed that she told her, that she viz the s'd Soams was the Instrumental Means of the death of Southwick, Upon

which s'd Soams casting her Eye on Warren struck her
into a dreadful fitt, and bitt her so dreadfully, that the
Like was never seen on any of the aflicted, which the
s'd Warren Charged the s'dSoams with doeing off,
saying that the s'd Soams told her this day she would be
the death of her. further Warren Affirms that she the
s'd Soams ran two pinns into her side this day, which
being plucked out the blood ran out after them. Goody
Gaskin being present att this Examination affirmed she
had kept her Bed for most parts these thirteen months--
Warren further affirms she told her that when she did
goe abroad att any time it was in the Night which Goody
Gaskin being present Confirmed the same, that that was
the Usual time off her goeing abroad --
furthermore Warren affirmed that this Abigail
Soams would have had her to have made a bargain with
her, telling her if she would not tel of her being a sickly
woman, she would not afflict her any more, and that
then she should goe along with her, for the
s'd Soams told her, she was her God, Upon
w'ch Warren answered she would not keep the Devils
Councel. Soams told her she was not a Devil but she was
her God. After this appearing three times more to her,
she s'd att one of those times she was as good as a God.
Q. Mary Warren is this true? A. It is nothing but the
truth. Soams being asked who hurt Warren in the time
of her fits she Answered it was the Enemy hurt her. I
have been said she myself distracted many a time, and
my senses have gone from mee, and I thought I have
seen many a Body hurt mee, and might have accused
many as well as she doth. I Really thought I had seen
many persons att my Mothers house at Glocester, and
they greatly aflicted me as I thought: Soams being
Commanded while Warren was in a dreadful fit, to

take Warren by the hand, the said Warren immediately recovered; this Experiment was tried three times over and the Issue the same. Warren after a Recovery being commanded to touch the s'd Soams although she assayed several times to do it with great Earnestness she was not able, But fell down into a dreadful fit, Upon which the s'd Soams being Commanded take Warren by the hand, she immediately recovered her again, Warren affirming she felt something soft in her hand, (her Eyes then being first shut) which revived her very heart. Warren being asked what the Reason was she could not Come to touch Soams affirmed she saw the apparition of Soams come from her Body, and would meet her, and thrust her with Violence back again, not suffring her to Come near her -- sometimes Soams would say it was distraction in talking she would often Laugh, upon which Laughing the aflicted person would presently fal into a fit. Soams being asked whether she thought this was witchcraft, or whether there were any Witches in the world, answered she did not know any thing but said itt was the Enemy or some Other wicked person or the Enemy himself that forces persons to afflict her att this time, presently this Warren fell into a trance, comeing out of which she affirmed, that, Soams told her in the time of her trance that she would thrust an Awl into her very heart and would kil her this night. Soams could never cast her Eye upon Warren, but immediately she struck her down, and one time she affirmed s'd Soams struck her such a Blow as almost killed, which made the s'd Warren break out into abundance of tears. Soams being Charged with it, instead of bewailing itt, Broke forth into Laughter. Warren being also afflicted by the wringing of her mouth after a strange, and prodigious manner, Soams being Command'd to look upon her in that fit, peremptorily answered she would not, same being by being ordered to turn her face about to look on the afflicted, which being accordingly done, she shut her Eyes Close, and would not look on her being then ordered to touch her she did and immediately Warren Recovered, which no sooner done but Soams opened her Eyes and looked on the afflicted, and struck her into another most dreadful and terrible fit, and in this manner she practised her Witchcrafts severall times before the Court. Mary Warren Looking on her affirmed this to be the very woman that had so often afflicted her dureing the Examination and Charged her with it to her face. sometimes dureing the Examination Soams would put her oun foot behind her Other leg, and immediately Warrens Legs would be twisted

[Reverse] that it was impossible for the strongest man there to Untwist them, without Breaking her Leggs, as was seen by many present--After this Examination Warren says the apparition of Proctor, Nurse and Burroughs that appeared before her, and Burroughs bitt her which bite was seen by many. Also Burroughs att the same time appeared to Margaret Jacobs who was then present, and told her as Jacobs affirmed, that her Grandfather would be hanged Upon which the s'd Jacobs wept. it was also Observed by the Rev'd M'r Noyse, that after the needle was taken away from Soams, that Warren was neither bit, not pinched by the s'd Soams, but struck so dreadfully on her breast, that she cryed out she was almost killed.

This is the first time an accused witch claimed herself to be a God, albeit Mary Warren's God. How this must have set with the Puritan judges, one can only guess. Was it worse to claim you were the Devil or a God? The blatant blasphemy must have set them aback, as they questioned Mary, asking "Is this true?" Mary confirmed Soames had said she was "as good as a God." Upon hearing Mary's claim that George Burroughs' specter had prophesied that George Jacobs Sr. would hang, Margaret Jacobs, broke down and sobbed.

Margaret was still in jail, saying that specters were still tormenting her. But, as the reality of where she was and all the lies she had proclaimed against her fellow neighbors overwhelmed her, she broke down. It was evil to bear false witness against thy neighbor. How much viler was it when those lies might result in their deaths? Fearing her actions had put her in the firm grasp of the Devil, Mary recanted her confession, deciding the magistrate's wrath was a lesser punishment than what the Devil could do to her.

It backfired on her. The magistrates were not pleased. They were close to having the charter back in their midst and the proper trials begun. They told her that by recanting her earlier confession, she was demonstrating a sudden relapse. She had wavered back and forth so many times. They ordered that she be put in a separate room with no time outside in the prison yard, a daily respite greatly cherished by those who spent their hours in the stench and darkness of the prisons. It was probably a pragmatic move as well. Away from the others, she could not influence them with her sudden turn of conscience.

Elizabeth Coleson was one of the names on the arrest warrants handed out two days earlier. Susanna Sheldon had claimed the specter of Coleson, along with George and

Rebecca Jacobs had threatened to stab her, and indeed claimed the Jacobs had wounded her on her left side. When Reading constable John Parker showed up and pounded on Elizabeth Coleson's door, he found she had fled, and guessed she may have headed to Boston to jump aboard a ship.

Martha Carrier, was the "Queen of Hell," according to Abigail William's report of her back in April. Abigail said she saw Carrier and the other witches dining in the parsonage pasture with the "King of Hell," George Burroughs at the head. Carrier's spirit was now suddenly increasingly active. Her specter attacked an eleven-year-old girl, Phebe Chandler, in an Andover meetinghouse. The girl said Carrier leaned over a pew and grabbed her shoulder, shaking her and asking her where she lived. This was odd, as Martha Carrier and Phebe Chandler were related by marriage and had even gone to mutual relatives during the smallpox epidemic. Phebe's father ran a tavern in southern Andover. The Carriers were just over the Andover line in Billerica.

It was a warm May afternoon in Andover. Phebe Chandler balanced the tray of beer from her father's tavern she was carrying to the farm hands. A voice suddenly hissed at her from the bushes to the side of the path. "Where are you going?" the voice whispered. Frightened, Phebe looked back over her shoulder at the tavern with the swinging wooden sign of a horseshoe. No one was in sight. Phebe broke into a run, foam sloshing from the mugs she carried, and told the farm hands what had happened. It was Martha Carrier's voice she heard, she told them. But Martha was in prison in Boston. That meant she had sent her witch shape to torment the girl.

Two hours passed, and the frightened girl hurried along the same path home. A breeze moved the branches overhead. Was that a voice or the rustling of leaves? The whisperings suddenly merged into one rasping voice. Martha's witch shape was now above her in the boughs.

"I'm going to poison you Phebe. You have only a few days to live."

Terrified, the young girl ran frantically to the house of her half-sister Elizabeth, who was living with her widowed mother-in-law, Faith Allen, Martha Carrier's mother. Elizabeth's husband had died of small pox two winters earlier. It was rumored Martha and her family had brought the deathly disease with them when they stayed that winter with the Allens.

While Carrier's spirit was abusing young girls in Andover, back in Boston, the legalities born of the new charter were carried out. Phips officially became Governor of Massachusetts, replacing old Governor Simon Bradstreet who had been a puppet official during the hurried overthrow of Andros. He was frail and often absent from church services and government business. Had he been of sound mind and body, able to carry out the mantle firmly placed upon his head, the witch madness might not have spiraled out of control. He had left matters to his deputy governor, Thomas Danforth. Had Bradstreet been in attendance at the inquisitions, it is possible he would have not allowed the admission of "spectral evidence," being a pragmatic man impatient with the folly of those who wasted his time.

The Charter was read, finally, in its entirety. It wasn't everything the colonists had hoped for, but the main concern of their property deeds becoming invalid was now at rest. A collective sigh of relief must have sounded throughout the room. Phips was now Governor, Vice

Admiral and Commander-in-Chief of all New England militias. His right-hand man, William Stoughton, was named Lieutenant Governor, and Issac Addington became Secretary. Samuel Sewall would become one of the councilors.

Mary Esty is Released

For this author, no story carries so much sympathy throughout the witchcraft chaos as that of the Towne sisters: Rebecca Nurse, Mary Esty, and Sarah Cloyce. It was obvious the magistrates looked at the calm pious faces of Rebecca and Mary during their examinations and their confidence in their guilt floundered. Hathorne in particular wavered and went beyond his usual full steam ahead method of coercing the accused into confessions. He asked the girls if they were sure this was the woman whose specter tormented them.

On Wednesday, May 18th, after John Willard was led away to jail, Mary Esty was brought into the court room to be re-examined. She had languished in Salem Jail for almost a month, while her sister Rebecca Nurse, sat shackled in Boston Prison. Mary was almost 20 years younger than her sister, and had left behind a large family in Topsfield—eight boys and four girls. Little Jeffery was only 12. Her husband Issac had been steadfast in proclaiming her innocence.

As Mary stood before the magistrates, her hair matted, clothes filthy from the dirty Salem Jail floor, the fear of what awaited her was tremendous. She waited for the usual shrieking of the afflicted girls as she stood there, still calm on the outside, but nerves threatening to abandon her. Oddly, there was no outcry. Only Mercy Lewis remained firm in her accusation that Mary Esty's specter had tormented her. The other girls were now not so sure.

Hathorne may have inwardly breathed a sigh of relief. He ordered the beleaguered woman released to the custody of her family.

Mary Esty walked out of the Salem Village meetinghouse into the May sunshine. It is probable that one of her family was in attendance at her hearing and was there to take her home. The mint-green of the new leaves opening, along with the blossoms that infuse Spring, must have been the most beautiful confirmation that she had been literally reborn; saved from the hangman's noose. Her joy was tempered only by the knowledge that her two sisters still sat chained in Boston Prison, awaiting their trials. Perhaps, she may have thought, if the Judges believed me innocent, they will see the same goodness in Sarah and Rebecca.

The welcoming chaos that ensued at the Nurse farm must have been heartwarming. All the loving arms flung about her neck, the joy of her neighbors who had anguished over her plight for the past month. How wonderous to feel fresh water and soap, and the luxury of cleanly washed clothes and bed sheets. She was home!

Mary Esty had missed being carted to Boston Prison by only one day. The following day, May 19th, the prisoners, who had been held in the watch house during their examinations, were tied to the cart rails of Ingersoll's wooden wagon, and herded to Boston. Jailer John Arnold, happy he had beefed up his jail house infrastructure, pulled out his trusty quill and entered in the new arrivals, posting the date of the commencement of their bill for room and board a day early.

The witchcraft madness filled the pockets of those whose fortune it fell to house the hapless victims—taverns and jails. Beadle's and Ingersoll's taverns, along with others, saw their coffers fill as they fed the magistrates and spectators filling each seat for every inquisition. In the back of their minds, they were no doubt aware that the circus was just getting started. The real trials would start the madness all over again.

As John Willard, Sarah Buckley, Mary Witheridge, Rebecca Jacobs, Roger Toothaker, Elizabeth Hart, and Thomas Farrar Sr. were looking about in horror at their new accommodations in Boston Prison, a full moon rose through the treetops. It hid its head, perhaps in shame, as pregnant clouds scudded across its face. Thunder rumbled overhead as Mercy Lewis lay in bed staring at the shadows darting about the ceiling from the thrashing trees outside her window. She was staying with Thomas Putnam Jr.'s cousin, Constable John Putnam, who lived nearby. Ann Putnam Sr., who had been somewhat quiet since March, was now suffering attacks from the specter of John Willard, even though he was freshly ensconced in Boston Prison.

John and Hannah Putnam had lost an infant daughter the month before, to witchcraft, they believed. It is unclear why Mercy was now living with them. It may have been to offer help, or to keep her away from Ann Sr., whose mind was becoming increasingly unhinged by the whole affair.

On May 20th, only one day after Mary Esty had been released and gone home, Mercy lay in the darkness watching the shadows, intermittent moonlight sending crazy shapes flying about the room. They had let Mary Esty go, she fumed. She was home, even now, celebrations and loving embraces shrouding the woman she had "cried out" against. The magistrates hadn't listened to her this time. She had been cast aside as witness. What if the other girls' silence came back against her? Would the court think she had made it up alone?

Suddenly the girl curled up in pain and yelled out. Hannah Putnam was the only adult present, as her husband John was in Salem Village's meetinghouse helping the magistrates record depositions against Sarah Bishop and Roger Toothaker that would be needed for their upcoming trials. Mercy's pains suddenly changed to a strange muteness. The girl lay pinned to her bed by some unseen force. Hannah asked Samuel Abbey, a neighbor who stopped by at 9 that evening, to fetch young Ann Putnam Jr. from her home down the lane. Perhaps Ann could see into the Invisible World and tell them who was harming Mercy.

Abigail Williams and Ann Jr.'s twenty-year-old cousin Sarah Trask (who had not joined the ranks of the afflicteds) accompanied Ann and Abigail back to John Putnam's house. As the moon dipped in and out of focus, Ann claimed she saw the specter of Mary Esty following them. She and Abigail said Esty told them she was taking her revenge on Mercy for still testifying against her at the re-examination.

When they entered the room where Mercy Lewis lay spellbound, Abigail and Ann wasted no time in "seeing" the specter of Mary Esty, along with John Willard and Mary Witheridge, choking and attacking Mercy Lewis as she lay helpless in the bed. At that time, Mary Walcott also entered the room. The three specters flew at the girls in a rage. Esty claimed Mary Walcott had blinded the other girls during the re-examination the day before, and only Mercy Lewis could see that she was really a witch. Esty then set upon Mercy again and choked her with a chain.

The witnesses in the room watched as Mercy fought for her life for hours. She cried out finally, "Dear Lord, receive my soul!" As the others watched, some in horror, some perhaps in appreciation of the grand performance,

Mercy screamed, "Lord, let them not kill me quite!" Her eyes flying open, she begged Abigail and the others in attendance to "Pray for the salvation of my soul, for they will kill me!" She claimed the spirit of Mary Esty had threatened she would kill her before midnight.

By the time John Putnam arrived home with Marshal George Herrick and Benjamin Hutchinson, Mercy's room was filled with concerned neighbors. The girl looked close to death. The men were told of Ann Putnam Jr.'s and Abigail William's testimony that it was Esty, Willard, and Witheridge who was attacking Mercy, and they had attacked them as well.

Hearing of the midnight deadline for Mercy's demise (and remembering the death of Daniel Wilkins), Putnam, Herrick and Hutchinson agreed the only thing to be done was to quickly arrest Mary Esty and return her to jail. They ran to Judge Hathorne in Salem and he signed the arrest warrant. It may have been with a sinking heart, or riddled with guilt that he had let a witch go free and now a poor girl was at death's door.

Marshal Herrick hopped his horse and rode through the turbulent night to Topsfield. The horror at seeing him, as he handed Issac Esty the arrest warrant for his wife Mary Esty, on the grounds that she had tormented Mercy Lewis, Abigail Williams, Ann Putnam Jr. and Mary Walcott, must have been knee-buckling. This couldn't be happening! Mary was going back to prison. She had been free only three days.

Back at the John Putnam house, Elizabeth Hubbard, not to be left out, arrived and was duly attacked by Esty, Willard, and Witheridge. She ramped up the ante by declaring more witches had flown into the room and joined in the attack above the bed of the "dying" Mercy Lewis. She cried out that the Proctor's daughter, Sarah, of Salem

Town, her aunt Sarah Bassett of Lynn, and Susanna Roots of Beverly were now tormenting Mercy and the other girls. At some point, Sarah Proctor's specter must have straddled her pole and headed over to Susannah Sheldon's home where she and her neighbor Elizabeth Booth were tortured by Sarah, her parents John and Elizabeth Proctor (who were chained in the Boston Prison), and Daniel Andrews (who was still at large.)

Marshal Herrick returned at midnight, out of breath from his ride through the moonlight, hoping to find the young girl alive. He quickly informed her that Mary Esty was once again in custody, hoping it would cure Mercy of her pains. To everyone's terror, she cried out that Esty was standing before her, threatening her with a winding sheet (the sheet the dead are wrapped in for burial). "I had rather go into the winding sheet than set my hand to the book," Mercy cried. Nauseated and racked with convulsions, she appeared to grow weaker.

The next morning, Saturday, May 21st, Putnam's neighbors found the authorities and told them the girl was barely alive. Esty's specter had tortured her all night. As Mary Esty sat huddled in the Salem Jail, mentally beaten down and frightened, the last degradation was added. The jailer unceremoniously entered the room and clamped eight pounds of shackles on her veined ankles. Her freedom, so shortly lived, was over. Mary Esty would never go home alive, again.

Almost the moment the chains were attached to Mary, Mercy miraculously recovered. Her seizures ceased and she lay calmly after two days of anguish. Based on the girls' complaints of the specters they saw in Mercy's room, John and Thomas Putnam Jr. entered complaints before Hathorne and Corwin against Sarah Proctor, Sarah Bassett, and Susanna Roots. Susanna Sheldon continued to be tormented by the specter of Sarah Proctor, who came to her along with the two fugitives George Jacobs Jr. and Daniel Andrews, and told her to sign the Devil's Book. When she refused, she claimed the three ghosts struck her until she was deaf, dumb, and blind. They left her in a darkness deeper than the oncoming night, she said later.

"Darkness deeper than the oncoming night" could not have been more deeply felt than by those sitting in the squalor of their stone rooms. Back in Topsfield, Mary Esty's family cried; some ranted against the unfairness of the system that had returned this angel to the misery of jail. All in all, it was a feeling of utter hopelessness. Speak out, and you could be accused of witchcraft as well. The nights were long; there would be many, many more before the gavel was finally silenced.

Chapter Twenty-Six

The Court of Oyer and Terminer

Mary Esty had been in Salem's Jail one day before she was ordered to be brought before the magistrates again for yet another examination. The charges this time concerned the heinous torture of Mercy Lewis. Hathorne had first ordered Mary to be brought to Beadle's Tavern in Salem Town to save himself a trip to the Village, but there were so many new arrests since her imprisonment, that he once again saddled his horse and made his way, along with his trusty side-kick Jonathan Corwin, to the chaos of Salem Village's meetinghouse.

The magistrates must have wondered, as they settled themselves into their familiar seats at the front of the room, just how many other times they would be summoned to hear witch accusations. It was the same excited faces they saw seated in the pews, the same hysterical "victims" writhing on the barren floor, and the same scribes scribbling furiously away on crackling parchment. The smells were the same—perspiration mixed with dust and the odor of field hands fresh from the plows. Light, speckled with floating particles of dust, danced through the diamond-paned windows, when they weren't blocked with people perched upon their sills. A gavel or rock, banging on the wooden table for quiet, and the screams of "Witch!" would soon fill the air.

Outside Essex County, the rest of the world went on, happy with the boring routine that was the 17th century in most Puritan households. Poppets were nothing more than dolls, and a sick animal's affliction was due to heat or eating something that didn't agree with it. Babies died because it was an all-too-common reality of an era without proper hygiene and medical facilities. Children acted out, but were punished with extra chores or additional Bible reading and repentance. A pole was a stick or broom handle that was as innocuous as a piece of paper, not a carrier of evil shapes through the night. Salem Village had rewritten the book on what was innocent and was not.

Mary Esty stood in hopeless resignation before the magistrates. Opening prayer was interrupted as all the girls showed signs of being choked, yet remained silent. When they found their voices, they cried out that Goody Esty was stabbing them with a spinning wheel spindle, one that had conveniently been missing from a house in the Village.

One of the clever girls had secreted the spindle in her clothing. She lunged at Mary Esty's specter to wrestle the *spectral* spindle away. Triumphantly, she held the real spindle aloft, where all agreed it was the missing item. Even after the spindle was safely locked away, the girls claimed they saw it in Mary Esty's spectral hands. In the classic story of *Sleeping Beauty*, the evil queen uses a spindle to cast her spell of death upon the princess. A prince's kiss of true love awakens and saves the heroine. There would be no salvation, on this earth, for Mary. Esty was led from the room.

Spinning wheel spindle.

Sarah Basset of Lynn (Elizabeth Proctor's sister-in-law) and **Susanna Roots** of Beverly were examined next. The only record of these two inquests related to Roots whose fellow boarder claimed he heard Susanna conversing with at least five other voices in a room empty of anyone other than herself. It was also alleged that she was seldom at family prayers.

As others were "cried out" upon, the magistrates ordered the arrest of Benjamin Proctor and his aunt Mary DeRich, along with Sarah Pease due to allegations of their specters tormenting Abigail Williams, Mary Warren, Elizabeth Hubbard, and the other usual cast of sufferers. The three were gathered up and brought to the meetinghouse for their questioning. The hurry was due to Hathorne and Corwin's schedule which would have them away for the next several days.

The speed at which these three were accused, arrests drawn up, apprehended, questioned, and jailed would have made their heads spin. In the course of only one day, they were dragged from their homes and sent to Salem Jail, only to be transferred to the Boston Prison the next day. The new group to travel via cart across the New England landscape were Mary Esty, Susanna Roots, Sarah Bassett, Benjamin Proctor, Abigail Soames, and Mrs. Elizabeth Cary.

One has to wonder about the reuniting of the Towne sisters in Boston Prison. As they clasped each other—Rebecca Nurse and Sarah Cloyce stained and dirty, and Mary Esty still dressed in her clean clothes from her short reprieve at home—were they resigned to their fate? As Christian women, did they comfort each other with the promise of God's love for them?

Jailer John Arnold billed Boston for additional shackles for the newly arriving prisoners from Salem Village's jail. The record proves the imprisoned "witches" were now being chained as an expedient deterrent to their spectral visits.

Iron shackle bolted to the floor.

Unsatiated by the last cartload of witches heading to jail, Mary Warren, the Proctor's maid, claimed two new specters were after her. **Mary Ireson** of Lynn, and **Mary Toothaker** of Billerica, whose husband Roger was already in prison. Toothaker had the dubious distinction of being the sister of Martha Carrier, the "Queen of Hell." Apparently, Mary Toothaker's specter came to Warren with all the accoutrements needed for a burial: a winding sheet, a coffin, and grave clothes. She also brought the ubiquitous Devil's Book for Mary's signature. As Warren was still in jail, one has to wonder where names of the new witches came from? Was it any wonder the magistrates were having a hard time dealing with the vacillating girl? One moment she was a confessed witch, and the next, new coven recruits were after her.

Captain Cary had managed to rescue his wife from the confines of Boston Prison and have her moved to a jail closer to their home in Middlesex county. If **Elizabeth Cary** thought her treatment would be more humane in the Cambridge Jail, she lost all hope when 8 pounds of shackles were clamped about her ankles. She fell into convulsions to the point that her husband feared she would not survive the night. He pleaded to have the restraints removed, but it fell on deaf ears. Elizabeth remained chained to the floor.

Thursday, May 26, saw some newcomers to the Salem Village Lecture Day at the meetinghouse. The new charter had arrived in Boston, and all were excited to hear what would happen next. Many, who had feared losing their land rights when the charter was revoked, were particularly eager to hear good news for a change. Most were there to hear the latest on the witches. If they were looking for more drama, they didn't wait long.

Mercy Lewis, Mary Walcott, and Ann Putnam Jr. screamed they were being attacked by new specters—those of Mrs. Bradbury of Salisbury, Goody Rice of Reading, Goody Read of Marblehead, and Goody Fosdick of Malden. Another woman in attendance at Lecture Day, Mary Marshall of Reading, joined in with the girls claiming the specters attacking them. Goody Fosdick's specter claimed she was also responsible for hurting the black woman working for the Putnams' relative, Peter Tufts.

The Court of Oyer and Terminer

Court of Oyer and Terminer. Photo courtesy of Tina Jordan and the Salem Witch Museum.

May 27, 1862, though already sweltering in the late May heat, found a certain type of relief. For Salem and the neighboring towns that had been overridden with witches riding throughout the night skies on poles, picnicking in the parsonage's pasture, and choking, pinching, stabbing, and murdering hapless victims everywhere, the final appointment of a legal court appeared as a rescuing Calvary. Now, the trials would ferret out those who were guilty of witchcraft...and they would hang.

Governor Phips had wasted no time in swearing in his dream team of authorities to oversee the proceedings. Secretary Issac Addington and the other councilors became justices of the peace, along with some magistrates, including John Higginson Jr. and Dudley Bradstreet for Essex County and Thomas Danforth for Middlesex. To expediate the trial proceedings (the jails were becoming overly crowded), Phips called a special court called the Court of Oyer and Terminer, meaning "to hear and to determine." The foundation of this court was based on laws of England, not Massachusetts. Phips had been appointed by the King of England to sit as Governor in Massachusetts, and he would, therefore, make sure the trials followed the ways of the sovereign. Justices Nathaniel Saltonstall of Haverhill; Peter Sergeant, John Richards, Wait-Still Winthrop, and Samuel Sewall of Boston; and John Hathorne, Johnathan Corwin and Bartholomew Gedney of Salem were all put beneath the supervision of Lieutenant Governor William Stoughton of Dorchester as acting chief justice.

Stephen Sewall (the brother of Samuel Sewall and Betty Parrish's host) was elected clerk of the court. Thomas Newton became the King's attorney general. George Corwin of Salem (son-in-law to Justice Bartholomew Gedney, and nephew of Justices Corwin and Winthrop, was elected to a new office, replacing his former station as Marshall. He was now Sheriff of Essex County. He was only twenty-five-years of age at the time of his election. George Herrick carried on as deputy sheriff.

Before the trials could begin, the girls remained active in their accusations of more and more people. Complaints were made out and arrests were made for Wilmot Read of Marblehead, Sarah Rice of Reading, and Elizabeth How of Ipswich.

On May 30th, Phillip English was finally located at his friend George Hollard's house in Boston. Deputy Marshall Jacob Manning picked him up and handed him over to Sheriff George Corwin. He had managed to hide out for a month, reportedly behind a pile of laundry in the cellar of his friend's home. For a wealthy merchant of Salem Town, it had been a humbling four weeks. Now, it was a terrifying transfer from Boston to Salem.

On this same day, Bridget Bishop's case was being compiled against her. Hawthorne and Corwin recorded the myriad depositions against the former tavern owner and accused witch.

The last day of May saw a few new faces seated at the head table of the meetinghouse in readiness for the questioning of newly accused witches. Bartholomew Gedney and General Thomas Newton were in attendance. Newton, in particular, was surprised at the proceedings, even though he had witnessed witch trials before. "I have beheld most strange things," he wrote, "scarce credible but to the spectators." Was this a hint of his incredulity at the girl's antics? Reverend Henry Gibbs was also there from Watertown and wrote that he "wondered at what I saw, but how to judge and conclude, I am at a loss." Judge Jonathan Corwin was Gibbs' step-father. Perhaps it took the cooler heads of men outside the fray to view the court's proceedings with some objectivity.

Phillip English was brought into the lion's den and accused of tormenting Mary Warren and Elizabeth Booth. Compared to many of the other complaints against menacing witches, English's were mainly spectral evidence and against only two of the afflicted, one of them in jail as a confessed witch. Granted, English was not a popular man among many with whom had conducted business. He had bought and sold many properties in the

Salem area, and repossessed many. He had also been a constable in charge of tax collection, another role that brought few fans. His wealth and style of living may have flown in the faces of many he out-shown.

Sarah Rice and Mary Toothaker were questioned next. No records of their questioning remain. Sarah was a long-time friend of accused witch Lydia Dustin. **William Proctor**, son of John and Elizabeth is believed to have been examined that day as well, along with **Captain John Flood** who had been arrested two days before. Flood had three strikes against him as he looked about him at the faces of Ann Carr Putnam Sr. and her husband Thomas. John had been the one to contest George Carr's will on behalf of the Carr and Putnam heirs. He had failed to get the results they so desperately hoped for. He had also failed in any attempt to save the villagers in York, Maine, during an Indian attack.

John Alden

(Examination of John Alden, as Published by Robert Calef)

[May 31, 1692]

John Aldin Senior , of Boston, in the County of Suffolk, Mar- iner, on the 28th Day of May, 1692, was sent for by the Magi- strates of Salem, in the County of Essex, upon the Accusation of a company of poor distracted, or possessed Creatures or Witches; and being sent by Mr. Stoughton , arrived there the 31st of May, and appeared at Salem-Village, before Mr. Gidney , Mr. Hathorn, and Mr. Curwin.

Those Wenches being present, who plaid their jugling tricks, falling down, crying out, and staring in Peoples Faces; the Magistrates demanded of them several times, who it was of all the People in the Room that hurt them? one of these Accusers pointed several times at one Captain Hill , there present, but spake nothing; the same Accuser had a Man standing at her back to hold her up; he stooped down to her Ear, then she cried out, Aldin , Aldin [Alden] afflicted her; one of the Magistrates asked her if she had ever seen Aldin , she answered no, he asked her how she knew it was Aldin ? She said, the Man told her so.

Then all were ordered to go down into the Street, where a Ring was made; and the same Accuser cried out, "there stands Aldin , a bold fellow with his Hat on before the Judges, he sells Powder and Shot to the Indians and French, and lies with the Indian Squaes, and has Indian Papooses." Then was Aldin committed to the Marshal's Custody, and his Sword taken from him; for they said he afflicted them with his Sword. After some hours Aldin was sent for to the Meeting-house in the Village before the Magistrates; who required Aldin to stand upon a Chair, to the open view of all the People.

The Accusers cried out that Aldin did pinch them, then, when he stood upon the Chair, in the sight of all the People, a good way distant from them, one of the Magistrates bid the Marshal to hold open Aldin's hands, that he might not pinch those Creatures. Aldin asked them why they should think that he should come to that Village to afflict those persons that he never knew or saw before? Mr. Gidney bid Aldin confess, and give glory to God; Aldin said he hoped he should give glory to God, and hoped he should never gratifie the Devil; but appealed to all that ever knew him, if they ever suspected him to be such a person, and challenged any one, that could bring in any thing upon their own knowledge, that might give suspicion of his being such an one. Mr. Gidney said he had known Aldin many Years, and had been at Sea with him, and al- ways look'd upon him to be an honest Man, but now he did see cause to alter his judgment: Aldin answered, he was sorry for that, but he hoped God would clear up his Innocency, that he would recall that judgment again, and added that he hoped that he should with Job maintain his Integrity till he died. They bid Aldin look upon the Accusers, which he did, and then they fell down. Aldin asked Mr. Gidney, what Reason there could be given, why Aldin's looking upon him did not strike him down as well; but no reason was given that I heard. But the Accusers were brought to Aldin to touch them, and this touch they said made them well. Aldin began to speak of the Providence of God in suffering these Creatures to accuse Inno- cent persons. Mr. Noyes asked Aldin why he would offer to speak of the Providence of God. God by his Providence (said Mr. Noyes) governs the World, and keeps it in peace; and so went on with Dis- course, and stopt Aldin's mouth, as to that. Aldin told Mr. Gidney, that he could assure him that there was a lying Spirit in them, for I can assure you that there is not a word of truth in all these say of me. But Aldin was again committed to the Marshal, and his Mittimus written.

Calef's account (above) of John Alden's inquisition is very powerful, as it shows, for the first time, a complete abhorrence of the girls' tactics. His opening statement says "Those Wenches being present, who plaid their jugling tricks, falling down, crying out, and staring in Peoples Faces," is one of pure disdain. It is apparent that Alden took on the court. Gedney was an old friend of his, and perhaps he thought he could appeal to him to show reason. "Why don't you fall down when I look at you?" is basically what he asked Gedney, a valid point if he was indeed casting about the "evil eye". His responses to Reverend Noyes, likewise, failed to impress. He was denied bail and held over.

Martha Carrier was next. As expected, the "Queen of Hell" was met with much excitement and wailings.

(Examination of Martha Carrier)

[May 31, 1692]

The Examination of Martha Carrier . 31. May. 1692

H) Abigail Williams w'o hurts you? W) Goody Carrier of Andover. H) Eliz: Hubbard who hurts you? E) Goody Carrier H) Susan:Sheldon , who hurts you? S) Goody Carrier , she bites me, pinches me, & tells me she would cut my throat, if I did not signe her book *Mary Walcot said she afflicted her & brought the book to her. H) What do you say to this you are charged with? C) I have not done it. *Sus:Sheldon cried she looks upon the black man .Ann Putman complained of a pin stuck in her. H)What black man is that? C) I know none. * Ann Putman testifyed there was.Mary Warrin cryed out she was prickt. H) What black man did you see? C) I saw no black man but your own presence. H) Can you look upon these & not knock them down? C) They will dissemble if I look upon them. H) You see you look upon them & they fall down C) It is false the

Devil is a liar. I lookt upon none since I came into the room but you *Susan:Sheldon cryed out in a Trance I wonder what could you murder 13. persons? Mary Walcot testifyed the same that there lay13. Ghosts. All the afflicted fell into most intollerable out-cries & agonies. Eliz: Hubbard & Ann Putman testifyed the same that she had killed 13. at Andover. H) It is a shamefull thing that you should mind these folks that are out of their wits. Do not you see them? C)If I do speak you will not believe me? H) You do see them, said the accusers. C) You lye, I am wronged. *There is the black man wispering in her ear said many of the afflicted. Mercy Lewes in a violent fit, was well upon the examinants grasping her arm. The Tortures of the afflicted was so great that there was no enduring of it, so that she was ordered away & to be bound hand & foot with all expedition the afflicted in the mean while almost killed to the great trouble of all spectators Magistrates & others.

*Note. As soon as she was well bound they all had strange & sodain [sudden] ease.

*Mary Walcot told the Magistrates that this woman told her she had been a witch this. 40 yeares.

Martha Carrier was bound hand and foot and taken from the room. As soon as she was without the meetinghouse walls, the afflicted recovered, although moments before they had been "almost killed" according to witnesses.

Wilmot Reed, the simple wife of a fisherman was from Marblehead. She was rough around the edges with a reputation for a salty disposition and a dislike of her neighbors' children. Her indictment was interesting. The complaint against her on May 31, 1892, listed Elizabeth Booth as the victim she was accused of tormenting. Yet, the complaint put forth during her official trial in September, lists Elizabeth Hubbard, not Booth, as the tormented girl. During the May examination, the tormented, including John Indian, thrashed about and were finally brought to Reed for the "Touch Test." Reed maintained her innocence, stating she felt the afflicted were "in a sad condition," but she had nothing to do with it. She was held over and led from the court room.

William Proctor, son of John and Elizabeth Proctor (both sitting in Boston Prison on the charges of witchcraft) was treated with a harsher persecution than his fellow accused. His examination is lost, but the complaint against him was for tormenting Elizabeth Hubbard and Mary Warren. He declared his innocence and was sent to Salem Jail where he was bound "neck to heel," a very painful torture. The victim was seated on the floor and bent in half, his head over his knees. A rope was tied about his neck and pulled to within inches of his feet, where it was secured around his ankles. Proctor was sentenced to 24 hours of this torture until he confessed of witchcraft. After many hours, blood gushed from his nose, and he was untied by some unnamed person.

All those questioned that day were assigned to Boston Prison. The official court trials of Oyer and Terminer would begin in a few days. The magistrates took advantage of those present and asked Mrs. Ann Putnam Sr. to fill out a deposition against Rebecca Nurse for the many times the specter of the elderly woman came into her home and attacked her. The magistrates read her words back to her so that she could swear to their accurate recording. Suddenly, the specter of Rebecca Nurse came shrieking at her through the court room. Before the astonished eyes of the spectators, it tackled Ann Sr. to the floor. Ann Putnam Jr. jumped up and yelled it was Rebecca Nurse's specter attacking her mother! Sarah Cloyce and Martha Corey's specters were hurting her as well.

The court adjourned and the magistrates headed up the hill to Ingersoll's where they had refreshments and gathered their horses for their ride back to Salem. Once home, Attorney General Thomas Newton wrote a report to Secretary Issac Addington, giving him a brief overview of the day's occurrences and commenting that the accused witches seemed to be among the poor, the rich, the military, and even the clergy. It was astonishing. Enclosed with the report was a list of the first prisoners to be tried in the Court of Oyer of Terminer. He requested that John and Elizabeth Proctor, Alice Parker, Rebecca Nurse, Susanna Martin, Bridget Bishop, John Willard, Tituba, and Sarah Good be brought from Boston Prison to Salem Town. Little Dorcas remained behind in prison. Tituba and a maid of Mrs. Thatcher were asked to be kept separated from the others, as they were confessed witches.

It is probable that Mrs. Thatcher's maid, mentioned in the documents, was Mercy Short, who had confessed of witchcraft. She was no doubt relieved to be kept away from Sarah Good as she had once thrown wood shavings in Good's face when Sarah asked her for some tobacco while she sat in the Boston Prison. Mercy had accused her mistress of witchcraft, and confessed of it herself. As yet, no charges were brought against Mrs. Thatcher.

In Boston, Cotton Mather once again warned about using "spectral evidence" to condemn people to death. He was also against torture to get a confession. He went so far as to advocate a lighter sentence than hanging, as it was, short of a confession, hard to truly establish one's guilt in the field of magic. Could they not look at the cases individually and take into account repentance and degree of perceived malice? He realized this was contrary to the one-size-fits-all legislature passed along from England's courts, but his dealings with Mercy Short and the Goodwin children had given him an insight that others might not have. His humane approach was not adopted, and within one week, the first "witch" would hang.

Chapter Twenty-Seven

The First to Hang

As preparations were made for the opening of the witch trials, the spectral attacks against the afflicted ramped up. Phillip English's shape stuck a pin into Mary Warren's hand, George Burroughs' specter had come after all who had testified against him, Martha Carrier and Bridget Bishop's ghosts were kept busy, and Rebecca Nurse terrified Ann Putnam Sr. with a nightly visit filled with corpses.

Ann Putnam Sr. awoke to find the specter of Rebecca Nurse threatening to murder her. Nurse had brought along with her the ghosts of Ann's dead sister Mary Bayley, and three of her deceased children, all shrouded in their burial clothes and floating before her. If that image weren't horrifying enough, the dead offspring of her other sister, Sarah Carr Baker, also clad in winding sheets, stared at Putnam, all claiming Rebecca Nurse, Elizabeth Cary, and an unnamed deaf woman of Boston (possibly Margaret Thatcher) had murdered them. Ann claimed the specter of Rebecca Nurse "tould me that now she was come out of prison she had power to afflect me."

Ann was not finished. She made up for the time she had been quiet in the former months. On the very morning the trials were to begin, her bedchamber was also visited by the ghosts of Samuel Fuller and Lydia Wilkins. They told her they would "tare me to pieces" if she didn't tell the magistrates that John Willard had murdered them. To emphasize their demand, their ghosts threatened to appear in court if Hathorne didn't believe her! At this point, the specter of John Willard floated into her room and declared with pride that he had indeed murdered them and her own children, along with children of her neighbors. He claimed William Hobbs had helped him.

The court would convene on June 2, 1692, and it was obvious the afflicted wanted to get in as many accusations against attacking specters as possible. The magistrates visited the "confessors" in jail to get the last of their information they could before the trials began. Mary English (imprisoned wife of Phillip English) took the opportunity to inform the magistrates that a month earlier, while in Salem Town, she had heard Mary Warren confess that she and the other afflicted girls were so distracted and distempered that they did not know what they said in their fits. Her words were ignored, either because the magistrates were hell bent on their current course of action, or, the words of an accused witch could not be believed. Besides, Mary Warren swung back and forth in her confessions as fast as a frenetic pendulum.

On May 30th, William Stoughton and Samuel Sewall called for the appointment of eighteen "honest and lawful men" for the grand jury, and forty more in case multiple cases had to be heard at one time, or other jurors fell away. It was probably not lost to those called that they would be incurring the wrath of the witches of which they sat in judgement. A vast portion of the area countryside was represented, as the jurors came from Topsfield, Ipswich, Boxford, Beverly, and Wenham. The foreman called was Thomas Fiske from Wenham.

The Court of Oyer and Terminer Convenes

No records remain from the actual trials that began on June 2, 1692. Cotton Mather wrote that "there was little occasion to prove the witchcraft, this being evident and notorious to all beholders." Obviously, the afflicteds' torments and the written depositions would suffice as "evidence." The earlier examinations would, sadly, be the foundation for the trials. The jury would hear the depositions and notes from the examinations. They would witness the obvious suffering of the girls as they screamed and tumbled about the floor. If the prisoners hoped for a second chance of redemption, it was a fool's dream granted only to a few.

Some business was conducted earlier that morning before the trials began. John Hathorne and Jonathan Corwin, after a three-day delay, wrote out arrest warrants for Elizabeth Fosdick and Elizabeth Paine. At ten o'clock, further degradation was heaped upon those who were to stand trial. Nine women and surgeon John Barton were sent to search the bodies of Rebecca Nurse, Alice Parker, Sarah Good, Elizabeth Proctor, and Susanna Martin for signs of witch's "teats." They testified that Bridget Bishop, Elizabeth Proctor and Rebecca Nurse each had an odd "excrescence of flesh" found in the anal area. Rebecca Nurse explained it was due to painful and prolonged child labor (it was probably a hemorrhoid, often a result of pushing during labor). One of the midwives said she saw nothing abnormal.

Bridget Bishop's examination was more detailed. Her body was thoroughly searched just before her trial and after. The midwives stuck pins into any mark that looked suspicious. They found a "witch's teat" between "ye pupendum and anus" just before she was taken before the magistrates. Three hours later (obviously after her lengthy trial) they once again searched the area and found the "teat" had withered, leaving behind a patch of dry skin. They took this to mean Bridget's familiar had been suckling there and drained it. They put their findings in writing. That the area had been previously pricked with a pin would cause it to "wither," but the natural explanation was not offered. As mentioned earlier, if a suspicious mole or other skin abnormality was pricked with a pin and bled, then it was deemed a natural skin occurrence. If, however, it was pricked and no blood came out, it was considered a witch's mark.

The trials were held in the Salem Town House on the second floor, only a block from the jail. Chief Justice William Stoughton presided. Samuel Sewall, John Hathorne, Bartholomew Gedney, John Richards, and Nathaniel Saltonstall sat the bench. The ubiquitous Jonathan Corwin was not presiding this time, but his services would be soon be required.

Bridget Bishop

The guards entered Salem Jail and clasped Bridget Bishop by the arms. They bound her wrists and hauled her roughly through the open door into the June sunlight. She squinted in the sudden brightness, and walked haltingly toward the Salem Town House only a block away. As they neared the building, she glanced angrily at it. Inside, waited those who would oversee her fate and jeer at her predicament. That glance, according to the guards, caused a nail-studded board to wrench from its place within the building and go flying across the room. The *bang* was heard from outside. Startled, the men led her into courthouse, nearly dragging her up the stairs to the second floor where her accusers waited.

Bridget Bishop's past had been one of upheaval. As mentioned earlier in this book, she had broken the town's peace with her tawdry taverns where shuffleboard was played, no doubt with bets in place. She was abrasive and seductive. Many of her accusers at the trial were men who gave reports of her specter coming to them in the night as they lay in the bedchambers. She blatantly rebuked the usual muted colors of the Puritan women by wearing a bright red waistcoat. She had been accused of thievery often throughout the years, but until the witchcraft outbreak of 1692, her charges had been old ones, including being accused of witchcraft in 1679.

While Bridget was being searched for witch's marks in Salem Jail, the court was already hearing testimonies from the witnesses who related stories of Bishop's *maleficium* in the past. Bridget's April 19th examination was brought up again and again as Thomas Putnam Jr., Nathaniel Ingersoll, and Samuel Parris related the torments the girls suffered as the magistrates questioned the "witch." Leaning largely on the English law requirement that at least two witnesses had to concur on an event, the men dutifully read off the indictments from April 19th, stating Goody Bishop had "Tortured Afflicted Pined, Consumed, wasted & tormented" Mercy Lewis, Betty Hubbard, Ann Putnam Jr., Mary Walcott, and Abigail Williams during her inquest a month-and-a-half earlier.

Cotton Mather, who was not in attendance at the trial, later described the proceedings from the written documents that are no longer extant. The result was a book called *Wonders of the Invisible World.* The problem, he said of the trials, was "to fix the *Witchcraft* on the Prisoner at the Bar." Thanks to this record, we have some idea of what happened on June 2, 1692, as Bridget Bishop faced off with a table flanked by men.

They began with the girls who testified "the *Shape* of the Prisoner did oftentimes vey grievously Pinch them, Choak them, Bite them, and Afflict them, urging them to write their Names in a Book, which the said Spectre called, *Ours.*" They claimed that Bishop's apparition had bragged of killing "sundry Persons, then by her named." Susanna Sheldon, never to be left from the spotlight for long, added a current report that she had witnessed that very day.

She said a confrontation had ensued between the specter of Bishop and the "Ghosts" of a pair of twins, who told her "to hir face that she had murthered them in setting them into fits whe of they dyed." In a side note, Mather conceded that the report was met with "much suspicion." Another witness reported that Bridget's specter had picked her up and taken her to a river where it tried to drown her if she did not sign the Devil's Book. The jury was reminded of the occasion when Abigail Williams had yelled out that Bridget Bishop's ghost had appeared, and

Jonathan Walcott had thrust his sword at it, tearing its coat. Bishop was accused of sitting at the Devil's sacrament in the parsonage meadow, and threatening Deliverance Hobbs with a whipping of "Iron Rods."

On and on the litany of accusations went, all the while the afflicted girls roared their torments before the startled jury. Mather wrote, "there were produced many Evidences of OTHER Witchcrafts by her perpetrated." Although some of the accusations went as far back as the 1670s, Bridget was charged with stealing money, strange accidents, unusual livestock maladies, the death or sickness of children, and her shape or that of an animal, appearing to men at night. These all followed some argument with Bishop of a perceived wrong. Reports of finding poppets hidden in a wall of her home, with pins stuck in them, were laid out before the court. Mather made a note that Bishop could not give a "reasonable or tolerable" explanation of the poppets.

Finally, the women who had searched Bridget reported finding "a preternatural Teat." Bishop was asked what her response was to the charges. The English law did not allow for counsel or an attorney, although the girls shouted out that the Devil was defending her that day. According to Mather's writings, she was caught in "gross Lying" seven times as she accosted her accusers and presented her claims of innocence to the all-male jury.

The testimony had been heard. Chief Justice Stoughton, in a move that mirrored the charge to the jury given by the Judge overseeing the trial of Lizzie Borden, instructed the jury not to look for any evidence of innocence, but with much bias, told them "they were not to mind whether the bodies of the said afflicted were really pined [stuck with a pin] and consumed, as was expressed in the indictment; but whether the said afflicted did not suffer from the accused such afflictions as naturally *tended* to their being pined and consumed, wasted, etc. This (said he) is a pining and consuming in the sense of the law." In other words, you don't need to see evidence of marks left by actual pins, or bruises from being choked. If the afflicted "tended" to show they were being hurt, that was good enough.

Cotton Mather did not list how long the jury took to reach its verdict. Bridget Bishop must have known in her heart, especially after hearing all the charges against her and Stoughton's biased admonition to the jury, that she was doomed. The men came back with their verdict. She was guilty and sentenced to hang.

Thomas Newton, the court's acting attorney felt the weight of the indictment, as did others. This was no longer a dozen crazed witnesses writhing on the floor and producing stories of incredible tortures by spirits only they could see. A woman was going to hang.

Bridget was taken back to jail, where the women searched her again. Judging by the reports of Bishop's temper, it can be supposed that by now she had had enough. She had been found guilty, and only the saving grace of God could prevent her from hanging.

While the court was still in session, the magistrates went ahead and took depositions against Rebecca Nurse and John Willard in preparation for their trials. But then something interesting happened. The trials stopped. Had it occurred to the magistrates that most of the evidence presented against the woman was decades old, and that it was all (with the exception of the thievery, some dolls found in a wall, and poor conduct charges) based on spectral evidence? You don't hang someone for stealing a spoon or running a shuffleboard game, not even for the wearing of red or having a foul temper. The day was June 2nd. The next trial would not occur for another 26 days.

It didn't stop a repeated search of the witches that had been brought over from Boston Prison. The magistrates had not informed the general population of their decision to take a hard look at what they were doing. At four o'clock that same day, right after Bridget was subjected to a second body search, Rebecca Nurse, Elizabeth Proctor, and Susanna Martin were stripped and probed. It was noted that Goody Martin's breasts, which had been full and firm that morning at ten o'clock, were now "all lank and pendant." Her familiars must have been suckling at her breasts and depleted them. John Proctor and John Willard were similarly searched by the male surgeon.

The delay between June 2nd and June 28th was not without its legal entanglements. Indictment after indictment, arrest after arrest was made until the prisons were bursting at the seams. Some prisoners were allowed to stay in jails within their county in an effort to alleviate the crammed conditions.

Six days after her guilty verdict was read, Bridget Bishop finally left jail for the last time. The reality of it would be hard to imagine as the guards led her to the waiting cart outside the Salem Town jail. Sheriff George Corwin tied her wrists to the upright cart support and the procession began. That the street was thronged with people to watch the first of the accused head to her execution was not reported but assumed. There was no fixed site of execution in Salem Town, as all capital offences were usually handled in Boston and the executions conducted there. That Bridget Bishop wasn't hauled away to Boston may have been an indicator that the town expected many more hangings in the days to come, and thus, a suitable location may as well be found now.

As the noon sun hung high in the June sky, humidity laced the faces and soaked the clothing of those making the

333

trek behind the cart. Bridget was probably taunted with shouts of "Witch!" She may have been pelted with fruit or small rocks as the creaking cart wheels floundered over rutted roadways. Sheriff Corwin steered his horse to the northwest of town.

Marilynne K. Roache, in her book *The Salem Witch Trials: A Day-By-Day Chronicle of a Community Under Siege*, set the scene of the promenade to the execution site:

"For now, Salem officials chose a spot of common pasture at the edge of town—away from the center of things, yet visible to passers-by. Like later condemned witches, Bridget Bishop was transported in a cart flanked by guards and mounted officers in a procession that drew onlookers as it passed from the jail, down Prison Lane, to the main street. They proceeded southwest of town where the road angled toward Salem Village and Boston, and the North River bent sharply to run between bedrock hills. A stream flowed from the height on the south into a salt marsh pool that met the river bend. The crowd headed north, crossing the stream on a causeway and bridge between the pool and the river (shallow now as its waters drained away to low tide). The procession turned left off the main road to a track that climbed the ledge about the salt marsh pool. Several of the afflicted were present, beaten, they said, by old Jacobs's specter, leaning on the Devil so it could use one of its staves as a club."

Even now, as the girls witnessed the result of their hard-fought battle against the Devil, they could not resist adding yet more tales of torment. No conscience seems to have weighed upon them that their actions were the cause of a human life being taken. The fact that Bridget Bishop had never met any of them before the inquest of April 19th, meant nothing to them. They marched on behind the cart, perhaps tingling with anticipation of what was to come.

Scholars over the years have posited their theories as to whether there was a scaffold constructed for the hanging, or if a ladder was merely placed against a tree for the condemned to be pushed from. As Bridget was the first, and no mention was made in any documents that a gallows had been constructed in the six days between her indictment and execution, this author tends to believe a ladder was placed against the thick branch of one of the trees growing along the crevice. It had to be a place where all could see the results of what happened to those who trifled in witchcraft.

Marilynne K. Roach, whose book was just cited, was one of a team of researchers and historians who located what they believe to be the precise location of the hangings. It sits at the forefront of Gallows Hill, and is called Proctor's Ledge. More about this will be talked about later.

The crowd assembled along the rocky crevice, and swelled out into the open ground. Bridget's hands were bound behind her back, and a rope tied around her skirt and legs. A hood may have been placed over her head for two reasons: an old suspicion that the "evil eye" from a witch, especially one about to die, could curse those whose gaze it fell upon. More pragmatically, it was to save those watching the grizzly effects of a hanging.

Bridget was carried or lifted up several steps of the ladder, far enough that a drop would cause her death and keep her feet from touching the ground. A noose, tied hurriedly to the tree bough, was placed around her neck. Witnesses say she proclaimed her innocence till the last. Beverly minister John Hale was present. He had been there at the first outbreak of witchcraft at Reverend Parris's house, and was, fittingly, here today, perhaps to offer a prayer.

The crowd looked on with mixed emotions. The small children in attendance were not shielded from the horror about to happen. It was better to instill in them the fear of the Devil and reinforce their desire for salvation. Hearts raced as they watched the heaving bosom of the prisoner, waiting for the final moments of life to flash before her. Sheriff Corwin paused, and then pushed the bound body of Bridget Bishop from the rung. After months of hysteria and screaming, the girls were finally silenced. The startled crowd watched as the form of Bridget Oliver Bishop convulsed and twisted, swinging from side-to-side as the tree bough creaked beneath her weight. After her feet jerked upwards a few more times, she was still.

An illustration of the hanging of Bridget Bishop.

The afflicted had extracted their pound of flesh. This was real. A body hung before them, turning slowly with the rope. Would this bring them out of the hysteria that had gripped them for more than four months? It is not recorded if Bridget's body was left to dangle in the heat of the day, or throughout the humid night, as a warning to others. If she followed suit of the others to come, she was eventually cut down and tossed into the crevice of rocks, a scant handful of dirt thrown over her.

Sheriff George Corwin appeared before the clerk of court later that day and turned in the first of the written documents reporting the execution's outcome: "I have taken the body of the within named Bridget Bishop…and caused the said Bishop to be hanged by the neck until she was dead."

Chapter Twenty-Eight

Death and Deliberations

The sobering reality of a public hanging did have its effect. Accusations of torturing spirits were silenced in the days following Bridget Bishop's execution. Prisoners, huddled in jails awaiting their turn at trial, must have panicked fully in the face of the reality the noose had just provided. The judges may have wished to follow Pontius Pilate's example and symbolically wash the blood from their hands. The laws they had followed to incriminate a witch now bothered many of them, particularly, the amount of weight put on "spectral evidence." They needed counsel on how to proceed. They needed something more than antiquated guidelines from a country they had deserted. They needed religious input.

A schism had formed among the judges. They argued amongst themselves. One stated that if spectral evidence had not been allowed in Bridget Bishop's trial, she would have hung for no more than the decades of gossip about her, wearing red, and running a "shovelboard" game. Governor Phips, still wet behind the ears in his newly-appointed post, felt the burden of dealing with ongoing threats of Indian warfare amongst the nearby villages, and the problematic scourge of witches sweltering in the prisons of his province. He was away much of the time in late May and early June, dealing with the Indian crisis. He basically decided to hand the whole witch business over to the clergy. Let them tell the court how to proceed. This was, after all, a battle being fought in the Invisible World of good and evil. He'd handle the physical issue of bloodshed amidst the colony, the church could handle the witches. He had not long to wait.

A large band of Wabanaki Indians attacked Wells, Maine on June 11th. Striking both the ships in the harbor, and the garrison of terrified villagers, the damage was small as far as lives lost. Thwarted in their attempts to breach the enemy's strongholds, they burned the town and butchered the livestock. One poor soul was captured and the wrath of the frustrated natives was taken out on him. They butchered him cruelly within the view of those holed up in the garrison. He was cut, castrated, scalped and tortured, burning sticks plunged into his wounds. Cotton Mather wrote "they Butchered One poor Englishman, with all the Fury that they would have spent upon them all." The irony of the hanging of one poor soul the day before in Salem Village, to satiate the outcry of witchcraft from a dozen distracted villagers, may not have been lost on all.

On June 15, 1692, with Bridget Bishop's hanging still clear in their minds, a conference of 12 ministers, including Cotton Mather, gathered to discuss the situation. If some of the imprisoned had been a fly on the wall during the early stages of the meetings, they might have felt some hope for the outcome of their predicament. The consensus was that "A very critical and exquisite caution" was needed "lest by too much credulity of things received only upon the devil's authority there be a door opened for a long train of miserable consequences." The trials, they advised, must be "managed with an exceeding tenderness towards those that may be complained of, especially if they have been persons formerly of unblemished reputation."

The latter words would have brought much hope to the likes of Rebecca Nurse and her sisters, Mary Esty, and Sarah Cloyce, all members of the church in good standing.

The problem with spectral evidence was hit hard during the ministers' gathering. This must be handled with care, they warned. Using words almost identical to the declarations of Rebecca Nurse and Susanna Martin, they stated that the "demon may assume the shape of the innocent." They hammered in the point that the evidence presented should be "certainly more considerable than barely the accused person being represented by a specter unto the afflicted."

The ministers next addressed the "Touch Test," where the afflicted were asked to touch the accused. If their afflictions immediately stopped, then the person was labeled a witch, as it demonstrated the curse had left the victim and gone back into the accused. This "proof" too was problematic and was discredited as "no infallible evidence...and frequently liable to be abused by the devil's legerdemain."

The document the clergymen drafted was labeled the "Return of Several Ministers." After casting dispersion on the use of "spectral evidence" and the "Touch Test" (which the exclusion of would have saved many from the gallows), they capitulated by praising the magistrate's structural dealing with the proceedings thus far.

"Nevertheless," they said, "we cannot but humbly recommend unto the government, the speedy and vigourous [sic] prosecution of such as have rendered themselves obnoxious, according to the directions given in the laws of God, and the wholesome statutes of the English nation, for the detection of witchcraft."

It was an ambiguous offering, that in effect, was worthless. Perhaps the weight of deciding the infrastructure of the trials was too odious for the ministers to take upon themselves. Out of fear of retribution—from man or God— they may have retreated with this basic offering that "giveth and taketh away." It was handed over to the magistrates, who probably deferred to William Stoughton for the final say in the matter. Robert Calef summed up the probable relief of the judicial body by saying the "Return of the Several Ministers" gave "as great or greater Encouragement to proceed in those dark methods, than cautions against them."

Astonishingly, the validity of the girls' afflictions was never called into question. Not even a hint that perhaps something other than witchcraft could be "distracting" these teenagers, children, and a few unstable adults. Even when two of the afflicted confessed that it had "been for sport," or that it came from "distraction and distemper," the trials went on. Sarah Churchill had even confessed to Sarah Ingersoll that it was all faked.

It was too much for one of the magistrates. Judge Nathaniel Saltonstall could no longer condone the proceedings. He had witnessed a trial and execution in which he had participated. He did not believe the antics of the afflicted that he witnessed, nor the "spectral evidence" that was being given so much credence. One man among many, who all seemed bent on a mission of cleansing the community of perceived demons, his voice was as one "crying in the wilderness." He resigned as magistrate and withdrew to his home in Haverhill, where it was rumored, he found solace in "drink." His seat was replaced by a familiar face—Judge Jonathan Corwin.

On June 16th, the persecution of witches claimed another victim—not by hanging, but by the toll imprisonment took.

Roger Toothaker, the self-proclaimed "Doctor" and healer, died in Boston Prison. He was 58-years-old. The coroner, Edward Wyllys, called in no less than twenty-four men to examine Roger's body. It seemed excessive, and the fact that one of the men, Benjamin Walker, questioned the other prisoners that were there when Toothaker died, makes one wonder if there was some concern that he had perished due to some kind of persecution from his fellow inmates or guards. Or, perhaps they were looking for any spectral visitors that may have tormented the man. The verdict was "he came to his end by a natural Death." He had been in jail since May 18th. After his arrest, all of his female relatives were accused as witches as well: his wife Mary; his eight-year-old daughter, Margaret; his eldest daughter, Martha; and his wife's youngest sister, Martha Allen Carrier, who was dubbed the "Queen of Hell."

Roger had several strikes against him. He had moved to Salem and set up his own practice, declaring himself a doctor, in a territory heretofore dominated by Dr. William Griggs (the same doctor believed to be called by Samuel Parris at the witchcraft outbreak to inspect his niece and daughter). It was Griggs' niece, Elizabeth Hubbard, and her two closest friends, Ann Putnam Jr., and Mary Walcott, who originally accused Toothaker. Whether it was his perceived competition with Griggs, or the fact that he had once bragged of teaching his daughter Martha how to kill a witch, it was enough to send him to prison. Counting Sarah Osbourne and Sarah Good's baby (both of whom died in prison), along with the hanging of Bridget Bishop, the girls could chalk up four deaths in their war on witchcraft.

The strange lull in spirit sightings following Bridget Bishop's death, slowly began to dissipate. It started with a Putnam...Constable Jonathan Putnam, who lived in the norther region of Salem Village, not far from several of the accused witches: Sarah Cloyce, Daniel Andrews, and some of the Jacobs. On June 18th, eight days after the first hanging, he suddenly felt ill. Mercy Lewis was asked to come and look into the Invisible World for signs of a specter tormenting the man. Beneath a full moon, Mercy made her way to Putnam's home. Samuel Parris and John Putnam Sr. had arrived to watch the proceedings. Oddly, the minute Mercy came into the house, she was suddenly unable to speak. Bewildered at her condition, the men finally settled on a solution. They told her to hold up her hand if she saw specters afflicting the Constable. Mercy looked at the man, and finally raised her hand. She suddenly went into a trance, before declaring it was the shapes of Rebecca Nurse and Martha Carrier torturing Putnam.

That same day in Boston, accused witches Lydia and Sarah Dustin were transferred via cart to the Cambridge Prison closer to their home in Middlesex. Others, not so lucky, were auspiciously taken from Boston to Salem Jail, a trip that could only mean they were up next for a trial. George Burroughs, Martha and Giles Corey, George Jacob Sr., Ann Pudeator, Sarah Cloyce, Sarah Wildes, Susanna Root, and Dorcas Hoar packed the wooden cart and were hauled along the town streets to the jail. Merchants and villagers alike stopped to watch the witches' trek. Had Bishop's hanging softened the spectator's gaze or enhanced the fear and hatred fueled by the scourge of evil they perceived inflicting their Puritan colony?

The females accused of witchcraft were not the only ones to be searched for witch's marks. In readiness for the next set of trials, Marshall George Herrick, Constable Joseph Neal, and jailer William Dounton stood old George Jacobs Sr. up upon his walking sticks and looked for witch's marks. They found a strange excrescence a quarter of an inch in size, on his right shoulder. They probed it with a pin, but nothing came out. This was a problem. They found two more on his right hip and inside his right cheek. The Devil was thought to often hide the teats (or marks) in places not obvious at first glance: under an eyelid, inside the mouth, in a person's "secret places." It was one of the reasons the prisoners were subjected to thorough and degrading searches of their persons. A committee of seven men next turned their attention to George Burroughs. Perhaps disappointedly, they found nothing.

As the prisoners awaited their fate, some of their families saw to it that they had a few creature comforts from home. If you could afford it, you were allowed to bring some provisions to the witches, which eased the cost of the jailer's feverous tabulations. Dorcas Hoar was one such prisoner blessed with a family who were trying to bring her some sense of normalcy and comfort. Her grandson John Lovett came with fresh clothes and some decent food. How the other prisoners must have coveted those gifts from home.

The Spectral Attacks Resume

Like a barometer registering the signs of an impending storm, the ensuing trials set the tides and winds of spectral gossip into high gear. The Devil, perched high on a hill in Salem Village, guided his playing pieces across an antiquated map as he maneuvered each to play its part in the defeat of a village's righteousness. The shadow of

Bridget Bishop's noose fell across the Pawns and Bishop, Knights and Castles that had all played their roles so well. One hanging had only whetted the appetites of those thirsting for death. The next move would require several ropes tied about the bough at one time. With a smile, he pushed the Pawns across the board toward the Castle that represented the seated court.

Jemima Rea, an eleven-year-old from Salem Village cried out that the specters of Rebecca Nurse and Sarah Cloyce were torturing her, along with Mary Black. Sarah was a neighbor, and it was she the young girl targeted in her seven consecutive seizures. "You cannot do it alone, and you brought this woman to help you? Why do you bring her? She was never complained of." She confessed that it was Sarah Cloyce tormenting her, and the innocent woman was Mary Black.

Susanna Sheldon, one of Satan's most-obliging pawns, went into overdrive with her afflictions only days before the next Court of Oyer and Terminer was to be convened. While working at William Shaw's in Salem Town, Susanna surprised visiting neighbors when she was found with her hands bound tightly with cord. Witnesses said the cord was so tight that they had to cut it away. Sheldon said it was the specter of Goody Dustin's specter. (It is curious that Sheldon accuses Lydia Dustin, who had just been transferred only a few days prior to this, to Cambridge Jail. Did the girl see the transfer as a sign that Dustin may be wiggling out of the noose? The perceived guilty were brought to Salem Jail, not farther away in Cambridge.)

Even more horrifying than Susanna's bound hands and the convulsions that followed, were the reports that she was found hanging from a hook, close to death. This hook-hanging happened on four different occasions. She accused Goody Destin of two of the attacks, and two on

345

Goody Good. More strange occurrences were reported along the line of teleportation or psychokinesis, for a broom suddenly appeared in an apple tree, and a shirt and milk tub turned up in the woods.

Four days later, only two days before the court would resume trying witches, Susanna was once again found by neighbors (supposedly at Shaw's farm) choking on the barren floor. Her head had been crammed behind a chest, and her hands bound tightly with a wheel band. As the adults cut away the band, she cried that it was Sarah Good who had done it.

John Proctor's specter came from his jail cell and tormented Abigail Hobbs. He promised she would not hang if she would touch "the book," and take a poppet and thorn he brought with him, with which to torture Ann Putnam Jr. It seems Hobbs wasn't safe, even in prison, from the persecutions of the witches.

Sarah Bibber accused the ghost of Rebecca Nurse for tormenting her, while Elizabeth Booth was attacked by Elizabeth Proctor's specter.

Meanwhile in Andover, a town that would claim more witches than any other, people were beginning to "cry out." Thirty-year-old **Timothy Swan** was being attacked at his father's home by an entire coven of witches. While most of the attackers were women (Toothaker, Post, Lacy, Foster, and others), Martha Carrier recruited her sons, as well as her daughter, and Richard Carrier, whose specters were all said to torment Swan grievously. Carrier burned Swan with a tobacco pipe and stabbed his knee with a red-hot iron spindle. It was the dreaded dark-haired man in the tall crown hat that was seen bearing the spindle to facilitate the torture. Shaw said the witches used poppets as well, to carry out their afflictions from a safe distance.

Reverend Samuel Parris, had kept a low profile throughout the chaos. He still performed his duties as minister, and tried to bring some sense of comfort to the congregation that was dwindling in numbers. Some were in prison, some were family members of those in prison, and others were wrestling with their own consciences over the whole witchcraft mess. Besides, some innocent people had been "cried out" upon while attending church. Was it safe to be there, in case one of the afflicteds' wandering gazes fell upon you and found disfavor?

Nevertheless, Parris stood before the fearful congregation nine days before the next scheduled court hearing, and claimed that they had not been abandoned in their hardships, for He is "the Father of mercies, and the God of all comfort. Which comforteth us in all our tribulation, that we may be able to comfort them which are in any affliction." The weathered faces looking up at him saw a man serving a dual purpose. On the Sabbath and certain Lecture Days, he was their spiritual leader and advisor. On trial days, he was the scribe furiously taking down the notes, or signing depositions, that would condemn their neighbors and family members to the gallows. Who was he really? And whose side was he on?

The Voice of Reason Silenced

Three days before the Court of Oyer and Terminer brought the next sacrificial lambs before the afflicted girls, one man took a stand against the legal proceedings he had witnessed so far. He was a Baptist minister, something that may have been against him to begin with. William Milborne, made out two petitions and presented them to Governor Phipps, a man Milborne had served with before under Governor

Andros' reign. "Several others" had signed the petitions and Milborne handed them to the council with hopes of making some difference in the upcoming trials.

"A woeful chain of consequences will undoubtedly follow" it read, in regards to the use of spectral evidence, that was seen as a means to condemn the innocent. "We therefore request that the validity of specter testimony may be weighed in the balance of our grace and solid judgements, it being the womb that hath brought forth inextricable damage and misery to this province, and to order by your votes no more credence be given thereto than the word of God alloweth."

Saltonstall had said as much as his reason for resigning from the court. The "Return of Several Ministers" had warned of it (before doing an about face and pretty much rendering their opinion moot). Many of the council had wrestled with their own consciences, but in the end, they validated the course they had chosen. They took offense at Melbourne's meddling and offering insight as his "very high reflections upon the administration of public justice." Governor Phipps had an arrest warrant drawn up against Melbourne for his "scandalous and seditious paper."

He was fined £200 bond and had to post two sureties that he would appear in court to answer to his "felonies." If he could not do both, he would sit in prison until the Superior Court convened (at no apparent scheduled date).

Even Increase Mather (fresh from his return to Massachusetts with the charter) sat with several of his Harvard constituents in the college library, and discussed the sticky issue: "Whether the devil may not sometimes have a permission to represent an innocent person as tormenting such as are under diabolical molestations?" They had weighed in with the "Return of Several Ministers" but may be regretting their vacillation in the document. After the fury metered out against Melbourne's latest supplication, they decided to sit on it, for now.

But time had run out. The day following their discourse, the next session of the Court of Oyer and Terminer took center stage in Salem Town. The lives of many would "hang" in the balance of the trial's outcome. Depositions would be read, the afflicted given free rein, with the accused getting only a breadth of a chance to contest the charges against them.

In the stagnant heat of that June night, only the rhythmic sound of crickets bound both the villagers sweltering in their bed sheets, with those of the accused stirring fearfully on their straw mats in Salem Jail. Crickets. A summer's night tune that brought a sense of continuity—the season would always be filled with such night sounds as these. But to Rebecca Nurse, Sarah Good, Elizabeth How, Susannah Martin, Sarah Wildes and others, it was only a reminder that this might be their last summer; it might even be their last night.

Chapter Twenty-Nine

"If it was the last moment I was to live..."

The "Return of Several Ministers" may have ended in ambiguity, but the tide had definitely turned within the conscious thoughts of those feeling the weight of the trial's outcomes.

Reverend Samuel Willard had come from behind the cloak of hidden meanings, and declared boldly in church, through consecutive sermons throughout June, exactly what his thoughts were pertaining to the trials. He lectured that Satan's "Subtilty" could deceive. "Don't believe the Devil," he admonished, "if it were possible he would deceive the very Elect." (Judge Sewall, seated in the congregation may have squirmed at this declaration.) His sermon went on to point out that the Devil was particularly interested in bringing down the righteous, and thus, the churches of Massachusetts had been targeted. Satan exhibited a "peculiar rage" against "the Children of God, and he improves every opportunity against them…where the Gospel comes, here he raises all his Powers and does his utmost to oppose."

Reverend Willard warmed to his subject and recited Biblical passages that flew directly in the face of the judicial system, especially the policy being used by Judge Stoughton. With the conviction of a man on a mission to upset the witchcraft proceedings, he put it all on the pulpit.

"The Devil may represent an inosent, nay a godly person, doing a bad ackt. It calls us to self examination, selfe abasing," he said, hearkening back to the Puritan code of "look to thyself first for blemish in thy conduct." The Bible, he said, made it clear that "the devil cane do this upon divine permission & will do it with out he be prevented by God." Satan could take "on the image of any man representing it." And then he delivered the blow that should have sent the magistrates back to their privy chambers to consider just what they were doing.

Satan "cane perswade the person afflicted that it is done by the person thus represented." In essence, Willard, without equivocation, stated that Satan didn't even need witches to carry out his evil plans. He could come in the shape of any person he chose, innocent or not, and afflict someone. Although he didn't directly quote from the Book of Job, he could have used that poignant story to underscore the fact that God had in the past allowed the Devil to afflict a righteous person for his own reasons. He closed by trying to assure the congregation that God was still with them, even in these "darke" and "unaccountable" times.

Boston minister, Reverend William Milborne, who had been scolded and fined for his words of warning, had focused upon the passages of the "Return of Several Ministers" that warned of judging people of heretofore impeccable reputations. There were "several persons of good fame and of unspotted reputation," he declared in his petition to the magistrates. Undoubtedly, he was speaking of Reverend George Burroughs, John Alden, John Floyd, Rebecca Nurse, Mary Esty, and Sarah Cloyce, among others. He once again attacked the ubiquitous charges seen only by the afflicted girls. "Bare spectral testimonie" against "many whereof we cannot but in Charity Judge to be Innocent...if said specter testimonie pass for evidence we have great grounds to fear that the Innocent will be condemned."

The man at the pulpit in Salem Village was trying to deliver messages of hope as well, to a congregation that had been divided toward their support of him from the beginning. The trials had done nothing to garner their good will. Reverend Parris offered words of encouragement, stating God was the God of comfort, "who comforteth us in all our tribulation, that we may be able to comfort them which are in any affliction." To the ears of those whose relatives and friends were in prison and fearful for their lives, Parris' definition of "affliction" may have been in question. Did he mean the afflicted girls, of which his niece and daughter were included, or did he mean the afflictions of the poor souls crammed into stone prisons? To many, his bias and affiliation was clear.

Sarah Good Goes on Trial

It had been almost a month since the trials of June 3rd. In the interim, admonitions from clergymen, petitions from the friends and family of the accused had been presented to the magistrates, and several people had come forward to show their own "evidence" that the afflicted persons were faking their torments. Yet, as the Court of Oyer and Terminer convened again on June 28, 1692, there was no discernable difference in the structure of the trial, or the weight given to spectral evidence.

Sarah Good had sat in prison awaiting her fate since March 1st. For almost three months, she had felt the seasons change from the bone-chilling cold of Spring, to the damp heat of Summer. She had gone through the pain of childbirth within the dirty walls of Boston's Prison, only to watch the child die from lack of nutrition and hygiene. Her young daughter, Dorcas, had finally been brought to her in Boston on April 12th. Dorcas had not only confessed to witchcraft, but had implicated her mother, Sarah as the one who had supplied her with "familiars."

Summons were sent out for the primary people who would testify against Sarah Good:

(Summons for Witnesses)

[June 27, 1692]

W'm & Mary By the grace of God of England Scotland France & Ireland King & Queen def'rs of the faith &ca.

To Samuel Abbey & his Wife Joseph Herrick & his Wife goodwife   Bibber Abigall   Williams Elizabeth Hubbard.   Mary   Wolcott   Ann   Putman   Mercey Lewis . Samuel Brraybrook   Wee comand: you and Every of you all Excuses set apart to appear at the Special Court of Oyer & Terminer to be held at Salem for the County of Essex on the 28th. of this Instant month at Nine of the Clock in the Morning there to testify the truth to the best of your knowledge on Severall Indictments then & there to be Exhibited against Sarah Good for Sundry acts of Witchcrafts by her Comitted & done. hereof make return fail not dated in Salem June.27.1692 *Step: Sewall Clerc. To the Constables of Salem or any of them Greeting Dat: 28 Jun1692.

I have warned the parsens.above.named accorden to

tener of this summonce by me. *John putnam. Const of salem
(Reverse) Subpena versus. Sa: Good.

Sarah Good's trial was held in the Salem Town House, where Bridget Bishop had heard her final conviction. It was nine o'clock on June 28, 1692. As the ragged women stood before the stoic faces of the five magistrates and the gaggle of jurymen, she must have realized she was in enemy territory. Who would stand for her? Her entire life had been one of hopelessness and men deserting her, either figuratively or literally. Now, her very life would be decided by these men who were rifling through parchment papers, filled with accusations from the afflicted seated to her right.

She waited, tension mounting in the court room. This was a much larger meeting room than that of Salem Village's meetinghouse. She tugged on her ratty apron, and adjusted her stained collar, the stale smell of pipe tobacco smoke wafting from each movement she made. Her past miserable life played before her: her father's suicide, the resulting loss of her inheritance due to a stepfather's greed, her first husband's death that left her mired in debt, and her present husband who had watched as she begged for food and shelter throughout Salem Village. She felt the eyes of the self-righteous gathering of wealthy Salem merchants behind her, and it took all she could do not to turn and lash out at all of them.

As the depositions against Sarah Good were read out, alleging each spectral attack against the afflicted (that continued even after her imprisonment), the demise of Samuel and Mary Abbey's seventeen head of cattle, as well as sheep and hogs (after the Abbey's kicked the Good's out of their home), and other various vagrancies, the afflicted girls did what had become the backdrop to the proceedings, they howled, writhed, and even produced a very real prop.

During the trial, one of the afflicted screamed out that Sarah Good had just stabbed her in the breast with a knife. She had thrust it so hard that the blade broke. Triumphantly, the girl held up a broken piece of knife blade. As the gathering of jurymen, magistrates and spectators looked on aghast, a young man stood up and made a startling accusation. He told the room that the blade had come from his knife that had broken the day before in front of the very girl claiming she had just been stabbed. Furthermore, he had discarded the broken piece in her presence. He held up the broken knife and the court compared the blade to it. It fit exactly.

Sarah Good's trial.

Shockingly, at a moment when the testimony of some of these afflicted witnesses should have been brought sharply into question, the magistrates only admonished the girl to stick to the facts, and continued on with the trial as if nothing had happened. This was just one more question at this point as to what mission these trials were on. These men were ignoring admonitions from ministers, and brushing away actual evidence of fakery to continue on with the trials that were becoming increasingly unpopular. Had they decided that to admit they had been wrong was too much to bear upon their respected stations in the colony? Would the blood of Bridget Bishop sign their removal from their exalted stations?

Reverend Samuel Parris, taking the opportunity to place the stigma elsewhere concerning his home as the original compass point of the outbreak, reaffirmed his complaint sworn out on May 23rd to Hathorne and Corwin. He, along with Thomas Putnam, Jr., and Ezekiel Cheever had witnessed the sufferings of Betty Parris and Abigail Williams on March 1st during the first examination of Sarah Good. They reminded the court of Tituba's accusations (after admitting to witchcraft herself) that Sarah Good and Sarah Osborne had "hurt the children" and ridden with her upon a pole through the night sky, to join the Devil's Sabbaths. Other indictments were for attacking Elizabeth Hubbard, Ann Putnam Jr., and Sarah Bibber. Little Dorcas Good's confession was also read out. The woman's own child had claimed Sarah Good was a witch.

Sarah was found "Guilty" on the charges of witchcraft; a verdict that surprised only a few. She had been the scourge of Salem Village, hounding the hard-working people for scraps of food and a place to stay the night. Most had helped her out of pity for the dirty-faced child she dragged about with her.

Sarah was taken back to Salem Jail, where she had begun her journey of hell in March. She sucked on her foul pipe and undoubtedly thought of Bridget Bishop. Bishop had been found guilty, and they had hanged her.

Susanna Martin's Trial

On June 29th, Susanna Martin was brought before the Court of Oyer and Terminer. After Sarah Good's trial the day before, evidence had been heard concerning Tituba. It was likely a reconstruction of her examination on March 1st. No record of her trial is extant. She was probably sent to Salem Jail, where she may have been kept separated from the other accused witches, as ordered during her transport from Boston to Salem Town for the trials.

Susanna Martin was a 71-year-old matron from Amesbury, Massachusetts. She had been associated with witchcraft for over 30 years, narrowly skating out of the noose more than once. Tales of her audacious behavior had been town gossip for ages, each story more brazen than the next. Deodat Lawson had made the trip from Boston to witness the trials that day. Even he, after watching the afflicteds' antics on many occasions, was horrified at the convulsions greeting Martin's arrival. The girls seemed to be twisted into contortions that threatened to pop their arms from their shoulder sockets. One of them threw up blood. It was so startling that someone actually dipped his finger into it to make sure it was not fake. It was not faked...it was real blood.

The depositions read against Martin were lengthy and hard to believe. Her neighbors from Amesbury had accused her of everything from drowning their cattle, to pitching cats at them from her second-story window to chew at their throats. Sarah Atkinson of Newbury took it a step further, accusing Martin of practically walking on water!

(Testimony of Sarah Atkinson
v. Susannah Martin)

[June 29, 1692]

Sarah Attkinson aged forty Eight years or thereabouts testifieth thatt Some time in the Spring of the year about Eighteen years Since Susanna Martin came unto our house att Newbury from Amsbury in an Extraordinary dirty Season w'n itt was not fitt for any [pbar]son to travell She then came on foot, w'n She came into our house I asked her whether She came from Amsbury a fot She Sayd She did I asked how She could come in this time a foott and bid my children make way for her to come to the fire to dry her selfe She replyed She was as dry as I was and turn'd her Coats on Side, and I could nott [pbar]ceive thatt the Soule of her Shows were wett I was startled att itt that she should come soe dry and told her thatt I should have been wett up to my knees if I Should have come So farr on foott she replyd thatt She scorn'd to have a drabled tayle. ["Scorned to have a draggled tail," meaning the tail of her dress becoming soiled.]

Susanna Martin had traveled on an especially foul day when the rain had made the rutted roads almost impassable. Yet, upon arriving at her friend's home, she was completely dry, not even the soles of her feet were wet. The implication was either she walked *above* the muddy terrain, or *flew*.

The rest of the depositions were from early May when Susanna Martin was first examined. The usual complaints of spectral attacks, pinching, choking, etc. were read aloud to the jury. Even Samuel Parris had put forth a complaint against Martin, on behalf of his niece and others.

(Deposition of Samuel Parris , Nathaniel Ingersoll and Thomas Putnam v. Susannah Martin)

[May 2, 1692]

The Deposition of Sam: Parris aged about. 39 years, & Nathanael Ingersoll aged about fifty & eight yeares and also Tho: Putman aged about fourty yeares all of Salem -- testifyeth & saith that Abigail Williams , Mercy Lewes Mary Walcot, Susannah Shelding and John Indian were much afflicted at the examination of Susannah Martin of Almsbury Widdow-before the honoured Magistrates the. 2. May. 1692 & that Goody Bibber (who before had not accused her) & some other of the afflicted then & there testifyed that there was a black man whispering in her ear, & also that the said Bibber Abigail Williams & Mary Walcot & John Indian could not come near said Martin when upon triall they were ordered by the Magistrates to attempt it, & their agonies & tortures they charged said Martin as the cause of, & also we farther saw that when she said Martin bit her lips they were bitten, & when the afflicted were ordered to go towards her they were knockt down.

Martin's inquest notes were read out. They included her obvious disdain for the proceedings and the girls' "afflictions." The magistrates reprimanded her for laughing at the obvious torment of the girls. They re-read her comments from her earlier questioning: "Well, may I laugh at such folly!" "What do you think ails them?" Hathorne had asked her. Susanna shrugged, obviously unimpressed by the whole performance. "I don't desire to spend my judgment on it," she had said off-handedly. Frustrated, Hathorne had pushed, "Don't you think they are bewitched?" "No, I do not think they are!" she spat. "If they be dealing with the black arts, you may know as well as I!"

Her irreverence only fueled the hysteria from the girls. The magistrates ordered her hand to be placed on the afflicted persons. The "Touch Test" was administered and the girls calmed. This seemed to amuse Martin even more.

Susanna managed to hit one solid stroke against the myriad accusations of her specter visiting the girls. "He that appeared in the shape of Samuel, a glorified saint, may appear in anyone's shape." This Biblical reference to the Witch of Endor was a powerful move. The pawn had pushed back a square in the Devil's board game. That the Witch of Endor had caused the shape of Samuel to appear before Saul, may have caused the magistrates to pause. She had used the Bible in her defense, and used it against "spectral evidence." After a moment's pause, they moved on. Her Biblical reference was but a sniffle to be ignored.

Like Bridget Bishop, she was accused of entering the windows of unsuspecting men at night, and climbing into bed with them. Others accused her of taking on amazing shapes, including "a marvelous light about the bigness of a half bushel." One witnessed her melt into an empty space only to emerge as a flock of birds that "pecked and pinched." She had appeared as a cat, and carried men away to feast and frolic with the Devil.

The haughty Martin was found "Guilty," and taken around the corner to Salem Jail to sit in the fumes of Sarah Good's pipe.

Sarah Wildes' Trial

The trial of Sarah Wildes that day received scant mention. The depositions had been gathered since her earlier examination on April 22nd. Even the testimony of Reverend John Hale of Beverly was put forth before the jury. It was entered into the court files July 2nd, a few days after the trial.

(Testimony of Rev. John Hale v. Sarah Wildes)

[July 2, 1692]

I John Hale of Beverly aged 56 years beeing summoned to appear & give evidence against Sarah Wiles of Topsfeild July .2. 1692; Testify that about 15 or 16 yeares agoe came to my house the wife of John Hirrek of Beverly w'th an aged woeman she said was her mother Goody Reddington of Topsfeild come to me for counsel beeing in trouble of spirit. when the said Reddington opned her greifs to me this was one that she was assaulted by witchcraft that Goody wiles her neighb'r bewitched her & afflicted her many times greiviously, telling me many particular storys how & when she troubled her, w'ch I have forgotten. She said allso that a son in law of said Wiles did come & visit her (shee called him an honest young man named John as I take it) & did pitty her the said Reddington, signifying to her that he beleived his mother wiles was a witch & told her storys of his mother. I allso understood by them, that this Goody Wiles was mother in law to a youth named as I take it Jonathan Wiles who about twenty yeares agoe or more did act or was acted very strangly Insomuch that I was invited to joyn with Mr Cobbet & others at Ipswich to advize & pray for the said Youth; whome some thought to counterfeit, others to be possessed by the devill. But I remember Mr Cobbet thought he was under Obsession of the devil. Goody Reddingtons discourse hath caused me to have farther thoughts of the said Youths case whether he were not bewitched.

Obviously, the words of a respected clergyman carried a lot of weight. Sarah Wildes was sentenced to death by hanging and led from the court room.

Elizabeth How's Trial

Elizabeth How's trial was held on June 30, 1692. The 50-year-old carried the distinction of Rebecca Nurse's sister-in-law, also from Topsfield. According to ignorant inhabitants, the Nurse genealogy chart must be filled with cauldrons and broomsticks.

How's main accusers were a family from the neighboring town of Ipswich. The Perley family accused Elizabeth How of afflicting their 10-year-old daughter until she was down to skin and bones. Reverend Samuel Phillips and Edward Payson, ministers of Rowley, did what Cotton Mather had recommended before. They took Elizabeth How to face the little girl.

"Did I hurt you?" asked Goody How, taking the child's hand in her own.

"No, never!" said the little girl. "If I did complain of you in my fits I knew not that I did so." The interview was conducted outside the Perley's house. The little girl's brother, listening through a window, hissed at his sister, "Say Goody How is a witch! Say she is a witch!" The little girl refused to say the lady whose hand she was holding was a witch. Reverends Phillips and Payson made note of it, and came away believing the charges were nothing more than that born of gossip or some misunderstanding. They put forth a deposition saying so before the magistrates.

Reverend Samuel Willard was of the same mind, and said so. The girls, feeling invincible, suddenly cried out against the Reverend, whose views on the afflicteds' antics were no secret. To the shock of the magistrates, and all gathered, the girls accused him of witchcraft. They had set their cap too high.

Samuel Willard had been the President of Harvard, fulfilling Increase Mather's role while Mather was in England lobbying for a new charter. He was a significant figure in Boston. The girls may have felt that if Reverend George Burroughs was fair game, and sat in prison at this moment on the charges of witchcraft, why not go for a clergyman who was proving to be problematic. It backfired.

"There will be no more of that!" one of the judges sternly admonished. "You are mistaken." As a hush fell over the court room, perhaps doubts beginning to form as to the validity of the afflicteds' charges against any of the witches, another magistrate jumped in, tempering his words in a more consoling tone. He suggested the girls must have mistaken Reverend Willard with Constable John Willard, who was, even now, sitting in prison awaiting his trial on witchcraft charges. All eyes swung toward the girls, who swallowed hard beneath the scrutiny. Yes! That must be it. They got the wrong Willard.

While the rescue line tossed to the accusing girl mollified the crowd for the moment, had it satisfied them? The judges couldn't confirm the afflicteds' accusations one minute, and toss them out the next. Either witchcraft was real, or it wasn't. You can't draw the line when someone of distinction is called into question. Unlike the examinations from early March, when a legal court had not been in charge, the Salem Witch Trials were finding themselves in murky water. It was becoming harder to sleep well at night, and not just from attacking specters.

Elizabeth How was found Guilty. Her life of hardship would be over soon. Her husband, James, whom she had married at 23, had been stricken with blindness seven years prior. She was left with six children and all the chores that came with running a farm. Her father had a large estate, of which she was in line to inherit. She would not see that day.

Many of her friends and family traveled from Topsfield to vouch for her. Her blind husband never forgot her during her imprisonment. Led by their daughters, Mary and Abigail How (due to his blindness), he traveled the distance from Topsfield twice-weekly to whichever jail his beloved wife was being held. Despite the expense of the trips, he came with food, drink, and clean linen. Her husband's 94-year-old father testified that Elizabeth is "very dutiful, careful, loving, obedient, and kind, tenderly leading her husband about by the hand in his want of eyesight."

It was the other depositions accusing How of witchcraft that overrode the many pleadings on her behalf. Accused of poisoning an apple, ruining cider and beer, causing the sickness and death of cattle, and even of bewitching one

Goodwife Sherwin to death, she sank beneath the testimonies. Her last words to the court, as they urged her to confess were, "If it was the last moment I was to live, God knows I am innocent of anything in this nature."

The magistrates had set their course, and it was obvious, they would not deviate from it. Only one accused witch threw them. Rebecca Nurse.

Chapter Thirty

Rebecca Nurse and Gallows Hill

The trial of Rebecca Nurse took place on June 29th. The Nurse family had been vigorously campaigning for her innocence since early May. No less than thirty-nine signatures appeared on a petition testifying to Rebecca's impeccable reputation. The harshest thing said about her was a rare squabble with a neighbor. Yet, this woman stood before the magistrates that sultry Wednesday morning, accused by Ann Putnam Sr. of murdering six children (who had appeared before Putnam in their winding sheets), and of the death of the husband of one Sarah Holten.

Three years earlier, Sarah Holten's husband Benjamin had gotten into an altercation with Rebecca when his hogs were once again found routing up her garden. According to Sarah, Rebecca stormed into their home "railing and scolding," threatening to have her son shoot the pigs. Sarah stated that even though her husband had handled the verbal attack with calm and decorum, his troubles had just begun.

Shortly after the altercation, Sarah claimed her husband began to suffer stomach pain, choking fits, and even blindness. This evidence, heard now in court as an indication of witchcraft, was refuted by several sources in support of Rebecca Nurse. Nathaniel and Hannah Ingersoll said, although it was true Holten had died while suffering violent convulsions, no one at the time said anything about witchcraft. Oddly, John Putnam Sr., who had voiced suspicions of Rebecca earlier, now stated that when their son-in-law John Fuller and daughter Rebecca Shepard had died during bouts with fever, witchcraft was never mentioned. Salem Town had been dealing with a plague of small pox at the time of the witchcraft outbreak, and fevers born of a variola virus ravaged many homes across the country. It was just another strange juxtaposition of the trials that one Putnam was condemning Rebecca Nurse, while another tossed a backhanded vote in her favor.

Rebecca was facing four indictments for witchcraft credited to her during her March 24th examination. She was accused of attacking Ann Putnam Jr., Mary Walcott, Betty (Elizabeth) Hubbard, and Abigail Williams. Strangely, Ann Putnam Sr.'s name was not among those noted. According to Ann Sr., Nurse's specter had come into her bed chamber on several occasions, showing her the bodies of murdered children, and even debating scripture verses. She had been choked and frozen in place by the menacing spirit.

Rebecca's trial was unprecedented in the number of people who came forward not just to attest to her pious character, but to cast doubt on the afflicted. The tide had definitely turned against the girls, at least in the court of public opinion. James Kettle stated that Betty Hubbard had told him "several untruths" during a Sabbath in late May. More disturbing was Joseph Hutchinson Sr.'s retelling of a conversation he had with Abigail Williams.

Abigail had been describing not one, but two different books the Devil had offered for her signature. They were both "red as blode," Abigail said, which "the black man" repeatedly pushed toward her. Hutchinson testified, "I asked her if shee was not afraid to see the devell. She said at the first shee was and did goe from him but now shee was not a fraid but Could talke with him as well as shee Could with mee."

If an accused witch had said the words attributed to Abigail's boasting, it would have been a crystal-clear indication that the person was on easy terms with the Devil, and probably in alliance with him. Yet, Abigail Williams sat unscathed, and unexamined.

The attacks on the girls' veracity continued. Former employers of Mercy Lewis testified that she had been known to tell "untruths." Robert Moulton went on record saying how Susanna Sheldon "Contradict[ed] herself when she told differing stories about how she traversed a stone wall. First, she said "the witches halled her Upone her bely though the yeard like a snacke and halled her over the stone wall." Her next version was much tamer; she stated that "she came over the stone wall her selfe." Sheldon also claimed "that she Rid Upone apoole (a pole) to boston and she said the divel Caryed the poole." (These testimonies were in written depositions, and the spelling is believed to be that of the one reporting the events, or taken down by a scribe.)

It is of interest, that here again, we have one of the accusers putting herself in a position that on the flip side was condemning others. Tituba testified she rode upon a pole, as did others. These were confessed witches. Yet, here we have Susannah Sheldon stating she had flown upon one, and it is filed away as the poor child being spirited away by the Devil.

Sarah Bibber, who had been an outspoken opponent of Rebecca Nurse, came under fire next. Nurse's family had collected depositions against some of the accusers. Two of Bibber's neighbors stated that Sarah was "unruly turbulent" who was "double tongued" and "could fall into fits as often as she plesed."

Perhaps, the most damning refutation of the afflicteds' authenticity came from Rebecca Nurse's daughter who had come to the trial along with many others of the matriarch's family. They watched in horror as the girls ramped up their performances. Even the jury and the magistrates were taken aback at the spectacle before them. Sarah Bibber suddenly screamed out that Rebecca Nurse had just stuck pins into her knees, and she showed the pins protruding through her dress to prove it.

Sarah Nurse, who had been watching the row of afflicted persons carefully throughout the trial jumped up and declared "I saw Goody Bibber pull pins out of her close and held them between her fingers and claspt her hands round her knees and then she cried out and said Goody Nurse pinned her. This I can testify!"

As to the witch marks found on Rebecca's body, two of her daughters, Rebecca Preston and Mary Tarbell, said that their mother had for many years dealt with the "infirmity" the midwives had found suspicious.

It should be mentioned here that the Nurse family was the only family of the accused witches that gathered documented testimony *against the accusers*, as well as going door-to-door and field-to-field to accrue 39 signatures in her favor. They are also the only family to ask Judge Stephen Sewall to see copies of the court trial records.

Several factors assaulted the jurymen's deliberation as they came to terms with what they had witnessed that day. They looked at the frail form of Rebecca Nurse, standing unsteadily before them, a confused look in her eyes, as though she could not comprehend what was happening to her. She seemed so meek and humble. They, no doubt, had heard of the admonitions of the "Several Ministers" as to the weight that should be given to "spectral evidence" and condemning those of unblemished reputations. Lastly, they had just heard testimonies *against* the *afflicted*, casting doubt on their veracity, a first of that magnitude.

The jury left the room and went off to deliberate. The strain amongst the Nurse family must have been formidable. Were they seeing their beloved mother and grandmother for the last time before this court of madmen hanged her?

Thomas Fiske, foreman of the jury, led the group of men back into the court, where the room waited in silence like a breath held in place. All eyes were on him, as he read the verdict. "Not Guilty!"

Several of the magistrates looked at each other in surprise. Had he really said "*NOT* Guilty?" After only a stunned moment of silence, the court room erupted in chaos. The girls shrieked out in unison so loudly, that all were stunned. They fell into contortions so bizarre that all thought they would never recover. It was eerily reminiscent of the backlash witnessed when Mary Esty—Rebecca's sister—was released.

The court ordered a temporary adjournment, a deeply-needed reprieve from the ear-splitting chaos inside the main room. The Nurse family may have grasped each other in happiness, only to feel a restless trepidation that it could all be taken away. Rebecca had a chance to rest. Due to her deafness and dazed condition, she appeared not to understand the drama playing out around her. She sank into a chair.

Outside the hearing of the anxious crowd, two of the judges voiced their displeasure at the jury's verdict, one judge declaring, based on the girls' torments in the court room, he would try Rebecca Nurse anew. Chief Justice

William Stoughton took a steady breath and fixed his gaze upon the jury (who sat in adjournment as well), coming to rest on Thomas Fiske. In an authoritative, yet measured tone, he told Fiske that, "I will not impose on the jury, but I must ask you if you considered one statement made by the prisoner? When Deliverance Hobbs was brought into the court to testify, the prisoner turning her head to her said, "What, do you bring her? She is one of us.""

That statement had been made during Rebecca's examination in May. Many of the jurymen were not even present during the questioning, as were some of the newer judges absent. Thomas Fiske, stammered. He was not certain as to what Judge Stanton was referring to. Fiske finally admitted he had forgotten the event, and asked if he could question Rebecca directly as to her meaning of the statement in question. The other jurors followed him.

Before he could even enter the court room, he could hear the wailing beginning anew from the bench of afflicted persons. It was unnerving, to say the least. He found Rebecca sitting in her almost trance-like condition, perhaps grateful for the first time in her life that she could barely hear the cacophony of voices accusing her of such heinous acts. She lifted her glazed eyes to the man before her and strained to hear him above the noise. Fiske repeated her statement from her earlier examination where she called Hobbs "one of us" and asked her to explain her meaning.

Rebecca did not know this man. She looked at him with uncertainty, a dull, foreign absence of comprehension behind her gaze. The noise in the room was deafening. Was he saying something to her? She was so tired. Fiske repeated the question, and Rebecca said nothing. He looked about him for some sign of what he was to do next. No one came to his aid.

He returned to the private room, a din of howling behind him, and reported that his query had been met with silence. The jury now had a dilemma on their hands. What did that silence mean? Why, if she was innocent, hadn't she come to her defense and answer him? The statement she had given that Deliverance Hobbs is "one of us" could mean two different things: That Hobbs was a witch like herself, or simply, that Hobbs was a prisoner under suspicion of witchcraft (like herself), and why bring her in as a witness?

The evident torment continuing from the court room next door may have swayed the jury. Thomas Fiske admitted that "these words (or lack thereof) were to me a principal Evidence against her." After all, this woman had been accused by more than one of attending the Devil's feasts, acting as Deacon to his Sabbath.

Within the hearing of the collected family of Rebecca Nurse, Thomas Fiske declared, that after careful deliberation, they were retracting their verdict. Beneath the pleased gaze of Chief Justice Stoughton, Fiske declared Rebecca Nurse "Guilty" of witchcraft and sentenced to hang.

It was reported that Rebecca collapsed after the trial. Whether she was carried around the corner to the jail, or she finally felt her strength leave her within the foul prison room, is not clear. She was informed, probably by her family, what exactly had just happened in the court room. It was explained to her that her failure to answer Fiske's question concerning her earlier statement at her examination had been the deciding factor in changing her verdict to "Guilty."

Rebecca, the gravity of her missed chance to defend herself, blurted out she had not heard him "being something hard of hearing, and full of grief." She, too late, told her audience that she "intended no otherways, than as they were Prisoners with us, and therefore did then, and yet do judge them not legal Evidence against their fellow Prisoners." Her family hastened to comfort her, assuring her they were not finished fighting for her.

Indeed, they pulled together all their forces. They went to Fiske and asked him what exactly had occurred to change the verdict; they presented Rebecca's statement they had just obtained, explaining why she hadn't answered Fiske's question in court; and they obtained copies of the court documents from Stephen Sewall. They took their information to the top—the office of Governor William Phipps. After hearing them out, and taking a short time to review the information, he ordered a reprieve for Rebecca Nurse. Away from the howling of the girls, and probably weighing the fact that the King of England was watching him in his new governing role, he did what he thought was fair.

Elated, the Nurse family ran to inform their mother that she was coming home. Robert Calef recorded that upon hearing of the reprieve "the Accusers renewed their dismal outcries against her," and "some Salem Gentlemen then persuaded him to rescind it." Chief Justice Stoughton was from Dorchester. Who were the "Salem Gentlemen" that pressured the Governor to think again? Hathorne? Corwin?

It has haunted scholars, and this author, why these educated men would overlook the obvious lies and ploys utilized by the afflicted girls and condemn church-covenanted members to the gallows? Over and over, they had ignored the evidence that the afflicted persons were faking their attacks, and that 90% of the "evidence" offered was of a spectral variety that could not scientifically be refuted.

These magistrates and members of the council may have felt that the troubles they were now embroiled in with the Indian attacks, and disputes with the French and Canada, were evidence the Devil was raging his own war with Massachusetts. The failed attempts to save the villagers of Maine lay on their doorstep. Many of that state's refugees huddled in broken homes throughout the Salem area. Is it not better to blame the Devil and his witches for the slaughter, and sabotage of their efforts? Here was a scapegoat on which they could lay their ineffectiveness.

Rebecca Nurse had witnessed her last hope of salvation, in more ways than one. Not satisfied to just condemn her to death, the congregation of the First Church of Salem, of which she was still listed as a member, decided to excommunicate her. She had been found guilty of aligning herself with the Devil. It fell to Reverend Nicholas Noyes to pronounce her sentence before a packed room on Sunday, July 3rd.

Unable to walk, Rebecca was strapped to a chair and carried from Salem Jail into the Sabbath meeting. Broken and bent, she bowed her head in defeat. Through the muffled sounds that managed to penetrate her ears, she listened in numb disbelief as Noyes read off her list of sins and offences. Before the congregation that had once been her peers, he finally announced on behalf of the entire church, that she was unclean and unworthy to continue to hold the ordinances to which she had once been privy.

They had stripped her of her home, as they pulled her from her bed and threw her into jail. They had stripped her of her decency, as they disrobed her and probed her nakedness. They had stripped her of her good reputation. And now, harder to bear than the threat of death, they had taken her beloved covenants from her, and declared her unworthy. The words she first uttered when she was told by Peter Cloyce (as she lay ill in her bed) that the girls had cried out against her, came back to torment her depressed mind: "As to this thing I am innocent as the child unborn," she had pleaded, "but surely, what sin hath God found in me unrepented of that He could lay down such an affliction on me in my old age?"

Samuel Parris witnessed the trial of Rebecca Nurse. Although a member of the First Church of Salem, she had been his parishioner for three years, as the Salem Village meetinghouse was much closer to her home. He would have known of her deafness and righteous character, yet he did nothing. He even bore witness against her in his depositions on behalf of the afflicted girls.

(Deposition of Samuel Parris, Nathaniel Ingersoll, & Thomas Putnam v. Rebecca Nurse)

[June 29, 1692]

The Deposition of Sam: Parris aged about 39. years & Nathanael Ingersoll aged about fifty & eight yeares & Thomas Putman aged about fourty yeares all of Salem -- testifyeth & saith that Ann Putman Sen'r & her daughter Ann, & Mary   Walcot & Abigail Williams were severall times & greviously tortured at the Examination of Rebekah Nurse wife to Francis Nurse of Salem before the Honoured Magistrates the. 24.March. 1691/2 & particularly that when her hands were at liberty some of the afflicted were pinched, & upon the motion of her head & fingers some of them were tortured; & farther that some of the afflicted then

& there affirmed that they saw a black man whispering in her ear, & that they saw birds fluttering about her.

Nathaniel Ingersoll bore witness to what he had seen, but past documents show he and his family were not happy with the witchcraft madness. His wife Hannah had scolded the girls in the past for their antics, and his daughter had testified to their lies. Samuel Parris posted a second deposition against Rebecca, always with a Putnam's name beside his own. Thomas Putnam Jr. was Parris's biggest supporter and instrumental in landing him the office of Salem Village's minister.

Gallows Hill

Tuesday, July 19, 1692, Sheriff George Corwin gave the final orders to the guards flanking a wooden cart with oversized wheels. The crowds had gathered as the blistering sun rose toward its noon zenith. There was almost a feeling of holiday as housewives left their chores, and farmers hurried to slop their pigs. Children, some too small to understand the gravity of the day, looked about at the expectant faces and wondered what the festivities were for.

Inside the jail, Rebecca Nurse was lifted from the floor, and her wrists tied. She may have been carried to the cart. Susanna Martin, Elizabeth How, Sarah Good, and Sarah Wildes were likewise bound and lifted up onto the cart. No record remains to testify of their mood as they looked out at the crowd who had come to witness their deaths. If the abrasive tongues of some of the prisoners lashed out, their remarks were not taken down, as the cart began its sojourn.

Along the same route that Bridget Bishop had been transported, the five rode over ruts so deep it threatened to throw them from the cart. They jerked along, the crowd keeping pace. Some jeered, some followed in sickened silence. Many had chosen to stay away. This was not, to them, the shining "city on the hill" they had escaped England to embrace. This was hell riding through their streets in a creaking wagon.

The nooses were slung over a thick tree bough, whether one at a time, or all five at once. As a later execution would prove, eight had been hung from the same limb, so it is not unreasonable to suppose there were five nooses.

Reverend Nicholas Noyes, who had passed the sentence of excommunication upon Rebecca Nurse less than three weeks ago, gave the prisoners one last chance to save their immortal souls by confessing to witchcraft. It would do nothing to keep them from the noose, but it might allow them some redemption in the next world.

Sarah Good, in her final defiance, snapped back at Noyes that she was not a witch. He chided her, saying he *knew* she was a witch. Fury spilling from her, she yelled, "You are a liar! I am no more a witch than you are a wizard, and if you take my life God will give you blood to drink." This may have been the only prophetic statement uttered by the woman. Nicholas Noyes did, indeed, die years later with his mouth filled with blood. He had hemorrhaged to death.

The five were hanged. All the efforts of the Nurse family had met with futility. The hopes that their mother would return to her home and take up her apron disappeared with the drop of a rope. The ravine at the edge of the hanging site made an easy burial place as it was a makeshift grave where bodies could be tossed and some rocks and dirt thrown over them.

According to Marilynne K. Roach's excellent book, *The Salem Witch Trials: A Day-to-Day Chronicle of a Community Under Siege*, Rebecca's body did not lay in that neglected sepulcher for long:

"By family tradition the Nurses waited for darkness (sunset was about a quarter after seven) then rowed up the North River to the bend by the ledge and exhumed Rebecca's body. According to another tradition Caleb Buffum (a distant relative) noticed this effort from his home nearby and helped carry the remains to the shore. From there a small craft could slip downstream past town on the midnight's high tide, then north up the estuary to Crane River and along its narrowing length to the Nurses' land, where they buried her privately on home-ground."

A loving memorial stands witness today at the Rebecca Nurse homestead in Danvers, Massachusetts, a permanent testament that this pious matriarch was brought home to rest.

Rebecca Nurse's grave monument at her home.

Chapter Thirty-One

Terror in Andover

An oppressiveness lay thick in the air, like sodden clouds threatening to burst. Hands faltered in the daily kneading of bread dough; tongues—once frantic with gossip—were suddenly still. The Bible's pages were searched anew in hopes of validation for what they had done. Even the clouds, hanging low and grey in the summer sky, reverberated with Shakespeare's' quote from almost a century earlier: *"A glooming peace this morning with it brings; The sun for sorrow will not show its head: Go hence, to have more talk of these sad things; Some shall be pardon'd, and some punished: For never was a story of more woe." (Romeo and Juliet, 1595)*

Francis Nurse, much in years, gathered his family around him. His wife Rebecca lay beneath the freshly-turned earth at the bottom of the small slope outside their home. Each sound of an approaching horse brought fear to the inhabitants of the large farmhouse. Would there be retribution for carrying away the body? Now, with a convicted family witch newly executed, would more of them be taken away? Other entire families had fallen beneath that sword. Their two aunts, Mary Esty and Sarah Cloyce, were still imprisoned awaiting their trials.

The knocks at their door were those of friends, bearing food and words of comfort, some sitting in silence with the

379

family, or sobbing softly. There were no words that could shine any light of reason upon this travesty of justice. It was a frightening, anxious feeling that hung like the scent of drying herbs beneath the beamed ceilings.

While the small world of Salem Village turned in a dazed aftermath of the hangings, some of the accused took action. The hangings spurred a panic among those waiting for a trial that promised no reprieve from the gallows. It was those with money who decided "the heck with justice."

John Alden, who had been examined and found probably guilty of witchcraft on May 28th, had been given permission to await his trial under house arrest. His reputation as an accredited soldier in the Indian wars had not been forgotten. His father and mother were John and Priscilla Alden, who would later be made famous as the romance of the Plymouth landing era.

Unfortunately, for John Jr., he was "a tall man from Boston," the very criteria needed to satisfy Tituba's description of the man who forced her to sign his book way back in February. The justice system seemed to swing between accusing George Burroughs (swarthy-skinned "black man") and John Alden ("tall man from Boston") as the person to whom Tituba attributed her tortures. Burroughs was now supposedly the ringleader of the witches, but not the Devil. What role did John Alden play in that chessboard of evil?

The day after the hangings a group gathered in John Alden's home for a day of fasting and prayer. Samuel Willard and Cotton Mather bent their heads with the anxious Alden. Judge Samuel Sewall was also in attendance, and noted in his diary that the clouds suddenly "burst open in a brave shower of rain." Sewall offered a prayer himself, a show of support for the prisoner. As John Alden thought over his predicament, weighing whether to flee or face his accusers, others of the accused opened their purses and fled.

Nathanial Cary was the first to take action. He had watched the examination against his wife and found it "a cruel mockery." The sobering reality of the hangings finally prompted him to facilitate her escape from prison on July 30th. Whether he bribed a guard, or found a means to smuggle her out, Cary "spirited" her away to Rhode Island. Fearing that was still too close to the proceedings, and hearing rumors that they were being pursued, the Cary's headed to New York.

Sarah and Edward Bishop, their name so closely aligned with the executed Bridget Bishop, decided not to wait for a benevolent outcome. They escaped and went into hiding.

Mary and Phillip English, also given better conditions than the other accused witches, were under guard in Boston and allowed some freedom during the daytime. The fact that they were friends with Governor Phips and his wife improved their situation. Thus, under what had been mixed feelings among the congregation, they attended church to hear Reverend Joshua Moody pontificate on a rather interesting subject.

Moody, no supporter of the witch trials murmurings against respected and prominent citizens, realized the dire straits in which Phillip and Mary English found themselves. There were already murmurings concerning perceived prejudice in the judicial system. Why was it that the elite, such as ex-Judge Saltonstall (of whom the girls had cried against once he denounced their theatrics) had not been imprisoned? The judges would be hesitant to let English go, a man who had been accused of wizardry and spoken out against the fakery of the girls.

Reverend Moody took the pulpit and looked down at the haggard faces of Phillip and Mary. Many were whispering behind their backs. How dare these accused people appear in church? It was blasphemy. In words that were intended for the English's ears, he quoted from Mathew 10:23, "If they persecute you in one city, flee to another." He continued on with a sermon, that did little to mask his meaning. Perhaps he felt safer in Boston than he would have preaching such scripture in Salem Village.

After the meeting, he and Samuel Willard visited with Phillip and Mary, and tossing subtlety to the wind, urged them to escape. Phillip resisted. Not only would running show as an indication of guilt, but his wealth of possessions would fall into the hands of Sheriff George Corwin...and English had *many* possessions. He would also forfeit the £4,000 bail that had allowed he, his wife Mary, and their six-year-old daughter Susanna to stay in better quarters in the Boston Prison jailkeeper's house. It also allowed them freedom during the day, as long as they returned at night.

"God will not permit them to touch me," he said, with less confidence than he was feeling. His wife Mary, who had endured more prison time than he, and was even now sick with consumption from the inhumane prison conditions, urged him to reconsider.

"Do you not think the sufferers innocent?" she pleaded. "Why not when we suffer also?"

Moody and Willard finally pressed him. If he would not look after his wife's wellbeing, they would carry her away. He finally capitulated. A letter of recommendation was hastily drawn up and a carriage sent for from Sir Benjamin Fletcher of New York. The letter admonished that Mrs. English was to be shown every courtesy. Once Phillip agreed to go as well, his name, and others, were added. New York, under the influence of the Dutch, was not suffering the witchcraft malady, and suddenly found itself harboring refugees from the noose.

Andover's Witches

In Andover, Massachusetts, the wife of Joseph Ballard lay in her bed, an invalid of many months. Local doctors had been brought in, but no remedy seemed to help her. With the witch hysteria going on in Salem, some began to look with fresh eyes at their loved ones dealing with fevers, aches, and other maladies. The afflicted girls of Salem Village had developed a reputation for their ability to see into the Invisible World and pluck out the witches tormenting the poor souls of God-fearing people. Their efforts had resulted already in ridding the Massachusetts Bay Colony of six accomplices of Satan. It was therefore decided to bring two of the more-gifted "seers" to Andover to see if they could discern who was afflicting their sickly.

The people of that town backed the decision of Joseph Ballard to bring in two of the girls and a man was sent to fetch them. Ann Putnam Jr., although only 12-years-of-age, and Mary Walcott, stepped into the cart and rode into Andover like rock stars. Villagers with ailing relatives were eagerly awaiting their arrival. They set up the sick rooms in readiness. For the two girls, this was a heady experience. The reverence with which they were met outshone those in Salem (Town and Village) who had were beginning to scold them as liars.

Ann and Mary were led into the house where they went into their trances and confirmed the fears of Andover, that there were witches sitting at the headboards and feet of the infirmed. To add to the ominous import of their visions, upon hearing there were witches among them, the younger inhabitants of the homes would suddenly fall into convulsions, their eyes open to the Invisible World, as well. But then, a predicament presented itself. Ann and Mary had never been to Andover. Unlike Salem Village, they were ignorant of the local gossip or the names of the usual suspects. In short, when asked "who" was afflicting the bedridden victims, they faltered.

It seems the girls were always able to skate away from anything that came close to the unveiling of their trickery. Rather than look askance at the afflicted duo's inability to name names, the good people of Andover, along with most of the church deacons, and Reverend Thomas Bernard, decided to conduct an experiment that would save time in discovering the witches of their town. They placed the two girls into the front of the Andover meetinghouse. Ann and Mary were still showing symptoms of their trances and afflictions garnered during their ordeal of going into so many houses and witnessing such a variety of witches. This was a perfect setting of the "Touch Test." No matter that the girls didn't know the names of the witches, they could touch them and "cry out."

A number of people from Andover were rounded up and taken to the meetinghouse where they were blindfolded. Some were the typical village miscreants, vagabonds like Sarah Good. Others were the fodder of gossip of one kind or another. To be fair, other citizens without blemish were added to the line-up to give an impartial "reading." One-by-one they were led to the two girls and their hands placed into the hands of the afflicted. If, at the point of "touch," either of the girls was suddenly cured of her symptoms, the person was accused of being a witch.

Simple enough. But the test went afoul. The church deacons figured a handful of people might fall beneath the test. But to their astonishment, and horror, almost every person failed the test. Former Deputy Dudley Bradstreet, who was responsible for Essex County, found himself suddenly writing out forty arrest warrants on the charges of witchcraft! As more people were placed before the gifted hands of the duo from Salem Village, other names were added. In exasperation, Bradstreet set down his quill and declared he could not with good conscience write out any more warrants based on this type of evidence.

The bloodthirsty among the gathering may have reminded him that Martha Carrier, the "Queen of Hell," was a resident of Andover, and even now was awaiting her trial. If one of Satan's leaders had lived among them, how many more might be passing themselves off as humble villagers?

Andover would soon have its first confessed witch. Widow Ann Foster was brought before the bar in Salem Village on a complaint of witchcraft, possibly from Joseph Ballard. At first, Goody Foster denied the charges, but she had not accounted for the gallery of afflicted girls and their outbursts. Mary Walcott, Mary Warren, Elizabeth Hubbard, and Ann Putnam Jr. all screamed that she was pinching and choking them. Beneath such an unnerving assault, she admitted that, Yes, the Devil had come to her "almost half a year since."

As usual, when the girls heard a confession in the works, they quieted and watched with a mixture of confusion (this woman was admitting to their accusations) and the thrill of the kill. Foster said the Devil had appeared to her in the form of a white-feathered bird with large eyes, that sat upon her table and promised her, like Tituba, many "pretty things." It had finally "vanished away black" and she found herself able to afflict others with only her glance. Foster then laid the blame at Martha Carrier's feet, the renowned witch of Andover. It was Martha, Foster said, who told her to hurt the girls seated to her left.

That same day, Goody Foster's granddaughter, Mary Lacy Jr., was accused by Timothy Swan of tormenting him.

Ann Foster was held over in Salem Jail where Reverend Hale questioned her further. She admitted she had actually been in the Devil's company for six years, not six months. She testified to attending the Devil's picnics on the Salem Village parsonage grounds, where George Burroughs and Martha Carrier held court. She said that now, due to her confessions, their specters had appeared to her from different parts of the prison and threatened to stab her to death with a "sharp pointed iron like a spindle, but four square."

Meanwhile, back in Andover, forty people who had awakened that day to their ordinary routines, were now accused as witches. Six of the women drew up a deposition stating "we were all exceedingly astonished and amazed and consternated and affrighted, even out of reason." Suddenly, these accused men and women were going over details of their past days, searching for some clue that might show the Devil had invaded their home or spirit. As always, the Puritan mantra that it must be due to their own sin or shortcoming, kept them searching for their failings. They remembered trivialities from eons past. Could that be when the Devil saw a fissure in their righteousness?

Andover denizen and confessor to witchcraft William Barker announced that he could understand why Salem Village had come under attack. Salem, he declared was cursed "by reason of the people being divided and their differing with ye minister." He went on to say he was fed up with the Puritan's obsession with damnation and hierarchy of the elite. Blasphemy be damned, he said he was seduced by the Devil for at least under his rule, all men were equal and "live bravely." And then he dropped his bombshell, perhaps almost gleefully. He claimed he knew the exact number of witches flying about Essex County— 307! That didn't include Connecticut's coven who had mounted poles and flown up to Massachusetts to help with the overthrow of churches.

Under warrants, others from Andover were taken to Salem Village and placed in the jail to await their initial examination. The official Court of Oyer and Terminer had returned to their various homes after the hangings of July 19th. One after another of the Andover accused witches confessed, largely due to pressure from their kinfolk, hoping they would be spared the gallows, and some believing their dear spouses must be witches after all. Samuel Wardwell, William Barker, Ann Foster, her daughter Mary Lacy, and her granddaughter (of the same name), all confessed before the magistrate's relentless barrage of questions.

The poignant case of Mary Tyler of Andover, shows the battery of pleadings for her to confess. As she rode to

Salem Village for her examination, her brother and Schoolmaster John Emerson accompanied her, ostensibly for support. But as they rode along, flanking her on either side, they hounded her to confess, to the point that she "wished herself in a dungeon than to be so treated."

Emerson reached over to her face and parodied beating the Devil away from her. When she remained stoic in her resolve, he pulled up on his horse and said, "Well, I see you will not confess. I will now leave you, and then you are undone, body and soul together."

After his departure, her brother took up the suit and railed against her in the ultimate act of betrayal. If you confess, "you cannot lye," he remonstrated her. In tears, Mary cried, "Good brother, do not say so. For I shall lye if I confess, and who shall answer to God for my lye?" It was her brother's retort that was like the sounding bell of so many others caught up in the witchcraft chaos. He said, "God would not suffer so many good men to be in error about it." Beneath his "long and violent" threats of hanging, and the spectacle of the meetinghouse examination, Mary broke down and confessed.

Later, in jail, away from her brother and the magistrates, and wailing of young women, she recanted her confession, rather than "belying herself." Samuel Wardwell, when given time and perhaps counsel from other accused men, also recanted his confession. Abigail Faulkner, whose father Francis Dane was urgently trying to reason with the inhabitants of Andover as to the ludicrousness of what was happening to them, would not confess, no matter how much pressure was brought upon her. The only thing she would admit to was that during the "Touch Test" in the meetinghouse in Andover, when she was told to clasp the afflicteds' hand, she had in defiance, struck her hands together. Perhaps, the Devil may have taken advantage at her act of irritation, she said, but "it was the devil and not I who afflicted them."

Andover was a different target than Salem Village. The evil had not crept up on it slowly, like an insidious Kudza vine of the south, crawling and snaking its way along until it devoured everything in sight. With the arrival of Ann Putnam Jr. and Mary Walcott, events happened so quickly, that people had scant time to react, other than to panic.

The recruits the two Salem Village "seers" left behind when they headed home, acted fast, fueled with the drama of what they had seen. Young women "cried out" on neighbors and animals in a flurry of accusations. John Bradstreet of Andover, brother of the Bradstreet who suddenly refused to sign any more arrest warrants, was accused of bewitching a dog on the street. Not waiting to be hauled into jail, he fled to New Hampshire. When his brother, Deputy Dudley Bradstreet, was "cried out" upon (not doubt in retribution for deserting his post during the arrest warrant debacle), he too left town and went into hiding with his wife. Afflicted girls had said they had spectral evidence confirming the Bradstreet couple had killed people.

The Andover incident produced something not yet utilized. Its effectiveness and legal ramifications should have been used long before. When some of the girls from that town cried out on a prominent man from Boston, it set off a hailstorm. Enough was Enough! Thought to be Robert Calef, the man took action and sent a "writ to arrest these accusers in a one-thousand-pound action of defamation." Defamation of character! 17th century slander at its finest. No one, not even some of the magistrates the girls in Salem Village had gone after, thought to use the legal system for anything other than hanging witches.

The writ had its effect. A thousand pounds was a lot of money. Calef had friends in Andover assigned to watch the girls in question. The outcry came to a slow, but final halt.

Andover benefited by the rapid rise and fall of the witchcraft hysteria there, even though 50 of their citizens were already in jails and facing hanging, should they be found guilty. Andover would carry the distinction of having more accused witches than the Salem province. Old Francis Dane, the father of accused witch Abigail Faulkner, became the sounding board of reason. Through his proclamations, Andover quickly recovered from the delusion it had been under. But now what? Fifty of their people would go before a court who had shown no mercy to even the most devout Puritans. It was a hanging committee that would interview six more prisoners in early August, and as it would be seen in only a few short weeks, one that would head for Gallows Hill once again.

Chapter Thirty-Two

The King and Queen of Hell

While Andover wrestled, literally, with its demons, Salem Town was still busy hearing testimony against various prisoners. The next Court of Oyer and Terminer would begin soon, and depositions and witnesses had to be examined in preparation for it. Several of these examinations were held in Thomas Beadle's tavern.

Seventy-seven-year-old **Mary Bradbury** was brought before the magistrates and the afflicted girls. The documents from this inquisition are lost, but for a few fragments contained in depositions. Bradbury hailed from Salisbury, the wife of Thomas Bradbury, a prominent resident of that town and a militia captain. She had been accused by the girls on May 26th, but not arrested for another month, perhaps due to her husband's influence.

During her examination, Ann Putnam Jr., Mary Walcott, Elizabeth Hubbard, Sarah Bibber, and Mary Warren all tumbled about and howled, on cue. It may have been Ann Jr. who instigated the arrest for Mary Bradbury. Salisbury was also the home town of Ann Carr Putnam Sr., and it's possible Ann Jr. had heard her mother speak of the woman before. Had the Bradbury's shunned Ann Sr., or was their wealth a source of jealousy to a woman who had been denied her own inheritance? It may have been no coincidence that Ann Jr. claimed to see a vison of her Uncle

John Carr "in a winding sheet," telling her that "mis Bradbery had murthered him and that his blood did Crie for venjance against her."

Seventy-year-old **Ann Pudeator** had been questioned before. She was brought in again to hear witness from Sarah Churchill who accused her of bringing the Devil's Book to her on June 1st. Ann swore she had never seen Churchill in her life. Another witness, Jeremiah Neal, was then brought forward with stronger stuff. He charged Pudeator with murdering his wife, after "often" threatening to kill her. When the afflicted went into their fits, the ever-popular "Touch Test" was administered. Mary Warren was cured immediately after touching Pudeator's wrist. Mary Walcott put on the finishes touches by adding she had seen Pudeator's specter in the company of Rebecca Nurse, who had hung for witchcraft.

Ann Pudeator and Mary Bradbury were taken to Salem Jail. While the magistrates were gathered at Beadle's Tavern, they decided to hear more cases. On Friday, July 1st, Thomas Putnam and his cousin John Jr. charged **Margaret Hawkes** and her slave **Candy** for tormenting Mary Walcott, Mary Warren, and Ann Putnam Jr. They had come to Salem Town by way of Barbados. It was during Candy's examination, that a new technique to discover witchery was employed.

Candy had turned on her mistress after being accused along with her. She told the court that Margaret Hawkes had made her a witch, and given her two poppets with which to torment people. She held up the dolls, and the afflicted went into hysteria. It was documented that Warren, Deliverance, and Abigail Hobbs were "greatly affrighted and fell into violent fits." Judge Hathorne noted that all of them "said that the black man, Mrs. Hawkes and the negro stood by the poppets or rags and pinched them, and then they were afflicted."

To the surprise of all, the magistrates, along with Nicholas Noyes, decided to perform some experiments that had not been done before. They took one of Candy's poppets and burned a portion of it. The afflicted girls screamed out that they had been burned. Noyes dunked the other poppet into a container of water, and the girls began choking as if they were drowning. One of them jumped up dramatically and ran from the building toward the river, as if to drown herself. It was one of the more visual effects they had seen; almost scientific under the controlled conditions by which it was executed.

A well-constructed poppet made from corn husks.

Needless to say, Margaret Hawkes and Candy joined the others inside the crowded prison.

By mid-July, the Court of Oyer and Terminer were sloughing through the old depositions and some new ones. After the hangings, the new accusations in Salem Village slowed, only to have the onslaught of prisoners from Andover ride in. That Salem Village's calling of *new* names had dwindled at this time, did not mean the afflicted had stopped complaining of spectral attacks from the witches they had already put into prisons weeks and months before. As if to make sure their charges stuck in the face of a new official trial hearing, they reminded the magistrates of attacks from Burroughs, Carrier, Foster, and others. It was obvious; the hangings had done nothing to slate their appetite for death.

Mary Lacey Jr., from Andover, who had confessed and been only recently incarcerated along with her mother Mary Lacey Sr. (whose brother had tormented her until she confessed to being a witch), gave enough damning evidence against Carrier and Burroughs to hang them. She also "cried out" against Richard Carrier and Andrew Carrier, claiming they were also witches.

"How many witches had Martha Carrier bewitched to death?" the magistrates asked the willing Mary Lacey Jr. The girl named seven, involving men, women, and children. When asked how she had killed them, Mary answered, "She Stabbed them to the hart with pinns needles & knitting needles," both "on their bodye[s]" and through the use of poppets.

The magistrates then went to the crux of the issue with "spectral evidence" and the Devil using the shapes of innocent people without their consent. They asked Mary Jr. "Doe you hear the Divil hurts in the Shap of any person without there consents?" Mary answered, "No."

Encouraged, hoping to refute Samuel Willard and other clergymen's objections from the prior month, they asked, "When any person Striks with a Sword or Staf at a Sprit or Spector will that hurt the body?" (How many testimonies had been born against prisoners pointing out tears in their clothing and cuts on their person from being struck during a spectral visit?)

"Yes," Mary answered, and then threw her mother and grandmother under the wagon cart by saying they had both been injured in such a matter within Salem Village recently.

Wanting to tighten the noose about Burroughs and Carrier's neck, Hathorne zeroed in and asked for more information about the two prisoners, whose trial was to begin shortly. Mary willingly added to their pyre, "Goody Carrier told me the Divell Said to her she should be Queen in Hell," and "The Minister" would be King. "What kind of a Man is Mr. Burroughs?" they asked her. "Why, a pretty little man and he has Come to Us Sometimes In his Spiritt in the Shape of a Catt & I think sometimes In his proper shape."

Mary Warren, who had obligingly suffered with fits initially during Mary Lacey Jr.'s interrogation, softened and took the girl's hands in her own, without suffering any harm. The scribe that day for the questioning said, "Mary Lacey did Ernestly ask Mary Warren Forgiveness for afflicting of her and both fell a weeping Together." Lacey Jr.'s mother was called for, and the emotional daughter begged her to "repent and Cal upon God."

Ann Foster, Lacey Jr.'s grandmother, was brought in, and although uncooperative at first, concurred with her granddaughter that Martha Carrier was responsible for many deaths. She added that Mary Allen Toothaker (whose husband had just passed away in prison awaiting his trial for witchcraft), and her daughter Martha Emerson, were both in attendance at the Devil's picnic in Parris' pasture, and it was here that both Lacey's and Foster signed the Devil's Book. At that point, Mary Warren fell into a fit and "cried out" against Richard Carrier. An arrest warrant was issued for him on the spot.

Richard Carrier was only eighteen-years-old. His brother Andrew, several years younger, was also rounded up and put into jail. With their mother being declared the "Queen of Hell," they were subjected to the heinous torture of "Neck and Heels." After only a short time of such torment, Richard confessed to signing Satan's Book, attending the witch meetings, and helping in the torment of Salem's villagers. He also, under pressure, declared his late Uncle, Roger Toothaker, his Aunt Mary Toothaker, and his cousin Martha Carrier, broke bread with the Devil at the meetings.

"I heard Sarah Good talk of a minister or two," Richard offered. "One of them was he that had ben at Estward & preached once at the Village, his name Is Burroughs and he Is a little man." When asked who else was at Satan's feasts, Richard Carrier provided a long list: Nurse, How, Bishop & Wildes—already executed; and prisoners Willard, the Proctors, the Coreys, and Bradbury. He admitted to the torment of several people, one of them, surprisingly was Reverend Parris's wife, who had been ill a long time. It was the first time Elizabeth Parris' name came up in the trials, and one wonders if Abigail Williams suggested her Aunt's maladies.

Richard Carrier was returned to jail, where John Proctor heard that Richard had testified against him. In a fury, realizing his trial date was imminent, he fought for his life. Along with some of the other prisoners, he drafted a letter from jail addressed to the Boston magistrates, specifically to Increase Mather, James Allen, John Bailey, Samuel

Willard and Joshua Moody alerting them that the two Carrier boys had been "tyed Neck and Heels till the Blood was ready to come out of their Noses." Proctor told them his own son had received the same torture and condemned it as "Popish Cruelties." His quill flying furiously across the page he entreated them to hear him out. The jury and magistrates, he said, have "Condemned us already before our Tryals, being so much incensed and engaged against us by the Devil."

John Proctor and the other men begged the clergymen to attend their upcoming trials, "hoping thereby you may be the means of saving the shedding our Innocent Bloods." The prisoners pleaded with the five clergy to show an enclosed letter to Governor Phipps, asking him to move their trials to Boston and have different Judges, other than the ones who had overseen the previous trials, sit the bench. Governor Phips made no move on their behalf, and the venue and magistrates remained unaltered.

(Petition of John Proctor from Prison)

Salem-Prison,

July 23, 1692.

Mr. Mather, Mr. Allen , Mr. Moody , Mr. Willard, and Mr. Bailey.

Reverend Gentlemen.

The innocency of our Case with the Enmity of our Accusers and our Judges, and Jury, whom nothing but our Innocent Blood will serve their turn, having Condemned us already before our Tryals, being so much incensed and engaged against us by the Devil, makes us bold to Beg and Implore your Favourable Assistance of this our Humble Petition to his Excellency, That if it be possible our Innocent Blood may be spared, which undoubtedly otherwise will be shed, if the Lord doth not mercifully step in. The Magistrates, Ministers, Jewries, and all the People in general, being so much inraged and incensed against us by the Delusion of the Devil, which we can term no other, by reason we know in our own Consciences, we are all Innocent Persons. Here are five Persons who have lately confessed themselves to be Witches, and do accuse some of us, of being along with them at a Sacrament, since we were committed into close Prison, which we know to be Lies. Two of the 5 are (Carriers Sons) Youngmen, who would not confess any thing till they tyed them Neck and Heels till the Blood was ready to come out of their Noses, and 'tis credibly believed and reported this was the occasion of making them confess that they never did, by reason they said one had been a Witch a Month, and another five Weeks, and that their Mother had made them so, who has been confined here this nine Weeks. My son William Procter, when he was examin'd, because he would not confess that he was Guilty, when he was Innocent, they tyed him Neck and Heels till the Blood gushed out at his Nose, and would have kept him so 24 Hours, if one more Merciful than the rest, had not taken pity on him, and caused him to be unbound. These actions are very like the Popish Cruelties. They have already undone us in our Estates, and that will not serve their turns, without our Innocent Bloods. If it cannot be granted that we can have our Trials at Boston, we humbly beg that you would endeavour to have these Magistrates changed, and others in their rooms, begging also and beseeching you would be pleased to be here, if not all, some of you at our Trials, hoping thereby you may be the means of saving the sheeding our Innocent Bloods, desiring your Prayers to the Lord in our behalf, we rest your Poor Afflicted Servants, JOHN PROCTER , etc.

(Robert Calef, *More Wonders of The Invisible World* [London, 1700], excerpted in Burr, Ed., *Narratives of the Witchcraft Cases*, pp. 362-364.)

Only days before the Court of Oyer and Terminer was to reconvene in Salem Town, Gedney, Corwin, Higginson, and Corwin ordered the arrests of Martha Emerson of Haverhill and her mother, Mary Toothaker of Billerica. These arrests followed hard on the testimonies and confessions of the Lacey's and Foster.   Three other warrants were issued for "witches" accused of torturing Elizabeth Ballard and Timothy Swan. One of the newly arrested, Mary Tyler Post Bridges of Andover, confessed. Martha Emerson, the Toothaker's daughter, also confessed, and named her Aunt Martha Carrier as a witch.

When Mary Allen Toothaker was questioned on July 30th, two days before the Court convened, she alluded to the stress of the Indian Wars as part of her "detached mental state." "This May last," she said, "I was under great Discontentedness & troubled with feare about the Indians, & and used often to dream of fighting with them." She said "the Devil had appeared to her in the shape of a Tawny man and promised to keep her from the Indians and she should have happy days with her son," who was a casualty of the Indian wars. "He promised if I would serve him, I would be safe from the Indians, and it was the fear of the Indians that put me upon it" (the signing of the Devil's Book).

Ironically, two days later, as Mary Toothaker sat in Salem Jail, a small party of Indians attacked Billerica. The inhabitants of two houses neighboring her own were butchered. Had she not been in prison, she too would be dead. Mary must have felt the Devil had kept his promise to her, and saved her from the attack. Perhaps, due to that covenant, she never did retract her confession.

The declarations of the five Andover prisoners, stating that all five of the recently hanged women had, indeed, been among the witches at the Devil's sacrament, gave the magistrates great relief. Here was proof they had not executed the innocent. If anything, it fueled their resolve for the next set of trials. Specifically, in their crosshairs were George Burroughs and Martha Carrier.

The Third Session of the Court of Oyer and Terminer

On Tuesday, August 2, 1692, the Court was again in session. There was a feeling akin to electrical charges surging through the room. The promise of more executions, too terrifying to admit to, ravaged the congregations' consciences like ravenous wolves. The stars of the show were seated in the front row of the Salem Town House, prim and proper in their white collars, aprons, and caps. A more unlikely lynch mob was never imagined. Yet the power they wielded inside that cavernous court room, would have impressed any leader of war.

The trials lasted four days. Martha Carrier went first on August 2nd and 3rd. John Willard, George Jacobs Sr., and John and Elizabeth Proctor were tried between the 3rd and the 5th. George Burroughs was saved for last, and was tried on August 5th. During these trial days, the magistrates also heard testimony against Mary Esty and Martha Corey. These two women were indicted from the "evidence" presented against them for their attacks on Mercy Lewis and Elizabeth Hubbard back in May. They were returned to jail to await their formal trials a month later in September.

Martha Carrier's Trial

We have Cotton Mather to thank for recording his thoughts of what happened during Martha Carrier's trial, as all the transcripts have been lost to time. Mather referred to her as "the Rampant Hag." The trials were no different than the others, as far as the structure of them went. Depositions were read from Martha's May 31st examination. The chaos that ensued at her exam was recalled. The torment of the girls had been so great that the magistrates had ordered Carrier's hands bound. Thomas Putnam Jr. was only too happy to remind the court of this as he said "had not the Honored Magistrats commanded hir to be bound we ware ready to think she would quickly have killed sum of them."

Elizabeth Hubbard, Mary Walcott, and Mercy Lewis all testified concerning Carrier's unrelenting torture. Abigail Williams and Ann Putnam Jr. added their sordid stories of Carrier's "witch" coming into their homes and tormenting them. Even a young twelve-year-old girl from Andover testified she had recently been attacked by the specters of Martha Carrier and her son Richard. Goody Carrier's tongue had done its own damage. Reports reminding the court of how Carrier had made fun of the girls' afflictions were presented. One witness spoke up and told of the time she spoke with Carrier the previous Spring. The woman had told Martha that a "maide" had reported seeing Carrier's specter outside Ingersoll's Ordinary and that her neck was "twisted almost round." To this, Martha remarked coldly, "it is no matter if hir nicke had ben quite of [off] if she sayd I was there."

Neighbors, and even her nephew, Allen Toothaker, testified against her. The Lacey's and Foster's statements concerning seeing Martha at the Devil's sacraments carried a lot of weight, possibly because these were new depositions taken only a few days prior. It gave the illusion that nothing had changed, and Carrier was still about Satan's business. To seal that concept, Susanna Sheldon reenacted the "pretty little trick" she had produced at Martha's examination in May. She showed how "her hands were uncomfortably ty'd together," and accused Carrier's specter of the deed.

It came as no surprise that Martha Carrier was convicted. If she left the court room without incident, or railed at her accusers, it was not noted.

John Willard's Trial

On May 18th, John Willard had been examined and indicted on witchcraft charges for torturing Mercy Lewis, Ann Putnam Jr., Abigail Williams, and Elizabeth Hubbard. Ann Carr Putnam told of the many ghosts that had hovered in her bed chamber, claiming Willard had murdered them. The written depositions from that exam show the names of Samuel Parris, Thomas Putnam Jr., and Nathaniel Ingersoll as the supporters of the girls' claims. Sarah Bibber also joined in with tales of affliction and witnessing Willard's specter attack Mercy Lewis and Mary Walcott on May 17th.

Much of the damning testimony concerned Willard's spectral attacks on the Wilkin's family, to which Daniel Wilkins finally succumbed, and Bray Wilkins was hounded. Once again, Ann Jr., Mercy Lewis, and Mary Walcott were the star accusers—they had witnessed Willard's ghost sitting on Daniel Wilkins's chest until the youth could not breath. Other Wilkins relatives reported being tortured by his hands and his specter appearing in their rooms threatening them.

Richard Carrier, newly confessed wizard, was called in to repeat his accusations against the man. Carrier, who had named Willard on July 22nd of being among those at the Devil's picnic in the parsonage, had accurately described John's specter as "a black hared Man of a Midle Stature." The usual accusations followed and he was convicted and sentenced to hang.

John and Elizabeth Proctor's Trials

The depositions against John Proctor would have filled a wooden crate. Every one of the afflicted people, either themselves or through their adult supporters, filed a complaint against Proctor. The usual accounts of spectral pinching, choking, pressing upon, etc. were levied against him. Some of the documents included his wife Elizabeth (who was also on trial this day) and even his son William and daughter Sarah. The Putnam names were affixed to many of them, as was that of Reverend Samuel Parris.

It was probably now that John Proctor regretted all the times he ridiculed the afflicted girls and called their antics "jugglers tricks." The words he had uttered all those months ago to Samuel Sibley about "beating the jade" (Mary Warren) and "tying her to the spinning wheel" until the foolishness left her, came back to haunt him now. Sibley's deposition was dated the day of Proctor's trial.

How often had he looked at these delusional girls and shaken his head in disbelief that grown adults were giving credence to their outbursts. He had even gone to Salem Village to drag his maid Mary back home after she spent a night at Ingersoll's after testifying in court. Now, he looked at their smug faces, and heard his name screamed, and knew he was doomed.

(Statement of Samuel Sibley v. John Proctor)

[August 5, 1692]

The morning after the examination of Goody Nurse.Sam: Sibly met John Proctor about Mr Phillips w'o called to said Sibly as he was going to sd Phillips & askt how the folks did at the village He answered he heard they were very bad last night but he had heard nothing this morning Proctor replyed he was going to fetch home his jade he left her there last night & had rather given 40d than let her come up sd Sibly askt why he talt so Proctor replyed if they were let alone so we should all be Devils & witches quickly they should rather be had to the Whipping post but he would fetch his jade Home & thresh the Devil out of her & more to the like purpose crying hang them, hang them. And also added that when she was first taken with fits he kept her close to the Wheel & threatened to thresh her, & then she had no more fits till the next day he was gone forth, & then she must have her fits again firsooth &. Jurat in Curia

Procter ownes   he   meant Mary   Warren attest. *St. Sewall. Clerk

Thirty-nine men submitted a signed petition to the magistrates, declaring they could not understand why God would let such a tragedy afflict the Proctors. They wrote "as to what we have ever seen or heard of them—upon our Consciences we Judge them Innocent of the crime objected." More than just a testament to the Proctors' character, the document attacked the spectral evidence so prevalent in the trials.

(Petition for John Proctor and Elizabeth Proctor)

[August 5, 1692]

The Humble, & Sincere Declaration of us, Subscribers, Inhabitants, in Ipswich, on the behalf of o'r Neighb'rs Jno Procter & his wife now in Trouble & und'r Suspition of Witchcraft.
To the Hon'rable Court of Assistants now Sitting In Boston. -- Hon'red & Right Worshipfull! The foresd John Procter may have Great Reason to Justifie the Divine Sovereigntie of God under thos Severe Remarques of Providence upon his Peac & Hon'r und'r a due Reflection upon his Life Past: And so the Best of us have Reason to Adoar the Great Pittie & Indulgenc of Gods Providenc, that we are not Exposed to the utmost shame, that the Divell can Invent und'r the

p'rmissions of Sovereigntie, tho not for that Sin fore Named; yet for o'r many Transgretions; for we Do at present Suppose that it may be A Method w'thin the Seveerer But Just Transaction of the Infinite Majestie of God: that he some times may p'rmitt Sathan to p'rsonate, Dissemble, & therby abuse Inocents, & such as Do in the fear of God Defie the Devill and all his works. The Great Rage he is p'rmitted to attempt holy Job w'th The Abuse he Does the famous Samuell, in Disquieting his Silent Dust, by Shaddowing his venerable P'rson in Answer to theharmes of WitchCraft, & other Instances from Good hands; may be arg'd Besides the unsearcheable foot stepps of Gods Judgments that are brought to Light Every Morning that Astonish o'r weaker Reasons, To teach us Adoration, Trembling. & Dependanc, &ca but - We mmust not Trouble y'r Honr's by Being Tedious, Therefore we being Smitten with the Notice of what hath happened, we Recoon it w'thin the Duties of o'r Charitie, That Teacheth us to do, as we would be done by; to offer thus much for the Clearing of o'r Neighb'rs Inocencie; viz: That we never had the Least Knowledge of such a Nefarious wickedness in o'r said Neighbours, since they have been w'thin our acquaintance; Neither doe we remember -- any such Thoughts in us Concerning them; or any Action by them or either of them Directly tending that way; no more than might be in the lives of any other p'rsons of the Clearest Reputation as to Any such Evills. What God may have Left them to, we Cannot Go into Gods pavillions Cloathed w'th Cloudes of Darknesse Round About. But as to what we have ever seen, or heard of them -- upon o'r Consciences we Judge them Innocent of the crime objected. His Breading hath been Amongst us; and was of Religious Parents in o'r place; & by

Reason of Relations, & Proprties w'thin o'r Towne hath had Constant Intercourse w'th us We speak upon o'r p'rsonall acquaintance, & observations: & so Leave our Neighbours, & this our Testimonie on their Behalfe to the wise Thoughts of y'r Honours, & Subscribe &c. *Jno Wise *William Story Sen'r *Thos Chote*John Burnum   sr *William   Thomsonn. *Tho.   Low Sanor *Isaac   Foster*John   Burnum   jun'r *William Goodhew *John Cogswell *Thomas Andrews *Joseph Andrews *Benjamin marshall *Isaac perkins*Nathanill Perkins *Thomas   Lovkine *William Cogswell *Thomas   Varny *John   fellows *William Cogswell sen * Jonathan Cogswell *John Cogswell Jr; *John   Andrews *Joseph   prockter *Samuell Gidding *John Andrews Ju'r *William Butler *William Andrews *Joseph Euleth. *Jems White

Even with a deposition in their favor listing the good men of Ipswich and Salem Village (which included the signature of Reverend John Wise), the words of small girls testifying to poppets, Devil's feasts, and specters flying about in the shapes of the Proctors, carried the most weight. They were convicted of witchcraft. Elizabeth Proctor let the court know that she was expecting a child. Witch or not, the Puritan court could not condemn an unborn child to hell. She was given a reprieve until the child should be delivered. No such mercy was given to John.

George Jacob Sr.'s Trial

No records, other than the original depositions made out at George Jacob's examination, remain. His servant Sarah

Churchill would have born witness that Jacobs had beaten her with his walking sticks. The other girls joined in with stories of abuse. John DeRich, the same youth who claimed old Jacobs had chased him into the river in an effort to drown him, also presented accounts of several ghosts appearing to him accusing Jacobs of murdering them.

George Jacobs Sr., leaning heavily upon his walking sticks, toothless, grey, and tired, listened to the accusations and watched as the girls went through their repertories of tricks. He was just as salty and argumentative as he had been during his examination. The notes from his exam were read and the events remembered:

"Here are them that accuse you of acts of witchcraft," the magistrate said. Before he could continue, Jacobs blurted out, "Well, let us hear who they are and what they are!"

He listened, glaring through rheumy eyes, as the afflicted, including newly-recruited sixteen-year-old John DeRich, recited their stories of torture. At the completion of the litany of accusations, the magistrate spat "Who did it?" "Don't ask me!" Jacobs fired back.

As the roaring of the afflicted rose to the wooden rafters overhead, he suddenly felt the weight of the hopeless position he was in. In a chastened voice, he pleaded, "Pray, do not accuse me. I am as clear as your worships." When the faces from the bar remained unchanged, he rallied again and shouted, "You tax me for a wizard; you may as well tax me for a buzzard!"

During his initial examination, the magistrates glanced over the depositions before them and came to rest on a hopeful loophole. They asked him why it had been reported he did not regularly hold family prayer. The old man shouted, "Because I cannot read!" "Well, surely," the magistrate said, the net closing in on the poor man,

"everyone knows the Lord's Prayer. Pray, recite it for us."
George Jacobs, walking canes quivering beneath his
unsteady weight, tried in vain, to recite the famous prayer
without faltering. It was one of the tricks inside the witch's
bag the court had at the ready.

Perhaps, the only mercy shown to George Sr., was the
court's declaration that his granddaughter, Margaret, who
had confessed to witchcraft and accused Jacobs of
unsavory acts, had recently recanted her confession and
wanted his forgiveness. The old man's heart must have felt
the only joy that horrid day offered. Her soul would be
saved, if not her life. He was convicted of witchcraft and
taken back to jail. Before the day of his execution, he
changed his will to include Margaret, just in case she was
spared.

George Burroughs' Trial

The last trial was that of George Burroughs. How it must
have rankled him to walk into the court where he had once
faced accusations from John Putnam for owing him money.
To feel the eyes of the Putnams, and the other Salem
villagers he had deserted when acting as their minister,
must have felt galling, and now, terrifying. The short,
dark-complexioned man approached the bar.

His trial had attracted the largest crowd. Among them,
adding to the air of importance of this particular
inquisition, was Deodat Lawson and Increase Mather from
Boston. Reverend John Hale had ridden down from
Beverly.

As the jury and magistrates took their seats, a heightened
feeling of excitement could be felt in the room. This was
not just another suspected witch. This man was accused of

being "the ringleader" of the coven trying to take over not only Essex County, but all New England churches. If George Burroughs was indeed Satan's right-hand man, was he also not responsible for the slaughtering of villagers at the hands of the Wabanaki Indians? Had he had a hand in spectrally thwarting the attempts of the militia to stop the warfare? His evil efforts may have even delayed a speedy return of a charter that could have steered a better course through the chaos now inflicting the area. Worst of all, he had posed as a *minister*, a man of God, and spouted his heresies from the pulpit. In short, all perceived evils seemed to be wrapped up in this one stout man from Maine.

It was afternoon on August 5th, when the afflicted stood, one-by-one to repeat their depositions of abuse. The court heard how Burroughs had once bragged of being a wizard, not just a mere witch. The usual litany of accusations of being pinched, tormented, pressured to sign his book, and even biting were put forth.

When the subject of biting came up, several of the girls presented their arms, showing bite marks. Here, like the poppets, was something tangible. The magistrates jumped on it. They had Burroughs put his teeth against the marks to see if they fit. In fairness, they had a few other men do the same. According to the triumphant judges, only Burroughs teeth fit the marks. Tangible proof—not just seeing things flying around in the Invisible World. Yet, it was Burroughs *specter* who had bitten them. Did they now have the proof they needed that spectral evidence was real, as anyone could see the bite marks, and "the pretty little man" had been the only one who seemed capable of making them?

The afflicted roared and fell convulsing to the floor throughout the proceedings, especially when Burroughs was speaking or testimony was being given. It was clear their pain increased when he was questioned. Chief Justice William Stoughton asked the little minister who he thought was hindering the witnesses? Burroughs responded that it was probably the Devil. Stoughton retorted, "How comes the Devil so loath to have any testimony born against you?" George had no answer.

The next performance offered by the afflicted was one that must be admired. If a fakery, then it was one they had practiced before the trial. For suddenly, all of the bench of afflicted victims froze, and went into a trance state. They all stared at the same spot, somewhere between Burroughs and themselves. The magistrates repeatedly asked them what was wrong, but none answered, only stared without blinking at one place. Then, as if on cue, they awoke and fell back in terror. Quickly, the judges ordered them separated into other rooms where each was asked what had just happened. Each girl, without the prodding of the others, recounted the same thing: there had been four ghosts glaring with red eyes at Burroughs and accusing him of their murders. The girls identified the ghosts as Burroughs first two wives, and the wife and daughter of Deodat Lawson.

This departure from the usual process of letting the girls all scream out their accusations as a group, is significant. The judges seemed to have taken the admonitions of the "several ministers" and others to heart. Not only did they have Burroughs test his teeth marks against those found on the girls' arms, they, for the first time, were separating them to get a fair accounting. It was obvious they were taking extra precautions to get it right with this prisoner, and make sure their findings were irrefutable.

When the judges related their findings to the packed courtroom, Burroughs hotly denied seeing any ghosts. What must Deodat Lawson have thought at hearing the deserting minister was responsible for the deaths of his late wife and daughter? The same deaths that many had felt were just retribution for Lawson himself leaving the ranks as minister of Salem Village.

Burroughs stood at the bar and listened as villager after villager accused him of everything from presenting with poppets and thorns to torment others, to neglecting prayer and not baptizing his own children. Reports that he had treated his wives harshly, almost "to the point of death" were blurted into the courtroom. No less than eight of confessed "witches" stood and told of how he had tricked them into signing his book and attending the parsonage picnics. These confessed witches, now joining the afflicted girls in their screaming, added to the overall deafening noise that met almost everything said that afternoon. Merchants going about their business in the streets of Salem Town must have paused in shock at the shrieks coming from the stately Town House.

And then came the line-up of people attesting to the minister's supernatural strength. Men, heads taller than Burroughs, stood and told of how they had witnessed (or heard second-hand) that Burroughs had lifted a heavy gun with a seven-foot barrel with only one hand in preparation for firing it at Casco Bay during the Indian attacks. He had, so they said, also lifted a large weighty barrel of molasses from a canoe, again, with one hand. Nine people testified of his unusual strength, their testimonies growing more ludicrous, ending with a man stating Burroughs had lifted the heavy gun reported on by placing only his finger into the gun barrel and hoisting it up. (This last report was allowed to slide.)

Burroughs was allowed to respond to the allegations. He scoffed at the molasses barrel story, and as for the gun, he answered with two versions: the first, was that he had picked it up before the gun's lock and pressed the butt of the gun into his chest to steady it. He then added that an Indian had steadied the long gun barrel for him. (Obviously, an Indian on their side of the warfare.) None of the accusers remembered seeing an Indian helping him. Some of the Gloucester men and Mrs. Roger Toothaker (also accused of witchcraft), claimed they saw specters helping Burroughs hold the gun.

As expected, John Putnam bore witness about Burroughs borrowing money from him for his late wife Hannah's funeral costs in 1681. The earlier reports given at his examination concerning the strawberry-picking expedition where he seemed to have preternatural hearing; his treatment of his second wife Sarah during her bed rest after childbirth, that resulted in her death, were all laid out.

Burroughs objected to each accusation and tried to offer his explanation of the events. They seemed trivial and baseless, a desperate man with desperate answers. Burroughs looked into the wooden face of Judge Hathorne and saw the brother-in-law of his second wife Sarah; the same Sarah he had just been accused of causing her death through harsh treatment. He could practically see the shadow of the hangman's noose against the beams.

George Burroughs final attempt to save himself from the gallows came in the form of a quote from a controversial book by Thomas Ady entitled *A Candle in the Dark*. It basically refuted that witches existed and that it was impossible to detect witchcraft, or sign a contract with the Devil and send others to do his bidding. When the magistrates accused him of quoting from the book that was held in disdain by many societies, Burroughs at first denied it, and then admitted he had seen the passage in the book, but he didn't actually own the book, merely transcribed it.

His vacillation on the book's passage only added fuel to the fire. Why was he trying to distance himself from a book that flew in the face of Puritan beliefs? He even claimed the word "witch" in the Bible was a different meaning than that used by the English today.

After listing all of Burroughs "contradictions and falsehoods," the verdict by the jury came back "Guilty." A great howl of approval rose from the confessed witches in the audience and the usual line-up of afflicted victims who had been accusing their neighbors since February. Reverend Increase Mather, seated among the agitated throng of spectators, admitted, that based on what he had heard and seen that sweltering August afternoon, "Had I been one of the Judges," he said, "I could not have acquitted him."

Burroughs had one last thing to offer as he was led out of the chaos—he claimed he would die due to false witnesses. While this statement may have felt like hollow words any condemned man would swear to, it bothered Reverend John Hale. He approached one of the confessed witches (we don't know which one) and said, "You are one that bring this man to death. If you have charged anything upon him that is not true, recall it before it be too late, while he is still alive." The answer was ambiguous. She merely stated she had nothing for which to blame herself.

For John Hale, a Reverend and man of the cloth, it may have been harder to believe a fellow clergyman, whom he may have himself heard preach, could be aligned with the Devil. He had heard of Burroughs many great works in Maine. He had saved many lives from brutal Indian attacks and administered to the sick and homeless. Could this man, so short in stature that it was hard to see him held up as a demonic "King," be guilty of the things of which he stood accused? What did this say for all clergymen? Were any of them safe from the temptations of evil? Had not the original witch outbreak begun in Reverend Parris' very household?

What was the deciding factor in George Burroughs' verdict? Was it the physical evidence of the bite marks? Was it the sequestered questioning of the girls who reported ghosts of murdered victims condemning the man? It was probably the sum of the parts. Six people had already hanged. Could they, with the ringleader in their grasp, ever conceivably let him go? He would hang from the gallows in two weeks' time.

Chapter Thirty-Three

The Lord's Prayer on Gallows Hill

After the verdicts of Guilty had been entered into the court documents on August 5, 1692, five witches, four men and one woman, sat in the Salem Jail and thought about their fate. John Proctor was still pleading for his life, while others, like George Jacobs Sr., were taking care of business.

Jacobs, after assessing the actions of his family, wrote a new will, one that would eradicate bequests to his daughter Ann and her husband John Andrews. They had done nothing to help him during the most tragic days of his life. He had originally disinherited his granddaughter Margaret as well, but after her repentance and recanting her confession of witchcraft, he penciled in a gift of £10 in silver for her. The bulk of his will went to his wife Mary during her pending widowhood. It included the farm and its holdings. George Jacobs Jr., old Jacobs' son, had escaped during witchcraft accusations and was still unaccounted for. Therefore Jacobs Sr., left him nothing. To his grandson George, he put him next in line to inherit the farm after Mary.

Based on the petitions written from jail, and wills drawn up, it is obvious the prisoners were allowed quill and paper. Whether this was brought from home, or paid for at the jailkeepers expense, is not known. Many a frantic parchment was etched within the walls of this stone prison.

Sheriff Corwin Rides Again

Even with Jacob's carefully-written document, it did nothing to allay the greed of Sheriff George Corwin. Not waiting for George Jacob Sr's., execution day, the Sheriff rode out to the Jacobs homestead in the section of Salem Village called North Fields. The farm was spitting distance to the North River, beautifully situated. Before anyone could stop him, he confiscated £79-13-0 worth of Jacob's farm and personal possessions. With carts lined up along the property, the sheriff and his men tied five cows, and one mare to the back of one of the wagons. They loaded up five pigs, and an assortment of chickens and geese. Sixty bushels of Indian corn, that had been handpicked and stored by the Jacob's family, along with crates of apples and eight loads of hay were thrown up onto the carts. While Mary Jacobs looked on in horror, the men slammed open her door and walked with heavy boots into the home bereft of her husband.

Without ceremony, they took brass kettles, furniture, and pewter. Twelve shillings in silver coin, a gold thumb ring, and Mary's wedding ring were eyed and placed into a small bag tied to the Sheriff's hip. The Sheriff even took their bedding and an "abundance of small things," Mary said, that were "took clear away." She would later petition and retrieve her wedding ring as it was not technically George's property, but hers. She had to buy some of the things they took from her pantry in order to survive. Some neighbors rallied around her after the sheriff and his men mounted their horses and rode off with heavy carts.

These were the actions that Phillip English so feared, when he was finally convinced to flee. For it was the male witches convicted that were fair game for Sheriff Corwin's looting. The female witches, who far outnumbered the men, were considered tied to their husbands. Their property became his property under the marriage covenant. Therefore, unless her husband was indicted too, as in the case of the Proctors (whom Sheriff Corwin looted upon their arrest and indictment), by law, her goods could not be taken. It would be this fear that forced Giles Corey to take tenacious measures when his turn came.

On August 17, 1692, only two days before the next executions, Margaret Willard hired a horse and rode to Boston to check on the status of a personal "replevin" that she had been granted for her husband John Willard. She had petitioned for it two weeks earlier and it had been approved. It would buy John a little time and temporarily reprieve him from hanging. The papers had still not shown up, so Margaret, desperate now with the hanging scheduled for day after tomorrow, made the long ride from Boxford to Boston. Despite her actions, it would come too late.

As the days dwindled down to the execution date of August 19th, the names of newly accused witches continued to arrive before the magistrates' desks. Frances Hutchins and Ruth Wilford of Haverhill had been complained on by Timothy Swan, Ann Putnam Jr. and Mary Walcott. This was only one day before the August 19th hangings. There would never be enough to satiate the need for carnage that raged inside these afflicted youth.

On the eve of the hangings, George Burroughs witnessed the odd juxtaposition of mercy and malice. Margaret Jacobs, granddaughter of old George Jacobs, Sr., was given permission to speak with Burroughs in prison. Tearfully, she begged his forgiveness for accusing him and bearing false witness against him, her own grandfather George Jacobs Sr., and John Willard. Burroughs was touched by her broken heart and fully forgave her. They prayed together and she left him there.

Meanwhile in Andover, the Salem Village girls, who were there helping in the indictment of their local witches, declared they saw George Burroughs specter holding another of his famous Satan's Sabbaths near the home of John Chandler. The said Burroughs encouraged his Andover coven to carry on his work and be secretive about their alliance with the Devil. His specter then departed to rejoin his physical form in prison.

One must wonder if Burroughs, his head bowed in prayer within the dirty confines of Salem Jail, had felt some glimmer of hope at Margaret Jacobs visit. Would the magistrates listen to the fact that she had confessed to lying about him? If her confession of witchcraft was fake, shouldn't that shed doubt on the others? It may have been a faint light in a gathering gloom that finally cloaked the room in darkness. The next day, he would be dead.

Five Hangings on Gallows Hill

The sun rose above the fields, rocky hillsides, and carefully constructed homes of Salem Village and Town. The sloshing of the ocean waves in the nearby harbor were drowned out by the excited cries of the crowd gathered outside Salem Jail. The guards were ordered to push the people back to allow for the prisoners to be brought out into the sudden glare of sunlight, and hoisted up onto the waiting cart.

John Proctor, his nerves failing him, had pleaded with Reverend Nicholas Noyes to pray with him in prison that morning. Noyes turned him down. One does not pray with a devil. Reverend Cotton Mather, who had finally made his way back to the area, may have offered Proctor some solace. Mather was haunted by the entire situation, even more so this grim day. "It would break a heart of stone," Cotton wrote later of the situation, "to have seen what I have lately seen…"

A conflux of magistrates and clergy were in attendance that day. Judges Hathorne, Gedney, and Corwin were there, along with ministers Reverend Nicholas Noyes, John Hale, Samuel Cheever, Zachariah Symms, and Cotton Mather. The formidable Stoughton and Sewall were away in Watertown dealing with church disputes.

Finally, the jail door opened and the prisoners were led out. Martha Carrier (frightened but refusing to let these liars see her tremble), John Willard (possibly scanning the crowd for a sign of his wife Mary holding the paper from Boston that would stay his execution), George Jacobs, Sr. (unsteady upon his walking sticks, stumbling over uneven ground), Reverend George Burroughs (meek and surprisingly calm), and John Proctor (the muscles jumping in his jawline and tears threatening to give him away), were walked to the cart and lifted up onto it. The wooden planks groaned beneath their weight, as their hands were tied to the cart.

Perhaps at the sight of Cotton Mather—the young man sitting quietly upon his horse, dressed in black with pained eyes—John Proctor suddenly felt a calm come over him. He had a few moments to look over the heads of the jeering crowd to the walls of the jail he had just vacated. Within, was his wife Elizabeth, carrying even now, their unborn child. Was she weeping? How had they come to this?

With a few shouted orders, Sheriff Corwin swung his leg over his saddle and motioned the cavalcade forward. Along the rutted roads of Salem Town, the cart jolted, its metal hubs creaking against the weight and the sudden jarring of frequent rocks that threatened to rip the wooden wheels apart. The five prisoners processed the long ride up to Gallows Hill in their own way. A mixture of sights, sounds, and smells were stamped onto their minds, as they realized this was the last they would see of the world in which they had participated. The smell of warm horse hides and dried leather wafted back to them from the team and trappings pulling the cart. Their own sweat, mixed with that of accompanying guards rose and fell on a fickle breeze. Faces peering from windows as they rode by, the incongruous sound of a child's laughter coming from somewhere in the crowd. Blotches of sunlight that pierced the eye, only to be blocked out again by buildings, and finally as the town fell away, by occasional trees.

It was this world of color and scent they may have focused on, choosing these simple sensations over the abrasive shouting of the people following their promenade of death. These were their neighbors, ministers, bakers and butchers. John Proctor had sold ale to some of them, and George Burroughs had preached hope to them from his pulpit. They had, no doubt, helped birth a calf or child, plough a field, or hold a hand during sickness. They prayed for some kind of numbness to turn it all into a calming blur.

The day was not with its asides in cruelty. As the progression was nearing its destination, they met the constable from Boxwood who was carrying Rebecca Eames (newly-accused of witchcraft) behind him pillion style. Not wanting to miss the hangings, he took his prisoner to the nearest house beneath the hanging ledge, and asked the owner John Macarter, to watch her. If Rebecca Eames looked out from the window, as indeed, might have John Macarter, she would have seen her future fate, doled out to her during her trial on September 17th.

The crowds jockeyed for position along the rocky flatland of Gallows Hill. It slopped upward, as indeed the road it flanked. The Sheriff had chosen the ledge at its edge, conveniently located where those passing could see the execution and the hanged witches. It also had a ravine with which to toss the victims after their death. It saved the Town the expense, the time, and man power needed to load up their bodies and find a burial place for them. You can't bury a witch in hallowed ground. There were a couple of cemeteries in Salem Town, none of which would accept the remains of one who associated with the Devil.

The condemned lined up beneath the large oak bough with five nooses affixed to it. All maintained their innocence, looking with the eyes of the damned into the faces of so many people who knew them, and should know their hearts. There were many weeping, some with hands placed protectively to their throats or faces. The glittering eyes of the afflicted girls may have been the hardest to see. They stood front and center, as if claiming this execution as their rightful due for ferreting out the evil in the community. Small children clung to their mother's apron, or innocently chased a butterfly as it darted among the farmers and housewives.

Cotton Mather, his maturity belying his youth, prayed with them. It may have rankled Reverend Noyes as he stood nearby. There was a perceived change in the air above the crowd. It had quieted. They looked with wonder at the calm of those waiting beside the ladder propped against the tree bough. The five earnestly begged to be forgiven, and then asked forgiveness for those who brought them here. And then they prayed aloud that theirs would be the last innocent blood spent.

Yet, it was as George Burroughs mounted the first step of the ladder, and turned to face his accusers, that consciences opened and faltered. This small man of Maine, this accused "ringleader" and "King of Hell," looked out at the throng with a supreme calm and prayed. He maintained his innocence, and closed with the perfect recitation of the Lord's Prayer. Letter perfect, without blemish or pause, he nullified the witch's test as he turned to mount the remaining rungs.

A murmur ran through the crowd. Many turned to each other in confusion and fear. This was supposed to be an unimpeachable proof that a person was not a witch, for anyone of the Devil could not recite the Lord's Prayer without stumbling. Excited faces turned toward the magistrates with the question hanging in the air. Many had wept at the tenderness of Burroughs's words and prayers. Now, he had faultlessly recited the prayer upon which so many indictments had hung.

One of the afflicted girls, seeing the turning of the tide, and not wanting to let the big fish get away, yelled out she had seen the black man whispering the prayer into Burroughs' ear. The confusion grew. That could not be, because the Devil wouldn't have been able to whisper the correct words either. The crowd began to surge forward, as if to rescue Burroughs from the ladder. Cotton Mather quickly mounted his horse, and with words that would later haunt him, reminded the crowd of Deodat Lawson's words that the devil is never more subtly himself than when he most appears like an angel of light. He gently admonished them that Burroughs was not even an ordained minister. He was not what he appeared to be.

Mather's words may have halted the crowd's attempt to disrupt the executions, but it did little to qualm their thoughts in the following days.

George Burroughs at his hanging.

Four men, and one woman, were hanged that day. One at a time, they dropped from the rope's end, their own weight betraying them as they struggled for breath. Finally, the girls were quiet. Some people stayed, rooted to the spot in their guilt, others as voyeurs of death. Finally, the bodies were cut down and carried or dragged to the ledge and tossed into the crevice. It was reported that Burroughs had been relieved of his good pants upon his death, as it was customary that the hangman could take the condemned person's possessions. With a final shred of decency not offered him before, he was hurriedly dressed in some other prisoner's pants, and thrown in amongst the others. Dirt and leaves were hurriedly flung in over them, so poorly, that it was recited later that Burroughs' chin and hand could still be seen, along with someone else's foot.

For days after the execution, the villagers murmured. Burroughs prayer haunted them. Wasn't that the supreme test of a witch? Cotton Mather was accosted wherever he went. People couldn't let it go. He was so hounded with their questions and his own growing doubts, that he uttered that he wished he had never heard "the first letters of his [Burroughs] name."

Rebecca Eames, the arrested witch who had just witnessed the hangings from the Macarter home, confessed at her later inquisition to spare herself the noose. Goody Macarter, who had also watched from her back window as the hangings took place, claimed a specter had stuck a pin in her foot. Clearly rattled at what she had just seen, and having an accused witch suddenly thrust into her home, it was clear she regretted her proximity to the newly-appointed hanging ledge.

Those that waited within prison walls may have breathed a sigh of relief that the next trial and executions would not happen for another eighteen days. Some would plan their escape, others would petition the court, their specters would fly, and more arrested witches would be crammed in next to them as impossible roommates.

Elizabeth Proctor would place her hand upon her belly and possibly feel the first stirrings of life. Word would have reached her that her husband was dead. She had, no doubt, heard that Sheriff Corwin had left little behind at her home in his wake of cruelty. Her world had been reduced to this stone prison, and the irony of a dead man's child growing within her.

Chapter Thirty-Four

Eight Firebrands of Hell

In the wake of the August 19th hangings, with the obvious introspection brought about by George Burroughs' heartfelt prayers from the gallows, there may have been a hope that a new perspective was needed pertaining to the witch trials allegations and the court system overseeing them. It was just the opposite.

Between mid-July and early September, the outbreak of witchcraft accusations had been coming mainly from Andover—thanks to the auspicious arrival of Abigail Williams and Mary Walcott. Other small towns bordering Salem Village had been infiltrated in smaller amounts, in that same time period, such as Rowley, Boxford, Haverhill, and Billerica. But, suddenly, beginning in early September (only three weeks before the third round of hangings), witches were reported flying about Gloucester, Reading, and Marblehead. Essex County had become Coven Central. Many of the accusers and accused had, in one way or another, been involved in the Maine Indian wars.

After the August 19th hangings, the largest explosion of witchcraft accusations flooded in. Not the usual retelling of old specters still out on nightly raids, but new names, to this point unheard of by the magistrates. 136 complaints, examinations, and confessions were noted immediately after the hangings and for months to come. It was as if every person wanting to rid themselves of a bothersome neighbor or relative (and it was shocking how many were relatives!), put forth complaints of being tormented by specters. Whether this was done to make the deadline for the monthly court of Oyer and Terminer, is not clear, but it shows an immediacy to jump on the bandwagon while the nooses were hot.

Constables from each town's faction were kept busy riding to terrified households with arrest warrants. The jails were literally bursting. One might think the jailkeepers were happy with the debts accruing, yet often, their bills to the magistrates went unheeded for long periods of time. Keeping prisoners was expensive, even if the food rations and accommodations were sparse.

Word had gotten out to the accused following the latest executions—confess and you may not hang. So far, this seemed to be the case. All five of the latest prisoners who were executed went to their deaths denying they were witches, as did Bridget Bishop when she was hanged alone. Thus, the number of people confessing to witchcraft after being hauled into court was astronomical. It caused Cotton Mather to pause once again in his uncertainty.

On September 9th, six witches were tried and condemned in the Court of Oyer and Terminer. On September 17th, nine more. Due to the influx of prisoners, the Court sat more than once that month. On September 22nd, eight of the fifteen found "Guilty" were hanged. It is worth noting that five of the fifteen who escaped the hangman's noose, had, indeed confessed: Rebecca Eames of Boxford, Mary Lacy and Ann Foster of Andover, Dorcas Hoar of Beverly, and Abigail Hobbs of Topsfield. Francis Dane's daughter, Abigail Faulkner from Andover was given a stay of execution due to her pregnancy. Mary Bradbury, one of the condemned was hidden from the authorities by her friends. Possibly due to her ill-health or her elevated station in life, it doesn't appear the magistrates spent much time looking for her.

While some felt the disinterest in hunting down Mary Bradbury, a confessed witch who was accused of even haunting ships at sea, as a bias for "rich folks," they were also disenchanted with the liberty given to Dorcas Hoar. This was the same woman who had shouted at the afflicted girls during her inquisition, "God will stop the mouths of liars!" Only days before her execution, she suddenly confessed, and was given a temporary reprieve by the magistrates offering her "a little time of life to realize and perfect her repentance for ye salvation of her soul." Many wondered, including the mild Reverend Hale, if Dorcas was confessing at the eleventh hour as a means to save her immortal soul or her tender neck.

The hearts and minds of Essex County were uneasy. The stark reality was that professing innocence would get you hanged, while the confessors gained a reprieve…albeit a temporary one for now. Why did so many suddenly come forward and confess? And not only confess their own sins, but point out even more witches the court had missed so far. Within families, living beneath the same roof, some confessed, and some held steadfast to their innocence. Reverend Hale tossed and turned over the notion that if people like Margaret Jacobs, who had named so many witches and confessed to her own involvement, could now recant that confession and be left from the gallows for now, what did that mean? Who were the liars and who were the truthsayers?

Samuel Willard had the dubious distinction of being the only male to stand before the court in September. The September 9th trials found **Martha Corey** of Salem Village, **Alice Parker** and **Ann Pudeator** of Salem Town, and **Mary Esty** of Topsfield "Guilty." On September 17th, **Mary Parker** of Andover, **Margaret Scott** of Rowley, and **Wilmot Redd** of Marblehead were also sentenced.

Ann Pudeator filed a petition, claiming the testimonies sworn out against her by Sarah Churchill, Mary Warren, and John Best were "altogether false and untrue." To back her claim, she pointed out to the court room that John Best had once been publicly humiliated by whipping in the town common on allegations of his being a "lyar." It all fell on deaf ears.

Martha Corey, still full of salt and vinegar, despite her long stay in prison, railed at the court. Samuel Parris, always willing to turn over a fellow parishioner, called upon Corey in prison to add pain to her already helpless position. He was about to make an announcement in Church. During his sermon on September 11th, he spoke from the pulpit saying, "Behold, the Devil shall cast some of you into prison that ye may be tried, and ye shall have tribulation. But be thou faithful unto death, and [earn] a crown of life."

The Reverend then asked the congregation to vote on the question of Martha Corey's excommunication, as she had been found guilty of witchcraft and aligning with the Devil. "By general consent" (not unanimous consent) she was voted out of the church. Parris, along with several others chosen from the Salem Village church, informed her on September 14th, only days before her hanging, that she would be excommunicated. Her name, along with that of Rebecca Nurse, would no longer be found among the church records. Martha Corey, like Nurse, had been a church-covenanted member. The Devil, his fingers placed upon the chess piece of the Bishop, had played the game well.

Parris, usually effusive in his notes, declined to write down the vitriol this announcement excited in Martha. He merely noted that she was "very obdurate, justifying herself and condemning all that had done anything to her just discovery and condemnation." The interview with her in jail had not lasted long. Parris only wrote that it was short "for her imperiousness would not suffer much." While poor Rebecca Nurse had been carried into church and forced to hear the dreadful words that she was no longer worthy to be among the elite of God, Parris chose, judiciously, to give Martha Corey the news in jail. The prison walls had heard such words as those that flew from her mouth, the church meetinghouse had not.

Mary Esty, ever compliant and meek, had nonetheless spent the preceding months petitioning the courts for trials that relied more on fairness and reason than had their examinations. It was too late for Rebecca Nurse, her sister, but she and her third sister, Sarah Cloyce, were still in danger of hanging. They begged that the magistrates listen to the myriad petitions and testimonies of their neighbors and families. They were God-fearing, church-going women. The fact that Sarah Cloyce had slammed the door in defiance at said church, was a minor detail.

Esty, in her submissive role as a mere village housewife, appealed to the power of the magistrates to help her and her sister in their pitiable positions. In writing, they asked "that you who are our judges would please to counsel to us, to direct us wherein we may stand in need." They asked that accusations against us as witches, either by those afflicted, or confessing witches, "not be improved to condemn us without other legal evidence." These were the exact guidelines the "several ministers" had advocated, yet it still failed to soften the hearts of the magistrates. Dated September 15th, 1692, Mary, probably realizing the court had not been moved by her first petition dated September 9th, showed her true depth of character by sending in her final words in hopes of saving the lives that came after her:

"I Petition to your honours not for my own life for I know I must die and my appointed time is sett but the Lord he knowes it is that if it be possible no more Innocentt blood may be shed which undoubtidly cannot be Avoydd In the way and course you goe in I question not but your honours does to the uttmost of your Powers in the discovery and detecting of witchcraft and witches and would not be gulty of Innocent blood for the world but by my own Innocencye I know you are in the wrong way the Lord in his infinite mercye direct you in this great work if it be his blessed will that no more Innocent blood be shed I would humbly begg of you that your honors would be plesed to examine theis Aflicted Persons strictly and keepe them apart some time and Like- wise to try some of these confesing wichis I being confident there is severall of them has belyed themselves and others as will appeare if not in this wor[l]d I am sure in the world to come whither I am now agoing and I Question not but youle see an alteration of thes things they say my selfe and others having made a League with the Divel we cannot confesse I know and the Lord knowes as will shortly appeare they belye me and so I Question not but they doe others the Lord above who is the Searcher of all hearts knowes that as I shall answer it att the Tribunall seat that I know not the least thinge of witchcraft therfore I cannot I dare not belye my own soule I beg your honers not to deny this my humble petition from a poor dy ing Innocent person and I Question not but the Lord will give a blesing to yor endevers."

Giles Corey's Death

Three days before the third execution was to take place, the husband of Martha Corey, Giles Corey, was sentenced to the cruel punishment of *"peine forte et dure"* (French for "hard and strong punishment"). He had stood as witness against his own wife, but knew now the girls were liars. The long months in jail had given him a new perspective of just how these wheels of justice turned. No matter what you said on behalf of your good name, it would not help you. He therefore, in a mind he had admitted belonged to "a poor man," he decided to "stand mute," and not answer to any allegations at all.

Thus, during his trial on September 9th, although he professed his innocence on all allegations, when he was asked the formal question of "How would you be tried?" he said nothing. The usual response is "By God and Country," upon which the court would then pass sentence. But Giles stood as a statue, glaring at the table of magistrates, and said nothing. They could not continue with the verdict without his participation. They asked him again, threatening the punishment of "pressing" (their definition of *"peine forte et dure"*), but he stood stoic.

It was not just in defiance of the court that had railroaded so many before him, it was a pragmatic way of keeping his possessions from the greedy clutches of Sheriff Corwin. Until he received an indictment of "Guilty," legally, the good Sheriff could not confiscate his goods. As stated, earlier, Giles Corey made out a renewed will in prison, hoping to thwart Corwin's band of looters.

On Monday, September 19th, Giles Corey was taken out to a field across from the jail and placed into a shallow pit. It was barely an indentation in the ground. His arms were outstretched and bound to stakes pounded into the hard ground. His ankles were likewise tied. A large board was placed upon his chest and the first massive stone was put upon the board. Beneath the blistering sun, he lay, a team of men surrounding him, awaiting his statement. As the day wore on, more large boulders were placed upon the board. Sheriff Corwin would come and go, asking if the prisoner had said anything. The answer was always "No."

The sun set, and nighttime brought with it a relief from the sun, but the gnawing of insects. To the surprise of those who watched the sunlight of Day Two wash across his pockmarked face, they found a man still resolute and unflinching. He was allowed a small portion of bread and a sip of water. Then more rocks were added to the board. The object of the "pressing" was to garner a confession or statement from a prisoner. Some surely died beneath the treatment, but most, their breathing becoming labored and their ribs threatening to crack, usually faltered. Not Giles Corey. Even the pleadings of his good friend Thomas Gardner would not sway Corey from his path.

A second day ended, his face blistered, his lips parched and his eyes blurred by sunlight. By morning, he was half-dead. It has been reported that both Judge John Hathorne and Sheriff Corwin came to Corey on the third morning and asked him again to answer the Court's questions. The prisoner's cracked lips moved, his dry tongue struggling to move inside a mouth devoid of moisture. One of the men leaned over him to hear his words. In a raspy, oxygen-deprived breath, he managed to utter, "More weight!" His tongue lolled to the side, and reports say that Hathorne or Corwin forced it back into his mouth with their walking cane. Sometime soon after, beneath the weight of multiple boulders, Giles Corey died. As it took three days for this stubborn farmer to perish, one wonders if the cart bearing his wife to the gallows may have passed by the site where he lay beneath a board of stones.

Giles Corey had withheld the two things the magistrates and Sheriff wanted most: to declare him a wizard and hang him; and for him to leave his door open to the thievery of the Sheriff. He died without giving them either. Corey's written will held. It was legal and binding and his property went to his heirs. Sheriff Corwin did ride out to the Corey farm to see what he could get. His son-in-law John Moulton gave him £11-6-0 and the matter was settled. Moulton also paid Giles and Martha's outstanding jail fees.

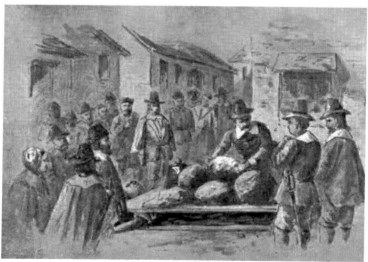

Giles Corey during the "pressing."

Several condemned witches were still in hiding, in hopes the whole hysteria would blow over. **Elizabeth**

Coleson had managed to escape and keep out of sight for a full four months. She was finally found in Charleston and brought back to face her fate. Constable Timothy Phillips brought her to Salem Town for her questioning. She was handed off to the Cambridge Jail to await her punishment along with her mother Mary Coleson, aunt Sarah Dustin, and grandmother Lydia Dustin.

During the week leading up the September executions, business went on as usual in the court room. Many depositions were heard, more prisoners brought in and questioned—it was a busy time for the scribes and judges. The jails continued to fill unabated. The pounding sound of the gavel pronouncing death was as evasive as the pounding of nails at a barn raising.

Eight Firebrands of Hell

The morning of Thursday, September 22nd, dawned with a promise of rain after a lengthy draught. As the cart, laden with seven witches and one wizard, made its way along the long and jolting road to Gallows Hill, a slight breeze brushed the sweating faces of the prisoners. There was a hint of fall in the air. The trees were turning, and the waters of Salem Harbor had become more of a gunmetal grey beneath the season's sky.

Mary Esty, Ann Pudeator, Alice Parker, Margaret Scott, Wilmott Read, Mary Parker, Martha Corey, and Samuel Wardwell listened to the rhythmic *thunk, thunk, thunk* of the wooden wheels as the cart rolled over the causeway at the North River. The road was deeply rutted and suddenly the cart lurched to one side. One of the wheels had sunk into a deep gouge in the earth. As men hastened to roll the wheels forward, several of the afflicted girls, who were following closely behind their victims, shouted out that it was the Devil that had caused the cart to stop. He was trying to save his followers from hanging!

The ledge came into view and the accused saw their Golgotha. There were no wooden crosses, only a large oak with eight nooses swaying in the fall breeze. The crowd scurried up the steep embankment and positioned itself for the best view. The long ladder was placed against the bough, and a silence fell over the throng. A prayer may have been offered. But again, it was the touching last words of the accused that moved many in the assembly.

Mary Esty, pious and meek until the end, said goodbye to her husband, children, and friends, whose faces were twisted in agony. All their petitions had not saved her. Many were weeping openly. Martha Corey, despite her recent excommunication, still proclaimed herself a "Gospel Woman" till the last. She declared her innocence and spoke briefly, her speech flying defiantly in the face of the Puritan rule that women did not speak in public. It was her final tenacious act and she "concluded her life with an eminent prayer."

Samuel Wardwell mounted the ladder and turned to say his piece, but smoke from the executioner's pipe blew on the breeze into Wardwell's face and choked away his final words on earth. The afflicted took advantage of this sad moment and yelled that the Devil had blown the smoke into the dying man's face to silence him.

Eight people dropped to their deaths. Mary Esty would not be coming home. Wilmott Read would be a fishmonger's wife no longer, cleaning his catch and tallying the books. Ann Pudeator, once wealthy and twice widowed, would not have her conviction reversed until 1957, centuries after the colony's General Court cleared the names of the other accused and executed witches.

Martha Corey, perhaps only minutes before seeing the body of her dead husband in the field across from the jail, followed him to whatever waited on the other side.

Alice Parker and Ann Pudeator had fallen beneath the sword of Mary Warren's "spectral evidence." She had seen the two local women sticking pins into poppets resembling Mercy Lewis and Mary Walcott.

Seventy-seven-year-old Margaret Scott had fallen on hard times in her life. Like Sarah Good, she had been reduced to asking for help from her neighbors. She was living on donated land, and occasionally was without firewood and food. She would no longer be a burden on the inhabitants. Samuel Wardwell of Andover, 49, had been accused of being a fortune teller with an uncanny ability to see into people's darkest secrets. "I wonder how Wardwell could tell so true," was said of him. One wonders if his crystal ball had shown him this day.

Reverend Nicholas Noyes looked up at the eight bodies twisting in the breeze and intoned, "What a sad thing it is to see eight firebrands of Hell hanging there." The tree branches suddenly thrashed about as a large gust of wind swept through the crowd. Eerily, the bodies swung in greater arcs. All eyes turned to the skies that were darkening quickly. Had it occurred to them that the scene was reminiscent of the events following the death of Christ, when the heavens opened and rain gushed down? Or by now, with all that had happened, were the scriptures forgotten? As the crowd hurried home to their families and pious prayers, the clouds let loose their heavy burden.

That night, seventeen-year-old Mary Herrick listened to the night sounds outside her second-story window in her home in Wenham, Massachusetts. Wenham, although a close neighbor to Salem, had been left unscathed from the witch hysteria. It was then quite frightening when through the shadowed recesses of the ceiling beams a form materialized and spoke to her.

"I am going upon the ladder to be hanged for a witch, but I am innocent and before a twelfth-month be past you shall believe it." The ghost identified herself as Mary Esty, and then disappeared.

Chapter Thirty-Five

The Tables Turn

For some time, Mary Herrick kept the vision to herself. She believed those that hung were indeed guilty of witchcraft and wanted nothing to do with it. Yet, shortly after Esty's prophecy, she began to experience unexplainable pains. A natural affliction was sought, but none was found. And then one night, just as Mary Esty had appeared to her, another shape appeared in the most unlikely guise—it was astoundingly the specter of Reverend John Hale's wife. After that, Mrs. Hale came on a regular basis and, according to Mary Herrick, choked and pinched her. After many spectral attacks, Mrs. Hale's apparition was joined by that of Mary Esty, who merely looked on quietly. Esty "made as if to speak and did not."

The specter of Mrs. Hale finally addressed Herrick. "Do you think I am a witch?" Hale asked. "No!" yelled Herrick, "You be the Devil!"

It was now that Mary Esty's specter spoke the words that began the fall of the witchcraft scaffolding. She told Mary Herrick "that she had been put to death wrongfully and was innocent of the witchcraft and she came to vindicate her cause." Esty "bid her to reveal this to Mr. Hale and Mr.

Gerrish and then she would rise nor more, nor should Mrs. Hale afflict her."

Herrick ran to her pastor, Reverend Gerrish of Wenham and related the tale of nightly visions and attacks to him. He questioned her at length and made a record of the account. She remained consistent in the telling of it, and he was convinced she was relating what she called "the delusion of the devil." Gerrish asked Reverend Hale from nearby Beverly to come to see him and related Mary's account to him.

Reverend Hale listened incredulously with a sinking heart as he heard his own wife had been accused. He knew his wife, knew her good heart and steadfast faith in God. There was not one ounce of truth that she was dabbling in witchcraft or would confer with the Devil.

As he sat there, dread running through him, he was suddenly hit with the clarity the imprisoned had prayed for. Knowing his own wife incapable of the things of which she had just been accused, then, how many others were also falsely accused? "Spectral evidence" was madness. How many innocent lives had been ripped from their homes, thrown into rotting prisons, and hanged? He felt physically ill.

As he sat in his study and looked to the scriptures and other writings for guidance, another thought hit him as hard as a first—if a witch, already hanged and dead, such as Mary Esty, could still come back and haunt the living, then what purpose did it serve to hang them to start with? Had the 8-pounds of chains clamped to their ankles kept them from flying about and attacking the girls? And now death had not purged Essex County of spectral attacks. It was indeed, complete madness! An exercise in futility built upon lies!

Reverend Hale did not keep these revelations to himself. He would speak out. He now knew in his heart how John Proctor must have felt when his own wife was accused. Proctor was dead by only a few days' time, but if Hale could help it, there would be no more death based on spectral evidence. Many ministers outside the reach of the Salem hysteria were already lobbying for the trials to halt. It was interesting to see towns like Plymouth, who did not allow a small circle of hormonal girls get out of control, look aghast at the desolation caused by these young people who should have been disciplined.

But, Plymouth, along with other Massachusetts provinces, lacked the likes of Mrs. Ann Carr Putnam, whispering the names of so many into the malleable minds of her daughter and friends. It was perhaps fortunate that many outlining towns were not on Mrs. Putnam's wooden rolodex. The towns like Boxford and Topsfield, where she knew the names of some that rankled, found their way into the afflicted girls' crosshairs. Andover, visited by Ann Putnam Jr. and Mary Walcott, were ransacked by a "hit and run" coven. Luckily, the town awoke from their nightmare quickly, albeit minus the largest portion of the accused victims in the Salem Witch Trial annals.

As the judges sat inside Boston chambers and looked toward the next session of the Court of Oyer and Terminer, scheduled to be held in October, the "cry and hue" from ministers, families, and even within their own ranks, grew. Winter was coming on. Many of the people had been sitting in unhealthy pen-like conditions for months. They were ill, and malnourished, and the fear was they might not last through a long, frigid New England winter. So many families bereft of their breadwinners were starving. Ploughs rusted in the fields, and children, bereft of their mother and caregiver, were suffering, or had been farmed out to other families who were buckling beneath the added cost of caring for them. In short, a pandemic was imminent.

The Quaker from Salem, Thomas Maule, came closest to hanging the shingle of blame on the Putnams' (and others') door. He said the witchcraft outbreak had been created by the petty hates and jealousies of the community. How many ministers had turned down invitations to preach in Salem Village as its ordained minister in the past, due to their knowledge that the bickering and battles among the neighbors there were unusually high? Maule asked what happened to "Love thy neighbor?"

Reverend Samuel Willard of Boston, whose viewpoints had already come under attack from the magistrates in favor of the trials, and from the afflicted themselves, pressed on with more vehemence than ever. He called the girls "scandalous persons, liars, and loose in their conversation." How could these people, not even close to being "humane witnesses," be afflicted and still be allowed to bear testimony? Wasn't their very affliction skating dangerously near the edge of being in cahoots with the Devil? He battled on: "God hath not granted to man such a power over another's lives."

Increase Mather, who had managed to stay under the radar, unless directly asked to participate, suddenly rankled when he saw a parishioner taking their ill child not to him, or the ministry, but to one of the afflicted to ask if they thought witchcraft was involved. Mather thundered, "Is there not a God in Boston, that you should go to the devil in Salem?" His very words aligned the afflicted with the Devil, if one was listening closely enough.

On October 3rd, possibly fearing another round of the Court proceedings, Increase Mather stood before a conference of ministers and read from a paper called *Cases of Conscience*, in which he laid out his objections to the Court protocol. He warned about placing too much weight on the credibility of spectral evidence. He attacked the "test of touch," and renounced white magic, such as in the making of a witch cake. "It is better that ten suspected witches should escape than one innocent person should be condemned." On October 19th, Mather asked to see the documents pertaining to prison "punishments," such as those John Proctor had ridiculed in his petition, specifically tying a prisoner "Neck and Heels" to coerce a confession from him.

There seems to be no mention in Mathers' *Cases of Conscience* concerning the court-ordered body search for witch's marks or "teats." He expounds mainly on those things ethereal, that cannot be bottled and tagged. Salisbury magistrate Richard Pike picked up the gauntlet on the contested witch's mark test.

The town of Salisbury had seemed to fall outside the witches' fly zone. Richard Pike's only involvement had been the occasional filing of a deposition against Susanna Martin, who was known there. As some farmers came to him with depositions concerning her witchcraft, he would often look up at them from his table and wryly say, "It's a pity you didn't tell the story four and twenty years ago when it happened."

When Saltonstall from neighboring Haverhill resigned his position as Judge on the Court of Oyer and Terminer, it peeked Pike's interest. Just what was all this hullabaloo about? He rode over and looked into it, especially reports concerning Mary Bradbury and Susanna Martin. What he saw did not please him. After witnessing the trial of George Burroughs in August, Pike wrote a letter to Judge Corwin (judiciously signing it only with his initials. No sense in risking being the next on the afflicteds' list). In the letter, Pike admonished the Judge that innocent lives were being handed over to the wrong people. He said the way the courts were currently operating only opened the doors "to the pleasure and passion of those that are minded to take them away...The witnesses were not only informers...but sole judges of the crime."

Pike was on a role, and perhaps gaining courage from the anonymity of signing the diatribe with only his initials, he attacked pretty much the entire infrastructure of the Court's platform.

How exactly could the Judge's prove witchcraft? By spectral evidence that actually showed people dining in the parsonage's pasture? The Devil had carried Christ to a mountaintop and promised him "pretty things" if he would join him, yet "left him innocent." And what of witch marks, Pike asked, finally addressing the elephant in the room. How often, he wrote, might "a superfluity of nature...as the piles..." be the cause of some blemish on a person's body? "Piles" or hemorrhoids, was exactly the abnormality found on Rebecca Nurse that she explained was the result of years of bearing children. Under these flimsy examinations, Pike wrote, it was recommended "to leave a guilty person alive until further discovery than to put an innocent person to death."

Pike then encapsulated the entire mad concept of what the judges were taking as "gospel." How, he basically asked, can you believe that people standing before you accused of witchcraft, who are direly trying to save their lives, would then send their shapes flying around the court room to torture the afflicted parties *right in front of you*? Would that be giving you just more of the evidence you are seeking? Would the Devil, trying to keep his witches from the scaffold, allow that to happen, if that is the notion upon which you hang your hats?

It was a salient point that no one had thought to point out. It made a mockery of the entire judicial process. The fact that the recipient of the letter, Judge Jonathan Corwin, had failed to heed the accusations against his mother-in-law, Margaret Thatcher, was another point not finding favor with the locals. If all the accusations of witchcraft were based on truth, why wasn't there an arrest warrant made out for the Judge's kinswoman?

Finally, Thomas Brattle of Boston, an intelligent man that boasted enough skills to land him as the upcoming treasurer of Harvard, also wrote a letter, signing his full name, and addressing it to include all the magistrates with a "Dear Sir." He backed up Pike's beliefs on the use of "spectral evidence." Without fear, Brattle attacked the Court writing that it was disgraceful that the magistrates had based their judgments on such evidence as common gossip, irresponsible "confessions," and the hallucinations of young girls, whom he condemned as liars. While addressing all those who had taken part in the persecutions of the innocent, he singled out Salem where "this sort of gentleman does most abound."

Lady Phips is Accused

While the Governor of Massachusetts, Sir William Phips, was away in Pemmaquid, dealing with business not related to witchcraft, his indomitable wife, Lady Mary Phips, took it upon herself to sign a pardon for one of the prisoners, who happened to be an acquaintance of hers. The woman was released and disappeared into parts unknown. On September 29, 1692, Sir William returned to Boston to find not only jails spilling over with inmates, but his own wife was now accused of being a witch! It seems the local witch-hunters frowned on Lady Phips illegal release of a prisoner accused of devilry.

The girls' accusations had now reached the level of ludicrous. Accusing Reverend Samuel Willard as an attacking specter (when the Reverend's preaching about what the Devil would and would not do came perilously close to denouncing the girls' accusations), was one thing. The girls had been corrected that time, with the Court covering its butt by saying they must have meant John Willard (accused witch). They had merely gotten the names mixed up…right? But now, they had aimed too high. They had accused the wife of the Governor of Massachusetts.

The Judges, wiping spectral egg from their faces, were beginning to blanch at the onslaught of criticism. They were coming off as idiots. Reverend Hale bottled it by saying, "It cannot be imagined that in a place of so much knowledge so many in so small a compass of land should abominably leap into the devil's lap at once."

The October session of the Court of Oyer and Terminer was delayed as the disgraced Judges decided to put the whole mess into the returning Governor's lap. They had a freshly-provided way to "encourage" the Governor's hand in the matter—his own wife was now in danger of the noose.

Sir William wrote to the King of England, with a vacillating missive; on one hand complimenting the magistrates on their handling of the witchcraft business, yet on the other hand, finding that "the devil had taken upon him to assume the shape of several persons who were doubtless innocent and to my certain knowledge of good reputation"—ahem, my wife—he had called off any further warrants be issued. He also told the Crown that he was putting a lid on any written material that might kindle "an inextinguishable flame," namely, Thomas Brattle's heated letter. In a whining tone, that may not have impressed the throne of England, he ended with a plaintive wail that people "are seeking to turn it all on me."

It was clear the fingers of blame were now pointing in every direction, and finally, at the ones who had started it all—several young girls from Salem Village, and the "afflicted" who joined their circle.

The outcry now was heard far and wide. Andover began it. On October 7th, 1692, seven of the town's inhabitants petitioned the court for the return of their women and children, citing the appalling conditions within the prison walls, the impending Winter, and their continued association with "poor distressed creatures as full of inward grief and trouble as they are able to bear up in life withal." Petitions came not only from Andover, but from Haverhill, Gloucester, Chelmsford, and Topsfield, asking for the release of their kin on bond.

When the Court balked, and it became evident the next trials had been postponed from the beginning of October, Andover residents became more forceful. On October 24th, twenty-four citizens wrote that they found the afflicted girls as "distempered persons" and condemned the weight their testimony had been given in court. "We know no one who can think himself safe if the accusations of children and others who are under diabolical influence shall be received against persons of good fame."

From Brattle's letter, to Governor Phips' address to the King, to this missive from Andover, one central theme remains: the belief in the Devil is absolute. The Puritan belief in the twin heads of Good and Evil never wavered. It was not in dispute that Satan was alive and well and targeting Essex County; it was the *evidence* presented to confirm he was using innocent people to advance his cause, and the suspicion that these young people were his harbingers. The girls had gone too far, and the tide of approval had turned against them in a big way.

The Court of Oyer and Terminer is Dismissed

The magistrates finally fell beneath the onslaught of disapproval and petitions for the release of prisoners. On October 26th, they did what they had always done, they laid the decision on the church's doormat. They called for a fast and "convocation of the ministers that may be led in the right way as to the witchcraft."

It was over. The Court was officially dismissed three days later. The orange and red leaves that crunched beneath the Villager's feet were somehow symbolic of the death of not only those who had been executed, or died in jail, but of a Court that had been, in the end, a mock trial. Yet, the fallout was far from over. The prison environment claimed two more lives, including that of confessed witch Ann Foster of Andover.

At least 150 "witches" had been arrested. What to do with them? As the dead bodies of prisoners were carried out and handed over to family members, the outcry increased. It was a legal mess, to say the least. Winter was a concern, and the prisons housing these poor creatures were rudimentary in structure and bursting with hungry and sick souls.

Governor Phips looked over the petitions from the neighboring towns of Massachusetts, asking for the release of their family members on bond, and chewed upon it. He ran a tired finger down the prison roster and blanched at the ages of some of the prisoners. Dorothy and Abigail Faulkner were merely ten and eight, respectively.

Nathaniel Dane and John Osgood were willing to put up £500 bond for them. Stephen and Abigail Johnson were thirteen and eleven; and Sarah Carrier only eight. After much time spent on reading the depositions against these children (and many adults), and finding the evidence to be mostly "spectral," he released the prisoners whose families could post bond.

For those whose families could not afford the bail money, the prisoners remained. Tituba Indian was one such person. Poor little Dorcas Good still huddled in a corner, her baby sibling dead and her mother hanged. It must have been gut-wrenching for those who watched as others walked out into the light of freedom, while they remained. Sir William admonished the Judges residing over the districts with imprisoned witches, to watch over their safety and welfare. Just how that was to be administered was left open.

In the wake of the superstition, lies, and hysteria, a new law was drawn up on December 14th, giving some guidelines as to what certain acts of witchcraft would bring in the weight of punishment. Incredulously, despite it all, witchcraft was still considered a very real thing; there just needed to be better laws to discern the *degree* of witchcraft used.

For those witches who conjured, or used charms to hurt or kill, for "any invocation or conjuration of any evil spirit," or for "taking up any dead man, woman, or child" from their graves, the penalty was death. (It's disconcerting to think this grave robbing must have been an issue, or it would not have required mention.)

For the practice of "white magic" (which was going on anyway in secret in many houses), the sentence was prison time or the pillory if you were using charms, etc. in an effort to find stolen property, buried treasure, the killing of cattle, or "to invoke any person to unlawful love."

Despite the dissolution of the Court, and the gradual release of prisoners, some towns held tight to the witch mania. Gloucester was one such town. It sent for the superstars of Salem Village to come and take a look at some afflicted people. The girls complied and four women were rounded up as witches, and ended up in Ipswich Jail when Salem turned them away.

In November, someone from Gloucester summoned the girls again. As they were crossing the Ipswich Bridge on their way to that town, they met an old woman that must have seemed like a perfect fit for a crone's image. The girls fell down into fits and cried out against her. But to their astonishment, the people who gathered to see what the fuss was about, looked at them in amusement, ignored them, and went about their business. Ipswich had no patience for such antics. The girls got up, dusted themselves off, and looked at each other as if to say "Now what?"

The girls continued their journey to Gloucester but their performance lacked conviction. The magician's curtain had been pulled back and they were exposed. No arrests resulted from their journey.

Salem Village turned its thoughts to the brutal cold of winter. The only thing that saved hundreds of households from freezing that season was that the majority of witches imprisoned were women, leaving the men to chop wood and forage for food. Still, so many field hands had left crops unattended during their time spent as spectators in court, and trying to fight off the Devil, that produce and meat were at a minimum. Sheriff Corwin had made off with cattle and food stuffs that were not that easy to replace. Jars that typically held preserves sat empty. Firewood was hastily gathered, where it could be found, for despite popular belief, Salem Village boasted mainly open fields, rocky ground, and marshes.

Old Nick pushed around the chess pieces on his map of Essex County to no avail. His pawns had fallen, leaving him deposed. His Bishop would soon be vanquished from the Village, and his Knights had fought their last battle. Even the Castles of Court were laid low. He looked about the destruction he had caused, and while 20 executions were not the massive total he had hoped for, the desecration of towns and churches had been encouraging. There would be other times, in other places.

Chapter Thirty-Six

What Have We Done?

As the Massachusetts Bay Colony looked about at the devastation wrought in a short year's time, it assessed the loss to its legislative coffers as well. The copious amount of time the magistrates, constables, and jailkeepers had spent on the witch trials had taken them away from other matters. The timing had been detrimental to the colony. They had only just received their new charter, and at a time when they had other important matters and legislature to conduct, they were instead traveling back and forth to Salem to watch children throwing tantrums on the floor, and hearing outrageous stories of flying ghosts and picnics in Samuel Parris's pasture. Their 17th century in-box was overflowing with petitions and legal documents demanding their attention. At this juncture, to sit on the bench overseeing a dispute about a land boundary or the cost of timber looked like heaven.

As prisoners were released to the families who could post bond, the Massachusetts' legal system put forth this statement on December 16th, when "Upon consideration of many persons now in Custody within the County of Essex, charged as Capital Offenders," a new Superior Court in the form of "a Court of Azzise and General Gaol Delivery" to be held on January 3rd, 1693.

With his proverbial tail between his legs, Governor Phips wrote to the Secretary of State in London, that some of the Judges "were convinced and acknowledged that their former proceedings were too violent and not grounded upon a right foundation," and so the 1693 trials would fly under a different judicial flag. Phips may have put forth the disclaimer that he had been in England when the whole mess started, and that many people were already questioned and in jail by the time he returned with the charter.

And so, in the new year of 1693, the snows fell upon Essex County. The mind-numbing routine that had witnessed the boredom and eventual hysteria of the winter prior, settled in once more. A year had passed since Abigail Williams and Betty Parris watched as Tituba dropped an egg white into a glass of water and the shape of a coffin appeared in the swirling albumin. As farmers, housewives, and children once more took up their daily chores and scripture study, did they miss the excitement that had added color to their gray days during the elevated state of hysteria of 1692? As their hands tied dried herbs, sewed a button, or wielded an axe, were they now freed from the miasma of psychoneurosis that had plagued the county?

Two court sessions were held in January and February under the new Court of Azzise, where fifty-two people were tried. Only three were convicted. Nine of the people appearing (including the wealthy Phillip and Mary English), were not even indicted. The list of those acquitted contained the names of Mary Toothaker, Mary Lacey Jr., Richard Carrier, and Mary Marston. Three confessed witches were convicted on the grounds of covenanting with Satan and afflicting others: Sarah Wardwell, Betty Johnson, and Mary Post.

Anthony Checkley, the Boston lawyer who had replaced Thomas Newton as trial attorney during the trials of Oyer and Terminer, informed Governor Phips, that technically, the three condemned women were "under the same circumstances" as "some of the cleared." Phips thought it over, and reversed his decision—he reprieved them as well. Lieutenant Governor Stoughton went through the roof. He had already signed their death warrants, along with five others who had recently been tried and found guilty. Phips, in a rare move of courage, stood strong and reprieved them all, stating his decision would stand "until their Majesties' pleasure be signified and declared." True, he had passed the buck to the head of England, but it was a stand of defiance all the same.

Stoughton stormed off the bench in early February, resigning his post. "Filled with passionate anger," he let it be known by this action of reprieving convicted witches "the Kingdom of Satan was advanced, & the Lord have mercy on this Country." He had been denied his pound of flesh. Thomas Danforth replaced him, although Stoughton returned in April to preside over the final set of trials.

By April, 1693, only a few remained who would stand before the bar. Hearing the Court of Oyer and Terminer had been dismantled, Alden had returned to Salem from his hiding place in New York on December 22nd, 1692. He posted bond on December 31st. On April 25th, he stood before a bench of Judges who lacked enthusiasm and were ready to move on to other matters besides witches and wizards. He was reprieved and left to go about his business. The majority of the other prisoners to stand before the Court of Azzise, filthy and thin from months of imprisonment, were Andover confessors. Those who had been home for a time, thanks to the bond release, looked far better off, with washed faces and clean clothes, and a color in their cheeks that was wanting in the others who spent their hours in darkness. Every one of them was acquitted and let go.

Tituba Indian sat within the crumbling stone walls and watched as one-by-one the others left and did not return. She had eaten the prison fare and inhaled the stench of sweat, urine, and feces for over a year. Babies had been born here...some lived, others did not. She had been here the longest. The other two arrested with her were long gone—Sarah Osbourne died before her eyes within the walls of Boston Prison, and Sarah Good had left her filthy pipe behind as she was dragged up to Gallows Hill and hanged. She had heard endless nights of weeping and prayers, hatred and swearing, hope and resignation.

On May 9th, 1693, an Ipswich Grand Jury finally granted her reprieve. The official document stated "Tittapa and Indian Woman Servant to mr Samuel Parris of Salem Village" had "Wickedly & feloniously...Signed the Devills Booke," and "become A detestable Witch." The court offered her one disclaimer as to her vulnerability to evil—they wrote "ignoramus" at the top of her reprieve.

If Tituba found the news of her pardon heart-warming, it was soon made known to her that her master, Reverend Samuel Parris had declined to pay her jail fees, thus leaving her there to rot. Many others, who had been formally granted their freedom, remained until their bills could be paid. Some, without relatives who would help them, or homes they could mortgage, waited in the dark nights. One such "witch" was Sarah Daston, who finally died waiting for some kind soul to ransom her out. Mary Watkins, finding herself in the same situation, hit upon the idea to ask the jailer if he might find her a master who would be willing to pay her jail fees in exchange for her servitude. A gentleman from Virginia was found, and she exchanged imprisonment for slavery.

Tituba, perhaps following her example, offered the same request, and a new master paid her fees in exchange for a lifetime of chores. With board at the jails (she had run up a tab at both Boston and Salem prisons) averaging about two shillings and sixpence a week, Tituba's bill of over a year, was formidable. She was lucky to find someone who would free her.

Margaret Jacobs, the granddaughter of old George Jacobs Sr., who had been hanged as a wizard, was still incarcerated. Her parents had fled the state during the witchcraft accusations, and not returned. It was a moot point anyway. The Jacobs' goods had been seized during their exile, and there was no money with which to pay the jailer. Although Jacobs Sr. had left Margaret £10 in his will, the inheritance had fallen through the cracks. Despite her bravery and recanting her confession of witchcraft, she stayed in jail as the seasons turned outside. Finally, a generous soul, hearing of her plight, paid her jail fees and Margaret went free—not as a servant, but as a young woman to find her way in the world.

For the prisoners handed their reprieves, it was on paper only. Despite reclaiming their places amongst their families, many did not reclaim their good names amongst the general population. They had been convicted of witchcraft, and an allegation such as that was hard to wear down. Elizabeth Proctor and Abigail Faulkner, both condemned witches who had been given extra time before their executions due to pregnancy concerns, walked out of jail with their babies. These women, and the others convicted, had no legal existence. They could not even claim their dowers. Proctor returned to a home desecrated of its possessions, only some of which her family had managed to buy back. Her husband had been hanged, and she had another hungry mouth to feed among a plethora of children.

The Aftermath

As the prisoners were released and wandered back to ruined lives, did the Villagers mark that the afflicted girls showed no signs of further tormenting? If, indeed, these people they had "cried out" against were witches, would they not still remain so? In fact, would they not now be free to inflict their wrath on the girls and adults who had caused their own torments and ruination? Yet, oddly, none of the afflicted posted reports of harassment after the prisons emptied.

Cotton Mather, defiled for his involvement in trying to help some of the afflicted, such as Mary Short, had remained faithful in putting his notes and insights of the trials into a manuscript. In his highly popular *Wonders of the Invisible World*, which came out in 1693 during the jail releases, he documented the events of the examinations and trials of George Burroughs, Bridget Bishop, Susanna Martin, Elizabeth How, and Martha Carrier, all hanged for witchcraft. For people who had not sat a pew during the proceedings, the manuscript offered their only version of the trials. Governor Phips had tried to prevent its publication, along with Thomas Brattle's inflammatory letter, but finally gave up when it was clear the public knew most of the culpability already. It became a journalistic masterpiece, lauded far and wide for its accuracy and reporting.

Sheriff George Corwin had continued his looting. Hardest hit was Phillip English. After he had been convinced to flee Salem, along with his wife Mary, what he had feared most, happened. Sheriff Corwin rode up with his men and his empty carts and fell upon English's possessions with relish. Corwin, having bagged a big bird, also went after English's wharves and warehouses, until the total amount seized totaled over £1500.

Phillip English, who eventually lost his wife, due to the conditions she had suffered while in prison, ranted and raved at the magistrates at the injustice of such tactics. It did little good. The new witchcraft law, which had been adopted in December while English was in hiding, left out the 1604 provision that preserved dower and inheritance for the heirs of executed witches. Many believe this omission was Phips way of protecting the Essex County Sherriff, who had already confiscated part or all of the estates of several of those who had been executed. Had Mary English's death been the loophole Corwin crawled through in order to snatch up English's goods, or was the looting of condemned witches allowed in the fine print?

At any rate, Corwin was exonerated from any wrong doing and the pleas of Phillip English in 1694 were ignored. Under the new bill, Corwin had done nothing wrong.

English was to have the last word on the matter. Sheriff George Corwin died in 1697. English, somehow, confiscated the dead man's body and hid it. While he couldn't do this for long, he held onto it until the funeral arrangements had been delayed enough for the Sheriff's family to finally pony up £60. Not nearly what English had lost, but a piece of justice, none the less.

Yet, it was the lineage of Judge John Hathorne, a man English hated equally as much as Corwin, who would thwart Phillip English's total revenge on the purveyors of the witchcraft trials. English left behind daughters, one of whom would marry one of Judge Hathorne's sons. This union would produce a lineage that included famed novelist Nathaniel Hawthorne, who added a "W" to his name in an effort to disassociate himself from the infamous Judge. Nathaniel, who was born in Salem Town in 1804, penned, among other novels, *The House of the Seven Gables* and *The Scarlet Letter.* These two literary masterpieces are filled with haunted images, where the ghosts of the witch trials can be seen woven throughout the inked lines.

God and the Devil

For New England Puritans, the deadly duo of Indian warfare and the visitation of hundreds of witches, was a devasting blow to the people who had escaped England to bring to this barren wilderness God's word, and erect their shining "city on the hill." These people, even third-generation Puritans, believed without doubt in the invisible world around them, where angels and demons battled over their welfare. The wonders of nature held signs of their righteousness or wrong-doing. You could be blessed by sun and rain for a bountiful harvest, or laid low by a hurricane or tornado. All acted as barometers of their standing with God.

Thus, when in 1692, a plague of Indian and witch attacks infiltrated New England, they turned to themselves to see what they had done to incur God's wrath. Why had he unleashed the Devil among them? It was this train of thought that the military commanders and magistrates hid behind during the ravaging of town and village by evil, appearing in the guise of spectral shapes, and the all-too-real physical bodies of hatchet-wielding natives. The militia's failed attempts to save butchered towns along Maine's coastlines could be attributed to the Devil, not ordinary men. They had not *failed*...evil had *prevailed*!

And what of the girls and the others who made up the circle of afflicted? How convenient it was to let these young innocents run the show. Not only did they (through coercion from adults), rid the Village of its unwanted souls, they had solved murders from long past through the appearance of specters in winding sheets crying out against their killers. These were murders in which the magistrates had failed to convict a perpetrator. The adults had but to whisper a name of someone who held land they coveted, or who had mistreated them, or held a rank higher than their own, and "Abracadabra," they were taken care of. It was not until the accusations hit too close to the Governor's door, that it all came falling down.

Is that partly why the magistrates overlooked the glaring evidence that the girls were faking their fits? Were they, like others, only too happy to see many of these people condemned? So many machinations were going on behind the scenes, that it is hard to say.

In the end, it was a group of "afflicted" people who would stand before the judgement of posterity. We look at this unseemly group with incredulity. Most were of the Puritan infrastructure that fell at the bottom of the hierarchy. Five were little girls, ages thirteen and under (three from Salem Village, and two who joined later from Andover).

The next group of accusers was comprised of young adults, fourteen and older, living in Andover and Salem Village, including one male. This age bracket fell within the parameters of being old enough to testify credibly in a court room, yet it was young Ann Putnam Jr. that brought about so many of arrest warrants, albeit with the support of her parents and some of the older girls.

Finally, there were the adults who made up the "inner circle," most-notably, Sarah Bibber and Ann Carr Putnam. These went on record with their depositions, but it was clear many males, such as Thomas Putnam, John Putnam, Samuel Parris, and Nathaniel Ingersoll, were only too happy to sign depositions attesting to the afflicted persons' torments.

It is the very make-up of this group that keeps historians and voyeurs from centuries into the future, gaping at the audacity of the girls, and the gullibility of a society. How did this happen? What have we done?

Chapter Thirty-Seven

Confessions and Compensation

Spring came to Salem Village in explosions of color, fragrance, and promise. The inhabitants looked out upon a world that seemed suddenly changed—not just in appearance, but in feeling. There were pews at the meetinghouse, glaringly emptied of the souls who once sat there on the Sabbath, now buried and mourned. One could not walk or ride past the rocky ledge of Gallows Hill without glancing with a shudder at the thick boughs of the trees there, one in particular void of its bark where weighted ropes had stripped it bare. Those most active in the accusations and trials searched for ablution; many never found it.

There was an unseen poison that still lingered here. As confessions began to immerge, admitting to falsified statements, the village of Salem was left reeling. What was real and what was fake? That the Devil lived was a certainty, but now they were being told that people had been executed due to false witness. Had witches infiltrated Salem, or had they not? Was it only by degree, or by mass? Neighbor had accused neighbor, husband had "broken charity" with wife, and children had testified against relatives. How would they ever rebuild a network of trust within these ruins?

Even the meetinghouse seemed less in the sunlight. Here, chaos had reigned in a house that was built for charity and a coming together of the community. As the people of the village walked past the pasture land of the parsonage, did they look and wonder if a bloody Sabbath was held there still? Was that the sudden bending of grass falling beneath an unseen footstep? Was that a witch's pole leaning against a tree or merely a broken branch dangling in the wind? How would they know now what to believe?

Reverend Samuel Parris' Last Days

Reverend Samuel Parris would take the brunt of the backlash as more and more people came to the conclusion that something very vile had happened under his watch. It was easier to lay the blame on someone else's doormat than to admit you had been party to the gossip, or had been one who had voted for Martha Corey or Rebecca Nurse's excommunication. The villagers did retain one area of consistency—they again refused to pay Parris' salary. He would have to find a way to make a living off the orchard and pasture where witches and the man in the "high crowned hat" had dined.

They went farther, and asked that Parris be removed, stating "Mr. Parris...has been the beginner and procurer of the sorest affliction not to the village only, but to the whole country." Many refused to set foot inside the meetinghouse if he was at the pulpit. In an effort to stem the tide of hatred, the Reverend looked out over the meager gathering in April of 1693 and offered a prayer of forgiveness for himself, along with the regret that the whole thing had begun beneath his roof. Yet, in typical fashion, he hurriedly made it clear he had no idea conjuring was going on, and that "I desire to lie low under this reproach and to lay my hand to my mouth."

Parris called his sermon "Meditations for Peace." He admitted in it that the Devil could take the shape of an innocent person and that it was wrong to allow the afflicted to name who was afflicting them, and use it as evidence. And laying it soundly back on the Devil, he offered his sympathy to the families who had suffered "through the clouds of human weakness and Satan's wiles and sophistry." To the end, Parris found scapegoats everywhere but his own threshold.

The congregation was not moved. Rebecca Nurse's family, in particular, were strong in their reproach of this man of the cloth. "If half so much had been said formally," stated John Tarbell, Rebecca Nurse's son-in-law, "it would never have come to this." One of Rebecca's sons, still trying to come to terms with his grief, said "We know not how to express the loss of such a mother in such a way."

The Nurse family, who had fought so valiantly to clear their matriarch, looked upon a man who took the word of hysterical children over that of a church-covenanted woman, and signed depositions that would hang her. Even Judge Hathorne had hesitated as he looked upon this frail, pious woman and tried to save her initially. But not Parris...not the shepherd of the flock.

The cry against him continued, until finally, in April of 1695, a council of churches of the North Shore met to mitigate the issue. After hearing the accusations against Parris, the assembly of ministers agreed with the opponents that "unwarranted and uncomfortable steps" had been taken by Parris during "the dark time of confusion." Many complained that his sermons during the witch trials had been "dark and dismal" and words of charity were never heard from his pulpit.

Finally, Parris bent to the majority. There was no point in preaching to a hostile gathering, or trying to subsist on paltry offerings from his land. He struggled on until June 21, 1696, when he made a formal announcement to his Salem Village congregation that he was resigning. Two weeks later, his wife Elizabeth, who had been ill throughout the witchcraft hysteria, died. His caveat for leaving was that the town pay him arrears of £79- 9s-6d. They happily complied and began immediately the search for a new minister.

Samuel Parris packed up what was left of his little family. Betty Parris, returned to her home, looked about at the emptiness left by the loss of her mother and Tituba, who had cared for her most of her life. She had a little brother now, Noyes, named after the infamous Reverend of Salem, and little else. It was rumored Noyes later died insane during his manhood. Samuel Parris remarried and moved three times more, first to Concord, then to Dunstable, and finally to Sudbury, where he died in February, 1720 at the age of sixty-seven.

Little Betty Parrish, the child who possibly began the witch crisis when her nervous disposition betrayed her over the conjuring with egg whites, went on to live a full life. She married and gave birth to five children while living in Concord, Massachusetts, where her father had first taken her. She, like her father, died at the age of seventy-seven.

Reverend Joseph Green Takes Over

Young twenty-two-year-old Joseph Green rode into town, fresh from his graduation from Harvard in 1695. A reformed "bad boy," he had found his faith renewed with the teachings of Cotton Mather's sermons. Filled with the charity and love that Parris lacked, he took up the reins of that ill-fated meetinghouse. His youth and cheerfulness served him well, for he undertook to engage the whole of the community. He could be called on for a barn-raising, or some happy talk over a mug of ale at Ingersoll's. He was good with a rifle and felled bobcat as well as bird. He was outgoing and optimistic, something the village had not seen before.

While in Wenham, his eye fell upon the lovely daughter of Mr. Gerrish, and he asked her to marry him. Elizabeth said "Yes," and soon the parsonage was filled with the laughter of little boys. Reverend Noyes wrote of them, "They were a lovely, loving pair."

Reverend Green encouraged Salem Village to set up a school and a new meetinghouse. He fought when Indian attacks came near their doorstep, and rode with the troop of horse. His bravest move was yet to come.

In a nod to reconciliation and a view to offering some kind of compensation to the injured families, Green reworked the seating arrangement in the Salem Village meetinghouse. Thomas Putnam's seat of honor was handed to Samuel Nurse, Rebecca's son. Rebecca Nurse's daughter, the Widow Preston, took the seat of Mary Walcott's mother, the Widow Walcott. Those who had played a role in the death of Rebecca Nurse, had been relegated to the second row. Oddly, there was no resistance in the new seating chart. Who would dare to now?

And so, began an uncomfortable coming together. It started out slowly, like the careful sewing up of an unraveled quilt. Reverend Green preached peace and forgiveness. And Rebecca Nurse's children, raised as they had been with a knowledge of the scriptures, looked at last at these people who had been their enemies and heard Jesus upon the cross: "Forgive them, for they know not what they do."

Reversing the Damage

On December 22, 1702, after repeated requests by her friends, Reverend Joseph Green approached his congregation in Salem Village and broached the subject of reversing Martha Corey's excommunication. This was a big ask. It was something that would require a good deal of soul-searching. Green reminded those in attendance that it was now common knowledge that the witchcraft trials had been found "problematic" at best. The members took to their knees and their conscience, and finally, over a year later, voted on February 14, 1703, to restore Martha Corey's good name to the church register.

A decade had passed since the witch trials and executions. Petitions had been arriving at the General Court beginning on March 2, 1703. "Several inhabitants of Salem Village and Topsfield" presented a petition with twenty-one names, including those of Andover. The document was signed by the children and spouses of the executed, along with three who were found "Guilty" but did not hang: Abigail Faulkner Sr., Elizabeth Proctor, and Sarah Wardwell. Listed were the names of those who perished: Rebecca Nurse, Mary Esty, Mary Parker of Andover, Elizabeth How, John Proctor, and Samuel Wardwell. The petitioners asked that "something may be publicly done to take off infamy from the names."

Abigail Faulkner Sr. sent another petition in June 1703 to remind the Court that although she had been reprieved, she was still legally "a malefactor convict upon record of the most heinous crimes that mankind can be supposed to be guilty of, which besides its utter ruining and defacing my reputation, will certainly expose myself to imminent danger by new accusations."

Eleven Essex County ministers asked the Court to reconsider the cases in an effort that something be "publicly done to clear the good name and reputation of some who have suffered" only "upon complaint of some young persons under diabolical molestations."

On July 21, 1703, Abigail Faulkner received what many hoped for. She, along with "sundry persons, were restored "their just credit and reputations as if no such judgement had been had." A bill was also drawn up to disallow "spectral evidence" in future trials.

Ever present was the Puritan belief that hardships were the turning away of God's providence and allowing the Devil to afflict the wicked. Thus, when in July of 1704, a mighty draught dried up the countryside, and war broke out in Europe (which would impact the New Englanders as well), many wondered if their part in the witch hangings was coming back to haunt them.

One such person was Reverend Michael Wigglesworth of Malden. He wrote to Increase Mather on July 22, 1704, "I fear that God hath a controversy with us about what was done in the time of the witchcraft. I fear that innocent blood hath been shed, and they may have had their hands defiled therewith." He threw the magistrates a bone by declaring the judges "did act conscientiously accordingly to what they did apprehend then to be sufficient proof, but since that, have not the Devil's impostures appeared?"

Wigglesworth believed more needed to be done, not just in word, but in deed. Many of the estates of those who were executed and jailed were in ruin. He stated, "the families of such as were condemned for supposed witchcraft, have been ruined by taking away and making havoc of their estates, and leaving them with nothing for their relief." He urged that some financial remuneration be given to the families. The Court, weighed down with the expense of Canadian attacks and the effects of the draught, balked. The witchcraft victims would have to wait.

Ann Putnam Jr. Confesses

It was August, 1706, when Reverend Green took the short stairs to his pulpit and looked out into the upturned faces. They were here to witness something extraordinary. Ann Putnam Jr., now twenty-six years of age, head bowed, stood to the right of the pulpit podium, as Reverend Green read a statement that had been taken down on her behalf. Ann had asked to be admitted to the Church of Salem Village. Green believed she needed to address the congregation and purify herself by asking for forgiveness for her part in the witchcraft trials. She needed clean hands and a clean heart to partake of the communion.

The meetinghouse walls may have still reverberated with Ann's screams as Rebecca Nurse stood there accused of witchcraft. The young Ann, along with her inner circle of afflicted girls, had shrieked with such torment and convulsions, that Rebecca, seeing the hatred toward her, had cried out "Oh Lord, help me!" There had been no help for Rebecca, and now her sons and daughters looked upon the chastened young woman before them, asking them to forgive her.

It was Ann's words, being read to a congregation made up of some the witch trial's surviving families. Reverend Green cleared his throat and began reading Ann's confession:

"I desire to be humbled before God. It was a great delusion of Satan that deceived me in the sad time... I did it not out of any anger, malice, or ill-will." The congregation, more knowledgeable now of some of the machinations that had put names of witches into the "mouths of babes," may have looked at Ann and seen the specter of her mother Ann Carr Putnam, hissing the names of those she loathed. Ann Sr., dead now for over six years, hovered over the meeting as surely as if she had been seated there.

Reverend Green continued to read Ann's confession: "And particularly, as I was a chief instrument of accusing Goodwife Nurse and her two sisters, I desire to lie in the dust and be humbled for it, in that I was a cause with others so sad a calamity to them and their families...I desire to lie in the dust and earnestly beg forgiveness of all those unto whom I have given just cause of sorrow and offense, whose relations were taken away and accused."

Reverend Green concluded his reading of the confession. All were quiet. Hearts were full with so many emotions. And yet, it was the feeling of forgiveness that won out. They voted Ann Putnam Jr. into their fold.

Ann's was not the first public confession. Others had come before her, though of higher rankings than the afflicted. The witch trial jury, on January 15, 1697, wrote a document in an effort to absolve themselves of wrong-doing. They, along with Thomas Fiske, the same foreman who had questioned poor Rebecca Nurse on that inflammatory statement and found her silent in its answering, wrote the following:

"We ourselves were not capable to understand nor able to withstand the mysterious delusion of the power of darkness and prince of air, whereby we feel we have been instrumental with others, though ignorantly and unwillingly, to bring upon ourselves the guilt of innocent blood." They begged forgiveness of the impacted families and expressed their "deepest sorrow."

Reverend Hale, present from the first outcry of Betty Parrish, wrote his confession in a thorough outpouring of the entire story in his manuscript entitled, *A Modest Inquiry into the Nature of Witchcraft*. Reverend Higginson of the First Church of Salem added his thoughts in the book's preface and also voiced his sympathy.

In 1711, the numerous petitions for some kind of restitution took effect. A sum of £578-12s was awarded to the survivors. Stephen Sewall headed the committee assigned to dole out the money. Some demands for compensation were merely that of the prison fees and travel expense of those of the imprisoned and their families. Others, such as Phillip English's claim of £1500 would have depleted the pot. In the end, he received nothing. His heirs, after his death, were finally awarded £200.

John and Elizabeth Proctor's family was awarded £150; George Jacobs Sr. was given £70, and George Burroughs £50. Martha Carrier's kin was awarded £7-6s, while Abigail Hobbs, a confessor who had not been put to death, received £10. Giles and Martha Corey's family received £21 collectively; while Sarah Good's descendants were awarded £30, perhaps as a means to offer some security to little Dorcas Good, who, from months of incarceration and the traumatic effects of her mother's hanging, was never quite right in the head thereafter.

And the Nurse family? Peter Cloyce had collected Sarah, Rebecca's church door-slamming sister, after she was released from jail and left the area. Rebecca Nurse's children had made it clear they did not want money, but a clearing of their mother's name. It was finally granted on March 2, 1712, when the First Church of Salem revoked her excommunication "that it may no longer be a reproach to her memory and an occasion of grief to her children." Giles Corey was likewise reinstated, posthumously.

The Devil Departs Salem Village

The destruction of lives, begun twenty years earlier, was slowly being restored, although the damage to families would never be repaired. A few silver coins would not undo the loss of lives, farmland, and livelihood, let alone bring about the full understanding of what had happened to this small community of 500 souls...and beyond.

Sir William Phipps returned to England in mid-November 1694, amidst the criticism of his handling of events as Governor in 1692. He died shortly thereafter in February 1695.

Thomas and Ann Carr Putnam died within two weeks of each other in 1699. Putnam's heirs received a small inheritance as Thomas left behind an estate heavily in debt.

Ann Putnam Jr. died unmarried in May 1715, at the age of thirty-five. Due to her confession, and membership of the church, she died with the forgiveness of her fellow man. God's forgiveness had already been granted.

Elizabeth Booth married Israel Shaw in Salem one day after Christmas in 1695. She bore two children. Her sister **Alice**, who had joined her as an accuser, married Ebenezer Marsh in Salem on November 25, 1700.

Abigail Hobbs married Andrew Senter of Ipswich on June 18, 1709. Her widowed stepmother **Deliverance** may have lived with them. She bore two sons after moving to Wenham.

Elizabeth (Betty) Hubbard, who had run from the wolf shape of Sarah Good all those years ago, married John Bennett in 1711 in Gloucester, and bore four children.

Sarah Churchhill married Edward Andrews on August 11, 1709, at the age of thirty-seven. If she had looked into the Venus Glass for some sign of her future husband's occupation, she would have seen the shape of a weaver's loom, for so he was. They were both fined for fornication before their union. They lived in Berwick, Maine, where he died. Sarah was still very much alive at the age of 67. She vanished from the records soon after.

Mercy Lewis, one of the more-vocal of the accusers, floundered after the trials. She moved to Greenland, near Portsmouth, New Hampshire, to live near her Aunt Mary Lewis Skilling Lewis. Mary was married to Jotham Lewis, and had a brother named Abraham Lewis. It was at the home of Abraham that Mercy bore a bastard son. One Charles Allen stepped forward during Mercy's prosecution, and testified on her behalf. It was believed the child was Allen's. He and Mercy married before 1701 and ended up in Boston.

Betty Parris, whose removal from the witchcraft delirium may have saved her, married Benjamin Barron in 1710 and had five children. He died in 1754, and she in 1760.

Susanna Sheldon fell on hard times after her fame as a professed seer met with disfavor. She wandered to Providence, Rhode Island, and lived with a relative, John

Sheldon, for a time. On May 8, 1694, she was ordered to court as a "person of Evill fame." She may have been forced from town, as many prostitutes were. There is no record of her after 1697.

Mercy Short, the young woman with whom Cotton Mather lavished so much time in an effort to relieve her afflictions, was married off by Mather to one Joseph Marshall on July 29, 1694. The happy union was not to last, as Mercy was excommunicated on the grounds of adultery with another man. She died before 1708.

Mary Walcott, the Parris' closest neighbor, and possibly one of the first brought into the accuser's circle, fared better than many of her constituents. She married Issac Farrar in Salem on April 29, 1696, only four years after the witchcraft outbreak. They ended up in Ashford, Connecticut in 1713 where they raised six children.

Abigail Williams and Mary Warren disappeared from the record books. If they had married, it would probably have been recorded. Some rumors had them falling in the way of Susanna Sheldon, where men paid for their services. There is little more known of them after the witch trials came to an end.

Deodat Lawson packed up his documents and went back to England in 1696. He published an extended version of his 1692 sermons, called *Brief and True Narrative* in 1704. His fortunes did not go as planned and he was enduring deep financial distress in 1714.

Cotton Mather died in 1728, outliving his much older father, Increase Mathers, by only five years. His celebrated works lived on and are still cherished by scholars of the witchcraft trials.

Nicholas Noyes fulfilled Sarah Good's curse from the gallows, when she told him he "would have blood to drink" if he hanged her. Noyes was old and fat in 1718, when a blood vessel burst inside his head, leaving his mouth filled with blood. He was seventy-years-old. It had taken twenty years for Sarah Good to extract her revenge…that is, if you believe in a "witch's" curse.

George Jacobs Sr.'s bones were found on his abandoned farm in a grave bulldozed by a developer in the 1950s. The developer put the bones in a box and handed it over to the Danvers Archival Center. Danvers was the new name given Salem Village when it finally became incorporated in 1757. In August 1992, the Tercentennial committee arranged to have Jacob's bones buried in the Nurse Homestead cemetery, near Rebecca's grave.

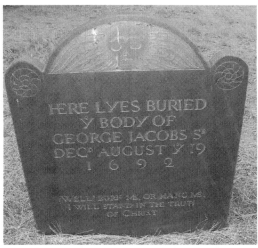

George Jacobs Sr.'s grave stone at the Nurse Homestead.

Danvers' Tercentennial Committee persuaded the Massachusetts House of Representatives in 1992, to issue a resolution for the "courage and steadfastness of these condemned persons who adhered to truth when the legal, clerical, and political institutions failed them." It was strong words coming from a body of legislative giants. The document listed the names that were omitted from the earlier Reversal of Attainder. The wording said the victims of 1692 were "worthy of remembrance and commemoration." Finally, on October 25, 2001, the missing names of Susanna Martin, Bridget Bishop, Alice Parker, Margaret Scott, and Wilmott Read were added to the 1957 Resolve.

The final ablution for the 1692 witchcraft victims was given 310 years after the hangings. Acting Governor Jane Swift signed the act that would officially clear all the names of those executed for witchcraft during the hysteria of 1692. On June 9, 2002, supporters and many descendants of the victims held an ecumenical service at Salem's First Church to honor them and restore their names as innocent of any wrong-doing.

The Devil, done with Salem Village, dropped the Bishops, Knights, Castles, and Pawns into a bag, and set his sights elsewhere. He crossed the Atlantic to England where he filled heads with nightmares and specters, tormented them and tortured, resulting in witches burning at the stake until the early 18th century. One of his chosen, Jane Wenham was tried as a witch in 1712, but was pardoned and set free. The last execution took place in England in 1716, when Mary Hicks and her daughter Elizabeth were hanged.

Scholars have wrestled over the centuries with the true cause of the Salem Witch Trial outbreak and what caused it. A popular theory is that of ergot poisoning. Ergot is a fungus blight that forms hallucinogenic drugs in bread. It thrives in a cold winter followed by a wet Spring. The problem with this theory, is if the ergot was infecting bread dough, then wouldn't every person eating it show signs of hallucinations? Why only a handful of girls. And if ergot appears on wheat in the Spring, after the winter thaw, then why were the first outbreaks in February when snow lay on the ground and the wheat had not been planted?

Other theories are mass hallucination among hormonal girls and equally hysteric women. In the 1800s, women suffering from hysteria were diagnosed as having symptoms due to their reproductive organs and "unmet needs." Hysteria was typically labeled a female's complaint, looked at by men with rolled eyes. Laudanum was an opiate so readily prescribed in that era, that practically every woman carried a bottle in her purse to relieve her "jittery" symptoms.

It is obvious from later confessions by the afflicted girls, as well as those told early on in the trials to adults who should have listened, that this was a contrived attack upon carefully selected victims. "We must have sport!" declared one of the afflicted girls in Ingersoll's Ordinary before the first person was executed. Faked props and mistaken names were overlooked as the wheels of justice surged forward. Finally, the confessions of Mary Warren and Ann Putnam Jr. put to rest any doubts that the girls were faking their symptoms and lying. Sarah Churchill had admitted to the fakery outside the Salem Town House when Sarah Ingersoll confronted her.

The question remains, what if only one dynamic had changed within this "wheel within a wheel?" What if

Parris, rather than encouraging Betty and Abigail's early signs, had punished them as had other parents in towns beyond the Salem Village borders when their adolescents acted up? Had he seen these early signs of witchcraft as a means to bring the people in his village to church, to God, to find need of him, to revere him…to pay his salary?

What if there had not been ongoing wars with the Wabanaki, leaving young girls like Mercy Lewis, Susanna Sheldon, Sarah Churchill, Mercy Short, and others, victims to nightmares of butchered relatives and homelessness? Did these horrific events leave them vulnerable to hysteria and a need to rid themselves of perceived wrongs?

What if the charter regulating Massachusetts had not been revoked, stirring up land disputes and the fear of losing one's farmland? What if the new charter had gotten to the shores of Boston much earlier?

What if the Putnams and Porters, and their constituents, had not warred over Salem Town and Village boundaries, meetinghouse and church affiliations, etc. If Salem Village had not felt like the ugly step-child, and had been granted rights of its own (like Andover, Topsfield, and so many others), would the divisive nature of those people involved have ended in death?

And, what if the magistrates had pulled the plug on the nonsense from the beginning, refusing, as others had always done, to listen to the fantasies of children? What if they had not seen their failures on the Maine frontier as something requiring a scapegoat—something ethereal and hard to track down—like diabolical infestations?

This perfect storm of conditions that hovered above Salem Village in 1692 might have been stemmed if only one of these components had been removed. If peace and love had been preached from the pulpit. If quarrels among neighbors had been mitigated quickly and fairly before they festered and split open. If supplies and men had been sent to the frontier in a timely manner and the militia better regulated. If the charter had not been revoked and there was a legal means to handle the witch trials' early examinations, before the prisons filled to overflowing. If the nightmares of little girls had been soothed away before a witch's cake gave credibility to the shadows that haunted their dreams.

It is, perhaps, this unequaled storm of happenstance and the culmination of so many factors, that leave us today peering into the Venus Glass in search of answers. It is almost too incredulous to have happened. Yet, it did. And there is nothing to say that a perfect alignment of planets and conditions couldn't bring it to pass again.

A View of the Witch Trials and Beyond:

Key Interviews, Maps, & Places

Pilgrim Woman

Coif

Waistcoat

Shift

Apron

Pettiooat

Shoes

Pilgrim Man

Felt hat

Ruff

Doublet

Cuffs

Breeches

Garters

Stockings

Shoes

Clothing worn in the 17th Century.

Massachusetts Bay Colonists arriving in New England and building
any shelter they could in the earlier days.

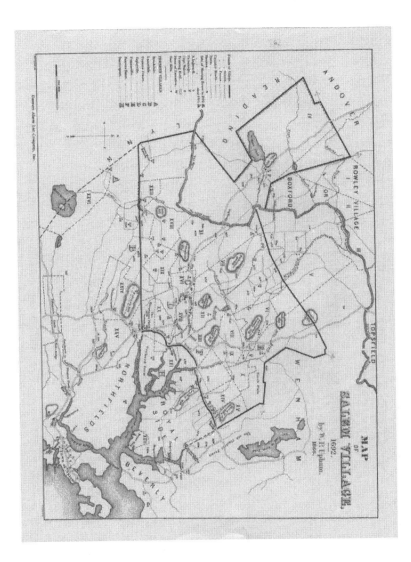

Map of Salem Village 1692, by W.P. Upham, 1866.

Proctor's Ledge

As mentioned in my interview with Marilynne K. Roach, a team of historians were assembled to determine the location of where the witch hangings probably took place. The nod is generally given to Sydney Perley's earlier research, but a great deal of time and effort went into not only verifying the location, but in constructing a memorial at the site. The Proctor's Ledge Memorial is a beautiful setting dedicated to the nineteen people who were executed there during the 1692 witch trials. The names and dates they were hanged are engraved in stones. The oak tree sapling is meant to symbolize endurance and dignity.

Proctor's Ledge Memorial, Salem, MA.

Martha Lyon is the landscape architect who designed Proctor's Ledge. It was built through a $174,000 Community Preservation Act grant and donations. Proctor's Ledge Memorial was built in 2017, during the 325th anniversary of the witch trials. In 2016, it was officially recognized as the site of the hangings.

The names listed in stone at the memorial are:

Bridget Bishop
Sarah Good
Elizabeth How
Susanna Martin
Rebecca Nurse
Sarah Wildes
George Burroughs
Martha Carrier
John Willard
George Jacobs, Sr,
John Proctor
Alice Parker
Mary Parker
Ann Pudeator
Wilmot Redd
Margaret Scott
Samuel Wardwell
Martha Corey
Mary Esty

The name of Giles Corey and those who died in prison while awaiting their trials are not listed here, as they were not executed at this site. Corey was pressed to death near the old Salem Gaol, and five others died in prison, both in Boston and Salem.

Rebecca Beatrice Brooks, in her wonderful blog *The History of Massachusetts*, offered a reference to the hanging location found in a notation in John Adam's diary in 1766:

It appears that in the late 18th century, locals still knew that Proctor's Ledge was the site of the executions because, in 1766, John Adams visited his brother-in-law in Salem and wrote in his diary that he had visited the ledge, which he referred to as Witchcraft Hill, a mentioned a number of locust trees that were later discovered to have grown on Proctor's Ledge:

"Returned and dined at Cranch's; after dinner walked to Witchcraft hill, a hill about half a mile from Cranch's, where the famous persons formerly executed for witches were buried. Somebody within a few years has planted a number of locust trees over the graves, as a memorial of that memorable victory over the 'prince of the power of the air.' This hill is in a large common belonging to the proprietors of Salem, & c. From it you have a fair view of of the town, of the river, the north and south fields, of Marblehead, of Judge Lynde's pleasure-house, & c. of Salem Village, &c" (Adams 199).

Yet, in 1867, historian Charles Wentworth Upham incorrectly identified Gallows Hill as the location of the Salem Witch Trials executions in his book, Salem Witchcraft, although he admitted in the book that it was only a guess and he might not be correct.

In 1911, a book titled *A Short History of the Salem Village Witchcraft Trials* by Martin Van Buren Perley was published and included a map that identified Proctor's Ledge as the site of the executions. The map also identified a rocky crevice alongside the ledge as the place where the bodies of the executed were temporarily placed.

THE PLACE OF EXECUTION
THE CREVICE FOR THE CORPSES

 Or the place where " The Witches" were hanged is on Proctor Street, Salem, marked off on this map by the dotted lines. The cross locates "The Crevice," where the corpses were thrown. To touch a witch corpse was malignant; yet some bodies were taken away for burial at home.

*The Place of Execution, illustration published in
A Short History of the Salem Village Witchcraft Trials, circa 1911.*

What Evidence Supports Proctor's Ledge as the Execution Site?

Rebecca Beatrice Brooks, in her blog *The History of Massachusetts*, stated that Sidney Perley's research indicates that similar evidence from another eyewitness, a nurse who was attending John Symonds' mother as she gave birth to him in 1692, also confirmed Proctor's Ledge as the site.

According to a letter written by Dr. Holyoke after the death of John Symonds in 1791, which was later published in Upham's book, the nurse who was assisting John Symonds' mother at his birth later told John that she could see the accused hanging at the execution site from the window of the Symonds house that day:

"In the last month, there died a man in this town by the name of John Symonds, aged a hundred years lacking about six months, having been born in the famous '92. He has told me that his nurse had often told him, that while she was attending his mother at the time she lay in with him, she saw, from the chamber windows, those unhappy people hanging on Gallows' Hill, who were executed for witches by the delusion of the times" (Upham 377).

Sydney Perley, during his extensive research, identified the location of the house where Symonds was born, on North Street. He found that other historians had been incorrect in identifying Gallows Hill as the execution site. Perley found that Gallows Hill is not visible from North Street because it is blocked by Ledge Hill, yet Proctor's Ledge was visible.

In Sydney Perley's book, *"Where the Salem Witches Were Hanged." Essex Institute Historical Collections*, Vol. 57, No. 1, Jan. 1921, pp. 1-18, he offers several wonderful interviews and clues to the Proctor's Ledge location. Edward F. Southwick lived with the great-great-granddaughter of John Proctor (hanged for witchcraft in 1692), Mrs. Nichols, and remembered as a boy that that

Nichols told him the accused witches were executed near the rocky crevice at Proctor's Ledge:

"When a boy, Edward F. Southwick lived with David Nichols at this place, from 1847 to 1852, Mrs. Nichols was a Proctor, and a granddaughter of Thorndike Proctor, who was grandson of John Proctor, who was executed for witchcraft. Mr. Southwick stated to the writer and others that both Mr. and Mrs. Nichols told him that the witches were executed near the crevice. Mr. Southwick also said that an old man, who lived with Mr. Nichols, and who was named Thorndike Proctor and was a relative of Mrs. Nichols, used to take walks with him, and he also told Mr. Southwick that the witches were hung near the crevice." (Perley pages 15-16).

Perhaps the most chilling report was one Perley related from an old family story from the Buffum family. Buffum states that after the executions on August 19, 1692, he could see, from his house on Boston Street, George Burroughs' exposed hand and foot sticking out of the rocky crevice, so he later went over that night to cover them so they were no longer visible. The Buffum house can be seen on maps sitting just below Proctor's Ledge in 1692. On the other hand, you cannot see Gallows Hills from his house.

Perley, from the same book:

"The distance from the house of Joshua Buffum to the top of the hill [Gallows Hill] would make it improbable that a slightly exposed hand or foot could be seen. In an air line the distance is about one hundred and twenty rods, which is considerably more than a third of a mile. Not only was the distance great, but the growth of the trees, which must have existed to a greater or lesser extent in the common lands, would necessarily have precluded such a view. From the house of Joshua Buffum to the crevice, in an air line, the distance is only about fifty-three rods, and the view unimpeded, as one had to look down the hill and over the marsh and river only." (Perley pages 14-15).

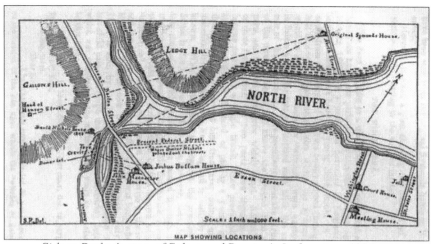
Sidney Perley's map of Salem and Proctor's Ledge circa 1921

From Rebecca Beatrice Brooks *The History of Massachusetts* blog, another piece of evidence is a local legend that states that after Rebecca Nurse's execution, her son Benjamin rowed a boat that night from a creek near the **Nurse homestead** into the North River right up to the base of the hill where the execution took place so he could claim his mother's body and give her a Christian burial on her property.

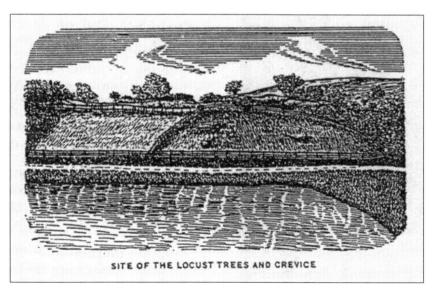
SITE OF THE LOCUST TREES AND CREVICE

489

There are no waterways, and never have been, leading to Gallows Hill or anywhere near it. Yet, at the time of the trials, the North River used to spill out into a large bay that pooled into Bickford's pond, which has since been filled in, at the base of Proctor's Ledge, thus allowing Benjamin Nurse direct access in his boat to the execution site.

In addition, Proctor's Ledge also has a rocky crevice running alongside the ledge and, according to Robert Calef, the bodies of the executed prisoners were temporarily placed in a rocky crevice at the execution site after they were cut down.

THE CREVICE

Sidney Perley at rocky crevice near
Salem Witch Trials execution site

All of the evidence confirms that Proctor's Ledge is the site of the Salem Witch Trials executions.

Please read Rebecca Beatrice Brooks' full account from her blog *The History of Massachusetts*. She has many wonderful articles spotlighting the fascinating history of Massachusetts. My thanks to her for allowing me to include excerpts from that blog.

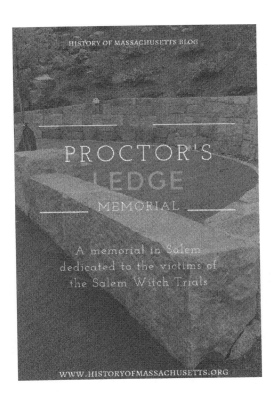

The Gallows Hill Project

The Gallows Hill Project prepared a series of questions and answers explaining how they confirmed Proctor's Ledge as the execution site for accused witches.

How did they pin down the site?

Marilynne Roach discovered a few key lines of eyewitness testimony in a Salem witch trials court record from Aug. 19, 1692. ... The record quotes the defendant Rebecca Eames, who had been on her way to the court in the custody of her guards and traveled along the Boston Road, which ran just below the execution site.

A few hours later, she appeared the Salem court for her preliminary examination. The magistrate asked Eames whether she had witnessed the execution that took place earlier that morning as she was passing by. She explained that she was at "the house below the hill" and that she saw some "folks" at the execution. Roach determined that the "house below the hill" was most likely the McCarter House, or one of its neighbors on Boston Street. The McCarter house was still standing in 1890 at 19 Boston St.

What other evidence is there?

Professor Benjamin Ray conducted research that pinpointed the McCarter house's location and worked with geographic information system specialist Chris Gist of the University of Virginia's Scholars Lab to determine whether, in fact, it was possible for a person

492

standing at the site of the house on Boston Street to see the top of Proctor's Ledge. Gist produced a view-shed analysis, which determined that the top of Proctor's Ledge was clearly visible.

Why did they rule out the top of Gallows Hill?

There are several reasons why the location at the top of Gallows Hill does not work. First, it would not have been visible from the McCarter house and its neighbors on Boston Street. It also would not have been visible from the Symonds house on North Street, where another person is known to have witnessed some of the executions. Furthermore, we know that the eight victims hanged on Sept. 22 were driven by cart to the execution site. It would have been next to impossible to get a cart full of eight victims up a steep and rocky slope that lacked a road.

Finally, executions were meant to be public events, so everyone could witness the terrible consequences that awaited those who committed witchcraft and other serious crimes. The top of Gallows Hill would be much more difficult to access than Proctor's Ledge.

Did the project find anything on Gallows Hill?

Professor Peter Sablock carried out geo-archaeological remote sensing on the site with a team of his geology students. Ground-penetrating radar and electronic soil resistivity do not disturb the soil, but can tell us about the ground underneath. His tests indicate there is very little soil on Proctor's Ledge. There are only a few small cracks in the ledge, and here the soil is less than 3 feet deep — certainly not deep enough to bury people.

This finding is in keeping with oral traditions that the families of the victims came under cover of darkness to recover loved ones and rebury them in family cemeteries. There is no indication that there are any human remains on the Proctor Ledge site.

What about the gallows?

The numerous surviving documents from the witch trials contain no mention of a gallows. Indeed, the only time Gallows Hill was used for executions was in 1692. Therefore, the team believes that the executions were carried out from a large tree, a common tradition at the time. The remote sensing research supports this conclusion, as no trace of structures were discovered, though admittedly a temporary wooden gallows would leave little evidence behind for archaeologists to discover.

Source: The Gallows Hill Project

The Interviews

The Salem Witch Museum
An interview with Rachel Christ
Director of Education

Rachel Christ
Photo courtesy of Rachel Christ

In the following interview with Rachel Christ, I will be using RP for Rebecca Pittman, and RC to designate Rachel Christ's comments:

RP: What is your capacity at the Salem Witch Museum?
RC: I'm the Director of Education. Within this role, I have my hand in a lot of pots. I do all of the outreach with students and teachers, authors, and journalists. I do a lot of working with teachers; I Skype into classrooms, do classes on the witch trials, and *The Crucible*. I buy all of the books for our bookshop and keep an eye out for new books on the witch trials. I also update all our exhibits. Currently, I'm working on updating our second exhibit, entitled "Witches: Evolving Perceptions." This exhibit focuses on the image

of the witch and how it has changed and evolved over time. This is an opportunity to step back from the Salem trials and focus on the history of witchcraft that led to 1692. This past winter we added a new timeline on the wall. We're working on updating our main presentation as well. So essentially, I work on keeping all the educational content up-to-date. It sounds odd, but the scholarship of the Salem witch trials is changing all the time, so my job is to keep us up-to-date with the scholarship. It's a very detailed piece of history.

RP: You have a theater in the round feeling there with the tableaus and vignettes. How did you filter down all the components of the witch trials into a 30-minute presentation? How did you choose the key elements?

RC: I wasn't here when that first presentation was created in 1972. We based the original presentation off of Marion Starkey's book *The Devil in Massachusetts*. It was one of the leading books on the Salem witch trials at the time. We are in the process of up-dating the presentation, simply because the scholarship has changed so much since that book came out in 1949. The idea was to take the big pieces of the Salem witch trials, for example, the trial of Rebecca Nurse, the hanging of George Burroughs, the pressing of Giles Corey, and combine them with some of the more refined aspects of the story, such as the girls sitting together in a kitchen, the environment of the Putnam house, prisoners languishing in jail. It was meant to give a snapshot of the trials. The trials were just a year. It's really quite a short period of time. It wasn't too challenging to encapsulate some of the big moments from that year; the big problem was we only have 30 minutes. There is so much more that could go into it.

RP: I thought it was interesting that you chose the Putnam house as one of the vignettes, instead of a scene in

Reverend Parris's house with Tituba. I thought it very appropriate to spotlight Ann Putnam Jr., as she was such a key feature in the trials, and to end the presentation with her apology was very strong. It was very easy to follow your narration by using the tableaus.

RC: It makes the Salem witch trials more accessible by presenting it with the tableaus. I think anyone can come in and grasp it. We see all ages, scholars, and people here with their families. We've tried to make it a clear presentation that encapsulates the basic theme.

From the Rebecca Nurse scene at the Salem Witch Museum. Photo courtesy of Tina Jordan and the Salem Witch Museum.

The Rebecca Nurse trial tableau at the Salem Witch Museum.
Photo courtesy of Tina Jordan and the Salem Witch Museum.

RP: You mentioned doing some updates, are you thinking of possibly updating the script, or changing the figures?

RC: It's mainly the script. I think the figures in the tableaus will remain relatively the same. We are in the process of updating the scholarship, as some theories have gone out of date. For example, Tituba's role in the trials has been debated by scholars rather extensively, so that's something we'll be looking at.

RP: When did you open the Salem Witch Museum?

RC: May of 1972.

RP: You seat how many people in the main theater room?

RC: About 120.

RP: Salem has a kind of love/hate relationship with the witch trial popularity. Do you have a personal feeling about it?

RC: I think Salem is a pretty unique example, our tourism industry really started in the early 20th century. There were vague whispers about it, but it didn't really start until *Bewitched* filmed here in the early 1970s. Arthur Miller came in the 50's to research *The Crucible* and that kind of shined a light on Salem. I personally think it goes so much farther. Obviously, Salem has become this big Halloween celebration. In the 20th century tourism started to grow here, and not just with the witch trial popularity. We have the New England draw and the House of the Seven Gables. When all the tourism dollars came in, it really helped the economy here. The history of witchcraft is so much more than the Salem witch trials. It's really living and breathing here. You see the stereotypical witch everywhere that Hollywood created, and then you also have *Bewitched* which is another definition of pop-culture witchcraft. We have a pretty healthy Wiccan population here, which is another example of a newer definition of the witch. In our museum we talk about the definition of a witch and how it's changed and evolved so dramatically over time. I think it's pretty interesting to see how this is still a living, breathing thing and how dramatically the term has changed over time.

RP: Is Wicca a religion?

RC: Yes. It's a legally-recognized religion in the United States. Wicca is a neo-pagan religion. These are based on older earth-based religions that go way back. It's a private practice typically. You won't see them making a show of themselves.

RP: We spoke of Hollywood stereotypes when discussing today's concept of a witch. I noticed in the witch trial transcripts that the word "broomstick" was never used when the girls stated seeing specters riding through the air. They always used the word "pole." It speaks once again to this stereotype we have of a witch.

RC: The broom is something you do see in other areas. In Europe, during the early modern period, which is the fifteenth to eighteenth century, that's when witch hunts were taking place, and there were reports of people flying on broomsticks.

RP: You have an amazing artifact there at the Salem Witch Museum—one of the actual beams from the Salem Jail where the prisoners were held during their questioning and trials. Do people comment on it?

RC: A lot of people comment on it. It's a surreal feeling to be able to see it. The original jail was constructed circa 1680. Around 1760 the original wooden jail was rebuilt, and it is said that some of the timber from the original structure was reused when building the new jail. The old jail site was demolished in the 1950's and at this time construction workers found seventh-century beams. Several of these beams were salvaged and given to the Peabody Essex Museum, the Witch Dungeon Museum and our museum.

RP: Have you noticed any paranormal activity inside the Witch Museum?

RC: This building was built in 1840, so it's very old. Yes, sometimes, odd things will happen, but you can almost always explain them. For example, books will fall off shelves, but it's because the floor is a little slanted.

A typical visitor experience in our museum takes 45 minutes to one hour. Visitors view two history presentations. Our first presentation is audiovisual and takes place in a large auditorium. Stage sets are illuminated in time with a narration which presents a point-by-point overview of the events of the witch trials that took place in Salem in 1692. This presentation is followed by a guided tour. This tour focuses on the history of the image of the witch and the European witch trials that led up to 1692.

You can visit the Salem Witch Museum's website at: salemwitchmuseum.com for ticket information, hours, and much more.

An Interview with Marilynne K. Roach
Author, Historian, & Artist

Marilynne K. Roach. Photo courtesy of
Marilynne K. Roach

For the purpose of this interview, Rebecca Pittman will be designated by the initials RP, and Marilynne K. Roach by the initials MR.

Marilynne K. Roach is the author of several books on the Salem Witch Trials, including *In the Days of the Salem Witchcraft Trials; Six Women of Salem: The Untold Story of the Accused and Their Accusers in the Salem Witch Trials;* and *The Salem Witch Trials: A Day-by-Day Chronicle of a Community Under Siege.* She has a large, hand-illustrated map of Salem Village in 1692, showing the location of all the homes and pertinent locations associated with the Witch Trials. I highly recommend it. You can purchase it at The

Salem Witch Museum in Salem, MA. Her drawings have blessed many archival websites, blogs, and books.

Marilynne was instrumental in the research used to discern the correct location of the Salem Witch Trial hangings, and was part of the team who instigated a memorial to the victims that now stands at Proctor's Ledge on Gallows Hill in Salem, Massachusetts.

RP: Your book, *The Salem Witch Trials: A Day-by-Day Chronicle of a Community Under Siege* is so amazing. I also bought your map of Salem Village in the Salem Witch Museum. How long did the map take you to create?

MR: Oh, years and years. It's based mainly on Sidney Perley's work..

RP: Do you have ancestors from the witch trials? Is that what got you interested in the Salem trials?

MR: I have ancestors from the era and that got me interested. I found relatives around the edges. There are two Uncles, Judge Samuel Sewall (who later apologized), and John Alden (who was arrested as a witch).

RP: Speaking of your map, when they took the prisoners from the Salem Jail up to Gallows Hill for their execution, did they cross the North River?

MR: There's a creek that came down from the upper part of Gallows Hill that flowed into where the river bends, sort of a right angle there—it's all filled in now—it was a tidal inlet at the time with a causeway and a bridge, so there was a bridge to go across.

RP: So, the cart carrying the prisoners did have to go across a bridge?

MR: Yes, it crossed that smaller creek, but it was still the main road from Salem to elsewhere. As they left the jail, they went along what is today Essex Street and then you turn into Boston Street.

RP: After reading several reports, including yours, it sounds like the spectators followed the cart all the way from the jail to Gallows Hill (or what we know now as Proctor's Ledge).

MR: I would assume so. It was supposed to be a lesson of what not to do, and it was also exciting, in a macabre way.

RP: I know the Wabanki Indians were mainly responsible for the attacks happening in Maine and New Hampshire. Was Salem afraid of imminent attacks?

MR: Oh yes. While some surviving members of the local tribes had scattered after King Phillip's War and joined larger groups of Indians to the north. When French Canada became involved you were never sure if you were going to be attacked. That's why Salem Village had a watch house where the militia had men stationed at night to watch for attacks. Andover was attacked, which is very close to Salem Village.

RP: There is so much woodland there in the area. It must have been very frightening to be in a remote farmhouse surrounded by trees that could be sheltering Indians.

MR: I'm not sure how much was cleared and how much was wooded. Obviously, they cleared trees for farming, and to build houses with the timbers. There are more trees there now than there were then, or even back to the Civil War. There was enough cover, certainly, to sneak up on a home.

RP: Poppets featured in the witch trials, in that they were supposed to be a tool of the devil to inflict pain on a victim. Were all poppets considered bad? Were children not allowed to have dolls in a home in 1692?

MR: They had toys. If it looks like a doll, I assume that was okay, but if it was crudely made, like you had thrown something together to use in magic, that would look suspicious. When they questioned Candy, the slave from Barbados, about poppets, her answer sounded like she just used something that she found lying around. The Lacy girl, when she was arrested, the deputy, or whoever it was to take her into custody, had orders to search the house, and they found some things that looked suspicious, like old scraps of cloth rolled up.

RP: We have an image of the Puritan way of life that shows them as strict, denying all pleasures or sense of frivolity. In your book, you mention that they did have dances, or played a game of Nine Pins. Would you elaborate on that, please?

MR: Men and women did not dance together, but they did dance. Even Increase Mather stated that dancing was a natural expression of joy, similar to dancing a jig. But couples did not dance together. Nine Pins is similar to what we call Bowling today, with smaller balls.

RP: Marilynne, for me, the turning point in the witch trials is when the adults asked the girls—who were just beginning to show signs of afflictions—"*Who* ails thee?" instead of "What ails thee?" which is what they had been asking them. It went from a general diagnosis of the girls being under "an Evil hand," to naming someone specifically for tormenting them through witchcraft. What are your thoughts?

MR: Yes. The girls assumed the adults knew best, when names were suggested, and that's when the spectral evidence began.

RP: I noticed several fortune telling devices mentioned during this period of history. The Venus Glass was the one mentioned as something Tituba was using to tell the girls' what occupation their future husband might have. What is a "sieve and shears?"

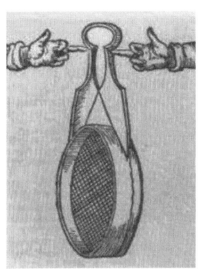

Sieve and Shears Divination

MR: It's like a Ouija board idea. The shears, then, were made out of one strip of metal so that the sharp blade and a hoop in the middle and then another sharp blade so that you're pushing them together to sheer, like with sheep. A sieve is a wooden hoop with woven mesh, possibly horse hair, on the bottom. It wasn't for delicate cooking. Apparently, you clutched the wooden hoop part with either side of the shears so that it's held up, and one person is pushing on one side of the springy part of the shears and the other one is pushing on the other side, so that they are suspending the hoop between the shear blades. It would turn in answer to their questions, like left or right. It was balanced delicately and any little movement of your hand would make it swing a bit. It's moving based on their slight movements that they aren't aware of, because it is so slight. "Turn clockwise if he loves me, turn counter-clockwise if he loves me not," kind of thing.

RP: It's similar to how a planchette reacts, correct? It's responding to the "ideomotor response?"

MR: Yes, it's the small muscle movements that we aren't conscious we are making, based on what's going on in the subconscious mind.

RP: What is the Bible and Key form of fortunetelling from that era?

MR: If you have a big door key, and you put it inside a big book, and tie it shut, so that the book is now somewhat convex, and lay it on the table, and it's now kind of rocking on the table, and you touch it, and your motor skills make it turn a bit. It was found that a tome of Shakespeare was used this way, and the key was inserted in a section of Romeo and Juliet, so someone must have been asking about love or romance.

Bible and Key Divination

RP: I noticed in your book that there were quarrels over land boundaries, especially between Topsfield and Salem Village. What was the main contention?

MR: The boundaries were not drawn up really well, and the land tended to overlap onto each other. There were disputes between the Endicotts and the Allens about the farm the Nurse family had bought. The contention was over who was to inherit the land.

RP: Salem Village had their own Watch House to keep a lookout for Indian attacks. Was it located across from Ingersoll's Ordinary where a church stands today?

MR: I believe so. It was on a little hill then, so they had a good view of all around them.

RP: Marilynne, I went to the Parris site in Danvers, where the stone foundation of his home can be seen. I believe in your book, you state that the house faced South to catch the sun, so that means that if you're standing at the foundation stones where the marker is now, you'd be facing the front door, correct?

MR: Yes, where the gate in the fence is.

RP: Do you find it interesting then, that the stairs to the cellar would be around the corner to the right of the front door, instead of at the back of the house?

MR: The cellar was under the parlor (the room to the left of the front door) and the stairs from it opened into the hall (to the right of the front door). The Hall was the all-purpose room, which would house the kitchen hearth. In the back of the Hall is a little foundation which might have been under the lean-to. The second cellar hole beyond the parlor was dug in the 18th century, when they put an addition on.

RP: Did the parsonage have a study? Different films show Reverend Parris as having a private study.

MR: I would think he would need one, and it's only a guess, but I think it was one of the upstairs' rooms. Yes, it was upstairs, because in his notes that he made after 1693, the Nurse family is mad at him, obviously, and they come upstairs to talk to him. He writes that they "all" came upstairs, instead of one-at-a-time. They were headed to his study. This was found in the Church Records, which you can see at the Danvers Archival Center's web-site.

RP: I'd love to ask you about your involvement with Proctor's Ledge. I read accounts that a few houses in 1692 could actually see the hangings from their windows. Is that true?

MR: Yes. Rebecca Eames was taken to the McCarter house on her way to the Salem Jail. The house was near the base of Gallows Hill. She said she saw the executions from the house. Perley saw it because that house was still standing until the 1914 fire which did so much damage to Salem.

RP: Were you one of the main people involved in the discovery of the Proctor's Ledge location?

MR: It was actually discovered by Sidney Perley back in 1901. And then he explained his reasons for assuming it was that location in 1921. In 1997, I found Rebecca Eames' comment on seeing the hangings, and then using Perley's articles on where the houses were in those days, I put it together that it had to be the lower ledges and not the top of the hill. I published a pamphlet on it back then. Elizabeth Peterson, director at the Witch House (Judge Jonathan Corwin's house) got a number of us who were obviously interested in the subject, to sit down together and discuss how the site could be better preserved: Professors Emerson Baker and Peter Sablock of Salem State University, Professor Benjamin Ray of the University of Virginia, film maker Tom Phillips, and myself. The site is on city land, purchased by Salem in 1936 to be a witch memorial. Nothing was ever done with it and it had trash all over it. We wanted it to be properly honored with some kind of a marker and to make sure the city didn't designate it as unnecessary land, which had almost happened a couple of times. We worked with the city to make sure everyone agreed that the site should be protected. You don't want to encourage large mobs of people coming up there, but you don't want it to be forgotten, either. Our press release to announce that the site had been found and verified went viral. The city hired landscape architect Martha Lyons to design a proper memorial. Benjamin Ray went to the computer department of the University of Virginia and used a mapping program to show if you were at the McCarter house (there's a laundromat there now), or several of the other houses that were along that stretch in 1692, if you could see the lower ledges and what was going on there, but you really couldn't see what was going on at the top of the hill...what we call Gallows Hill. And the thing about the computerized program is that you could really see what was going on without the trees and today's apartment buildings getting in your way. That helped to verify it. The memorial's dedication was appropriate and moving. A lot of descendants of the accused were there to honor their ancestors who had died on that spot.

RP: Do you think there was a gallows erected for the executions, or do you feel it was a ladder propped up against a tree bough?

MR: If there was a convenient tree, there would be no reason to waste time and money to build a scaffold. Locust trees are not very strong and they are a bit brittle, so I don't think it was a locust tree as many have suggested. Whatever it was, it had to be big enough to accommodate "eight firebrands of hell." That implies something horizontal that might be a good oak tree. I've seen illustrations from other eras that show a ladder going up into a tree and the victims would have to be carried up the ladder.

RP: Do you believe the victims were merely thrown into a ravine and some dirt thrown over them after they were hung, rather than a proper burial? We know some of the bodies were taken home by the families, such as Rebecca Nurse, but what of the others?

MR: I do believe it was a hasty temporary burial. I don't see Sarah Good's husband exerting much energy to dig her up and bring her home.

RP: When I read that George Burroughs' pants came off as they dragged his dead body to the ravine, it was such a heart-wrenching image.

MK: Yes, it was. Traditionally, the victim's clothes belonged to the hangman, so he could keep it or sell it. So, if you were wearing nice clothes, they would remove them and put older clothes on you. It was mentioned that another prisoner's pants were put on Burroughs, so presumably, not as nice a pair as he was wearing.

RP: I heard rumors that the Salem Jail would flood at times during the witch trials. Do you think that's true?

MR: No. I think there were some problems with the later jail. There's not much of a description of the Salem Jail where the prisoners were held. There were a couple of reports of prisoners tunneling under the wall and escaping before 1692, which would imply you were at ground level, not down below the surface. The river would have been a lot closer then because the terrain has changed, but the jail was on a small hill. There were bills from the jailer for firewood, which shows they probably had some form of heat in the winter. Candles were expensive and there was probably straw on the floor, so it's doubtful they were given candles for light at night.

RP: How in the world did some of those people endure an entire year in that environment? Through the frigid winters and humid summers?

MR: (Facetiously) They had good immune systems.

RP: What could the families of the prisoners bring them while in jail?

MR: There were reports that they brought them food and clothing, if they could afford it. It was a minimum of items.

RP: Bridget Bishop's apple orchard is said to have been where Turner Seafood is today. Is that correct?

MR: Approximately there, yes.

RP: I've heard there are pirate tunnels under Salem, is that true?

MR: That came later. There were access tunnels and I have seen pictures of doors and easements as if there had been something there.

RP: So many components came together to form the environment of the Salem Witch Trials: Indian warfare, Parris' dire warnings of the Devil from the pulpit, the absence of a charter through much of it, the Magistrates not being formally trained at law, the boredom of winter, etc. If only one of those components had been missing, do you think it would have turned into the wildfire that it did?

MR: Possibly not. It was so many things all at once—a critical mass of things going wrong. If one was removed, maybe it wouldn't have. I don't go with the conspiracy theories some people advance, as if Parris and the Putnams got together and planned it.

An Interview with Richard Trask

Town Archivist and Curator of the Danvers Archival Center.
Author of *The Devil Hath Been Raised: A Documentary History of
the Salem Village Witchcraft Outbreak of March 1692.*

*Richard Trask as an extra on the set of the film, Three Sovereigns for Sarah, a
movie depicting the Salem Witch Trials.*

*Danvers (Salem Village) Archival Center. Photo courtesy of
Richard Trask and the Center.*

The Archival Center houses a wonderful and diverse collection of two–dimensional materials that relate to the history of Salem Village and Danvers from the 17th century to the present. Our books, manuscripts, maps, photographs, newspapers and other materials are available to anyone interested in finding out more about Salem Village witchcraft, any aspect or era of Danvers history, local architecture, and local genealogy. Interested persons are urged to call, email or visit us during our open hours.

The Danvers Archival Center   www.danverslibrary.org.
15 Sylvan Street, Danvers, MA.   978-774-0554

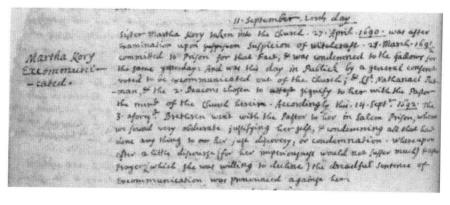

Martha Cory's examination transcript. Only one of copious documents from the witch trials you will find at the Danvers Archival Center. Photo courtesy of Richard Trask & the Center.

For this interview, RP will represent Rebecca Pittman, and RT will designate Richard Trask:

RP: Richard, I was fascinated with your research into the location of the parsonage where Reverend Samuel Parris lived. I understand you were the one that instigated the task to find it and excavate the stone foundation. How did you go about locating the site?

RT: I used what was available to me at the time. Back in 1970 we didn't have the archives, we didn't have a lot of the information in one location, the Charles Upham book *Salem Witchcraft* had a general location and some other secondary sources also gave me an idea of where it was located, off of Centere Street, which was the main roadway in Salem Village. And I got some aerial maps in Danvers to see if it would show up there, and it didn't. There was also some oral history and tradition that said it was located behind 67 Center Street. There was a sign that had been put up in the 1930s, pointing to a cart road that led to a large empty lot. The sign read that at the end of this cart road was the location of the Parris house site.

So, I had a general location of where it was and found out that the owner was a school teacher by the name of Alfred Hutchinson who was related to Rebecca Nurse. I asked if it would be possible to do a little probing on his property and he said "Yes." I contacted an author whose book was called *Hidden America* that had been written maybe 10 years earlier by a fellow named Roland W. Robbins. Among other accomplishments he had located the birth place of Thomas Jefferson and had done a major excavation in Saugus, Massachusetts, which is not too far from Danvers, of 17th Century iron works. He also discovered the location of Thoreau's dwelling at Walden Pond. He was not a professional, he was not University-trained, but he had an innate ability to be able to discover things. I wrote to him. He lived in Lincoln, Massachusetts, about twenty miles from here and asked him if he would like to help me discover the site of the Parris house. He did, and for the first year or so, he basically did it out of the goodness of his heart. I got some of my friends, including my future wife Ethel, and we would spend one or two days a weekend on the open space in the back yard of Mr. Hutchinson. Robbins would probe with an iron rod which he was famous for, and by holding onto the rod and sticking it into the ground, he could determine the kind of soil. He would obviously hit rocks, and if he found a pattern then it could be a foundation. We also dug little test trenches and we finally came across a few holes with fragments of glass and pottery in it, so we knew that we were in an occupied area. We followed along every foot-and-a-half until we hit upon what was a foundation which was about 3 feet below the surface. From there we began excavating. I wasn't that knowledgeable in archeology, other than what reading numerous books. Archeology is a very specific science, as once you disturb something, you must have documented your work, or it will be lost.

When the house was torn down, all they did was throw dirt and rubble into the foundation itself. So, we excavated it and it took about two seasons and we came up with three foundations associated with the 1681-1784 house. The original thought was to dig it up, take pictures and notes, and fill it in again. But we found it so interesting, and Mr. Hutchinson agreed, that he allowed us to leave the excavation open. Eventually, we got a stone mason to put the foundation back to the top of the soil and put a split-rail fence around it. Mr. Hutchinson allowed people to go onto his property for many years, and then in the late 1980s, he was going to move to Maine, and we able to, with a grant from the state, as well as local volunteer money, purchase that portion of the property and make it into a small mini-park for the town. It's been like that since we dedicated it in 1990. It was a great project that involved a lot of kids and adults over many years. Two of the kids who worked on the project eventually became professional archeologists.

So, it's there...a little bit out-of-the-way. All of the artifacts we found, tens of thousands of artifacts, most of them pretty much small fragments, gave us a good idea of a Colonial parsonage that had about a 100-year occupancy. It was a very interesting project, and one that allowed me to do other things later in town, including the establishment of the archives here. It's unusual for a municipality to have a tax-supported archives.

Archaelogist Roland W. Robbins at the excavation site.

Danvers fourth-graders listen to Richard Trask
tell of start of witch hunts at this location.
Boston Sunday Advertiser--June 20, 1971

Richard Trask at the Parris excavation site.

517

Richard Trask (above and below) with artifacts found at the Parris site excavation. Below, he is holding the neck of an 18th century wine bottle.

Artifacts found at the Parris parsonage site. The metal plate fragment
(bottom left) shows the initials SPE for Samuel and Elizabeth Parris.

Don Hayes and Ethel Boghosian-Trask cleaning artifacts at the
Danvers Archival Center.

When I was growing up in Danvers, witchcraft was kind of a taboo subject. It was always a subject centered around sadness concerning the witchcraft, and Danvers was always happy to let Salem have the credit and the tourists.

When I began the excavation process, there were a lot of people in town who were not happy about it because it was like bringing up a sore subject. There were two matronly ladies who lived on the street on the other side of the cart road that lead into the parsonage, and I can remember we tried to get the local schools involved, especially the local Highland School. We would invite the kids to come down and watch us, and in some cases, sift for some artifacts in the soil we had taken out of the cellar hole itself. As the kids were coming into the site, the two ladies across the street were shaking their fists at them and saying "Why are you bringing this up? You shouldn't be talking about this."

So, because it was related to the witchcraft and we were doing things that excited the public and unearthing things that hadn't been seen for 300 years, it became a fairly well-known project. The Associated Press picked it up and did a feature piece with photographs which circulated around the country. Walter Cronkite talked about it on the *CBS Evening News*. It brought a lot of positive publicity and I think it helped change the minds of a lot of the townspeople. We were trying to say, Yes, the witch trials were a very bad thing. All of the institutions failed, but what you did have, was individuals, some nice, some not so nice, who actually became heroic when they believed that truth was more important than life itself. That's something that should be remembered and emulated. We put a positive spin on it and later, during the 300th anniversary, the whole town got involved and we able to have a year-wide commemoration of the witchcraft. Thirty years earlier, that never would have happened.

RP: You make such a beautiful point. The integrity of these people who would not renounce their faith, even in the face of death, is so much more poignant than the actual madness that went on during the witchcraft outbreak. You have done a lot to be proud of, Richard.

RT: Well, thank you. It was an amazing project to be part of.

RP: Why do you think the Parris house was set so far back from the road?

RT: They wouldn't have considered it that way. A lot of houses sat back. It always faced in a southerly direction to get the best exposure to the winter sun. It could have been because the well was located there. It wasn't like a neighborhood like we think of today. It was scattered homesteads along a somewhat well-traveled street.

RP: Would the Walcott's have been the Parris' closest neighbor?

RT: Yes, the Walcotts were two stones throw away from the parsonage, and in the opposite direction was Ingersoll's Ordinary, which was about the same distance away.

RP: And the Walcott house is no longer standing, correct?

RT: No, we have an approximate location for it, and it also sat back from the road to Andover…quite a way back from the road.

RP: Would the Parris family have trekked down the cart trail to the road, turned left, walked to Ingersoll's and turned left again to get to the meetinghouse where Parris spent so much of his time, or would they have cut through the woods next to the parsonage?

RT: At that time, in 1692, there weren't as many trees. Everything was open. The cart road, which now leads into the parsonage actually went all the way through to what is now Forrest Street which was an old Indian trail. That was another roadway in the 17th Century, so Parris would have just gone down the cart road to Forrest Street and taken a right and he would have been at the meetinghouse. The corner of Forest Street is about where the meetinghouse was.

RP: There was a lot of testimony about Satan's spectral picnics behind the parsonage in the meadow there. What do you think the word "behind" meant? To the right of the parsonage, to the left, behind it?

RT: It's what now is known as Whipple Hill and it's a little way from the parsonage. Saint Richard's Church is located at the foot of Whipple Hill today. Apparently, there were some trees on the hill there and its where the witches' Sabbaths were supposed to take place.

RP: Are there still quite a few homes still extant from the witch trial era in Danvers?

RT: Salem Village was not just Danvers, but spread out to Middleton and Peabody. In Danvers, we have approximately a dozen or more houses that date to that time period. Salem Village (Danvers) was a farm community so the homes are spread out. Ipswich, which is about 15 miles from Danvers, has the largest cluster of houses dating to that period. They have the largest concentration of First Period houses that survived. There are several First Period houses here on Centere Street. I live in the Haynes house which is a 1681 house and that's right up the road. The next three houses up the road from the parsonage date to that time period as well.

RP: The church across the street from Ingersoll's is where the Watch House was located in 1692, correct?

RT: Yes. It would have been about 30- to 40-feet higher than it is now.

RP: Is there anything else you'd like to share that you find interesting?

RT: There was a very quirky book done a few years back called *A Season with a Witch*. It was by J. W. Ocker (a pen name). He came to Salem and spent a month taking in the Halloween events, and talked about what it was like there and a socio-economic description of the area. He wrote a lot about me and my projects. It's a book that goes into things that haven't been described before. It's available on Amazon.

I've done a lot of projects on Salem witchcraft. I was the chairman of the Tercentennial Committee in Danvers, and we did a year's worth of events, with major programs covering every one of the execution days. We did a sight-and-sound program for the meetinghouse at the Nurse Homestead. We buried the bones of George Jacobs Sr., which I had in my custody since the 1960s, at the Nurse Homestead. I was one of two consultants for the PBS movie *Three Sovereigns for Sarah*, which I still feel is the best rendition of the Salem Witchcraft events. The barn at the Nurse Homestead is the actual frame of the house that belonged to Endecott who gave testimony at the witch trials. His house was going to be torn down, but a group of friends and I dismantled and preserved the 1681 frame. We found some hex symbols which was a way of warding off evil when we were dissembling the house.

The John Proctor House
An Interview with Barbara Bridgewater
(Owner)

Barbara Bridgewater and her two daughters. Photo courtesy of Barbara Bridgewater.

For the purpose of this interview, I will use RP to designate Rebecca Pittman, and BB to designate Barbara Bridgewater.

RP: When did you purchase the Proctor home?

BB: We purchased /closed escrow on the Proctor House near the end of December 2018 (approx. 12/24/18).

RP: What is your understanding of the house's makeup? What are the original structural features you can see that were there in 1692?

*Additional notes – The sign on the front of the house states

1638. There was a dendrochronology report done by William Flynt for a TV documentary done by the Smithsonian which aired in March 2019. In this report, Flynt dates some of the beams in the house to 1726 which is after Proctor was hanged. However, in that same report it also appears beams were dated to 1674. John Proctor leased the land from Emmanuel Downing from 1666-1692. Flynt's sketch of the house places it in approximately 3 different time periods that he believes it was constructed.

With this being said; the realtor when selling the house, also did extensive research and is not completely convinced of the accuracy of the dendrochronology report.

The John Proctor house is very old and it depends on which version of history you care to believe as to the date of the house. Our family met with Kelly Daniel, Curator for the Peabody Historical Society and she stated that she believes that John Proctor did live on the land. It is hard to determine if he lived in the house. His subsequent relatives/ family did.

The house at one point was alleged to have burned (approx. 1645) but I believe even if it did burn the house was rebuilt on its current foundation. It was very unlikely in those days that they would dig a new basement when there was one or two already in existence. Additionally, there has not been any testing done in the basement area so the only way to really date the house and land is to deconstruct the house.

The realtor mentioned that at some point the occupants of the house were doing some digging in one of the basements and found some artifacts. When artifacts are found, the State Historical Commission is supposed to be notified, which is believed to have happened. I have been told that artifacts were removed and not returned. I do not know what the artifacts were since it was not disclosed. However, when I visited the Witch House in Salem, MA, a fork from John Proctor was displayed but it did not say where it was found.

RP: Do you believe the main room on the first floor could have been used as a tavern? We know he ran one.

BB: Yes, he ran a tavern & house / farm. There was originally over 300 acres. It's hard to tell where the tavern was but we may be able to narrow it down by looking at the drawing.

RP: How many acres are there now?

BB: Currently the home is on approximately a half acre.

RP: Do you plan on opening the house for tours, overnight stays or events?

BB: I would like to do tours, overnight stays, and community or special events. Perhaps a reading room or small museum or art gallery in a part of the home. I have lots of ideas. I just need to see what works.

RP: How many rooms are there? How many are bedrooms? We know there were 9 children there in 1692, plus John and Elizabeth, and Mary Warren (their maid).

BB: There are lots of rooms. Starting from the bottom:
2 separate basements,
1st floor:
1 kitchen
1 dining room (fireplace)
1 family room (fireplace)
1 other room (fireplace)
2nd floor:
Great room (fireplace)
Master bedroom (no fireplace)

2 bedrooms (both with fireplaces)
3rd floor:
Great room only back of fireplace visible.
2 bedroom (no fireplaces)
There is also an attic above the 3rd floor.

RP: What are your plans for the house? Will you be opening it to the public?

BB: Our plans for the house are to give tours, host private & community events & prepare for overnight stays whether it be a bed & breakfast or other form of stay. We ultimately want to share this unique & wonderful house with the community/public. We have plans to further restore and furnish it. The prior owners did a great job & we want to continue what they started.

We have established an Instagram (@thejohnproctorhouse), Facebook (thejohnproctorhouse) and our websites are currently under construction
(JohnProctorHouse.com & johnproctorhouse.org).

Brief Report of the Inspection of the John Proctor House, 348 Lowell Ave, Peabody, MA Inspection by Myron O. Stachiw and William A. Flynt, July 18, 2017

The inspection was conducted in advance of filming at the house later the same day by Lone Wolf Media. William Flynt was there to carry out sampling of the timbers as part of the dendrochronology study to determine if the **Phase 1** building is old enough to have been actually owned and occupied by

John Proctor, one of the Salem residents accused of witchcraft and executed in August 1692. Myron Stachiw, an architectural historian, was engaged to evaluate the architectural features, sequence of construction, etc., with the hope of determining the age of the building. The result of the inspection and evaluation of the building is an alternative interpretation to current knowledge about the building. For more than a century, it has been postulated, and repeated over and over, that the house was built in the 17th century and occupied by John Proctor and his family when he was accused and executed. Some have claimed that it was built in 1638; others that the building was occupied by Proctor as a tenant and after his purchase in 1682; others that the house was constructed c.1700 after his death. An inspection of documentation in the hands of the property owners resulting from a brief building inspection in 1988 by Chris Eaton of the Society for the Preservation of New England Antiquities (SPNEA) offered an interpretation that identified four phases: • **Phase 1** consisted of a two-story structure with end chimney and one room per floor. It was postulated that the present west half of the house, including the chimney bay at the east end, was the original structure. • **Phase 2** was the addition of the present east front room and room over it. • **Phase 3** was the addition to the rear of the Phase 1/Phase 2 two-story structure of several rooms that extended from the west wall of the building about two-thirds of the distance to the east end of the structure. Eaton suggested that this addition was beneath a long lean-to roof, forming a saltbox-form structure. • Phase 4 was the construction of a two-story, gable-roofed addition on the northeast corner of the house, erected against the rear and east sides of the alleged Phase 2 addition. The east wall of the addition projected out beyond the east gable end of the alleged Phase 2 section approximately 5 feet; the north gable end of the alleged Phase 4 addition extended northward about 3 feet beyond the north wall of the alleged Phase 3 addition; the south elevation ended about eight feet north of the south elevation of the house. Easton postulated that Phase 1 was constructed in the last quarter of the 17th century; Phase 2 possibly during the opening decades of the 18th century; Phase 3 during the 3rd quarter of the 18th century; and Phase 4 during the 19th century, perhaps in conjunction with the construction of a wrap-around Victorian era porch added to the south façade. Eaton viewed the building prior to subsequent remodeling of the house which removed much of the interior finishes which masked most early framing, fireplaces, and other early features of the house. Results of July 18, 2017 inspection. The inspection by Stachiw and Flynt revealed at least three major phases of construction based on the revealed evidence. No removal of any interior fabric or finishes was carried out, so this assessment must also be considered, in part, conjectural. However, Stachiw and Flynt are very confident of their identification of the nature of the original Phase 1 building. Phase 1 The house as initially constructed consisted of a two-story, one-room deep, center chimney house. The hewn oak frame is chamfered with a simple, narrow, bevel chamfer with simple triangular stops cut at a 45-degree angle at the end of the chamfer. The posts are splayed on the second floor. On the ground floor summer beams in both rooms are situated longitudinally; on the second floor the summer beams – actually tie beams supporting principal rafter pairs – run from front to rear plate. The frame of the structure to either side of the central chimney is identical in terms of material, treatment, joinery, and dimension; even the intervals between the posts and braces in the rooms on both sides of the central chimney are virtually identical. The roof frame consisted of six large, hewn, principal rafter pairs, with three purlins on each slope of the roof let into the top of the rafters and pegged, together with a ridge purlin. Inspection of the roof frame revealed with complete certainty that it was of a single build spanning the full width of the center chimney building. At present only the south slope of the original roof remains. A door located centrally on the south façade opened into an entry lobby located south of the central chimney; a staircase to the second floor rose along the south face of the chimney stack, rising from west to east. Scars of a staircase remain on the plastered south face of the chimney behind the existing staircase, which dates to the middle decades of the 19th century. A cellar lined with stone walls was dug beneath the west room; a staircase was located in the south end of the east wall, rising to the east to the ground floor level beneath the staircase to the second floor. It entered the ground floor through a doorway that opened either into the entry lobby or into the east room through the west wall of that room. Two early fireplaces in the west rooms on the first and second floors remain; each fireplace has side walls set perpendicular to the back wall, but the inner corners are curved. The fireplace in the ground floor west room is much larger, at least five feet wide and nearly 4 feet high with a large wooden lintel. A portion of the brickwork in the back wall is set back the thickness of one brick, forming a channel or "throat" for improved air draft through the firebox and into the chimney. The bricks of both fireboxes, as well as the bricks forming the chimney mass, are laid up in yellow clay. The fireplace in the ground floor room shows no evidence of having a bake oven in its back or side walls, suggesting this room was not the hall or kitchen, but likely the parlor of the hall-parlor house. The fireplaces in the two east rooms have been altered with later remodeling. On the second floor, a new brick firebox appears to have been erected within an earlier firebox; removal of the new firebox might reveal whether the original – or at least earlier – firebox remains intact, and whether it too has curved inner corners. The revealed details of this Phase 1 section of the house support a construction date as early as the 4th quarter of the 17th century or as late as the 1st quarter of the 18th century. Phase 2 The second phase of construction identified appears to be the two-story, gable-roofed addition erected onto the northeast corner of the Phase 1 house. The roof ridge runs perpendicular to the phase 1 roof. The framing is very similar in form and treatment to the Phase 1 structure: hewn oak, splayed corner posts, tie beams on the second floor spanning from plate to plate and supporting hewn principal rafters, spanned by purlins supporting vertical roof sheathing boards. However, there are several differences: the posts are about 10 inches taller than the posts of the Phase 1 structure, thus creating higher ceilings than in the Phase 2 structure; the framing elements of the Phase 2 structure were not chamfered, suggesting that from the beginning they were intended to be enclosed in casings, hidden from view. This similarity in general framing methods does not imply that the structure was built soon after the completion of Phase 1, although it may have been constructed within a few decades. This manner of framing likely continued in this region well into the 3rd quarter of the 18th century, if not even into the 4th quarter of the 18th century. A brick chimney was located at the north end of the structure; this has been rebuilt by the present owners. The section of the Phase 2 structure extending southward along the east gable end of the Phase 1 structure contains a winding staircase that rises from the ground floor to the second floor, and also descends to a second stone-walled cellar beneath the Phase 2 ground floor room. The staircase is assembled using wrought nails, suggesting its construction sometime during the 18th century. Due to all framing being cased in the entry, it was not possible to ascertain with absolute certainty that this bay is of the same vintage as the framing immediately to the north, but it is suspected that it is. At present only a small section of the west roof slope of the Phase 2 structure remains in place; other portions were either removed or replaced with modern material. The surviving section of roof reveals important evidence regarding the sequence of construction of the Phase 2 structure and the Phase 3 structure. The portion of the roof that was covered by the present Phase 3 roof contains a number of shingle nails, indicating that it preceded the present large roof structure over the building. Phase 3 Phase 3 involved the construction of the present enlarged roof covering the house. This appears to have been erected during the second half of the 19th century, likely sometime during the last quarter of the century. The south slope of the Phase 1 structure was not dismantled, but new, circular-sawn, 2 inch by 10 inch rafters were added extending the south slope upward to a new 1-inch-thick ridge board, with new similar rafters forming the new north slope of what is now the present roof structure. The original north slope of the Phase 1 structure was dismantled at this time. A series of rooms were created in the new enlarged attic. Unidentified Phase There is evidence that an additional phase exists, possibly constructed between the Phases 1 and 2 described above, against the north wall or rear of the Phase 1 structure, and extending across two-thirds of the rear wall from the west gable end of the Phase 1 house. If so, this is likely the Phase 2 structure identified by Chris Eaton during the 1988 assessment. However, it is not clear whether this structure was in fact a salt box-like addition, or a one-story structure under a shallow shed roof. Nor is it clear whether its depth or width was the same as the present structure occupying the area west of the Phase 2 structure as identified above. No evidence was found on the rear plate of the Phase 1 structure to suggest that rafters were added to form a saltbox-shaped roofline over this section of the house. Another factor supporting the existence of this unidentified phase of construction is the statement by the current owners that a firebox exists behind the current south wall in the kitchen/dining room. Evidence of an added firebox to the north side of the Phase 1 chimney stack and facing into the rear rooms can be seen through an access port in the west front room. As access to this firebox and its original form was not available, the nature of this firebox and any conclusions about its age, was not possible. The exposed framing in this room indicates a mix of old and newer framing; it is not clear whether this was created in an "old-timey" manner when the present roof over this structure was erected in the 2nd half of the 19th century, or whether it is truly old, a part of an earlier construction. The pattern of framing visible in the ceiling does not reveal a framing logic that is familiar or reflective of rear addition framing in known early 18th century buildings. The framing of the rooms on the second floor does not at all reflect that of the ground floor ceiling. Most timbers are circular-sawn, and either replaced earlier deteriorated timbers, or represent the raising of a one-story rear addition to two full stories beneath the new mid- to late-19th century roof. Thus, there must remain some uncertainty about the full sequence of construction. If there was a one-story lean-to addition built against the rear of the Phase 1 structure, it is likely that it was constructed prior to what has been identified above as Phase 2, and that the Phase 2 structure identified above was really the third phase of construction. This would fourth phase of construction, raising the earlier one-story addition to two full stories beneath the new roof. Can this be confirmed? Probably, but it would require removal of considerable fabric of the existing interior finishes to expose scars and other evidence on the rear walls of the Phase 1 structure and also on the west wall of the addition identified above as Phase 2. The results of the dendrochronology study, if successful, can provide absolute dates for the felling of the trees used in the construction of the frames of the various components of the house. In the absence of this data, we can only speculate on the date of this building – unless new documentary research and a careful review and new interpretation of the existing documentary records might provide more accurate information.

John Proctor House Inspection July 18, 2017 Myron O. Stachiw and William A. Flynt

Proctor House Exterior. Photo courtesy of Irene Moreira & Joseph Cipoletta with Barret Realty, Peabody, MA.

Proctor House Interior. Photo courtesy of Irene Moreira & Joseph Cipoletta with Barret Realty, Peabody, MA.

Proctor House Interior. Photo courtesy of Irene Moreira & Joseph Cipoletta with Barret Reality, Peabody, MA.

Proctor House Interior. Photo courtesy of Irene Moreira & Joseph Cipoletta with Barret Realty, Peabody, MA.

Proctor House Interior. Photo courtesy of Irene Moreira & Joseph Cipoletta with Barret Realty, Peabody, MA.

The House of the Seven Gables

An Interview with David Moffat
Courtesy of Julie Arrison-Bishop
Special Projects Manager at The House of Seven Gables

The House of the Seven Gables in Salem, MA.

RP: Is Manning Mansion on Herbert Street still standing? Are there any images available?

DM: The Manning House still stands today, at 10 ½ Herbert Street. It is a residential building, but a plaque on the exterior marks its significance. I've attached an image of the house, c. 1998, from the Massachusetts Cultural Resource Information System (MACRIS), and several historic images of the house from the early 20th century can be seen in the collections of the Phillips Library.

Richard Manning House where Miriam Lord Manning
(Hawthorne's maternal grandmother) lived. Photo courtesy of David Moffat.

RP: Do you believe the novel *The House of the Seven Gables* is based on Hawthorne's unresolved issues with his great-great-grandfather's role in the witch trials? Does *The Scarlet Letter* go even farther to describe his obsession with the "family curse"?

DM: *The House of the Seven Gables* drew from several historical sources for Hawthorne's interpretation of the Salem Witch Trials and I personally think that his great-great grandfather's connection to the trials was an inspiration for Hawthorne. We know from the introduction to *The Scarlet Letter*, that Hawthorne was greatly concerned with the sins of his ancestors:

> "His son, too, inherited the persecuting spirit, and made himself so conspicuous in the martyrdom of the witches, that their blood may fairly be said to have left a stain upon him. So deep a stain, indeed, that his old dry bones, in the Charter Street burial-ground, must still retain it, if they

have not crumbled utterly to dust! I know not whether these ancestors of mine bethought themselves to repent, and ask pardon of Heaven for their cruelties; or whether they are now groaning under the heavy consequences of them, in another state of being. At all events, I, the present writer, as their representative, hereby take shame upon myself for their sakes, and pray that any curse incurred by them—as I have heard, and as the dreary and unprosperous condition of the race, for many a long year back, would argue to exist—may be now and henceforth removed."

The House of the Seven Gables directly concerns a family grappling with their ancestors' misdeeds and haunted by the legacy of their past. I think the moral of the novel, being to break away from the past, was therapeutic for Hawthorne. Many critics have missed about the dark secret of Hawthorne that inspired the brooding tone of much of his work and the plot of *The Scarlet Letter*. One plausible explanation is that Hawthorne was himself deeply haunted by the acts of his ancestors William and John Hathorne.

RP: The House was built in 1668 for Captain John Turner and enlarged in 1676. This means it was present during the witch trials. Is there any record that it was ever used as a Common House or lodging for the Magistrates or the accused while waiting trial?

DM: The connections between the House of the Seven Gables and the Salem witch trials are quite limited, as far as we know. John Turner II owned the house at the time. He was only 21-years-old and not present in the testimony at the trials, but someone named "John Turner," perhaps John Turner II, was pushed out of a tree by Ann Pudeator, and this was used as a charge against Pudeator when she was hanged for witchcraft.

RP: Did Hawthorne pen any of his works at the house while visiting

Susannah Ingersoll?

DM: As far as we know, Hawthorne never wrote any of his works at The House of the Seven Gables. He was a frequent visitor and was inspired by the house and his cousin Susanna to write two of his works, the novel *The House of the Seven Gables*, and *Grandfather's Chair*, a collection of short stories. *The Scarlet Letter* was written while Hawthorne lived on Mall Street in Salem, in a house which still stands, and he wrote *The House of the Seven Gables* while in Lenox, Massachusetts.

RP: Please describe unique elements of the house (Batten door, hidden staircase, etc).

DM: The House of the Seven Gables is truly a gem of early American architecture. There are no other houses from the era on a comparable scale and few houses remaining with the level of period detail maintained in many parts of The Gables. Highlights include the wealth of original features in the attic, including surviving nogging or insulation from the 17th century. The Georgian paneling in the dining room, great chamber, and parlor is some of the earliest surviving in the United States, and dates from the early 18th century.

The fragment of the batten door was discovered on the outside of the house during the 1909-1910 restoration and a reproduction was made to show the impressive design of the original door, with approximately 500 nails to show off the wealth of the Turner family.

The secret staircase was long reported to be an original feature of the house, allegedly uncovered by Henry Upton during his removal of the original chimney, but the staircase as it exists today was built in 1909-1910 by Caroline Emmerton and her architect Joseph Chandler, to help the house conform to Hawthorne's novel and also to make the site more attractive to visitors. Until 2004, guests were told that the staircase dated back to the building of the house. Subsequently, new research has determined that its current iteration is not original. Joseph Chandler's other Colonial Revival restorations are architectural innovations in their own right, as he made much of the progress in the field of historical restoration. The view panel showing an early post in the great chamber may be the earliest example of such a concept in a historic house museum in the country.

RP: Hawthorne's works show an obsession with ghosts, the grave, witches, etc. Has any paranormal activity been reported at the house or his birthplace home on the grounds?

DM: Some guides have experienced alleged paranormal experiences, but the majority of guides believe that the House of the Seven Gables is not haunted. As for the birthplace, more paranormal activity has been allegedly spotted there, but no definitive claims have been made. As an organization, we do not promote ourselves as a haunted attraction, and many of our staff, including myself, are hard skeptics regarding the paranormal.

RP: Please tell me what fascinates you about the house and the Salem history surrounding its time during the 17th and 18th centuries. Feel free to introduce any topic or information that would interest the reader.

DM: The early history of Salem is fascinating because it is foundational to our identity as a nation. The Puritan experiment, the Witchcraft Trials, and the Great Age of Sail all left their mark on the history, the Revolution, and consciousness of Americans, though the latter era has been largely forgotten. My personal interest in Salem's history is partly aesthetic—I'm drawn to the forms and arts of the seventeenth and eighteenth century, especially their use of clean lines in furniture and gravestone carving, and the domestic history that accompanies the building, changing, and destruction of houses which often gets at the life of the ordinary person in history.

The house where Nathaniel Hawthorne was born. It is part of the House of the Seven Gables property at 115 Derby St., Salem, MA.

The House of the Seven Gables is an incredible piece of history with breathtaking gardens, history, and unparalleled views of the harbor. Please visit their website at 7gables.org for tour information and hours of operation. The address is 115 Derby St., Salem, MA.

The Interviews

Places of

Interest

Peabody Essex Museum
East India Square, Salem, MA.

The Peabody Essex Museum
Photo courtesy of Whitney Van Dyke

ABOUT THE PEABODY ESSEX MUSEUM
Over the last 20 years, the Peabody Essex Museum (PEM) has distinguished itself as one of the fastest-growing art museums in North America. Founded in 1799, it is also the country's oldest continuously operating museum. At its heart is a mission to enrich and transform people's lives by broadening their perspectives, attitudes and knowledge of themselves and the wider world. PEM celebrates outstanding artistic and cultural creativity through exhibitions, programming and special events that emphasize cross-cultural connections, integrate past and present and underscore the vital importance of creative expression. The museum's collection is

among the finest of its kind boasting superlative works from around the globe and across time -- including American art and architecture, Asian export art, photography, maritime art and history, Native American, Oceanic, and African art, as well as one of the nation's most important museum-based collections of rare books and manuscripts. PEM's campus affords a varied and unique visitor experience with hands-on creativity zones, interactive opportunities and performance spaces. Twenty-two noted historic structures grace PEM's campus, including Yin Yu Tang, a 200-year-old Chinese house that is the only such example of Chinese domestic architecture on display in the United States. **HOURS**: Open Tuesday-Sunday, 10 am-5 pm. Closed Mondays, Thanksgiving, Christmas and New Year's Day. **ADMISSION**: Adults $20; seniors $18; students $12. Additional admission to Yin Yu Tang: $6 (plus museum admission). Members, youth 16 and under and residents of Salem enjoy free general admission and free admission to Yin Yu Tang. **INFO**: Call 866-745-1876 or visit pem.org.

Whitney Van Dyke
Director of Communications
PEABODY ESSEX MUSEUM
East India Square | Salem, MA 01970 | 978.542.1828

The Rebecca Nurse Homestead & Meetinghouse

149 Pine Street, Danvers, MA.

Rebecca Nurse Homestead. Photo courtesy of the Danvers Library.

Richard Trask, Danvers (Salem Village) town historian and curator at the Danvers Archival Center was kind enough to tell me about the Rebecca Nurse Homestead, as he was a former curator there, and responsible for the creation of the meetinghouse reproduction found on the Nurse property, among other things, as you shall see.

RP: How much of the Nurse Homestead is the original building from 1692?
RT: It's hard to tell. The traditional date on that house was 1636. Probably the old house was torn down, the posts re-used, and a new house was put there. It probably dates to circa 1678, which is the date when the Nurse family started renting the property. It is a First Period house. Any First Period house is our most ancient properties. There is probably less than 400 of them in the entire country. First Period means anything built before 1720. The rarest of any houses in America are First Period houses. Danvers has sixteen of them. The largest community to have a number of them is Ipswich, which

is about twenty miles from Danvers. They are all clustered together, whereas Danvers was a farming community, and they were all spread out. Ipswich was a major town in the 17th century.

RP: How many acres was the Nurse farm when Rebecca Nurse lived there?

RT: About 300 acres. The sons-in-law would take portions of that property and build homesteads of their own. Today, there is 25 acres left of the original 300-acres plat.

RP: The meetinghouse replica found on the Nurse property is due to your research of the what the 1692 meetinghouse must have looked like, correct?

RT: I designed that for the movie *Three Sovereigns for Sarah*. There are three remnants of meetinghouses left, but the structure of the original building isn't evident. One of my jobs as the consultant for the film was to design the meetinghouse. That's a pretty good representation of what the Salem Village meetinghouse probably looked like.

Completed meetinghouse found on the Nurse farm.
Photo courtesy of Richard Trask.

RP: It mentions in the Salem witch trial transcripts that the trials would become so packed with spectators, that some would sit on the window sills. Were those windows glass or open?

RT: They had a combination. The majority of the windows were open windows with interior shutters. They had vertical bars on the windows themselves. There were six casement windows in the meetinghouse and they had been taken from an earlier Salem Town meetinghouse.

RP: And the sermons in 1692 were three hours long in the morning and three hours in the afternoon?

RT: Yes. One of the deacons had the responsibility to go around with a pole that often had a feather or animal tail on one end and a knob on the other and he would prod members of the congregation to keep them awake or stop them from fooling around. It sounds like a lot of time today to spend in church, but you have to remember that was one of the big breaks they had. They got an awful lot of theology, but they also got a noon break where they could meet-and-greet people. It was nice to see your neighbors and a lot of socialization took place there as well.

RP: Ingersoll's Ordinary was well-positioned. At the noon break, everyone headed up the road for something to eat or drink.

Back to the Nurse Homestead, there is a family grave yard there at the bottom of the small hill and we believe Rebecca Nurse is buried there, along with the bones of George Jacobs, Sr. who was also hanged for witchcraft. I believe you were instrumental in bringing his bones there, is that correct?

RT: Yes. When the executed witches were cut down, they were given just a cursory burial near the place of execution. It wasn't necessarily legal to take the bodies and bury them elsewhere. If the families were local, they probably would have taken the bodies. We know from family tradition that at least some of the bodies were taken. One was Rebecca Nurse and we assume she was buried in the family grave yard, one was George Jacobs, Sr. and the other was John Proctor. The marker for Rebecca Nurse was a late 19th century addition.

I got possession of George Jacobs remains back in the 1960s, and we decided that would be an appropriate place to bury him. Originally, he was buried on his family farm. During the excavation of that property, the bones turned up, and I was given custody of them.

RP: Was the Nurse house considered large for that era?

RT: No. It was not as large as you see it today. In 1692, it was probably three rooms in the house: a first-floor great hall, a hall chamber above it, a lean-to on the back, plus the little entry, which they called the porch, although it was not like what we call a porch today.

RP: I understand the main bedroom was always on the first floor. Was that so they would be closest to the door in case of an Indian attack or other intrusion?

RT: Yes. And because that was the warmest part of the house, because that is where you would have the fireplace going probably 24-hours a day.

RP: Would other rooms be clustered there, or would there be some on the second floor?

RT: First Period houses had the chimney on the end, the great hall on the first floor and then what was called a hall chamber on the second floor. In the attic, which they called the garret, you would have living space as well there. Later on, they would often build two other rooms onto the other side of the chimney. They would also add a lean-to onto the outside of the house. So, you basically have three different styles that could be built all at once, which was pretty unusual, or styles that could be built one at a time over different periods of time, depending upon how affluent they were and how easy it was to add onto the house. There would be a fireplace opening in every room. There's a central fireplace and each room has an opening, as will the lean-to at the back of the house.

Rebecca Nurse house main floor fireplace.

Rebecca Nurse house main floor.

Rebecca Nurse house bedroom upstairs.

RP: Did they have outhouses, or did they rely on chamber pots?

RT: Probably both. Chamber pots for nighttime, or if you were sick, and outhouses for the daytime.

RP: Is the herb garden in front of the Nurse home today indicative of what they would have had in 1692?

RT: They usually would have some kind of vegetable garden with herbs and they would have had the kind of vegetables such as corn or rye, and sometimes wheat. It's usually at the back of the house, like the Nurse homestead. You wouldn't find vegetables such as sweet potatoes. They are often raised gardens. The house has a root cellar for storage. You could keep potatoes there.

The Nurses lived in it until the 1780s, and then the Putnam family bought it. It was acquired by a Nurse descendent in 1909. It was one of the earliest restorations of a First Period house. They gave it to a Boston preservation agency known as The Preservation of New England Antiquities. They owned about 75 properties throughout New England. When I was doing a house tour with the Director, and showing him some of the First Period houses in Danvers, he mentioned they couldn't handle all the First Period houses here, so I asked him if he would transfer the Nurse home to the Danvers Alarm List Company. We purchased the property in 1976 from that Boston organization.

Photograph of inside the meetinghouse at the Nurse farm showing the pulpit and sacrament table. Photo courtesy of Richard Trask.

RP: The following are the wonderful drawings of Marilynne K. Roach who was interviewed earlier in the book. They are of the

Salem Village meetinghouse as it would be seen in 1692:

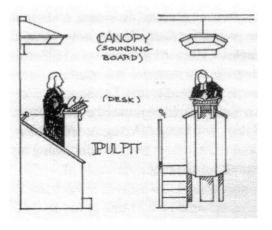

Drawings by Marilynne K. Roach.

I want to thank Richard B. Trask so very much for his time in talking with me. His book *Pictures of the Pain: Photography and the Assassination of President Kennedy* contains his incredible history of the photographs taken at the Kennedy assassination. It's a result of 10 years of research and contains 360 illustrations, many never before published. It is considered the classic book on the photography of the event. He wrote three books on the subject. I highly recommend them. He is justly proud of the work and the accolades involved with the books. *National Nightmare on Six Feet of Film: Mr. Zapruder's Home Movie and the Murder of President Kennedy*, and *That Day in Dallas: Three Photographers Capture on Film the Day President Kennedy Died* are the other two books in this collection. They are available on Amazon.

The Hawthorne Hotel

18 Washington Square West

The Hawthorne Hotel in Fall.
Photo courtesy of Donald Gerolamo

In 1925, Frank Poor, founder of Hygrade/Sylvania Lighting Company, envisioned a grand hotel in the heart of Salem that could accommodate the traveling businessman. Word got out about this "modern hotel for Salem," resulting in half a million dollars' worth of stock being sold in one week in 1923. The hotel was open for business on July 23, 1925. The Salem Chamber and Salem Rotary led the festivities at a flag-raising ceremony and city-wide parade. It towered six stories, the tallest building in Salem, Massachusetts.

The Hawthorne evolved with the times, including a dance school in the 1960s led by Miss Harriet James in the Grand Ballroom. But it was the 1970s that put the Hawthorne Hotel in Hollywood's spotlight when the TV series *Bewitched* came to call. The popular show broke the ugly witch stereotype by casting Elizabeth Montgomery in the lead role. Two shows were filmed in the "Witch City" and the cast stayed at the hotel during filming. One iconic photo shows Elizabeth Montgomery as Samantha and Dick York as

Darrin getting into the Hawthorne elevator.

A statue in her honor was later placed at the corner of Essex and Washington Streets, amid controversy. Salem was still coming to terms with its relationship with the Halloween aspect that had descended upon a town that was trying to show respect and reverence for the events of 1692.

9-ft. bronze statue of Bewitched donated by TV Land on June 15, 2005.

On Halloween Eve, 1990, a group of hopefuls assembled at a séance in the Hawthorne Grand Ballroom in an effort to summon Harry Houdini back from the grave. It was the 64th anniversary of his death. Houdini had promised his wife that if he died, he would find a way to communicate with her from beyond the grave. And so, the lights dimmed, the voices intoned his name, but, alas, he did not appear.

Promotional ad for Harry Houdini.

The Grand Ballroom at the Hawthorne.
Photo courtesy of Lightshed Photography.

The Hawthorne Lobby. Photo courtesy of Lightshed Photography.

The Hawthorne Lobby.
Photo courtesy of Lightshed Photography.

In 1991, the Hawthorne embraced the Halloween spirit that marched past its door in full regalia every October (and to be honest), other months as well. It instituted its first annual Halloween party.

In 2015, Hollywood once again came knocking. The movie *JOY*, starring Jennifer Lawrence, Bradley Cooper, and Robert DeNiro offered scenes filmed in the Hawthorne Grand Ballroom, Mezzanine, and a guest room. The stars stayed at the Hotel during the filming.

The movie ad for JOY.

My sincere appreciation to KrisTina Petty Wheeler, *Assistant to Claire Kallelis, General Manager;* and to Claire Kallelis, *General Manager at the Hawthorne,* for submitting these beautiful photos of their hotel.

In 2015, the Hotel received one the most prestigious awards given in the hospitality business. It was presented with the "2015 Best City Center Historic Hotel Award" from Historic Hotels of America. This major award is in recognition of the Hawthorne's continued achievement in excellence. The Hotel is noted for its beauty, service, cuisine, elegant rooms, weddings, events, and…even a few ghosts, which we will deal with in the Haunted section of the book.

The Witch House

310 Essex Street

The Witch House in Salem, Massachusetts is a touchstone to the events of 1692. It is the only extant house in Salem with direct connections to the witch trials of that era. It is also known as the Jonathan Corwin house, as it was here, during the trials, that Judge Corwin lived.

The house has gone through several changes during its long life. It stands two-and-a-half stories and is made of timber. Its current location is only 35 feet from where it originally stood in 1692. Judge Corwin was an affluent merchant, dealing in the exportation of timber and fish to the East Indies and England. Salem was a flourishing seaport in those days and the money he made, along with a sizeable inheritance from his wealthy family, allowed him to purchase wharves, ships and farmland.

The Corwins bought the house in 1675. They immediately hired Daniel Andrews (the same man who would be arrested for witchcraft almost twenty years later. He fled before he could stand trial before the magistrate who was now hiring his services). Andrews was to make many changes to the house which included digging a cellar beneath the East Room, taking down chimney flues and rebuilding them, and adding an additional five chimneys to this

3-gabled home. He was tasked with providing Dutch tiles for the bedroom chamber fireplaces, building a fireplace and furnace for the kitchen, and general plastering and finishing work. For this, he was payed the handsome sum of 50 pounds in English currency.

As discussed in my interview with Richard Trask earlier in this book, First Period houses are rare, with only 400 standing in the United States. The Corwin house is a First Period house and an exquisite example of 17th century architecture. The home barely escaped demolition in 1944 when the road was to be widened. Salem citizens raised $42,500 to move the house back from the road to its current location. In 1948, it opened a museum. Today, the home offers exhibits and tours, not only discussing the history of Judge Corwin's involvement in the witch trials, but the fascinating legacy of the house. The docents there give the visitor a real taste of life as it was in that era, and even earlier during the Davenport's time.

You can find ticket and tour information at their website at www.thewitchhouse.org, or call 978-744-8815.

Pioneer Village

Salem's Forest River Park

Pioneer Village in Salem represents how the early Puritans lived during the 1630s. It was built in 1930 during the Tercentennial of Massachusetts. It is considered America's only living history museum. It sits on three acres and portrays the various living structures the early Massachusetts Bay colonists built. When first arriving from England, their need for shelter resulted in dugouts, wigwams, and thatched roof cottages. The Governor's Faire House is also depicted at Pioneer Village.

The Village gives visitors an idea of the culinary fare of that era and the medicinal gardens grown. A blacksmith is also part of the Village. The movie *Hocus Pocus* filmed an early scene here where Emily is lured by the witch into the woods.

The Pioneer Village sits in Salem's Forest River Park and is a ten-minute drive from downtown. You can rent the Village, or ask about using it for a period event or re-enactment, by contacting www.thewitchhouse.org.

Danvers Witch Trial Memorial

176 Hobart Street, Danvers, MA.

Danvers was Salem Village in 1692, and the home of the original outbreak of the witch hysteria. Hobart Street has the distinction of housing many of the places most-closely tied to the trials and examinations. It is here, on the corner of Hobart and Centere Streets that you will find Ingersoll's Ordinary, where the first three witches—Tituba, Sarah Good, and Sarah Osborne—were taken for their first examination. Across from Ingersoll's Ordinary (which is still standing) was the location of the Watch House where Village inhabitants took turns watching for Indian attacks.

Only a few yards down Hobart from Ingersoll's was the infamous meetinghouse where the examinations were held. The trials were held in Salem Town for the convenience of the magistrates and the need for a large hall in which to hear testimony amid a crowd of spectators. The Salem Village meetinghouse location has been taken over by homes, but a large marker across the street from its original location, stands. This is also the location of the Danvers Witch Trial Memorial, a large and touching tribute to the people who lost their lives during the witchcraft hysteria.

On May 9, 1992, the Salem Village Witchcraft Victims' Memorial of Danvers was dedicated before an audience of over 3,000 people. It was the first such Memorial to honor all of the 1692 witchcraft victims, and is located across the street from the site of the original Salem Village Meetinghouse where many of the witch examinations took place. The Memorial serves as a reminder that each generation must confront intolerance and "witch hunts" with integrity, clear vision and courage.

This memorial project was undertaken by the Salem Village Witchcraft Tercentennial Committee of the Town of Danvers which commemorated the 300th anniversary of the witch prosecutions during 1989-1993. The Memorial itself was designed by Committee members Richard B. Trask; Robert D. Farley, CSI; and Marjorie C. Wetzel. Finance Chairman Ralph E. Aridff, Jr. raised money for the project through donations of numerous town, civic, patriotic, business, and ethnic organizations, and by individuals. The property was donated and is now maintained by the Town of Danvers, and the Memorial is open to the public daily from dawn to dusk.

Memorial Design and Symbolism

The design of the Memorial is highly symbolic in nature. On a light-colored Barre granite sarcophagus measuring 4' x 8' x 4' rests an oversized representation of a slant-top bible box. In colonial times such boxes were used as storage containers for precious volumes and papers. The positioning of the block with the bible box on top is reminiscent of a colonial pulpit and its juxtaposition and correct alignment with what would have been the original Meetinghouse pulpit across the street is purposeful. Yet the bible box, a domestic item of furniture, better represents individual home-inspired devotion, rather than communal, ecclesiastical worship, denoting the significance of personal beliefs and morals.

The box is composed of Canadian Pink granite, and on its front is carved several different and local style rosettes, typical design features found in both Puritan furniture and gravestones. The five rosettes banded together by a serpentine vine are Puritan symbols for eternity. Resting on top of the bible box, and composed of the same brown-reddish granite as the box itself, is an open book with an inscription in 17th century typeface reading, "THE BOOK OF LIFE." In biblical language this phrase represented the record of those who should inherit eternal life. During the witch trials numerous persons testified that the accused had signed the "Devil's book" thus becoming witches and doing the work of the devil. Those who were executed for witchcraft refused to confess to being witches, for they wanted to be inscribed in "The Book of Life." At the time almost all in the Puritan community believed the accused to be guilty, while today the historical record, a modern-day "book of life" of sorts, has rectified the former deadly falsehoods of 1692.

The weight of truth, symbolized in the granite box and book, is also represented smashing through the falsehood of history, depicted by a pair of large-scale reproduction metal shackles divided in two by the book and resting broken upon the block of granite. Curtis M. White, a talented blacksmith, staff member of the Saugus Ironworks National Park and at the time the resident overseer of the Rebecca Nurse Homestead, hand-forged the chains. Carved on the face of the block granite is the inscription "In memory of those innocents who died during the Salem Village witchcraft hysteria of 1692."

To the rear of this granite piece stands a three-panel 12-feet long by 8-feet high granite memorial wall containing in 17th century spelling form the names of the 24 men and women and one child who died as a result of the witch hysteria. Also included are the towns of origin of these people which include besides Salem Village, Salem Farmes (Peabody), Salem, Andover, Billerica, Amesbury, Reading, Topsfield, Marblehead and Rowley. Above the center panel on a granite ellipse is carved the Tercentennial Committees logo featuring a man grasping an open book. The man's hair style, robe and neck bands are reminiscent and symbolic of a 17th century cleric with an open bible or a magistrate with an open law book trying to come to understand and interpret the witch hysteria which had overtaken much of Massachusetts. The logo was designed for use of the Tercentennial Committee and donated by Jim Barina, founder of 'Spellbound,' a Salem, Massachusetts, advertising agency.

On each side of the Memorial wall stands at a 45-degree angle to it a wall inscribed to include in their own words brave statements made by eight of the accused witches during their harrowing examination just across the street from the memorial location.

Danvers Witch Trial Memorial Bible Box

Salem Custom House

176 Derby Street

The Salem Custom House was built in 1813 and housed offices for the officers of the U.S. Customs Service, as well as attached warehouses, and the Public Stores used for the storage of bonded and impounded cargo. There has been a Custom House in Salem since 1649, pre-dating the Witch Trials. Its primary use was for collecting taxes on imported cargos first for the British Government during the Colonial period, then for the American Government after the establishment of the U.S. Customs Services in 1789.

Today, the U.S. Custom House in Salem is home to exhibits on the tools of the Custom Service, the work of the Customs Inspectors, and the office of Nathaniel Hawthorne, who worked there during his youth. He later penned the famous novels *The House of the Seven Gables*, and *The Scarlet Letter*. The inspiration for the latter came from Hawthorne's three-year-stint at the Custom House.

There are many more Places of Interest in Salem and the surrounding areas, but as a good deal of them report "shades from the past," they will be covered in our next section:

The Haunting

The

Haunting

The 1692 Salem Witch Trials left a stain on American History that impacted the New England cities and hamlets surrounding it. Most were, in some way, touched by the witchcraft outbreak, whether directly or indirectly. The names of the accused were from counties all the way up into modern-day Maine, which was, in 1692, part of Massachusetts. You cannot visit these places without a stirring in the soul. Remnants of that past tragedy still finds it mark on historic homes, monuments, tombstones, and memorials. This "stirring" goes beyond our perceived idea of a haunting. While strange occurrences are reported in many properties throughout Salem and Danvers, it is an overlying atmosphere that one most feels here. And, perhaps, a warning that the culmination of superstition and unforeseen events could begin it all again.

I will admit, I have deviated somewhat from the usual accounts of paranormal activity that make up the Haunting section of my books. The research and reporting of the witch trials touched me more than any book I've written. I've stayed my hand more in this section than normal, out of respect for the lives lost.

I do continue to believe that places carry shadows of events, and science is corroborating the fact that energy can be retained and transmitted through certain conditions. I have no issue with that. I have witnessed too many unaccounted-for events to know "there are more things in heaven and earth, Horatio, than are dreamt of in your philosophy." Many places in Salem lay claim to paranormal events, and I will give them a cursory mention here. It is also more daunting to report the occurrences of an entire community than it is to zoom in on one venue, as I've done in the past. I hope you will not be disappointed with the treatment of the topic. As I said, the telling of the witch trials carried a weight and a certain responsibility I could not walk away from.

-- The Author

572

The John Proctor House
348 Lowell Street, Peabody, MA.

While interviewing Barbara Bridgewater, current owner of the John Proctor house in Peabody, MA., I asked if she had noticed any paranormal activity in the home, she was kind enough to share this with me:

Barbara: There have been a fair number of occurrences. My youngest daughter who is close in age to Mary Warren (the Proctors house servant) has experienced at least 3 nose bleeds and believed she was pushed or pulled down one of the staircases.
   The first time we stayed there my husband and both daughters heard female voices around 2:00-3:00 am and they felt it was in the house downstairs on the first floor. They said the voices were distinctly female and they know the voices did not come from the outside since it was late December and very cold outside.
   I have heard the player piano play in the late hours of the night (2/3 am) at least 2 times. And on my most recent trip in late August, we had an additional occurrence with the piano. The Travel Channel was filming interviews of me and my youngest daughter during the

day. The crew was there a couple of days. The day they left, my older daughter and I went around the entire house to close things up since we were going to leave for a short getaway to Rhode Island early the next day. We closed all the windows, doors, and the piano. When we returned late the next night from RI, we checked around the first floor again before we went to bed. We did this together and found that the piano keyboard had been opened. There was no way for anyone to get in the house and no way it could have opened. We both looked at each other and asked if the other had opened it. Neither of us had. We don't know how that happened but we almost left the house to stay at a local hotel. We would have left if it wasn't so close to midnight.

Each time we are there we sleep on the second floor and hear the house settling and what sounds like people walking up on the third floor above us.

I know there is energy there but feel that it is not bad or malicious.

The Hawthorne Hotel

18 Washington Square West

The historic Hawthorne Hotel holds court in the middle of Salem, towering six stories above the streets that once saw horse and rider, oxcarts and pillories. Built in 1925, it once boasted a secret society on its rooftop for seafaring mariners called the Salem Maritime Society. From 1766 on, they held their clandestine meetings, and a few of their ghosts are said to haunt the hotel.

Like all historic hotels who have watched the parade of life amble through its long corridors, the Hawthorne has some particularly infamous rooms that seem to have put out the welcome mat for those from the Invisible World.

Michael Teleoglou stayed in Room 325 and sent me this account:

Michael: I wanted to pass along this story about room 325 at the Hawthorne hotel. In my opinion, the room had a creepy vibe to it. My mom and I felt the same atmosphere. There was a constant smell of perfume, and my Mom was not wearing any. Although we did not have anybody hop in bed with us, my Mom did think she heard someone walk across the room at night. I left 2 recorders running throughout our time there and both had a good amount of audio on them. In my bedroom of the 2-bedroom set-up, I felt as if I was being watched. The chance to be there was a night I will always remember. I turned off my recorders several times to change the batteries. The last time I turned them off in the morning, something strange happened. Seconds after I turned the second one off, I could have sworn I heard a female saying my name.

This author stayed in the Hawthorne in 2015, in Room 628. This room's window faces the Salem Witch Museum and the statue of Roger Currant. It's a gorgeous view at night when the Museum's red spotlights showcase the stone structure.

I was reading in bed and glanced over at the hotel's digital clock. It read 10:45 in glowing red numerals. I took a drink from a plastic bottle of water on the nightstand where the clock sat, and turned off the lights. I glanced at the clock again in the dark, and faded off to sleep. Sometime, during the night, I was awakened by a sharp cracking sound. I was still groggy, but I know a strange sound had awakened me. Then it came again…a sharp crackling noise. I turned to look at the clock and felt confused. It had been clearly in view when I went to sleep, but now, looking at the red glowing numerals, it was like trying to see them through a blur. Something was blocking the view, yet I could see them in a distorted way.

I reached for the nightstand lamp and turned it on. The water bottle I had placed back on the nightstand, after taking a drink before bed, had moved a good foot away from the lamp where I set it. It was now blocking the clock, and it was through the water in it that I was seeing the distorted clock's dial. I hesitantly picked it up. As my grasp closed around the thin plastic, it made a sharp cracking sound, the way plastic does when compressed or bent. I nearly dropped it. Whatever moved it had caused it to make the noise that awakened me. I'm not ashamed to say I placed the bottle in the bathroom and closed the door.

Many ghost stories swirl about the Hawthorne Hotel. Perhaps, it is its location adjacent to **Washington Square**. In the 17th century, Washington Square was a typical New England Common. It was used to allow livestock, such as sheep to graze, and later was used as a militia training ground. The pillories, where public humiliation was carried out, may have been here as well. Today, it is a 9-acre park with odd angles, surrounded by stately homes and the gateway to the stores and restaurants that fill to the brim in Fall. Many people have felt strange sensations in the park. Several stories have been reported of visitors feeling pressed against by unseen presences as they walk through the Common. One man said, "It's as if you just walked through a crowd of people, and they are bumping up against you."

Some reports have surfaced stating Ann Pudeator's ghost was seen walking through the 17th century Common *before* she was hanged for witchcraft. I have had emails from people saying they have looked down from the Hawthorne Hotel onto the Square and seen strange lights and shimmering forms. Whoever the spirits are, several seem to have checked into the Hawthorne Hotel.

In 1766, the Salem Marine Society was founded by local seafaring men. It's building where the Society met sat where the hotel stands today. Their meeting place was razed to allow room for the hotel's construction. The caveat to such a situation, was the hotel was to supply a meeting place for the displaced captains and other sea-faring souls. The hotel agreed to construct a small structure on the rooftop, whose interior is an exact replica of the cabin of a ship called the *Taria Topan*. It still stands today and houses the secret society's meetings.

Many people have reported seeing shapes of sea captains in the Lower Deck of the hotel which carries a nautical theme. They are caught from the corner of the eye, walking across the room, only to disappear into a paneled wall. It would seem there are more secrets to the Marine Society than we know.

Ropes Mansion
318 Essex Street

The Ropes Mansion is a Georgian Colonial home located in the McIntire Historic District in Salem. The Peabody Essex Museum now owns the home and offers it as one of their tours. The house was built for Samuel Barnard, a wealthy Salem merchant in the 1720s. It was later purchased by Judge Nathaniel Ropes from Barnard's nephew. It underwent renovations over the years, but still retains much of its original structure. In 1907, the house was given to the Trustees of the Ropes Memorial for public use. A lovely garden is found behind the house and is worth seeing.

Rope's Mansion, circa 1918 with gardens.

During the Revolution, Judge Ropes lived in the mansion. He was loyal to the Crown, which incited the local colonists, and they reverted to the witch trial days—they decided to hang him. Storming his house, they found the Judge withering away with small pox, a plague that had impacted Salem in the 17th century. The poor man was so far gone, they departed and left it to other forces to deal with him. He did die in the home, but his was not the only tragic death reported.

One night in 1839, his wife Abigail passed too close to a fireplace in her bed chamber on the second floor and her long dressing gown caught fire. Although she screamed for help, she finally succumbed to the flames and smoke.

Tour guides have reported that some photos taken for insurance purposes have shown indentations suddenly appearing on a sofa cushion as though someone just sat down. Teeta Moss, owner of the Myrtles Plantation in Saint Francisville, Louisiana, accidently captured the ghost of a slave girl from another era while taking photos for insurance purposes. The photograph was submitted to a professional photographer & archivist who found it to be authentic. You can clearly see the figure of a black woman in a turban standing next to the building. Adding to the shivers is that you can see the plantation's clap boards through her shape.

Wraiths have been seen on the stairways and in the gardens at Ropes Mansion. *National Geographic* was shooting photographs at the mansion in the 1970s and was surprised to see the ghostly torso and feet of a man standing before one of the sofas. The mansion sits along a ley line that runs along Essex Street in Salem. Ley lines are natural energy lines below the ground's surface and can purport extra activity in a location.

Disney's 1993 film *Hocus Pocus* used the house as the home of Max's love interest, Allison.

Joshua Ward House

148 Washington Street

The Joshua Ward house in Salem has garnered the reputation as the most-haunted home in the "Witch City." With roots going back to 1692 and the dreaded Sheriff George Corwin, is it any wonderful ghost hunters are fond of coming here. George Corwin was so notorious for his dealings with the imprisoned "witches" that his family feared that, after his death, the townspeople would take the body and tear it to pieces. As noted in the History section of this book, Phillip English did indeed steal Corwin's body and held it for ransom while trying to recoup some of the money stolen from him while he was hiding from the trials. He gave it back only a few days later.

Apparently, the family buried the Sheriff's corpse in the cellar of the house, as they feared his grave would be ravaged if interred at a local cemetery. The Sheriff's house is no longer there, and a three-story Federal-style building was constructed over the foundation. It was a grand home, and in 1789, George Washington asked to stay there while visiting Salem. A white bust of the President can be seen on the second floor. The home once boasted a view of the South River, but it was filled in, in 1830. It was listed on the National Register of Historic Places in 1978.

Carlson Realty moved in, in the 70s, and reports began circulating of strange things happening in the house. When the staff for the Realty Company arrived at work in the morning, they would find trash cans turned upside down, chairs had been moved, lampshades were up-ended, and strangest of all, the candlesticks would be found lying on the floor twisted into an "S" shape. The security alarms went off inexplicably. It was reported they went off over sixty times in two years, when there was no cause to do so. One of the office rooms remained artic cold despite efforts to warm it.

Tales of a strange woman in a long black coat with frizzy hair and translucent skin have been told by more than one person working at the Ward House. When Christmas photos of the Carlson Realty's employeee were taken one year, a very strange photo emerged from the camera. Standing before a Christmas wreath hanging on a door, is a blurry shot of a woman in a long black coat with what appears to be frizzy black hair. *Unsolved Mysteries* saw the picture in the 1980s and had it tested for authenticity. Once it appeared on their show, it became a sensation. Julie Tremblay, one of the employees at the time, was suggested as the person in the photo, standing before the wreath, which made her dark hair appear "wild and frizzy." The person taking the photo argued that what he saw in the viewfinder, and what emerged from the camera were not the same thing. As blurry as the picture is, it is very hard to discern the details.

Photo taken at Carlson Realty in the Joshua Ward House during a Christmas party.

George Corwin's body was later moved to the Broad Street Cemetery. Corwin died on April 12, 1696, only three years after the Salem Witch Trials ended. His wife, Lydia, was hounded by Phillip English for restitution of the goods Corwin had stolen from him. She paid him off partially in silver in linens. When Lydia died a few years later, Corwin's estate was worth £73-8-4. His outstanding debts of £33-17-3 diminished the sum. If it is Corwin, or perhaps his wife Lydia haunting the old home site, it does not look like they are interested in leaving anytime soon...at least according to Salem tour guides who call it the most-active place in Salem.

Gardner-Pingree House

128 Essex Street

Across the street and down a block from the Peabody Essex Museum is the Gardner-Pingree House. Owned by the Museum, it is an exquisite mansion built in 1804. This author toured this beautiful home and was impressed with the retention of its 19th century architecture and warmth. If you tour the house, be sure and notice the "brag button" on the newel post at the bottom of the grand staircase. In the 1700s and 1800s, if an owner was rich enough to pay off the mortgage of his home, he would often drill a hole in the newel post of the main staircase and either insert the deed to the house, or pour its ashes there. The hole was then capped with a "button," usually of ivory. Wealthier owners sometimes used jewels. This way, visiting guests could simply glimpse the "button" and know how wealthy the owner really was. It was a way of saying

"That's right! We own it!" without "bragging" out loud. I've seen brag buttons at the Myrtles Plantation in St. Francisville, Louisiana, and at the Whaley House's back staircase in San Diego, California.

While the furnishings and architecture are wonderful, the house was also the site of a brutal murder that was quite the sensation at the time. Eighty-year-old Captain Joseph White was a shipmaster and trader. He was attacked one evening and beaten over the head with a twenty-two-inch piece of refurbished hickory, also called an "Indian Club." If that wasn't enough, the poor elderly man was stabbed thirteen times near his heart.

As the story goes, Joseph (Joe) Knapp, Captain White's grandnephew, had recently learned that the Captain had just completed a will, leaving $15,000 to Mary Beckford, White's niece, housekeeper, and next of kin. Mrs. Beckford had a daughter, also named Mary, who was living in Wenham with her husband, the same Joseph Jenkins Knapp Jr. Joe figured that if old White died before the will could be notarized, half of his $200,000 fortune would go to his mother-in-law Mrs. Beckford, rather than a paltry $15,000. His wife Mary Jr. would benefit indirectly.

Joe and his brother John set upon a plan. They hired a man of questionable character, Richard Crowninshield, from a prominent family, to do the deed. For $1,000, Richard was to kill the old man in his sleep. Joe Knapp had access to the mansion, and on April 6, 1830, he stole the will and left a back window open for the murderer's entrance. Crowninshield played his part, entering the mansion through the window and climbing the staircase to the second floor, where he found the old man in bed. He killed him with one blow of the Indian Club to the left temple. Why he continued with a stabbing is unknown. He hid the murder weapons under the steps at the former Howard Street meetinghouse.

The police had suspicions from the beginning. For one thing, nothing was missing from the wealthy sea merchant's home. The will was not common knowledge and so its absence went undetected. The Knapp brothers came up with an alibi to make it look like a family attack by saying they were robbed that same night by three men on their way to Wenham. It was a puzzling mystery. Somehow, Richard Crowinshield was found out and arrested. Rather than face conviction, he hung himself in prison. Suspicion fell upon the Knapp brothers and they were arrested.

None other than Daniel Webster took on the "Case of the Century," acting as prosecutor against the Knapps. He called the murder "a most extraordinary case" and a "cool, calculating, moneymaking murder." The Knapp brothers were convicted, after finally confessing to the murder-for-hire. Rumor had it that Webster's oration during the trial inspired Edgar Allen Poe to pen his famous *The Tell-Tale Heart*, whose plot centered around the grisly murder of an old man, and the guilt that followed after.

On September 28, 1830, John Francis Knapp was hanged in front of the old Salem Jail (Gaol), sending Salem back nearly two hundred years. Joseph Knapp, the mastermind behind the murder, was likewise hanged in November, 1830.

The Peabody Essex Museum houses the Indian Club from the murder in a location not open to the public. But, as mentioned earlier, you can tour the house. In a strange twist of irony, the Crowninshield-Bentley House was moved next door to the Gardner-Pingree House in 1959, so that now, the murderer's home, and the victim's are side-by-side. Many report seeing the specter of old man White peering down from his second-story window on the anniversary of his murder, on April 6, 1830.

The John Ward House

9 Brown Street in the Federal Garden Area

Directly behind the Gardiner-Pingree house sits the John Ward house. This was not its original location. Built ca. 1684, the timber house literally sat across the street from the Salem Jail (Gaol) during the witch trials. The house stood on a one-acre lot with a kitchen garden and an outhouse. It witnessed the throngs of spectators pressing into its yard as oxcarts, loaded with condemned "witches," rode off down Prison Lane toward Gallows Hill. It was also in close proximity to Giles Corey's execution site in a nearby field. The house was moved to its present site behind the Gardiner-Pingree House in 1910.

As nearby houses and taverns were sometimes used to take prisoners while searching for witch marks, it has been rumored the John Ward House may have served such a purpose. Today, it used by the Peabody Essex Museum for storage. Reports of screams coming from the house have been reported, as well as glimpses of specters if one peers through the diamond-paned windows.

Samuel Pickman House

Corner of Charter and Liberty Streets

The Samuel Pickman House is located on Charter Street in Salem, Massachusetts, behind the Peabody Essex Museum. The house, built in 1664, abuts the Witch Memorial dedicated in 1992 on the 300th anniversary of the Salem witch trials and is also next to the second oldest burying ground in America, Old Burying Point. These properties form part of the Charter Street Historic District. The Pickman House boasts American colonial architecture from the First Period. The style of the large central brick chimney is an excellent example of First Period craftsmanship. The house was restored by Historic Salem in 1969 and purchased by the Peabody Essex Museum in 1983. The Pickman House is not open to the public.

A story continues to circulate about the spirit of a young girl who looks down from the attic window. It is based on urban legend surrounding a tale of a father going berserk and killing his daughter and wife. No documents have been found to substantiate the story, yet a great number of people say they see the little girl's pale face looking down woefully from the attic where she was supposedly murdered.

The Salem Inn

7 Summer Street

The Salem Inn is actually one of three bed-and-breakfasts owned by Richard and Diane Pabich. The West House is the largest and sits across from the Witch House on Summer Street. Salem Inn emblazes a plaque hanging from the beautiful Greek Revival building. It offers 22 guest rooms and is the only pet-friendly Inn in Salem. It has a very haunted reputation, based, perhaps, on the fact that it is sitting on the land once owned by Judge Jonathan Corwin, while he resided across the street in what is now known as the Witch House.

The land Salem Inn was built upon was purchased in 1811 by Captain Nathaniel West. In 1834, he built three townhouses. He died while living in one of the townhomes. When the Pabich's purchased the townhouses in 1983, they combined them, keeping the Victorian air for which the Inn is known. Antiques grace each room and common area.

The other two Inns owned and operated by the Pabich's are nearby. **The Peabody House** was built as a single-family Dutch Colonial home in 1874 by John P. Peabody, a purveyor of ladies' fine furnishings. The House offers four large suites with kitchenettes, along with two romantic rooms with king-size four poster beds. All rooms offer European walk-in showers in the en-suite modern bathrooms and most offer working fireplaces.

The Curwen House is an Italianate Revival building built in 1854 by James B. Curwen and his brother Captain Samuel R. Curwen. The brothers are related to the Corwins who acted as Judge and Sheriff in the 1692 witch trials. Each of the 11 guest rooms in the Curwen House offer private baths. It is an adult-only Inn. The other two houses in the Salem Inn conglomerate welcome children, and as mentioned, the West House of Salem Inn allows pets. The rooms here offer three deluxe suites with a whirlpool bath, fireplace, and queen-sized bed. All rooms are handsomely furnished with antiques.

Many stories of paranormal happenings have come from Salem Inn. Room 17 seems to be its most-haunted location. Many guests have reported a transparent apparition of a young woman in 17th century period clothing. She has been seen in the breakfast room and gliding about the hallways. The sound of a gunshot has been reported, along with doors opening and closing by themselves, and electrical devices turning on by themselves. Guests say things move about the room and even disappear. The TV remote control has been tossed to the floor and the lights extinguished at very inconvenient times—such as when one is taking a bath in the Jacuzzi tub. People say they have felt pressure as they lay in bed, as though something has decided to lay down as well, on top of them.

Rooms 12, 13, and 15 have their own ghostly showings. Doorknobs rattle when no one it there, the sound of long skirts swishing along the floorboards is heard, and even makeup cases have been flung through the air while the female guests are dressing for dinner.

Room 16 seems to have spirits in the room who do not mind announcing themselves. They knock on the door, turn the water off in the sink, and even make appearances in the form of shimmering shapes walking about the room. Room 40 reports muffled voices, stomping and knocking sounds.

The Peabody House and the Curwen House tout their own ghost stories, but it is agreed Salem Inn holds the record.

The Stephen Daniels House

1 Daniels Street

The Stephen Daniels House was built in 1667 by Stephen Daniels with a "new" addition added in 1756. The home was a private residence for a direct descendant of the Daniels family for nearly 300 years. It was converted to a two-family home for a short time before becoming a Bed & Breakfast. The home was converted to a restaurant and inn in 1945 by the Hallers. Current owner Catherine Gill, affectionately known as Kay, purchased the inn in 1962 and has proudly served as innkeeper and caretaker for 49 years, making it Salem's oldest running Bed & Breakfast.

The house sits near The House of the Seven Gables and Pickering

Wharf. It is named after Stephen Daniels, an affluent sea captain who built the three-story wooden structure in 1667. The home was purchased in 1962 by Thomas and Kay Gill of Chicago. They ran it as a bed-and-breakfast and operated a restaurant there as well. William Shatner is said to have dined there. Although Thomas has passed away, Kay continues to run the Inn, serving continental breakfasts to guests and happily telling her stories of the history of the house.

The playwright Arthur Miller stayed here in one of the four upstairs bedrooms. The house has nine fireplaces, which is not unusual for a First Period home. Each room needed its own fireplace.

Guests most-often report seeing a ghost in a shiny black hat and coat. He is suspected of opening and closing windows, and rolling up window blinds. Guests have seen the wraith of a woman falling down the stairs, and the apparition of a man resembling one of the many portraits adorning the walls of the home. Yet, the Stephen Daniel's house most-famous ghost is that of a tabby cat. One guest painted a portrait of a cat she had never seen before visiting Salem. She was shocked to see a cat exactly resembling the picture she had painted on the grounds of the Daniel's house. More disturbing, was that the creature disappeared before her eyes. Kay Gill, the proprietor, does have a cat (let alone one that disappears) and says she has yet to see the specter of the feline that reportedly jumps up onto guests' beds and offers to cuddle with them.

The Salem Athenaeum

337 Essex Street

The name "Athenaeum" is derived from "Athena," the Greek

goddess of wisdom. It's no wonder, as the building's history includes the Social Library in 1760; and the Salem Philosophical Library in 1781. By 1810, the two libraries merged to create the Salem Athenaeum. When the Athenaeum was founded, there were more libraries in Salem than in Boston. Salem had become a center of learning and culture. The Library of Arts and Sciences and the Fourth Social Library were also open. The Essex Institute housed extensive holdings of maritime information, artifacts, and curiosities.

The Salem Athenaeum today.

For the first four decades of its existence, the Athenaeum had no permanent home, occupying quarters at four different locations at Salem. In the 1850s, a bequest from Caroline Plummer enabled the Athenaeum to erect a brick building in the Italianate style at 132 Essex Street. It later sold the building to the Essex Institute (now the Peabody Essex Museum) in 1905, and with the proceeds constructed the building it now currently occupies at 337 Essex Street. It was dedicated in 1907. Today the Athenaeum is home to over 50,000 volumes in its circulating and research and research collections. Cultural programs including concerts, readings, lectures, performances, and lively social gatherings are offered, along with a reading room and gardens for quiet work.

Speaking of quiet work, Nathaniel Hawthorne spent each noon break from his work at the Customs House reading at the Athenaeum. He was not the only one who found the library a welcome retreat, amid the books and quiet. An eighty-year-old gentleman, Reverend Harris, frequented the reading room as well, always nodding in quiet recognition to young Hawthorne who shared the space with him. Years later, old Harris passed away. It was then, with some shock, that for the next five consecutive days after the man's death, Hawthorne would look up to see Reverend Harris seated in his favorite place in a chair by the fireplace in the library reading room.

It so impacted the author, that Hawthorne documented it in some of his papers. His fascination with ghosts was threaded throughout many of his great works.

The Morning Glory Bed&Breakfast
22 Hardy Street

Morning Glory Bed & Breakfast is a beautifully restored Georgian Federal home, circa 1808, located in historic Salem MA. The inn is owned and operated by Bob Shea, a native of Salem. The home is ideally situated on a very quiet, dead-end street, a stone's throw away from beautiful Salem Harbor, across the street from the historic House of the Seven Gables, and an easy walk to all of the seaside restaurants, museums, and attractions Salem has to offer. The view of Salem harbor from its rooftop deck is a treasured bonus to staying here.

A few spirits must agree. A guest once asked the owner if the Inn was haunted. They were at breakfast at the time. Before he could answer, a teakettle suddenly flew off the stove and onto the floor. Mr. Shea left the room, finding the kettle had answered the question for him. Another guest reported seeing a young woman of about 17-years-of-age peering in at her from the upper outside balcony. When she checked, there was no one there. It would seem the kettle was not the only thing that could fly.

The Old Salem Witch Jail (Gaol) Site
10 Federal Street

All that remains of the jail that held many of the witch trial prisoners is a plaque on a modern brick building in the middle of Salem. The structure sits across from a large parking lot, adding to the odd juxtaposition of eras.

It sits now at the corner of Federal Street and St. Peter's Street—once called Prison Lane during the witch trial period. It was here that innocent people who had been "cried out" against from the afflicted girls languished as they awaited their trials, and after, their executions. 19 people were hanged for witchcraft, one man (Giles Corey) crushed to death, and at least five others died in the jail while awaiting their fates.

The conditions were horrific. The jailers and town profited by charging the families of the accused for everything from their food to the irons that shackled their ankles. When Ann Foster died in the jail while awaiting her fate, her son was charged two pounds, sixteen shillings just to remove her body. The jail was only 70 feet by 280 feet, made of rough, hand-hewn timbers. It was frigid in the winter and stifling in the summer. Rats ran rampant, and torture was not an uncommon occurrence as prisoners were constantly "urged" to confess to witchcraft. Families could bring clean clothes, blankets, and fresh food, but many homes had been left destitute by the witchcraft outbreak, and many just couldn't afford the trip, or the care package.

While the site is today a modern one, one can still pause and imagine the oxcart waiting outside the jail door to deliver the condemned to Gallows Hill, amid the shouts of hundreds of spectators there to witness the executions. The original jail was razed in 1956, after being abandoned in 1813 as a jail. In Francis Hill's book *Hunting for Witches*, she states "In the 1930s, a house stood on the site, built with timbers from the jail. In that decade it became Salem's first Witch City attraction, when the Goodell family who owned it, constructed a replica of the dungeons and charged tourists admission. The Old Witch Jail and Dungeon, as it was known, drew tens of thousands of visitors before being bulldozed to make way for the telephone company building. The attraction then moved to Lynde Street, becoming the "Witch Dungeon," which is still there today. The original timbers from the jail were donated to the Peabody Essex Museum but are not on display." One beam from the original jail can be seen at the Salem Witch Museum, and one can be found at the Witch Dungeon.

The Witch Dungeon

16 Lynde Street

The mood is set from the moment you enter the Witch Dungeon Museum. You are there - in Salem Village in 1692, and you are guaranteed a unique educational experience with a chill or two. You'll experience the acclaimed performance of a Witch trial scene adapted from the 1692 historical transcripts, showcasing the trial of

Sarah Good, one of the three "witches" first accused. Professional actresses in repertory reenact the electrifying scene.

The preamble to the Dungeon states: Welcome to Salem Massachusetts, where in the year 1692 something very unusual took place. The Reverend Parris' daughter Betty and niece Abigail began acting very strangely. The minister asked Dr. Griggs to examine the girls, but he could not find anything wrong with them. Abigail and Betty continued their strange behavior and other children began to copy them. Some of the odd things they did were bark like a dog, while others would throw themselves on the floor and have fits. One child tried to crawl into the fireplace. Another child said the Devil was after her. The adults now believed that the Devil had come to their little village.

A tableau in the Witch Dungeon showing the Parris home.

The children began to say that some of the people in the village were witches and had cast spells on them. The villagers gathered at the meetinghouse to find and punish the people who were bewitching the children. The children began to accuse their neighbors. They said they were witches. Fear spread through the village. The Devil had come to Salem. The trials lasted for thirteen months. One hundred and fifty-six people were accused. Nineteen were hanged. One man was pressed to death. Two dogs were hanged because the children said they gave them the "evil eye".

The Witch Dungeon Museum is a former church and many visitors and staff have said they've seen the specter of a hooded monk in the Dungeon section of the tour. He is often seen near the "Crushing Death of Giles Corey" exhibit. The basement of the attraction has been turned into a walking tour of over a dozen vignettes depicting the witchcraft events. It is a very chilling feeling to be below ground in a darkened tunnel-like atmosphere with realistic settings. People have reported hearing whisperings, things moving about, and the ubiquitous monk, who seems to join tour groups. The original support beam from the jail is found here and photographs have picked up images of strange people standing beneath it in period clothing.

This author has written about the Stone Tape Theory in my book *The History and Haunting of the Stanley Hotel.* It has been scientifically proven that some types of minerals and other components can retain energy, and play it back under certain conditions. Many castles in Europe have quartz in the stonework. Quartz is used in radios to transmit signals. Signals are frequency. Energy is frequency. Human beings are 99% energy and light. Is it so far-fetched to think that when we die our energy continues on, and is, in fact, a frequency? Quantum physicists are saying every human being has their own frequency that goes out and interacts with other frequencies. Sometimes, that energy imprints on cameras and video recorders. For one thing is certain—energy cannot be destroyed. It can only change forms. Thus, when we die, and our physical bodies are laid to rest, the energy that comprises us must go on. We call it ghosts, or hauntings.

It appears the Witch Dungeon and other places in Essex County have some excess energy going on.

If you're looking to see how a pillory works, there is one in front of the Witch Museum. I have witnessed many a hapless husband "trapped" there with his head and hands protruding from the openings. It makes for a fun Photo Op. I'm sure to the Puritans who were locked into these devices during their "public humiliation," it was not much fun. You could be sent to the "stocks" for stealing, berating your husband (if you were female), and other sundry offences.

The pillory stocks in front of the Witch Dungeon.

The Witch Trials Site

70 Washington Street

*Plaque commemorating the location of the meetinghouse
where the Salem Witch Trials were held.*

A plaque, standing literally in the middle of a modern-day Salem Street, marks the location of the Town House where the witch trials were conducted. The building is long gone, but the stigma of what happened at this location will last for decades to come. The plaque reads:

> **Nearly opposite this spot, in the middle of the street,
> stood a building devoted to, from 1677 to 1718, to
> municipal and judicial uses. In it, in 1692, were tried
> and condemned for witchcraft most of the 19 persons
> who suffered death on the gallows. Giles Corey was
> here put on trial on the same charge, and refusing to
> plead, was taken away and pressed to death. In January
> 1693, 21 persons were tried her for witchcraft, of whom**

18 were acquitted and three condemned, but later set free, together with about 150 accused persons, in a general delivery which occurred in May.

Nicholas Noyes, the infamous reverend who played an integral part in the witch trials, lived only steps from the Town House. He was in attendance, and even took notes during the trials. Noyes also witnessed the hangings, and it was to him that Sarah Good shouted, "I am no more a witch than you are a wizard. And if you take my life, God will give you blood to drink!" Noyes died of a hemorrhage, and it was reported his mouth was filled with blood.

Salem Witch Trial Memorial
98 Liberty Street

Located just off Charter Street, on Liberty Street, is Salem's simple yet dramatic memorial to the 20 victims of the witch trials of 1692. Four-foot-high granite walls surround three sides, with granite benches representing each victim cantilevered inward from the wall. Etched on each bench is a name, means of execution, and execution date. One can read, on the stone threshold of the memorial, words of the accused taken directly from court transcripts. Visitors will note that the words – among them, "God knows I am innocent" – are cut off in mid-sentence, representing lives cut short and indifference to the protestations of innocence.

A public design competition, juried by five noted professionals, resulted in 246 entrants. The winning entry, designed by Maggie Smith and James Cutler of Bainbridge Island, Washington, was presented to the press and public by renowned playwright Arthur Miller on November 14, 1991. Among the notable works by Miller is *The Crucible*, which used the Salem Witch Trials as an allegory for the McCarthyism of the late 1940s and early 1950s.

The Witch Trials Memorial was dedicated on August 5, 1992 by Nobel Laureate, Holocaust survivor, and author Elie Wiesel, who noted, "If I can't stop all of the hate all over the world in all of the people, I can stop it in one place within me," adding, "We still have our Salems."

This quiet and peaceful memorial, located in the very center of Salem, provides a place for people to pay their respects, to reflect on tolerance and understanding, and to remember the inspiring stories of personal courage revealed in 1692.

Just over the wall of the Memorial is the Old Burying Pointe Cemetery. Ironically, the graves of witch trial judges John Hawthorne and Bartholomew Gedney are buried here. One wonders if the names carved in the stone benches of the Salem Witch Memorial ever whisper on the night breeze and linger over the grave markers of the two magistrates responsible for signing their death sentences? The haunting found here is one of personal reflection. A stirring that picks at the scabs of conscience. Are we of better temperament today than the souls of 1692? Would we condemn another based on jealousy, greed, or grievances? It should be the stuff that haunts our dreams. Could it happen again?

The Cemeteries

St. Mary's Cemetery
Route 114, Salem

St. Mary's Cemetery is located on Route 114. It is reported to be New England's most-haunted cemetery. Dating back to the 19th century, the large resting place is home to politicians, and other notables. It also lays claim to a phantom dog that has been seen and heard running amidst the tombstones. Many have said they feel an oppressive atmosphere and the feeling that they are trespassing.

Old Burying Point
Charter Street, Salem

In 1637, the town of Salem set aside an area of land to be used as a burial place. It is the oldest cemetery in Salem and the second-oldest in America. Tombstones mark the graves of Judge John Hawthorne and Judge Bartholomew Gedney, famous for their roles in the Salem witch trials. Giles Corey's first wife Mary is buried here, along with more recognizable names, such as Captain Richard More who arrived in New England via the Mayflower, and Governor Simon Bradstreet. Reverend John Higginson, who played a part in the witchcraft hysteria, is also buried here.

The cemetery was a favorite place for local author Nathaniel Hawthorne to spend his meditative moments. He often wandered through Old Burying Point and studied the markers. He used a few of the names in his novels, notably Dr. Swinnerton and his own relative, John Hathorne who appear as characters in *The House of the Seven Gables*. In his novel *Dr. Grimshaw's Secret*, he mentions the graveyard. Grimshaw House is still standing at 53 Charter Street. It was here Nathaniel met his wife Sophia, in 1837.

The usual phenomenon is attributed to the cemetery: mysterious lights, a glimpse of something floating amidst the stones, and hushed voices. The Witch Trial Memorial sits on the other side of the stone wall.

Howard Street Cemetery

Howard Street near 50 St. Peter's Street

Howard Street Cemetery sits just on the other side of an iron fence that was the site of the Old Jail. This is not to be confused with the Salem Gaol (Jail) which is on Federal Street. A new jail was built in 1813 (now called the Old Jail), long after the area had been nothing but open field. It was here that Sheriff Corwin and Judge Hathorne took Giles Corey and laid him on the ground to be crushed to death beneath a board laden with large rocks.

Howard Street is a narrow avenue, flanked by the cemetery on one side and apartments on the other. Standing there, looking out in the crumbling markers, one can't help but step back to the year 1692 and picture the poor man lying there alone for three days, given only a mouthful of water and some bread. The idea was that he would finally cave beneath the torture and confess to witchcraft. They underestimated Corey, and his resolve. He died with the final statement "More weight!" St. Peter's goes right by the location where Corey died. In 1692, St. Peter's was called Prison Lane, and it is very possible Gile's wife, Martha Corey saw him lying there as the cart bearing her to Gallows Hill passed by.

There is a legend that Corey cursed Salem with his final breath. I could find no mention of it in the transcripts.

According to Nathaniel Hawthorne, there was a legend that Corey had cursed the town in his final moments. One such account says his actual words were "Salem will burn." Over the years, the word spread that whenever a calamity was about to befall Salem, Corey's ghost would appear in the old cemetery. Nathaniel Hawthorne wrote, "Tradition was long current that at stated periods, the ghost of Giles Corey, the wizard, appeared on the spot where he suffered as the precursor of some calamity that was impending over the community, which the apparition came to announce." It was reported that Corey's ghost was seen before the Great Fire of June 25, 1914. If Corey had cursed Salem with destruction by fire, he came close—the fire of 1914 destroyed one-fourth of the city.

Broad Street Cemetery
A small mound bordered by Broad, Summer and Gedney Street

Although Broad Street Cemetery is the smallest cemetery in Salem, it is home to the graves of two of the most-reviled participants in the witch trials. It is here that the body of Sheriff George Corwin was finally buried after his family hid him in the basement of the home for fear the enraged inhabitants of Salem would desecrate his body. Barely had the body of Giles Corey been removed from the field, but Sheriff Corwin descended upon Corey's property and began carting off his goods. Others also lost their life's work to the Sheriff once their arrest warrants were posted for witchcraft. The Proctor family was left destitute after Corwin took everything, including the copper pot filled with the family's broth for the day's meal.

His father, Judge Jonathan Corwin is also buried here. Together, the two Corwin's went down in history as the most-despised members of the trials. It is reported that either Hathorne or Corwin were responsible for forcing Gile's Corey tongue back into his mouth as he lay dying on the hard ground. The cemetery is said to host strange lights at night and the ubiquitous floating specter.

Haunted Eats

Turner's Seafood at Lyceum Hall

43 Church Street

Turner's Seafood's catch phrase is "Anything fresher still swims!" As it has been awarded Best of Northshore Magazine four years straight, it seems the general populace agrees with them. James F.

Turner opened Turner Fisheries in 1954. He was committed to supplying only the freshest New England seafood. With the growth of the commercial airline industry and the ability to fly fresh seafood anywhere in the United States, the country's finest restaurants and clubs began advertising "Today's fish flown in fresh from Boston's Turner Fisheries." Likewise, Turner Fisheries proudly displayed its new title "The nation's leading quality seafood house."

In 1994, John's four sons opened Turner's Seafood Grill & Market in their hometown of Melrose, MA. This authentic New England seafood house is complete with a fresh fish market and turn-of-the-century oyster bar. The Turners expanded their retail operation to historic Gloucester, the nation's oldest fishing port, in 2006. In 2010, the Turner family launched its on-line Dock to Door Seafood Market shipping fresh fish daily overnight from Gloucester to anywhere in the continental USA. In November 2013, historic Lyceum Hall in Salem, Massachusetts became home to the family's latest seafood experience. With an authentic shuck and serve oyster bar, the city's only seafood market, classic lunch and dinner fare, and a top choice for wedding rehearsal dinners, it's safe to say, Turner's is having an impact in Salem.

It appears that something may be impacting Turner's, as well. It is said Turner's Seafood at Lyceum Hall sits on the previous site of Bridget Bishop's apple orchard. Bishop was the first person to be hanged during the 1692 witch trials. She ran a tavern in Salem, making ale from her apples, and was a rather notorious figure with her flashy clothes and sharp tongue. Many odd occurrences have happened at Turner's, especially in the stairwell and upstairs rooms. Michael Teleoglou was dining at Turner's in September of 2018. He asked if he might see the upstairs, and a staff member willingly obliged. The picture on the following page shows a white wraith on the right side of the upper staircase.

Stairwell of Turner's Seafood.
Photo courtesy of Michael Teleoglou

While visiting the upstairs' room, Michael captured a rather large orb which appears at the right of the picture on the drapes.

Upstairs at Turner's Seafood. Photo courtesy of Michael Teleglou.

In Sam Baltrusis' book *Ghosts of Salem: Haunts of the Witch City.* He states, "I have had several odd experiences outside of Lyceum Hall, which was believed to be Bridget Bishop's orchard. An apple mysteriously rolled out of nowhere in the alley behind what is now Turner's Seafood. I looked up. No one was there. I accepted it as a peace offering from Bridget, who later became one of my favorite characters on the tour."

Turner's Seafood is located on the first floor of **Lyceum Hall**. A lyceum is a public hall where lectures, programs, and concerts are offered. They were very popular in England, and as the Puritans set sail for America, they brought the tradition along. The Salem Lyceum was created in 1830 by Josiah Holbrook and it quickly became a hit. Salem boasted the first lyceum hall in America. The theater offered 700 seats and two weekly lectures. This was something new. An educational series that was not just for the elite, but for everyone.

Salem witnessed some of the greatest artists and feats in American History. The first long-distance phone call was made within the Salem Lyceum walls. As the audience listened in astonishment, Alexander Graham Bell made a long-distance call to his partner Thomas Watson eighteen-miles away in Boston. When Watson's voice came back through the newly invented telephone, the applause was thunderous. Other greats graced the hall: Henry David Thoreau, Daniel Webster, Oliver Wendall Holmes, John Quincy Adams, and Horace Mann, to name a few. With Salem's close proximity to Boston, it was able to pluck from the notables that visited the capital for both business and cultural events.

While the original wooden building caught fire in 1894, and burned to the ground, the current structure of brick was built atop the original location. The second floor is now used for events hosted by Turner's Seafood. It would seem not all things went up in smoke. Stories of missing glassware, things being hurled down the stairs, the smell of apple blossoms, and the figure of a woman seen on the second floor, are all reported today. The third-floor coatroom and attic have an oppressive feeling at times, and things have been found to be moved around.

Perhaps, the spirits that linger here know great seafood when they see it.

Rockafellas

231 Essex Street

Rockafellas is lovely restaurant housed in the old Daniel Low building. Daniel Low once operated a large jewelry store here, so large, that he had a tunnel built between the building and the one across the street, that he used as a warehouse. His jewelry business became such a huge success, that he operated the original mail-order catalogue and offered the first silver witch spoon of Salem.

One of the other proprietors of the Daniel Low building was John P. Peabody, the name sake for the Peabody House that is part of the Salem Inn conglomerate. His popular fine furnishings store was here.

Today, Rockafellas restaurant holds court. Its patio service is very popular in the summer, while the interior boasts warm wood paneling and great service. Built in 2003, it has become a popular eatery. Obviously, a few ghosts find it tempting as well. The Blue Lady specter is seen here, along with a somber minister in dark clothing.

Hollywood and Salem

With the rich history of Salem, is it any wonder movies and plays have been written about witches? Several prove as faithful documentaries of the 1692 witch trials, while taking some dramatic license. Others are tongue-in-cheek iconic films, and still more adaptations made the TV streaming circuit. Here are a few notables:

Three Sovereigns for Sarah

Photo courtesy of Richard Trask

Three Sovereigns for Sarah is a PBS special TV series that aired June, 2005. It is a realistic depiction of the witch trials of 1692, using a fictionalized account in the opening and closing scene where Rebecca Nurse is appealing to the magistrates for the clearing of her sisters' names. Despite the fact that liberties were taken with the actual scene, it is fact that many families applied for compensation after the loss of their loved ones and ruination of their homes. The cast is stellar, and the background represented in minute detail.

Richard Trask, town historian and curator at the Danvers Archival Center (see his interview earlier in the book), was approached for the film, due to his acumen with regards to the witch trials. These are his words:

"Because the Danvers Archival Center houses the largest collection of imprints concerning that witch hysteria, it was not surprising when back in 1981 a polite, self-assured, curly haired young man named Victor R. Pisano visited the archives looking for witchcraft material. Pisano explained that he was interested in the witch era and wanted, through a film, to tell the story of some of the witchcraft trials' victims. My enthusiasm was not overflowing. Several film groups had visited us before, and I had usually been disappointed with their finished product.

"Pisano indicated an interest in Rebecca Nurse and asked if I could suggest other victims whose lesser-known stories would also have dramatic interest. I said that he might look into the story of one of my ancestors, Mary Esty. Though she was executed as a witch, her written plea to the court – not for her own life, but to save others – is a selfless document that is dramatic in its wording even centuries later.

"Though I had my doubts that I would ever see Mr. Pisano again, several months later he returned with a script outline and a request that I comment on it. As I read the outline, my enthusiasm rose. He had not chosen to write principally about Mary Esty or about her better-known sister Rebecca, but instead he had focused on their youngest sister, Sarah Cloyce.

"Although she also was accused of being a witch, forty-seven-year-old Sarah lived through her ordeal, unlike Rebecca and Mary, who were hanged. Though not much about Sarah has come down to us in history, interesting glimpses do survive. Sources reveal that she created a stir during religious services on a day following the witchcraft examination of her sister Rebecca. When village minister Samuel Parris announced the text of his sermon, which alluded to devils in Christ's church, Sarah could not bear the vicious comparison. She rose from her pew and walked out on the minister and congregation, purportedly slamming the door. As Pisano later would comment, "The more I looked into it, the more Sarah's story leaped out at me."

"That Pisano had been doing his homework was evident from his story outline. A first-draft screenplay followed in early 1983. I read it one Sunday in my 1681 home, only a few hundred feet from where the witchcraft hearings had actually taken place."

Richard Trask was asked to design a meetinghouse that would closely resemble the one in Salem Village in 1692 where the witch examinations took place and where Reverend Samuel Parris preached each Sunday. He did so, and the building now stands today on the Rebecca Nurse Homestead site where much of the movie was filmed. Trask continued:

"Eminent historian Stephen Nissenbaum, a professor at the University of Massachusetts and coauthor of the award-winning book, Salem Possessed, joined as the other historical consultant, concentrating primarily on character development and interpretation. I was mainly responsible for historical detail and accuracy. Stephen Nissenbaum has an intellect and inquisitiveness of the highest order, yet matches it with a kind and gentle spirit. He was both a joy and inspiration, and I was honored to work closely with him.

"During the ensuing months, Pisano, who now served both as writer and producer of the film, met with Nissenbaum and me on numerous occasions for page-by-page examination of the script, picking up on inaccuracies of speech, objects, settings and facts. Our comments went like this: "This date in the script for Rebecca's preliminary hearing is incorrect;" "During scenes of Sunday attendance at the meetinghouse, the men and the women must be separated into men's and women's sides of the building;" "Sarah should not drink tea in a china cup, but cider in an earthenware mug;" "You can't call a farmer's wife 'Madame' because her status would not allow it, you must call her 'Goodwife' or 'Goody.'"

The result of all this painstaking work is a wonderful movie that is available on Amazon.com, and in the Nurse Homestead Gift Shop, among other places. Here are some photos from the film, which starred Vanessa Redgrave, Kim Hunter, Will Lyman, Buffy Baldauf, and Wes Lyman, among others. It was directed by Phillip Leacock and written by Victor Pisano. Here are some photos of the film's production, courtesy of Richard Trask, who also played a role in the film as a guard.

Director Philip Leacock (left) with screenwriter/producer Victor Pisano at the Nurse Homestead on the final day of shooting in January 1985.

The finished meetinghouse, built from Richard Trask's drawings and research, aged for the film. Vanessa Redgrave is in the foreground.

Actress Sylvia Anne Soares portraying Tituba in jail.

Richard Trask in full costume, wig, and hat on the set.

Patrick McGoohan in his full bottomed wig, with original volumes and reproduction props cluttering the table at the Saugus Ironworks location.
Photo by Douglas Miller.

Noted actor and voice-over artist Will Lyman portrayed the Rev. Mr. Samuel Parris, whose miniature oval portrait is at right.
Photo by Douglas Miller.

Phyllist Thaxter as Rebecca Nurse (L) & Kim Hunter as Mary Esty.

Elizabeth Trask (daughter of Richard Trask) with other extras; and Vanessa

Redgrave as Sarah Cloyce getting ready to storm out of the church.

The three sisters, Sarah Cloyce (back), Mary Esty (L) & Rebecca Nurse (R). Photo courtesy of Douglas Miller.

Salem Witch Trials

Salem Witch Trials is a made for Television Mini-Series starring Kirsti Alley, Rebecca DeMornay, and Shirley MacLaine. It's focus on the Putnam families is educational, as it is tough sometimes to keep the Putnams straight. It also depicts Issac Porter's role in the separation of the Putnam fortune. Kirsti Alley and Shirley MacLaine turn in superb performances, as do the afflicted children. Bridget Bishop is wrongly portrayed as the village witch living in a hut in the woods, but it adds color to the story. You come away with a good idea of the basics of the witch trials, and feel deeply for the victims during the jail and execution scenes. Peter Ustinov, as Chief Justice William Stoughton, oversees the strip search of Rebecca Nurse (played by Shirley MacLaine) and gives an appropriately uncomfortable performance. You can buy the DVD at Amazon.com.

The History Channel Salem Witch Trials

The History Channel takes on the witch trials with their usual attention to detail. It is a good overview of the 1692 hysteria, done in stills and narration. It is available on Amazon.

The Crucible, based on the play by Arthur Miller

The Crucible movie has done more to sensationalize the witch trials than any movie or play on the event. It is still shown in High Schools today, and performed on every stage platform. If it is a student's first baptism into the details of the witch trials, they come away believing Abigail Williams was a lusting teenager who has tempted John Proctor to bed. Scenes depicting the girls conjuring with Tituba in the woods, and Abigail's naked dancing, are pure Hollywood.

The Crucible was written in 1953 as a play by American playwright Arthur Miller. It was meant as an allegory for McCarthyism, when the United States Government persecuted people accused of being communists. Miller was brought up before the House of Representatives' Committee on Un-American Activities in 1956 and convicted of contempt of Congress for refusing to identify others present at meetings he had attended.

Enjoy the movie for its touching drama between Elizabeth Proctor (played by Joan Allen) and John Proctor (played with aplomb by Daniel Day-Lewis), and the heartbreak of Abigail Williams (played by Winona Ryder).

Salem, the TV series uses the witch trials only as a broad backdrop.

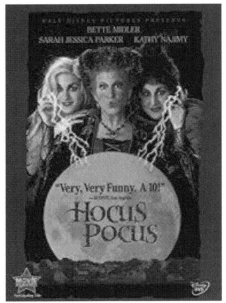

Hocus Pocus

Let's face it... Hocus Pocus grabbed the imagination of the

American public and has become an icon in the movie industry. Disney Productions knocked it out-of-the-park on July 16, 1993, with this hilarious romp through Salem. For every die-hard Halloween fanatic that ever wanted to see into a witch's hut, or fly on a broomstick (or Hoover), Bette Midler, Sarah Jessica Parker, and Kathy Najimy are the perfect tour guides. Many scenes were shot in Salem. It is surprising to me how often I have heard tourists in the Salem Gift Shops ask cashiers where they can find the Sanderson Sisters' Witch House in Salem. The hapless clerks always smile indulgently and say, "You do realize the witch hut was a movie set? It isn't real." They then offer to tell them of the "real" locations that were used during the filming of the movie.

Here is a brief tour of the locations used in the movie:

Max and Dani Dennison's house. 4 Ocean Dr. (Private residence)

Rope's Mansion, home of Max's love interest, Allison. 318 Essex St.

Salem's Old Town Hall. 32 Derby Street.

Phillips Elementary School, which depicted Jacob Bailey HS in the film.
86 Essex St.

Washington Square where Max followed Allison from school.
Adjacent to the Hawthorn Hotel.

Pioneer Village where Sarah lures Emily Binx away. 98 West Avenue

Old Burial Hill in Marblehead, MA, where Max meets
Ernie (ICE) and Jay.

Other scenes were Disney film sets, including the cemetery where they meet Billy Butcherson (or what's left of him), and the Sanderson Sisters' house.

"On All Hallow's Eve, when the moon is round,
A virgin will summon us from under the ground.
We shall be back!
And the lives of all the children of Shall be mine!"
--Winifred Sanderson
October 31, 1693

Witch Trial Accusers

Name	Age	Town
1. Abigail Booth	14	Salem
2. Elizabeth Booth	18	Salem
3. Richard Carrier	18	Andover
4. Sarah Churchill	25	Salem
5. John DeRich	16	Salem
6. Rose Foster	13	Andover
7. Abigail Hobbs	--	Topsfield
8. Deliverance Hobbs	--	Topsfield
9. Elizabeth Hubbard	17	Salem Village/Ryal
10. John Indian	--	Salem Village
11. Mercy Lewis	19	Salem Village
12. Abigail Martin	19	Salem Village
13. Mary Marshall	--	Andover
14. Elizabeth Parris	9	Salem Village
15. Sarah Phelps	12	Andover
16. Ann Putnam Jr.	12	Salem Village
17. Ann Putnam Sr.	30	Salem Village
18. Margaret Rule	17	Boston
19. Susannah Sheldon	18	Salem Village
20. Mercy Short	17	Boston
21. Martha Sprague	16	Andover
22. Timothy Swan	30	Andover
23. Sarah Bibber	36	--
24. Mary Walcott	17	Salem Village
25. Mary Watkins	20s	Milton
26. Abigail Williams	12	Salem Village

627

Witch Trial Victims
Key:
H=Hanged, P=Pressed

Name	Age	K	Town
1. Bridget Bishop	50s	H	Salem
2. George Burroughs	42	H	Wells, Maine
3. Martha Carrier	40s	H	Andover
4. Giles Corey	70s	P	Salem Village
5. Martha Corey	70s	H	Salem Village
6. Mary Esty	56	H	Topsfield
7. Sarah Good	38	H	Salem Village
8. Elizabeth How	50s	H	Topsfield
9. George Jacobs Sr.	80s	H	Salem Village
10. Susannah Martin	71	H	Amesbury
11. Rebecca Nurse	71	H	Salem Village
12. Alice Parker	--	H	Salem Village
13. Mary Parker	55	H	Andover
14. John Proctor	60	H	Salem Village
15. Ann Pudeator	70	H	Salem
16. Wilmot Reed	50s	H	Marblehead
17. Margaret Scott	77	H	Rowley
18. Samuel Wardwell	49	H	Andover
19. Sarah Wildes	65	H	Topsfield
20. John Willard	20s	H	Salem Village

Died in Prison

1. Lydia Dustin	79	Reading
2. Ann Foster	70s	Andover
3. Sarah Good's baby	--	Salem Village
4. Sarah Osborne	40s	Salem Village
5. Roger Toothaker	58	Billerica

*Over 150 people were accused during the witchcraft hysteria.

Recommended Reading, Websites & Maps

Baker, Emerson W. *A Storm of Witchcraft*. Oxford University Press.

Baltrusis, Sam. *Ghosts of Salem*. Haunted America.

Beard, George M. *The Psychology of the Salem Witchcraft Excitement*. G. P. Putnam & Sons.

Boyer, Paul & Stephen Nissenbaum. *Salem Possessed*. Harvard University Press.

Burr, George Lincoln. Editor *Narratives of the New England Witchcraft Cases*. Dover Publications.

Foulds, Diane E. *Death in Salem: The Private Lives Behind the 1692 Witch Hunt*. National Book Network Dist.

Goff, John. *Salem's Witch House*. History Press.

Guiley, Rosemary, Ellen. *Haunted Salem*. Stackpole Press.

Hill, Frances. *Hunting of Witches*. Commonwealth Editions.

Jackson, Shirley. *The Witchcraft of Salem* Village. Random House.

Lawson, Deodat. *A Brief and True Narrative of Some Remarkable Passages Relating to Sundry Persons Afflicted by Witchcraft at Salem Village*. Kissinger Publishing.

Macken, Lynda Lee. *Haunted Salem & Beyond*. Black Cat Press.

Mather, Cotton. *The Wonders of the Invisible World*. Bell Publishing.

Norton, Mary Beth. *In the Devil's Snare*. Vintage Books.

Perley, Sidney. *The History of Salem Massachusetts*. 3 vols. Record Publishing Company; Haverhill.

Perley, Sidney. *Where the Salem Witches Were Hanged*. Essex Institute Historical Collections.

Roach, Marilynne K. *The Salem Witch Trials: A Day-by-Day Chronicle of a Community Under Siege*. Taylor Trade Publishing.

Roach, Marilynne K. *Six Women of Salem: The Untold Story of the Accused and Their Accusers in the Salem Witch Trials*. Da Capo Press.

Starkey, Marion L. *The Devil in Massachusetts*. Doubleday

Anchor Book.

Trask, Richard B. *The Devil Hath Been Raised: A Documentary History of the Salem Village Witchcraft Outbreak of March 1692.* Danvers Historical Society.

Woodward, Elliot W. *Records of Salem Witchcraft.* Vol. 1. Sagwan Press, Inc.

Websites

1. **Danvers Archival Center**.
https://www.danverslibrary.org/archive

2. **University of Virginia. Salem Witch Trials Documentary Archive & Transcription Project**.
http://salem.lib.virginia.edu/17docs.html

3. **History of Massachusetts blog.**
https://historyofmassachusetts.org

4. **Peabody Essex Institute**.
https://www.pem.org

Maps

1. **Roach, Marilynne K.** *A Map of Salem Village and Vicinity in 1692.* Watertown, MA.: 1985, 1990. (Large parchment map showing all the homes and businesses during the Salem Witch Trials of 1692. You can purchase it at the Salem Witch Museum in Salem, MA.)

2. **Perley, Sidney.** Various maps of Salem Village locations during 1692, as well as sight lines for the location of Proctor's Ledge. (These various maps are found in Perley's books and transcripts.)

Other Books by Rebecca F. Pittman:

Historical & Paranormal Non-Fiction:

The History and Haunting of the Stanley Hotel,
1st & 2nd Editions
The History and Haunting of the Myrtles Plantation,
1st & 2nd Editions
The History and Haunting of Lemp Mansion
The History and Haunting of Lizzie Borden
The History and Haunting of Salem
The History and Haunting of the Palace of Versailles (June, 2020)

Self-Help Books:

How to Start a Faux Painting or Mural Business,
1st & 2nd Editions
Scrapbooking for Profit,
1st & 2nd Editions
Troubleshooting Men, What in the World Do They Want?
(A Dating & Marriage Advice Book of Secrets for Women, based
on Ms. Pittman's TV Talk Show by the same name.)

Supernatural Thrillers/Fiction:

T.J. Finnel and the Well of Ghosts (Book One of a Five-Book
Series)

Coming Soon in Fiction:

Don't Look Now!
The Diamond Peacock Club

Sign-up for Ms. Pittman's free email newsletter *Ghost Writings* at
her website, www. rebeccafpittmanbooks.com for the latest news
on her new book releases & paranormal articles.

Haunted History Paranormal Card Game.
Lizzie Borden Murder Mystery: Case 1.

A rummy-style card game based on real evidence & crime scene photos from the famous Borden Murder Case of 1892. It's never the same game twice. Gets yours at www.rebeccafpittmanbooks.com.

About the Author

Rebecca F. Pittman is an historian who just happens to find herself in the middle of paranormal activity while writing about America's iconic venues. Her series of books in the *History and Haunting* series have garnered her a faithful following. You can see her list of publications under the Recommended Reading section of this book.

Her book *The History and Haunting of Lizzie Borden* was highlighted in 2019 on the Travel Channel's *Legend Hunter*, and the CW's *Mysteries Decoded*. Radio and podcast interviews center around her experiences while researching, and her fascination with things that "go bump in the night." This love of mystery led to the creation of her first paranormal card game in the *Haunted History* series, *Lizzie Borden Murder Mystery Paranormal Card Game*. She has two other games on the drawing board, and is interested in creating a subscription-style murder mystery series.

Ms. Pittman's website, www.rebeccafpittmanbook.com offers a sign-up for her popular *Ghost Writings* newsletter that is emailed out monthly to subscribers. It's free and always interesting. From stories of the paranormal to contests, new book and game release information, and specials, it's a fun way to keep abreast of all things mysterious. You can sign-up through your laptop at the lightbox that appears as soon as you enter the site.

Rebecca makes her home in the foothills of the Rocky Mountains. Her passions are her growing family, golf, boating, travel…and of course…mysteries.

Made in the USA
Monee, IL
30 October 2021